Lonely planet

BEST ROAD
EUROPE

ESCAPES ON THE OPEN ROAD

DUNCAN GARWOOD, ISABEL ALBISTON, OLIVER BERRY, STUART BUTLER,
JEAN-BERNARD CARILLET, FIONN DAVENPORT, MARC DI DUCA, BELINDA DIXON,
PETER DRAGICEVICH, ANTHONY HAM, PAULA HARDY, CATHERINE LE NEVEZ,
JOHN NOBLE, SALLY O'BRIEN, JOSEPHINE QUINTERO, KEVIN RAUB, DANIEL ROBINSON,
BRENDAN SAINSBURY, REGIS ST LOUIS, ANDY SYMINGTON, RYAN VER BERKMOES,
KERRY WALKER, NICOLA WILLIAMS, NEIL WILSON

Contents

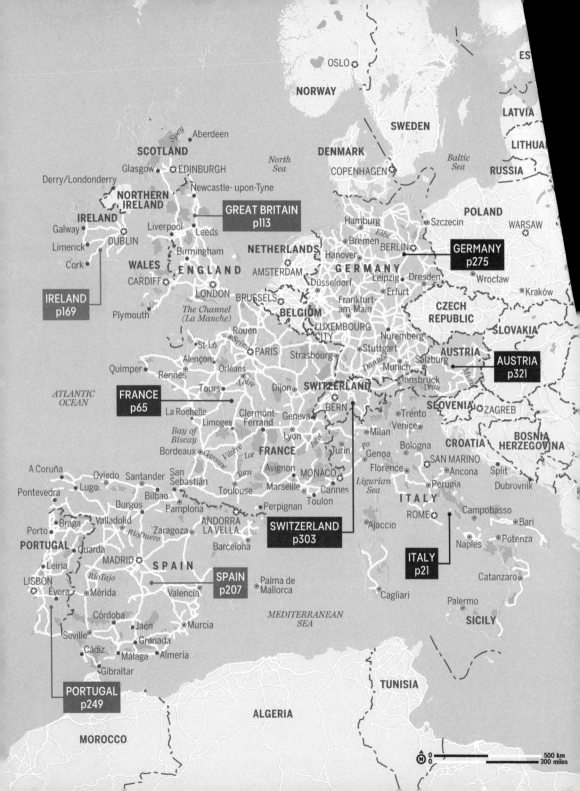

Welcome to Europe

Few destinations can rival Europe's intoxicating mix of culture, beauty and joie de vivre. The sight of its artistic masterpieces and iconic monuments will stay with you for life, while cosmopolitan streets, cutting-edge fashion and national cuisines will leave you hungry for more. Out on the road, you'll find mountainous landscapes and thrilling coastlines equally as inspiring.

The 41 trips detailed in this book run through nine countries, leading from the big-draw cities of London, Paris and Rome to medieval Bavarian towns and remote Irish villages, from sun-kissed Portuguese beaches to soaring Swiss Alps. They take in ancient ruins and fairy-tale castles, royal palaces and cosy pubs.

So buckle up and enjoy the ride whether that's a grand tour of Italy, an adventure in the Austrian Alps, a Spanish pilgrimage or a riverside Rhine cruise.

Tuscany, Italy

Our Picks

BEST ART & ARCHITECTURE DRIVES

Europe's astonishing artistic and architectural legacy is writ large across the continent's diverse lands and historic cityscapes. Roman amphitheatres stand alongside Gothic cathedrals and baroque palaces, while avant-garde landmarks and contemporary skyscrapers give new shape to urban skylines. World-famous museums showcase masterpieces by a who's who of major-league artists, from Renaissance maestros to impressionist pioneers and experimental surrealists. For art lovers, there really is nowhere better for an unforgettable road trip.

GUIDES

Audio, video and VR guides can really add to a visit, particularly at ancient sites that might initially seem confusing.

DOMINGO LEIVA/GETTY IMAGES ©

Italian Grand Tour

A whistle-stop tour of Italy's headline cities and their priceless treasures.

P.24

Châteaux of the Loire

Marvel at the fairy-tale châteaux that line the Loire.

P.106

Mediterranean Meander

Cruise Spain's Mediterranean coast, admiring Picassos in Málaga and modernist architecture in Barcelona.

P.210

The Historic South

Explore cathedrals, castles, London landmarks and prehistoric icons in southern England.

P.134

Wonders of Ancient Sicily

Discover Greek temples, baroque basilicas and Byzantine mosaics in sun-baked Sicily.

P.54

EQROY/SHUTTERSTOCK ©

ONLINE BOOKING

Book tickets online for popular attractions. Many places now require it, and it will save queuing at the site.

Château d'Azay-le-Rideau (p108), France

Christ Church Cathedral (p118), Oxford, England

Our Picks

BEST HISTORY DRIVES

Europe's history has played out to tumultuous effect across the continent, leaving a trail of historic cities, sites and monuments. Stone circles and ancient ruins recall early civilisations; castles and battlefields tell of war and bloody conflict; and cathedrals, châteaux and palaces testify to the might of former monarchs, despots and popes. Everywhere you go in the old continent you're surrounded by reminders of the past.

PRE-TRIP PREP

Prep yourself for your trip by dipping into the vast literature of European history or taking in a history-inspired film.

World Heritage Treasures

Roman monuments and medieval cityscapes star on this epic Italian odyssey.

P.48

D-Day's Beaches

See where the bloody events of D-Day played out on Normandy's shores.

P.74

Edinburgh Castle (p125), Scotland

Historic Castilla y León

Tour Spain's Castilian heartland, taking in medieval cities and historic architecture.

P.236

The Best of Britain

From Edinburgh to London, Britain's headline cities promise history and drama.

P.116

The Romantic Road

Discover quaint medieval towns in a picturesque corner of Bavaria.

P.286

Semana Santa procession, Zamora (p238), Spain

Our Picks

BEST FOOD & WINE DRIVES

Superb produce, deep-rooted culinary traditions and a passion for the finer things make Europe a dream destination for food and wine lovers. Every country has its own specialities and way of doing things, so whether you're sipping Champagne in a French cellar, snacking on tapas in a Spanish bar or tearing into pizza in an Italian pizzeria, magical moments await at every stop.

WINERY VISITS

Book ahead as walk-ins are not always accepted. Buying a bottle or two is a polite way of thanking your host.

 1

Champagne Taster

Break out the bubbly on this tour of France's celebrated Champagne region.

P.100

 2

Tuscan Wine Tour

Savour fine dining and noble reds in Tuscany's Chianti wine country.

P.36

 3

Roving La Rioja Wine Region

Search out bodegas, restaurants and historic vineyards in northern Spain.

P.242

 4

Douro Valley Vineyard Trails

Explore the wineries and terraced vineyards of Portugal's culinary Eden.

P.252

 5

Along the Danube

Austria's meandering river leads to fabled beer- and wine-producing monasteries.

P.330

AUTUMN JOYS

Autumn is a prime time for foodies, with earthy woodland foraging, food festivals and the annual grape harvest.

APROPOS IMAGES/SHUTTERSTOCK ©

Douro Valley (p252), Portugal

Our Picks

BEST SEASIDE DRIVES

Stretching from the Atlantic to the Adriatic, from wild Welsh beaches to sun-kissed coves in the Algarve, Europe's coastline is a stunning spectacle. Whether you want to bask on idyllic Mediterranean beaches or hole up in a remote fishing village, marvel at romantic seascapes on the Amalfi Coast or hang out with celebs on the French Riviera, you're sure to find somewhere to suit your style.

SUN LOUNGERS

To use the sun loungers and umbrellas that cover many Mediterranean beaches, you'll have to pay a daily (or weekly) fee.

Amalfi Coast (p42), Italy

BALATE DORIN/SHUTTERSTOCK ©

Amalfi Coast

Bask in the sublime beauty of Italy's celebrated coastline, a classic Mediterranean pin-up.

P.42

Ring of Kerry

Featuring Atlantic beaches, loughs and islands – this Irish drive promises magical scenery.

P.186

Alentejo & Algarve Beaches

Dreamy beaches and great surf await on Portugal's southern coast.

P.258

Riviera Crossing

Swoon at the cinematic seascapes and chic towns of France's Côte d'Azur.

P.92

West Wales: Swansea to St Davids

Plunging cliffs and wild sandy beaches in west Wales.

P.160

Our Picks

BEST MOUNTAIN DRIVES

Europe's mountains set the stage for some of the continent's most exhilarating driving. Stunning roads snake over high-altitude passes in the Pyrenees, past towering Alpine peaks and through remote Scottish glens, revealing magnificent views at every turn. The going can be challenging at times, but you're rewarded with breathtaking scenery and opportunities for epic year-round sport – hiking and cycling in spring, summer and autumn, and skiing in winter.

CAR EQUIPMENT

If heading to mountainous areas between October and April, check your car is equipped with winter tyres and/or snow chains.

The Swiss Alps

Buckle up for Switzerland's legendary Alpine peaks – the Matterhorn, Eiger, Jungfrau.

P.306

Grossglockner Road

This roller-coaster trip promises white-knuckle driving and majestic scenery in the Austrian Alps.

P.324

The Pyrenees

Meander through beech forests and verdant valleys in the French Pyrenees.

P.86

Royal Highlands & Cairngorms

Tour rugged mountains and pine forests in the Scottish highlands.

P.150

The Graceful Italian Lakes

Snowcapped Alpine peaks provide the backdrop to Italy's romantic lakes.

P.30

MOUNTAIN PASSES

Many high-altitude mountain passes close in the snowy winter months, typically between October and May.

Furka Pass (p308), Switzerland

Pyrenees (p86), France

When to Go

Europe's roads are good year-round but spring and early summer are best for long days, sunny weather and gorgeous colours.

Europe is at its most festive in summer. The sun is out, the festival season is in full swing, and everyone is on holiday, particularly in July and August. Of course, with the good weather you also get high-season prices, the risk of congested roads and, depending on where you're headed, some very hot days.

Spring and autumn are quieter and cooler, ideal for road-tripping, city sightseeing and hiking, especially in the hotter southern climes.

Winter is good news for skiers who flock to Alpine resorts; otherwise it's a cold, wet time of year. Heavy rain, fog and ice

TOMMY LAREY/SHUTTERSTOCK ©

Carnival, Nice (p94), France

Festival Watch

CARNIVAL

The run-up to Lent sees revelry break out across the continent. High-profile destinations include Nice in southern France, Venice in Italy, and the German Rhine lands. **February/March**

LAS FALLAS DE SAN JOSÉ

Pyrotechnics and partying go hand in hand at Valencia's explosive bash. Top billing goes to the giant *fallas* (effigies), which are burned on the last night. **March**

PRIDE

LGBTQ Pride events take to the streets of Europe's cities throughout the summer. Huge crowds turn out to celebrate, with colourful displays and raucous festivities. **June/July**

FESTIVAL D'AVIGNON

France's premier arts festival rolls into the Provence city of Avignon in July, heralding three weeks of high drama and world-class dance performances. **July**

Warth-Schröcken ski resort, Austria

RED-HOT SUMMERS

Europe's hottest recorded summer was 2021 – until the summer of '22 proved even hotter. In that sweltering year, the mercury topped 40°C in Britain and a record-breaking temperature of 48.8°C was recorded in the Sicilian coastal city of Syracuse.

can make driving challenging, even if major roads are generally well maintained.

Accommodation

Accommodation rates fluctuate with demand, so expect to pay full whack on the coast in July and August and in popular cities in spring and autumn. Major festivals and seasonal events also push prices up. As a general rule, book as early as possible for the best deals.

SODDEN STEREOTYPES

As you shelter from the drizzle in Dublin, console yourself with the fact that it could be worse – you could be in Rome. It actually rains more in the Eternal City than in many other European capitals, including London, Lisbon, Vienna, Paris and Berlin.

SNOW CHARTS

High winter temperatures played havoc with Europe's 2023 ski season. But if there's one place that can be relied on to have snow, it's the Warth-Schröcken resort in western Austria. This snowy area gets about 10.5m of the white stuff each year.

PALIO DI SIENA

Medieval rivalries play out in thrilling style at Siena's historic horse race. Action centres on the city's main square where bareback riders gallop for glory in front of baying crowds. **2 July and 16 August**

ZÜRICH STREET PARADE

There's dancing on the streets of Zürich as huge crowds kick off to thumping techno during the city's celebrated street party. **August**

EDINBURGH FESTIVAL

Artists, comedians, musicians and performers play to packed houses in the Scottish capital. The main festival is shadowed by its alternative twin, the Fringe Festival. **August**

OKTOBERFEST

Beer lovers from across the world descend on Munich for the city's colossal knees-up. Around 7.5 million litres of locally brewed beer are consumed during the two-week event. **September**

Get Prepared for Europe

Useful things to load in your bag, your ears and your brain.

WATCH

Inspector Montalbano
(1999–2021) Hugely
popular Italian TV
series starring a food-
loving detective in
southeastern Sicily.

La Vie En Rose
(Olivier Dahan; 2007)
Marion Cotillard gives
an Oscar-winning
performance as French
chanteuse Edith Piaf.

Dolor y gloria
(Pedro Almodóvar; 2019)
Almodóvar's deeply
personal reflection on
art, love and loss.

**The Banshees
of Inisherin**
*(Martin McDonagh;
2022)* A compelling
study of friendship
breakdown on a
remote Irish island.

A Lisbon Story
(Wim Wenders; 1994)
Wenders' love letter
to Lisbon starring
Teresa Salgueiro.

Clothing

Shoes: Comfy shoes are a must, particularly in historic towns and cities where cobblestones can wreak havoc on unprotected feet. Pack a pair of shoes or trainers for daytime use and a smarter pair for the evening. Flip-flops are good for summer beach-going; walking boots are essential for hiking.

Smart casual: For evenings out in Europe's fashion-conscious cities, smart casual is the way to go. For driving and daytime sightseeing, comfort is key so go with what works for you.

Swimming gear: Whether for beach bathing or wild swimming, you'll need a costume or two and a beach towel.

Accessories: Sunglasses are essential for long hours behind the wheel, particularly on the coast and in the mountains. A hat can be a lifesaver too, especially in summer when it can get ferociously hot.

Dress codes: Some big religious sites enforce dress codes, so it pays to play it safe and cover your shoulders, torso and thighs.

Wet weather kit: Bring a light waterproof jacket for spring and autumn, and cold weather gear for winter. A small umbrella is always a good idea.

Multi-language sign, Mt Titlis (p308), Switzerland

LISTEN

London Calling
(The Clash; 1979) The energy of this punk classic will fire you up for the English capital.

Mariza
(Mariza; 2018) Portuguese fado by the Mozambique-born superstar.

Concierto de Aranjuez
(Joaquín Rodrigo; 1939) A classical-guitar concerto brilliantly conveying Spain's simmering passions.

Autobahn
(Kraftwerk; 1974) A homage to Germany's autobahns by the legendary pioneers of electronic music.

READ

The Old Ways
(Robert Macfarlane; 2012) Britain's ancient trails inspire this lyrical homage to the joys of walking.

The Marseille Trilogy
(Jean-Claude Izzo; 1995–98) Izzo brilliantly evokes Marseille's gritty atmosphere in his detective story trilogy.

Eggshells
(Caitriona Lally; 2015) Lally's inventive debut centres on a lonely protagonist wandering the streets of Dublin.

My Brilliant Friend
(Elena Ferrante; 2012) An international bestseller chronicling the friendship between two young girls in postwar Naples.

Words

Six major languages are spoken in the countries covered in this book – English, French, German, Italian, Portuguese and Spanish. In addition to these, there are a whole host of minority languages, such as Welsh, Irish, Catalan, Basque and Romansch, as well as hundreds of local dialects.

Road signs reflect this linguistic diversity. In Wales, for example, place names are indicated in Welsh and English. Similarly, Swiss signs feature a combination of German, French and Italian, while in the South Tyrol you'll see signs in both Italian and German.

In non-English-speaking countries, you can usually get by with English in major cities and popular tourist destinations. In rural areas, English is less widespread and you might have to try the local language. In fact, wherever you go, people will appreciate efforts to speak their language, so it pays to have a few phrases up your sleeve. This is when Google Translate or a similar app can come in handy.

If all else fails, you can, of course, resort to hand signs. Gestures speak volumes and many native speakers use them to great effect, particularly in Mediterranean countries where non-verbal communication sometimes appears to be a form of performance art.

ROAD TRIPS

Grossglockner High Alpine Road (p326), Austria
RYYW/SHUTTERSTOCK ©

Contents

Selinunte (p56)

Italy

Explore

Italy

There's no better country for an epic road trip than Italy. With your own wheels, you can take in romantic cities, iconic monuments, regional cuisines and a landscape that encompasses snowcapped peaks, plunging coastlines, gorgeous lakes and vine-clad hills.

Our Italian trips run the length of the country, leading from Alpine lakes to southern volcanoes, from hilltop towns in Tuscany to fishing villages on the Amalfi Coast. They stop in high-profile cities and under-the-radar gems, and cover a wide range of experiences. So whether you want to tour gourmet towns and historic vineyards, idyllic shorelines or pristine national parks, we have a trip tailor-made for you.

Rome

Many people get their first taste of Italy in Rome, the country's capital and main gateway. The city sits in the heart of the Lazio region, providing a convenient geographical base for exploring Italy's central territories. From the city the main A1 autostrada leads north to Umbria and Tuscany, and south to Naples, about 200km away.

Rome is, of course, a destination in itself, and it's well set up for visitors with excellent transport links, accommodation for all budgets, and no end of bars, cafes, trattorias and restaurants. It boasts a lifetime's worth of sights, certainly too many for a single trip, but you won't want to miss the Colosseum, Pantheon and Sistine Chapel.

Milan

Many trips to northern Italy pass through Milan, the area's historic powerhouse. A fast-paced, forward-looking metropolis renowned for its fashion, design and high-end shopping, it's a city of trendsetters, start-ups and sharply dressed financiers. Among its many banks and boutiques, it also harbours some celebrated masterpieces including its fairy-tale Gothic Duomo and Leonardo da Vinci's *The Last Supper*.

To reach the city you can fly to one of its two airports (Malpensa and Linate) or get a national or international train into Stazione Centrale. For drivers, autostradas strike out in all directions – the A4 is a principal artery, connecting the city with Turin, Verona,

WHEN TO GO

Spring and autumn are best for road-tripping, sightseeing and seasonal food. The weather is pleasant and, away from the main cities, the driving is pretty easy-going. Summer is good for festivals and beach-going, but watch out for heavy traffic on the coast and on the main north–south arteries. Winter brings the risk of snow and ice in mountainous areas.

Padua and Venice. To the north, lakes Maggiore and Como are accessible by train or car.

Naples

First port of call for many travellers to southern Italy is Naples. Italy's third-largest city makes an immediate impression with its in-your-face energy and Dickensian backstreets. And once you've found your feet, you'll discover there's a lot to love here with priceless art packed into regal palaces and sweeping bay views over to Vesuvius on the horizon. Accommodation is plentiful and the food is magnificent – a pizza margherita in Naples' historic centre is one of Italy's quintessential eating experiences.

Transport-wise, Naples is well connected with its own international airport and excellent rail and road links. To the south of the city, urban development skirts the Gulf of Naples as it curves around to the Sorrentine Peninsula and the sunny resort

TRANSPORT

Flights serve airports throughout the country. Italy's main intercontinental airports are Rome's Fiumicino (officially Leonardo da Vinci) and Milan's Malpensa. Both are well connected by public transport and offer a full array of services, including car hire. There are also excellent rail and bus links, especially to destinations in northern Italy, and ferries to Italian ports from across the Mediterranean.

of Sorrento. This animated seaside town heaves in summer and serves as a local transport hub with buses and seasonal ferries to the Amalfi Coast, hydrofoils to Capri and a direct rail service to Pompeii.

 WHAT'S ON

Pasqua

Rome's Easter celebrations culminate in the Pope's traditional blessing on Easter Sunday.

La Biennale di Venezia

(May–November; labiennale.org) Europe's premier arts event sets up stall in Venice.

Verona Opera Festival

(late June–late August; arena. it) Verona's ancient amphitheatre provides the stage for summer opera.

Grape Harvest

(September and October) Italy's vineyards are a hive of activity during the annual *vendemmia* (grape harvest).

Resources

Agriturismi (*agriturismi. it*) Listing and booking site with thousands of farm stays across the country.

ACI (*aci.it*) Information on driving in Italy from the country's main automobile association.

Italia (*italia.it*) Italy's official tourism website with comprehensive info on the whole country.

 WHERE TO STAY

From dreamy villas to chic boutique hotels, family-run B&Bs, campgrounds and apartment rentals, Italy offers accommodation to suit every taste and budget. Options are plentiful in headline cities and popular coastal resorts but places fill quickly, especially at peak periods when prices shoot up to reflect the high demand. To avoid disappointment, book as early as you can. Out in the countryside, *agriturismi* (farm stays) are a great bet for the period between April and October. Another option, particularly popular in religious centres, is a convent or monastery, many of which offer basic, inexpensive lodgings.

01

Italian Grand Tour

BEST FOR HISTORY

Rome, the repository of over 2500 years of European history.

Palazzo Reale, Turin

DURATION	DISTANCE	GREAT FOR
12–14 days	1390km / 865 miles	History, food and drink

BEST TIME TO GO	Spring (March to May) is perfect for urban sightseeing.

From the Savoy palaces of Turin and Leonardo's *Last Supper* to the disreputable drinking dens of Genoa and pleasure palaces of Rome, the Grand Tour is part scholar's pilgrimage and part rite of passage. Offering a chance to view some of the world's greatest masterpieces and hear Vivaldi played on 18th-century cellos, it's a rollicking trip filled with the sights, sounds and tastes that have shaped European society for centuries.

Link your trip

03 Tuscan Wine Tour

Linger in the bucolic hills around Florence and enjoy fine gourmet dining and world-renowned wine tasting.

04 Amalfi Coast

Play truant from high-minded museums and head south from Naples for the Blue Ribbon drive on the Amalfi Coast.

01 **TURIN**

In his travel guide, *Voyage Through Italy* (1670), travel writer and tutor Richard Lassels advocated a grand cultural tour of Europe, and in particular Italy, for young English aristocrats, during which the study of classical antiquity and the High Renaissance would ready them for future influential roles shaping the political, economic and social realities of the day.

First they travelled through France before crossing the Alps at Mt Cenis and heading to Turin (Torino), where letters of introduction admitted them to the city's agreeable Parisian-style social whirl. Today

(cenacolovinciano.net). Advance booking is essential.

From his *Portrait of a Young Man* (c 1486) to portraits of Duke Ludovico Sforza's beautiful mistresses, *The Lady with Ermine* (c 1489) and *La Belle Ferronière* (c 1490), Leonardo transformed the rigid conventions of portraiture to depict highly individual images imbued with naturalism. Then he evolved concepts of idealised proportions and the depiction of internal emotional states through physical dynamism (*St Jerome*), all of which cohere in the masterly *Il Cenacolo*.

While you're here, take time to walk around other parts of the city, too.

02 GENOA

Despite its superb location, mild microclimate and lush flora, Genoa (Genova) has a dubious reputation. Its historic centre was a warren of dark, insalubrious *caruggi* (alleys), while the excessive shrewdness of the Genovese banking families earned them a reputation, according to author Thomas Nugent, as 'a treacherous and over-reaching set of people'.

And yet with tourists and businesspeople arriving from around the world, Genoa was, and still is, a cosmopolitan place. The **Rolli Palaces**, a collection of grand mansions originally meant to host visiting popes, dignitaries and royalty, made Via Balbi and Strada Nuova (now Via Giuseppe Garibaldi) two of the most famous streets in Europe. Visit the finest of them, the **Palazzo Spinola** (museidigenova.it/en/palazzo-spinola) and the **Palazzo Reale** (museidigenova.it/en/royal-palace-genoa). Afterwards stop for sweets at **Pietro Romanengo fu Stefano** (romanengo.com).

Turin's tree-lined boulevards retain their elegant, French feel and many gilded cafes, such as **Caffè Al Bicerin** (bicerin.it), still serve its signature coffee and chocolate drink – as it has since the 1760s.

Like the Medicis in Florence (Firenze) and the Borghese in Rome (Roma), Turin's Savoy princes had a penchant for extravagant architecture and interior decor. You suspect they also pined for their hunting lodges in Chambéry, France, from where they originated, as they invited André Le Nôtre, Versailles' landscaper, to design the gardens of **Palazzo Reale** (museireali.beniculturali.it) in 1697.

🚗 THE DRIVE

The two-hour (170km) drive to Genoa is all on autostrada, the final stretch twisting through the mountains. Leave Turin following signs for the A55 (towards Alessandria), which quickly merges with the A21 passing through the pretty Piedmontese countryside. Just before Alessandria turn south onto the A26 for Genoa/Livorno.

🧭 DETOUR

Milan
Start: 01 Turin

No Grand Tour would be complete without a detour up the A4 to Milan (Milano) to eyeball Leonardo da Vinci's iconic mural *The Last Supper*

THE DRIVE

This 365km drive takes most of the day, so stop for lunch in Cremona. Although the drive is on autostrada, endless fields of corn line the route. Take the A7 north out of Genoa and at Tortona exit onto the A21 around industrial Piacenza to Brescia. At Brescia, change again onto the A4 direct to Padua.

03 PADUA

Bound for Venice (Venezia), Grand Tourists could hardly avoid visiting Padua (Padova), although by the 18th century international students no longer flocked to **Palazzo Bo** (unipd.it/en/guidedtours), the Venetian Republic's radical university where Copernicus and Galileo taught class.

You can visit the university's claustrophobic, wooden anatomy theatre (the first in the world), although it's no longer de rigueur to witness dissections on the average tourist itinerary. Afterwards don't forget to pay your respects to the skulls of noble professors who donated themselves for dissection because of the difficulty involved in acquiring fresh corpses. Their skulls are lined up in the graduation hall.

Beyond the university the melancholy air of the city did little to detain foreign visitors. Even Giotto's spectacular frescoes in the **Cappella degli Scrovegni** (Scrovegni Chapel; cappelladegli scrovegni.it), where advance reservations are essential, were of limited interest given medieval art was out of fashion, and only devout Catholics ventured to revere the strange relics of St Anthony in the **Basilica di Sant'Antonio** (Il Santo; basilicadelsanto.org).

THE DRIVE

Barely 40km from Venice, the drive from Padua is through featureless areas of light industry along the A4 and then the A57.

04 VENICE

Top of the itinerary, Venice at last! Then, as now, La Serenissima's watery landscape captured the imagination of travellers. At **Carnevale** (carnevale.venezia.it) in February numbers swelled to 30,000; now they number in the hundreds of thousands. You cannot take your car onto the lagoon islands so leave it in a secure garage in Mestre, such as **Garage Europa Mestre** (garageeuropamestre.com), and hop on the train to Venice Santa Lucia where water taxis connect to all the islands.

Aside from the mind-improving art in the **Gallerie dell'Accademia** (gallerieaccademia.it) and extraordinary architectural masterpieces such as the **Palazzo Ducale**, the **Campanile**, Longhena's **Basilica di Santa Maria della Salute** and the glittering domes of the **Basilica di San Marco** (St Mark's Basilica; basilicasanmarco.it), Venice was considered an exciting den of debauchery. Venetian wives were notorious for keeping handsome escorts *(cicisbeos),* and whole areas of town were given over to venality. One of Venice's best restaurants, **Antiche Carampane** (antichecarampane.com), is located in what was once a den of vice, so called because of the notorious brothel at Palazzo Ca'Rampani.

Eighteenth-century tourists would inevitably have stopped for coffee at the newly opened **Caffè Florian** (caffeflorian.com)

and paid a visit to the opera house, **Teatro La Fenice** (teatro lafenice.it), to hear groundbreaking concerts now being revived by the **Venice Music Project** (venicemusicproject.it).

THE DRIVE

Retrace your steps to Padua on the A57 and A4 and navigate around the ring road in the direction of Bologna to pick up the A13 southwest for this short two-hour drive (154km or so). After Padua the autostrada dashes through wideopen farmland and crosses the Po River, which forms the southern border of the Veneto.

05 BOLOGNA

Home to Europe's oldest university (established in 1088) and once the stomping ground of Dante, Boccaccio and Petrarch, Bologna had an enviable reputation for courtesy and culture. Its historic centre, complete with 20 soaring towers, is one of the best-preserved medieval cities in the world. In the **Basilica di San Petronio** (basilicadisan petronio.org), originally intended to dwarf St Peter's in Rome, Giovanni Cassini's sundial (1655) proved the problems with the Julian calendar, giving us the leap year, while Bolognesi students advanced human knowledge in obstetrics, natural science, zoology and anthropology. You can peer at their strange model waxworks and studiously labelled collections in the **Palazzo Poggi** (sma. unibo.it/it/il-sistema-museale/ museo-di-palazzo-poggi).

In art as in science, the School of Bologna gave birth to the Carracci brothers, Annibale and Agostino, and their cousin Ludovico, who

were among the founding fathers of Italian baroque and were deeply influenced by the Counter-Reformation. See their emotionally charged blockbusters in the **Pinacoteca Nazionale** (pinacoteca bologna.beniculturali.it).

🚗 THE DRIVE
Bologna sits at the intersection of the A1, A13 and A14. From the centre navigate west out of the city, across the river Reno, onto the A1. From here it's a straight shot into Florence for 100km, leaving the Po plains behind you and entering the low hills of Emilia-Romagna and the forested valleys of Tuscany.

06 FLORENCE
From Filippo Brunelleschi's red-tiled dome atop Florence's **Duomo** (Cattedrale di Santa Maria del Fiore; museumflorence.com) to Michelangelo's and Botticelli's greatest hits, *David* and *The Birth of Venus,* in the **Galleria dell'Accademia** (galleriaacca demiafirenze.it) and the **Galleria degli Uffizi** (Uffizi Gallery; uffizi.it), Florence, according to Unesco, contains the highest number of artistic masterpieces in the world.

Whereas Rome and Milan have torn themselves down and been rebuilt many times, incorporating a multitude of architectural whims, central Florence looks much as it did in 1550, with stone towers and cypress-lined gardens.

🚗 THE DRIVE
The next 210km, continuing south along the A1, travels through some of Italy's most lovely scenery. Just southwest of Florence the vineyards of Greve in Chianti harbour some great farm stays, while Arezzo is to the east. Exit at Orvieto

and follow on the SR71 and SR2 for the final 45km into Viterbo.

07 VITERBO
From Florence the road to Rome crossed the dreaded and pestilential *campagna* (countryside), a swampy, mosquito-infested low-lying area. Unlike now, inns en route were uncomfortable and hazardous, so travellers hurried through Siena, stocking up on wine for the rough road ahead. They also stopped briefly in medieval Viterbo for a quick douse in the thermal springs at the **Terme dei Papi** (termedeipapi.it), and a tour of the High Renaissance gardens at **Villa Lante** (polomusealelazio. beniculturali.it).

🚗 THE DRIVE
Rejoin the A1 after a 28km drive along the rural SS675. For the next 40km the A1 descends through Lazio, criss-crossing the Tevere River and keeping the ridge of the

TOP TIP:

Jump the Queue in Florence

In July, August and other busy periods such as Easter, long queues are a fact of life at Florence's key museums. For a fee of €4 each, tickets to the Uffizi and Galleria dell'Accademia (where *David* lives) can be booked in advance. Book at firenzemusei.it.

Apennines to the left as it darts through tunnels. At Fiano Romano exit for Roma Nord and follow the A1dir and SS4 (Via Salaria) for the final 20km push into the capital.

08 ROME
In the 18th century, Rome, even in ruins, was still thought of as the august capital of the world. Here more than anywhere the Grand Tourist was awakened to an interest in art and architecture, although the **Colosseum** (Colosseo; parco colosseo.it) was still filled with debris and the **Palatino** (Palatine Hill) was covered in gardens, its excavated treasures slowly accumulating in the world's oldest national museum, the **Capitoline Museums** (Musei Capitolini; museicapitolini.org).

Arriving through the Porta del Popolo, visitors first espied the dome of **St Peter's Basilica** (Basilica di San Pietro; vatican. va) before clattering along the corso to the customs house. Once done, they headed to **Piazza di Spagna**, the city's principal meeting place where Keats penned his love poems and died of consumption.

Although the **Pantheon** (pantheonroma.com) and **Vatican Museums** (Musei Vaticani; museivaticani.va) were a must, most travellers preferred to socialise in the grounds of the **Borghese Palace** (galleriaborgh ese.beniculturali.it). Follow their example and mix the choicest sights with more venal pleasures such as fine dining at **Aroma** (manfredihotels.com/aroma) and souvenir shopping at antique perfumery **Officina Profumo-Farmaceutica di Santa Maria Novella** (smnovella.com).

🚗 THE DRIVE

Past Rome the landscape is hotter and drier, trees give way to Mediterranean shrubbery and the grass starts to yellow. Beyond the vineyards of Frascati, just 20km south of Rome, the A1 runs 225km to Naples, a two-hour drive that can take longer if there's heavy traffic.

09 NAPLES

Only the more adventurous Grand Tourists continued south to the salacious southern city of Naples (Napoli). At the time Mt Vesuvius glowed menacingly on the bay, erupting

Photo Opportunity

Florence's multicoloured marble *duomo* (cathedral).

no less than six times during the 18th century and eight times in the 19th century. But Naples was the home of opera and *commedia dell'arte* (improvised comedic drama satirising stock social stereotypes), and singing lessons and seats at **Teatro San Carlo** (teatrosancarlo.it) were obligatory.

Then there were the myths of Virgil and Dante to explore at **Lago d'Averno** and **Campi Flegrei** (the Phlegrean Fields). And, after the discovery of **Pompeii** (pompeiisites.org) in 1748, the unfolding drama of a Roman town in its death throes drew throngs of mawkish voyeurs. Then, as now, it was one of the most popular tourist sights in Italy and its priceless mosaics, pornographic frescoes and colossal sculptures filled the **Museo Archeologico Nazionale** (mann-napoli.it).

SERGEY NOVIKOV/SHUTTERSTOCK ©

Duomo, Florence

02

The Graceful Italian Lakes

Isola Bella

DURATION	DISTANCE	GREAT FOR
5–7 days	213km / 132 miles	History, food and drink, nature

BEST TIME TO GO	April to June, when the camellias are in full bloom.

Writers from Goethe to Hemingway have lavished praise on the Italian Lakes. They have an enduring natural beauty, dramatically ringed by snow-powdered mountains and garlanded by grand villas and exotic, tropical flora. At Lago Maggiore the palaces of the Borromean Islands lie like a fleet of fine vessels in the gulf, while the siren call of Lago di Como draws Arabian sheikhs and James Bond location scouts to its discreet forested slopes.

Link your trip

01 Italian Grand Tour

From Stresa take the A8 to Milan (Milano) and the A4 on to Turin (Torino) from where you can commence your own Grand Tour of Italy.

38 The Swiss Alps

From Verbania head northeast for the greatest of the great outdoors: perfect peaks, gorgeous glaciers and verdant valleys.

01 **STRESA**

More than Como and Garda, Lago Maggiore has retained the belle-époque air of its early tourist heyday. Attracted by the mild climate and the easy access the new 1855 railway provided, the European *haute bourgeoisie* flocked to buy and build grand lakeside villas. The best of them are paraded in the small but select lakeside town of Stresa.

From here it's a short punt to the palace-punctuated **Borromean Islands** (Isole Borromee; isoleborromee.it), Maggiore's star attractions. **Isola Bella** took the name of Carlo III's wife,

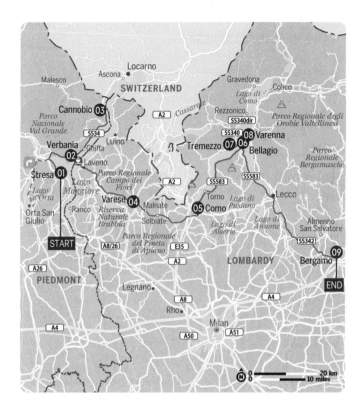

Photo Opportunity

The cascading gardens of Palazzo Borromeo.

lake in a day. The focal point is the captivating medieval village of **Orta San Giulio**, which sits across from Isola San Giulio, where you'll spy the frescoed, 12th-century **Basilica di San Giulio**. Come during the week and you'll have the place largely to yourself.

02 VERBANIA

There are two Verbanias: Pallanza, a waterside maze of serpentine streets that serves as an embarkation point for the Borromean Islands, and Intra, the broader, newer ferry port. Between them sits the late-19th-century **Villa Taranto** (villataranto.it). In 1931, royal archer and Scottish captain Neil McEacharn bought the villa from the Savoy family and started to plant some 20,000 species. With its rolling hillsides of purple rhododendrons and camellias, acres of tulip flowers and hothouses full of equatorial lilies it is considered one of Europe's finest botanical gardens. During the last week in April, **Settimana del Tulipano** takes place, when tens of thousands of tulips erupt in magnificent multicoloured blooms.

THE DRIVE

Pick up the SS34 again, continuing in a northeasterly direction out of Verbania, through the suburbs of Intra and Pallanza. Once you've cleared the town the 20km to Cannobio are the

the *bella* Isabella, in the 17th century, when its centrepiece, **Palazzo Borromeo**, was built. Construction of the villa and gardens was thought out in such a way that the island would have the appearance of a vessel, with the villa at the prow and the gardens dripping down 10 tiered terraces at the rear. Inside, you'll find the work of countless old masters.

By contrast, Isola Madre eschews ostentation for a more romantic, familial atmosphere. The 16th- to 18th-century **Palazzo Madre** includes a 'horror' theatre with a cast of devilish marionettes, while Chinese pheasants stalk the English gardens.

THE DRIVE

Leave Stresa westwards on the Via Sempione (SS33), skirting the edge of the lake for this short, 14km drive. Pass through Baveno and round the western edge of the gulf through the greenery of the Fondo Toce natural reserve. When you reach the junction with the SS34, turn right for Verbania.

DETOUR
Lago d'Orta
Start: 01 Stresa

Separated from Lago Maggiore by Monte Mottarone (1492m) and enveloped by thick, dark-green woodlands, Lago d'Orta would make a perfect elopers' getaway. At 13.4km long by 2.5km wide you can drive around the prettiest on the tour, shadowing the lakeshore the entire way with views across the water.

03 CANNOBIO

Sheltered by a high mountain and sitting at the foot of the Cannobina valley, the medieval hamlet of Cannobio is located 5km from the Swiss border. It is a dreamy place. **Piazza di Vittorio Emanuele III**, lined with pastel-hued houses, is the location of a huge Sunday market that attracts visitors from Switzerland.

You can hire stand-up paddleboards, canoes and small sailing boats from **Tomaso Surf & Sail** (tomaso.com) next to the town *lido* (beach). A good boat excursion is to the ruined **Castelli della Malpaga**, located on two rocky islets to the south of Cannobio. In summer it is a favourite picnic spot.

Alternatively, explore the wild beauty of the **Valle Cannobina**. Trails begin in town and snake alongside the surging Torrente Cannobino stream into the heavily wooded hillsides to **Malesco**. Just 2.5km along the valley, in Sant'Anna, the torrent forces its way powerfully through a narrow gorge known as the **Orrido di Sant'Anna**, crossed at its narrowest part by a Romanesque bridge.

🎡 THE DRIVE

The next part of the journey involves retracing the previous 22km drive to Verbania-Intra to board the cross-lake ferry to Laveno. Ferries run every 20 minutes. Once in Laveno pick up the SP394dir and then the SP1var and SS394 for the 23km drive to Varese.

LAGO MAGGIORE EXPRESS

The Lago Maggiore Express (lagomaggioreexpress.com) is a picturesque day trip you can do without the car. It includes train travel from Arona or Stresa to Domodossola, from where you get the charming Centovalli train, crossing 100 valleys, to Locarno in Switzerland and a ferry back to Stresa. The two-day version is perhaps better value if you have the time.

04 VARESE

Spread out to the south of the Campo dei Fiori hills, Varese is a prosperous provincial capital. From the 17th century onwards, Milanese nobles began to build second residences here, the most sumptuous being the **Palazzo Estense**, completed in 1771 for Francesco III d'Este, the governor of the Duchy of Milan. Although you cannot visit the palace you are free to wander the vast Italianate gardens (open 8am to dusk).

To the north of the city sits another great villa, **Villa Panza** (fondoambiente.it), donated to the state in 1996. Part of the donation was 150 contemporary canvases collected by Giuseppe Panza di Biumo, mostly by post-WWII American artists. One of the finest rooms is the 1830 **Salone Impero** (Empire Hall), with heavy chandeliers and four canvases by David Simpson (b 1928).

🎡 THE DRIVE

The 28km drive from Varese to Como isn't terribly exciting, passing through a string of small towns and suburbs nestled in the wooded hills. The single-lane SS342 passes through Malnate, Solbiate and Olgiate Comasco before reaching Como.

05 COMO

Built on the wealth of its silk industry, Como is an elegant town and remains Europe's most important producer of silk products. The **Museo della Seta** (Silk Museum; museosetacomo.com) unravels the town's industrial history, with early dyeing and printing equipment on display. At **A Picci** you can buy top-quality scarves, ties and fabrics.

After wandering the medieval alleys of the historic centre take a stroll along **Passeggiata Lino Gelpi**, where you pass a series of waterfront mansions, finally arriving at **Villa Olmo** (villaolmocomo.it). Set grandly facing the lake, this Como landmark was built in 1728 by the Odescalchi family, related to Pope Innocent XI, and now hosts blockbuster art shows. On Sundays you can continue your walk through the gardens of **Villa del Grumello** and the **Villa Sucota** on the so-called Chilometro della Conoscenza (Kilometre of Knowledge).

On the other side of Como's marina, the **Funicolare Como–Brunate** (funicolarecomo.it) whisks you uphill to the quiet village of **Brunate** for splendid views across the lake.

Palazzo Estense, Varese

Seaplanes on the Lake

For a touch of Hollywood glamour, check out Aero Club Como (aeroclubcomo. com), which has been sending seaplanes out over the lakes since 1930. The 30-minute flight to Bellagio from Como costs €280 for two people. Longer excursions over Lago Maggiore are also possible. In summer you need to reserve at least three days in advance.

THE DRIVE

The 32km drive from Como to Bellagio along the SS583 is spectacular. The narrow road swoops and twists around the lakeshore the entire way and rises up out of Como giving panoramic views over the lake. There are plenty of spots en route where you can pull over for photographs.

06 BELLAGIO

It's impossible not to be charmed by Bellagio's waterfront of bobbing boats, its maze of stone staircases, cypress groves and showy gardens.

Bellagio is a place best absorbed slowly on your own. You can pick up three self-guided walking tour brochures from the **tourist office** (bellagiolakecomo. com). The longest three-hour walk takes in neighbouring villages, including **Pescallo**, a small one-time fishing port about 1km from the centre, and **Loppia**, with the 11th-century Chiesa di Santa Maria, which is only visitable from the outside.

The walk to one of Como's finest mansions, **Villa Melzi d'Eril** (giardinidivillamelzi.it), heads south along the lakeshore from the Bellagio ferry jetties, revealing views of ranks of gracious residences stacked up on the waterside hills. The grounds of the neoclassical Villa Melzi run right down to the lake and are adorned with classical statues couched in blushing azaleas.

For on-the-lake frolics, **Barindelli** (barindellitaxiboats. it) operates slick, mahogany

IAN LAKER PHOTOGRAPHY/GETTY IMAGES ©

Bellagio

cigarette boats in which you can tool around the headland on a sunset tour.

 THE DRIVE
The best way to reach Tremezzo, without driving all the way around the bottom of the lake, is to take the ferry from Piazza Mazzini. The journey takes 10 minutes, but for sightseeing you may want to consider the one-day central lake ticket, covering Bellagio, Varenna, Tremezzo and Cadenabbia.

 07 TREMEZZO
Tremezzo is high on everyone's list for a visit to the 17th-century **Villa Carlotta** (villacarlotta.it), whose botanic gardens are filled with orange trees knitted into pergolas and some of Europe's finest rhododendrons, azaleas and camellias. The villa, which is strung with paintings and fine alabaster-white sculptures (especially lovely are those by Antonio Canova), takes its name from the Prussian princess who was given the palace in 1847 as a wedding present from her mother.

 THE DRIVE
As with the trip to Tremezzo, the best way to travel to Varenna is by passenger ferry either from Cadenabbia (1.3km north of Tremezzo's boat dock) or Bellagio.

 08 VARENNA
A mirror image of Bellagio across the water, Varenna is a beguiling village bursting with florid plantlife, narrow lanes and pastel-coloured houses stacked up on mountain slopes that defy the laws of physics.

You can wander the flower-laden pathway from Piazzale Martiri della Libertà to the gardens of **Villa Cipressi** (hotelvillacipressi. it), now a luxury hotel, or undertake a 40-minute walk up to the 13th-century **Castello di Vezio** (castellodivezio.it), high above the terracotta rooftops of Varenna. The castle was once part of a chain of early-warning medieval watchtowers. These days it hosts alfresco temporary exhibitions of avant-garde art and holds falconry displays in the afternoons – daily except Tuesdays and Fridays. There's also a small cafe.

 THE DRIVE
Departing Bellagio, pick up the SS583, but this time head southeast towards Lecco down the other 'leg' of Lago di Como. As with the stretch from Como to Bellagio, the road hugs the lake, offering spectacular views along the whole 20km to Lecco. Once you reach Lecco head south out of town down Via Industriale and pick up the SS342 for the final 40km to Bergamo.

09 BERGAMO
Although Milan's skyscrapers are visible on a clear day, historically Bergamo was more closely associated with Venice. The Venetian-style architecture can be seen in **Piazza Vecchia** and, more stridently, in the **City Walls** that were included as part of a Unesco World Heritage Site in 2017.

Behind this secular core sits the **Piazza del Duomo** with its

modest baroque cathedral. A great deal more interesting is the **Basilica di Santa Maria Maggiore** next door. To its whirl of frescoed, Romanesque apses, begun in 1137, Gothic touches were added, as was the Renaissance **Cappella Colleoni**, the mausoleum-chapel of the famous mercenary commander, Bartolomeo Colleoni (1696–1770). Demolishing an entire apse of the basilica, he commissioned Giovanni Antonio Amadeo to create a tomb that is now considered a masterpiece of Lombard art.

Also like Venice, Bergamo has a grand art academy. The seminal **Accademia Carrara** (lacarrara.it) is both school and museum, its stunning collection of 1800 Renaissance paintings amassed by local scholar Count Giacomo Carrara (1714–96).

03

Tuscan Wine Tour

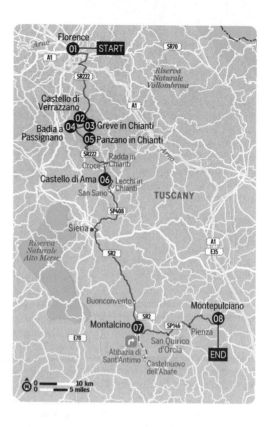

DURATION	DISTANCE	GREAT FOR
4 days	185km / 115 miles	Wine

BEST TIME TO GO	Autumn (September to November) for earthy hues and the grape harvest.

Tuscany has its fair share of highlights, but few can match the indulgence of a drive through its wine country. This classic Chianti tour offers a taste of life in the slow lane. Once out of Florence, you'll find yourself on quiet back roads driving through wooded hills and immaculate vineyards, stopping off at wine estates to sample the local vintages. En route, you'll enjoy soul-stirring scenery, farmhouse food and some captivating towns.

Link your trip

01 Italian Grand Tour

From Florence head either north or south to embark upon your own Grand Tour of Italy.

05 World Heritage Treasures

Also from Florence, pick up the A1 to Siena and towards Rome, for Unesco-listed beauties.

01 FLORENCE

Whet your appetite for the road ahead with a one-day cooking course at the **Cucina Lorenzo de' Medici** (cucinaldm.com), one of Florence's many cookery schools. Once you're done at the stove, sneak out to visit the **Chiesa e Museo di Orsanmichele**, an inspirational 14th-century church and one of Florence's lesser-known gems. Over the river, you can stock up on Tuscan wines and gourmet foods at **Obsequium** (obsequium.it), a well-stocked wine shop on the ground floor of a

BEST FOR GOURMETS

Tuscan *bistecca* (steak) in Panzano in Chianti.

Vineyard, Chianti

medieval tower. Or explore the old town on foot before you hit the road.

THE DRIVE
From Florence it's about an hour to Verrazzano. Head south along the scenic SR222 (Via Chiantigiana) towards Greve. When you get to Greti, you'll see a shop selling wine from the Castello di Verrazzano and, just before it, a right turn up to the castle.

02 CASTELLO DI VERRAZZANO
Some 26km south of Florence, the **Castello di Verrazzano** (verrazzano.com) lords it over a 230-hectare estate where Chianti Classico, Vin Santo, grappa, honey, olive oil and balsamic vinegar are produced. In a previous life, the castle was home to Giovanni di Verrazzano (1485–1528), an adventurer who explored the North American coast and is commemorated in New York by the Verrazzano-Narrows Bridge linking Staten Island to Brooklyn.

At the *castello* (castle), you can choose from a range of guided tours, which include a tasting and can also include lunch with the estate wines. Book ahead.

THE DRIVE
From the *castello* it's a simple 10-minute drive to Greve in Chianti. Double back to the SR222 in Greti, turn right and follow for about 3km.

03 GREVE IN CHIANTI
The main town in the Chianti Fiorentino, the northernmost of the two Chianti districts, Greve in Chianti has been an important wine centre for centuries. It has an amiable market-town air, and several eateries and *enoteche* (wine bars) that showcase the best Chianti food and drink. To stock up on picnic supplies, head to

Wine Tasting Goes High Tech

One of Tuscany's biggest cellars, the **Enoteca Falorni** (enotecafalorni.it) in Greve in Chianti stocks more than 1000 labels, of which around 100 are available for tasting. It's a lovely, brick-arched place, but wine tasting here is a very modern experience, thanks to a sophisticated wine-dispensing system that preserves wine in an open bottle for up to three weeks and allows tasters to serve themselves by the glass. Leave your credit card as a guarantee or buy a nonrefundable prepaid wine card (€5 to €100) to test your tipples of choice at the various 'tasting islands' dotted around the cellar. Curated tastings are also available.

Antica Macelleria Falorni (falorni.it), an atmospheric butcher's shop-bistro that the Bencistà Falorni family has been running since the early 19th century and which specialises in delicious *finocchiona briciolona* (pork salami made with fennel seeds and Chianti wine). The family also runs the Enoteca Falorni, the town's top cellar, where you can sample all sorts of local wine.

🧭 THE DRIVE

From Greve turn off the main through road, Viale Giovanni di Verrazzano, near the Esso petrol station, and head up towards Montefioralle. Continue on as the road climbs past olive groves and through woods to Badia a Passignano, about 15 minutes away.

04 BADIA A PASSIGNANO

Encircled by cypress trees and surrounded by swaths of olive groves and vineyards, the 11th-century **Chiesa di San Michele Arcangelo** (Abbey of Passignano) sits at the heart of a historic wine estate run by the Antinoris, one of Tuscany's oldest and most prestigious winemaking families. The estate offers a range of guided tours, tastings and cookery courses. Most require prior booking, but you can just turn up at the estate's wine shop, **La Bottega** (osteriadipassignano. com), to taste and buy Antinori wines and olive oil.

🧭 THE DRIVE

From Badia a Passignano, double back towards Greve and pick up the signposted SP118 for a pleasant

AGENZIA SINTESI/ALAMY STOCK PHOTO ©

Castello di Ama

15-minute drive along the narrow tree-shaded road to Panzano.

05 PANZANO IN CHIANTI

The quiet medieval town of Panzano is an essential stop on any gourmet's tour of Tuscany. Here you can stock up on meaty picnic fare at **L'Antica Macelleria Cecchini** (dariocecchini.com), a celebrated butcher's shop run by the poetry-spouting guru of Tuscan meat, Dario Cecchini. Alternatively, you can dine at one of his three eateries: the **Officina della Bistecca**, which serves a simple set menu based on *bistecca* (steak); **Solociccia**, where guests share a communal table to sample meat dishes other than *bistecca;* and **Dario DOC**, a casual daytime eatery. Book ahead for the Officina and Solociccia.

 THE DRIVE
From Panzano, it's about 20km to the Castello di Ama. Strike south on the SR222 towards Radda in Chianti, enjoying views off to the right as you wend your way through the green countryside. At Croce, just beyond Radda, turn left and head towards Lecchi and San Sano. The Castello di Ama is signposted after a further 7km.

06 CASTELLO DI AMA

To indulge in some contemporary-art appreciation between wine tastings, make for **Castello di Ama** (castellodiama.com) near Lecchi. This highly regarded wine estate produces a fine Chianti Classico and has an original sculpture park showcasing 14 site-specific works by artists including Louise Bourgeois, Chen Zhen, Anish Kapoor, Kendell Geers and Daniel Buren. Book ahead.

WJAREK/SHUTTERSTOCK ©

Wine shop, Montalcino (p40)

TUSCAN REDS

Something of a viticultural powerhouse, Tuscany excites wine buffs with its myriad full-bodied, highly respected reds. Like all Italian wines, these are classified according to strict guidelines, with the best categorised *Denominazione di Origine Controllata e Garantita* (DOCG), followed by *Denominazione di Origine Controllata* (DOC) and *Indicazione di Geografica Tipica* (IGT).

Chianti
Cheery, full and dry, contemporary Chianti gets the thumbs up from wine critics. Produced in eight subzones from Sangiovese and a mix of other grape varieties, Chianti Classico is the best known, with its Gallo Nero (Black Cockerel) emblem, which once symbolised the medieval Chianti League. Young, fun Chianti Colli Senesi from the Siena hills is the largest subzone; Chianti delle Colline Pisane is light and soft in style; and Chianti Rùfina comes from the hills east of Florence.

Brunello di Montalcino
Brunello is among Italy's most prized wines. The product of Sangiovese grapes, it must be aged for a minimum of 24 months in oak barrels and four months in bottles, and cannot be released until five years after the vintage. Intense and complex with an ethereal fragrance, it is best paired with game, wild boar and roasts. Brunello grape rejects go into Rosso di Montalcino, Brunello's substantially cheaper but wholly drinkable kid sister.

Vino Nobile di Montepulciano
Prugnolo Gentile grapes (a clone of Sangiovese) form the backbone of the distinguished Vino Nobile di Montepulciano. Its intense but delicate nose and dry, vaguely tannic taste make it the perfect companion to red meat and mature cheese.

Super Tuscans
Developed in the 1970s, the Super Tuscans are wines that fall outside the traditional classification categories. They are often made with a combination of local and imported grape varieties, such as Merlot and Cabernet. Solaia, Sassacaia, Bolgheri, Tignanello and Luce are all super-hot Super Tuscans.

WHY I LOVE THIS TRIP

Duncan Garwood, writer

The best Italian wine I've ever tasted was a Brunello di Montalcino. I bought it directly from a producer after a tasting in the Val d'Orcia and it was a revelation. It was just so thrilling to be drinking wine in the place it had been made. And it's this, combined with the inspiring scenery and magnificent food, that makes this tour of Tuscan wineries so uplifting.

THE DRIVE:

Reckon on about 1½ hours to Montalcino from the *castello*. Double back to the SP408 and head south to Lecchi and then on towards Siena. Skirt around the east of Siena and pick up the SR2 (Via Cassia) to Buonconvento and hilltop Montalcino, off to the right of the main road.

07 MONTALCINO

Montalcino, a pretty medieval town perched above the Val d'Orcia, is home to one of Italy's great wines, Brunello di Montalcino (and the more modest, but still very palatable, Rosso di Montalcino). There are plenty of *enoteche* where you can taste and buy, including one in the **Fortezza**, the 14th-century fortress that dominates the town's skyline.

For a historical insight into the town's winemaking past, head to the **Museo della Comunità di Montalcino e del Brunello** (fattoriadeibarbi. it/museo-del-brunello), a small museum at the Fattoria dei Barbi wine estate, one of the oldest in the region.

THE DRIVE

From Montalcino, head downhill and then, after about 8km, turn onto the SR2. At San Quirico d'Orcia pick up the SP146, a fabulously scenic road that weaves along the Val d'Orcia through rolling green hills, past the pretty town of Pienza, to Montepulciano. Allow about an hour.

☑ TOP TIP:

Driving in Chianti

To cut down on driving stress, purchase a copy of *Le strade del Gallo Nero,* a useful map that shows major and secondary roads and has a comprehensive list of wine estates. It's available at the tourist office in Greve and at Casa Chianti Classico (chianti classico.com), the headquarters of the Consorzio di Chianti Classico in Radda.

⬦ DETOUR
Abbazia di Sant'Antimo
Start: 07 Montalcino

The striking Romanesque **Abbazia di Sant'Antimo** (antimo.it) lies in an isolated valley just below the village of Castelnuovo dell'Abate, 10.5km from Montalcino.

According to tradition, Charlemagne founded the original monastery in 781. The exterior, built in pale travertine stone, is simple but for the stone carvings, which include various fantastical animals. Inside, look for the polychrome 13th-century *Madonna and Child* and 12th-century *Crucifixion* above the main altar. The abbey's church, crypt, upper loggia, chapel, pharmacy and garden can be visited with a rented video guide.

08 MONTEPULCIANO

Set atop a narrow ridge of volcanic rock, the Renaissance centre of Montepulciano produces the celebrated red wine Vino Nobile. To sample it, head up the main street, called in stages Via di Gracciano nel Corso, Via di Voltaia del Corso and Via dell'Opio nel Corso, to the **Enoliteca Consortile** (enolitecavinonobile.it), a modern tasting room operated by local wine producers. Housed on the ground floor of the town's **Medicean fortress**, it offers over 70 wines for tasting and purchase.

Montepulciano

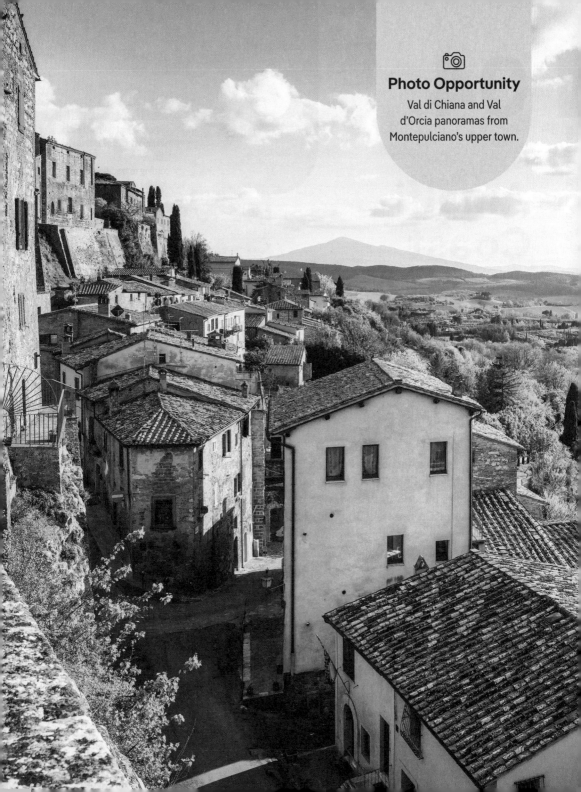

04

Amalfi Coast

BEST FOR THE OUTDOORS

Hiking Ravello and its environs.

Marina del Cantone

DURATION	DISTANCE	GREAT FOR
7 days	100km / 62 miles	Food and drink, nature

BEST TIME TO GO	June or September for beach weather without the peak summer crowds.

Not for the faint-hearted, this trip along the Amalfi Coast tests your driving skill on a 100km stretch, featuring dizzying hairpin turns and pastel-coloured towns draped over sea cliffs. Stops include the celebrated coastal resorts of Positano and Amalfi, as well as serene, mountain-top Ravello, famed for its gardens and views. Cars are useful for inland exploration, as are the walking trails that provide a wonderful escape from the built-up coastal clamour.

Link your trip

01 Italian Grand Tour

It's a short hop north to Naples, from where you can start your search for enlightenment and adventure.

06 Wonders of Ancient Sicily

While you're in the south, why not head to Sicily for Arab treasures and Greek splendours?

01 **VICO EQUENSE**

The Bay of Naples is justifiably famous for its pizza, invented here as a savoury way to highlight two local specialities: mozzarella and sun-kissed tomatoes. Besides its pretty little *centro storico* (historic centre), this little clifftop town overlooking the Bay of Naples claims some of the region's top pie, including a by-the-metre version at cult-status **Ristorante & Pizzeria da Gigino** (pizzametro.it).

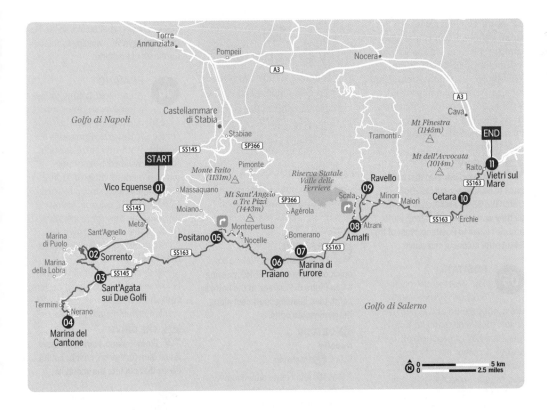

 THE DRIVE
From Vico Equense to Sorrento, your main route will be the SS145 roadway for 12km. Expect to hug the sparkling coastline after Marina di Equa before venturing inland around Meta.

02 SORRENTO

On paper, cliff-straddling Sorrento is a place to avoid – a package-holiday centre with few sights, no beach to speak of, and a glut of brassy English-style pubs. In reality, it's strangely appealing, its laid-back southern Italian charm resisting all attempts to swamp it in souvenir tat and graceless development.

According to Greek legend, it was in Sorrento's waters that the mythical sirens once lived. Sailors of antiquity were powerless to resist the beautiful song of these charming maiden-monsters, who would lure them to their doom.

 THE DRIVE
Take the SS145 for 8km to Sant'Agata sui Due Golfi. Sun-dappled village streets give way to forest as you head further inland.

03 SANT'AGATA SUI DUE GOLFI

Perched high in the hills above Sorrento, sleepy Sant'Agata sui Due Golfi commands spectacular views of the Bay of Naples on one side and the Bay of Salerno on the other (hence its name, Saint Agatha on the Two Gulfs).

The best viewpoint is the **Convento del Deserto**, a Carmelite convent 1.5km uphill from the village centre. It's a knee-wearing hike, but make it to the top and you're rewarded with fabulous 360-degree vistas.

 THE DRIVE
From Sant'Agata sui Due Golfi to Marina del Cantone it's a 9km drive, the last part involving some serious hairpin turns. Don't let the gorgeous sea views distract you.

04 MARINA DEL CANTONE

From **Nerano**, where you'll park, a beautiful hiking trail leads down to the stunning Bay of Ieranto and one of the coast's top swimming spots, Marina del Cantone. This unassuming village with its small pebble beach is a lovely, tranquil place to stay as well as a popular diving destination. The village also has a reputation as a gastronomic hotspot and VIPs regularly catch a boat over from Capri to dine on super-lative seafood at **Lo Scoglio** (hotelloscoglio.com).

🛞 THE DRIVE
First, head back up that switch-back to Sant'Agata sui Due Golfi. Catch the SS145 and then the SS163 as they weave their way along bluffs and cliff sides to Positano. Most of the 24km offer stunning sea views.

05 POSITANO
The pearl in the pack, Positano is the coast's most photogenic and expensive town. Its steeply stacked houses are a medley of peaches, pinks and terracottas, and its near-vertical streets (many of which are, in fact, staircases) are lined with voguish shop displays, elegant hotels and smart res-taurants. Look closely, though, and you'll find reassuring signs of everyday reality – crumbling stucco, streaked paintwork and occasionally a faint whiff of prob-lematic drainage.

Photo Opportunity
Positano's vertiginous stack of pastel-coloured houses cascading down to the sea.

John Steinbeck visited in 1953 and was so bowled over that he wrote of its dream-like quali-ties in an article for *Harper's Bazaar*.

🛞 THE DRIVE
From Positano to Praiano it's a quick 6km spin on the SS163, passing Il San Pietro di Positano at the halfway point, then heading southeast along the peninsula's edge.

➤ DETOUR
Nocelle
Start: 05 **Positano**

A tiny, still relatively isolated mountain village above Positano, Nocelle (450m) commands some of the most memorable views on the entire coast. A world apart from touristy Positano, it's a sleepy, silent place where not much ever happens, nor would its few residents ever want it to. If you want to stay, consider delightful **Villa della Quercia** (villalaquercia.com), a former

monastery with spectacular vistas. No-celle lies eight very winding kilometres northeast of Positano.

06 PRAIANO
An ancient fishing village, a low-key summer resort and, increasingly, a popular centre for the arts, Praiano is a delight. With no centre as such, its whitewashed houses pep-per the verdant ridge of Monte Sant'Angelo as it slopes towards Capo Sottile. Exploring involves lots of steps and there are several trails that start from town, in-cluding the legendary **Sentiero degli Dei**.

For those who'd rather venture below sea level, **La Boa** (laboa.com) runs dives that explore the area's coral, marine life and grottoes.

🛞 THE DRIVE
From Praiano, Marina di Furore is just 3km further on, past beautiful coves that cut into the shoreline.

07 MARINA DI FURORE
A few kilometres further on, Marina di Furore sits at the bottom of what's known as the fjord of Furore, a giant cleft that cuts through the Lattari mountains. The main village, however, stands 300m above, in the upper Vallone del Furore. A one-horse place that sees few tourists, it breathes a distinctly rural air despite the presence of colourful murals and unlikely modern sculpture.

🛞 THE DRIVE
From Marina di Furore to Amalfi, the sparkling Mediterranean Sea will be your escort as you drive eastward along the SS163 coastal road for 6km. Look for Vettica Minore and Conca dei Marini along the way, along with fluffy bunches of fragrant cypress trees.

WALK OF THE GODS
Probably the best-known walk on the Amalfi Coast is the three-hour, 12km **Sentiero degli Dei**, which follows the high ridge linking Praiano to Positano. The walk commences in the heart of Praiano, where a thigh-challenging 1000-step start takes you up to the path itself. The route proper is not advised for vertigo sufferers: it's a spectacular, me-andering trail along the top of the mountains, with caves and terraces set dramatically in the cliffs and deep valleys framed by the brilliant blue of the sea. You'll eventually emerge at Nocelle, from where a series of steps will take you through the olive groves and deposit you on the road just east of Positano.

WHY I LOVE THIS TRIP

Cristian Bonetto, writer

From Richard Wagner to Gore Vidal, the Amalfi Coast has bewitched some of the world's most illustrious figures. This is Italy's most arresting coastline, with a natural beauty that borders on the ethereal. While this trip takes in the fabled, sun-drenched towns the Amalfi Coast is famous for, it also sees you hitting the sleepy, hike-friendly hills above, where the views demand a symphony.

08 AMALFI

It is hard to grasp that pretty little Amalfi, with its sun-filled piazzas and small beach, was once a maritime superpower with a population of more than 70,000. For one thing, it's not a big place – you can easily walk from one end to the other in about 20 minutes. For another, there are very few historical buildings of note. The explanation is chilling – most of the old city, along with its populace, simply slid into the sea during an earthquake in 1343.

One happy exception is the striking **Cattedrale di Sant'Andrea**, parts of which date from the early 10th century. Between 10am and 5pm entrance to the cathedral is through the adjacent **Chiostro del Paradiso**, a 13th-century Moorish-style cloister.

Be sure to take the short walk around the headland to neighbouring **Atrani**, a picturesque tangle of whitewashed alleys and arches centred on a lively, lived-in piazza and popular beach.

THE DRIVE

Start the 7km trip to Ravello by heading along the coast to Atrani. Here turn inland and follow the SR373 as it climbs the steep hillside in a series of second-gear hairpin turns up to Ravello.

09 RAVELLO

Sitting high in the hills above Amalfi, polished Ravello is a town almost entirely dedicated to tourism. Boasting impeccable artistic credentials – Richard Wagner, DH Lawrence and Virginia Woolf all lounged here – it's known today for its ravishing gardens and stupendous views, the best in the world according to former resident the late Gore Vidal.

To enjoy these views, head south of Ravello's cathedral to the 14th-century tower that marks the entrance to **Villa Rufolo** (villarufolo.it). Created by Scotsman Scott Neville Reid in 1853, these gardens combine celestial panoramic views, exotic colours, artistically crumbling towers and luxurious blooms.

Also worth seeking out is the wonderful **Camo** (museodelcorallo.com). Squeezed between tourist-driven shops, this very special place is, on the face of it, a cameo shop. And exquisite they are too, crafted primarily out of coral and shell. But don't stop here; ask to see the treasure trove of a museum beyond the showroom.

Cetara

THE DRIVE

Head back down to the SS163 for a 19km journey that twists and turns challengingly along the coast to Cetara. Pine trees and a variety of flowering shrubs line the way.

DETOUR

Ravello Walks
Start: 09 Ravello

Ravello is the starting point for numerous walks that follow ancient paths through the surrounding Lattari mountains. If you've got the legs for it, you can walk down to **Minori** via an attractive route of steps, hidden alleys and olive groves, passing the picturesque hamlet of **Torello** en route. Alternatively, you can head the other way, to Amalfi, via the ancient village of **Scala**. Once a flourishing religious centre with more than 100 churches and the oldest settlement on the Amalfi Coast, Scala is now a pocket-sized, sleepy place where the wind whistles through empty streets, and gnarled locals go patiently about their daily chores.

10 CETARA

Cetara is a picturesque, tumbledown fishing village with a reputation as a gastronomic delight. Since medieval times it has been an important fishing centre, and today its deep-sea tuna fleet is considered one of the Mediterranean's most important. At night, fishers set out in small boats armed with powerful lamps to fish for anchovies. No surprise then that tuna and anchovies dominate local menus, including at **Cetara Punto e Pasta**, a sterling seafood restaurant near the small harbour.

THE DRIVE

From Cetara to Vietri sul Mare, head northeast for 6km on the

Amalfi Coast

THE BLUE RIBBON DRIVE

Stretching from Vietri sul Mare to Sant'Agata sui Due Golfi near Sorrento, the SS163 – nicknamed the **Nastro Azzurro** (Blue Ribbon) – remains one of Italy's most breathtaking roadways. Commissioned by Bourbon king Ferdinand II and completed in 1853, it wends its way along the Amalfi Coast's entire length, snaking round impossibly tight curves, over deep ravines and through tunnels gouged out of sheer rock. It's a magnificent feat of civil engineering – although it can be challenging to drive – and in certain places it's not wide enough for two cars to pass, a fact John Steinbeck alluded to in a 1953 essay.

SS163 for more twisting, turning and stupendous views across the Golfo di Salerno.

11 VIETRI SUL MARE

Marking the end of the coastal road, Vietri sul Mare is the ceramics capital of Campania. Although production dates back to Roman times, it didn't take off as an industry until the 16th and 17th centuries. Today, ceramics shopaholics can get their fix at the **Ceramica Artistica Solimene** (ceramica solimene.it), a vast factory outlet with an extraordinary glass and ceramic facade.

For a primer on the history of the area's ceramics, seek out the **Museo della Ceramica** in the nearby village of **Raito**.

05

World Heritage Treasures

DURATION	DISTANCE	GREAT FOR
14 days	870km / 540 miles	History, food and drink

BEST TIME TO GO	April, May and September for ideal sightseeing weather and local produce.

Topping the Unesco charts with 58 World Heritage Sites, Italy offers the full gamut, ranging from historic city centres and human-made masterpieces to snowcapped mountains and areas of outstanding natural beauty. This trip through central and northern Italy touches on the country's unparalleled artistic and architectural legacy, taking in ancient Roman ruins, priceless Renaissance paintings, great cathedrals and, to cap it all off, Venice's unique canal-scape.

Link your trip

02 The Graceful Italian Lakes

Branch off at Verona and take the A4 for some refined elegance and mountain scenery.

03 Tuscan Wine Tour

From Florence head south to Tuscany's Chianti wine country to indulge in some wine tasting at the area's historic vineyards.

01 **ROME**

An epic, monumental metropolis, Italy's capital is a city of thrilling beauty and high drama. Its historic centre, which according to Unesco has some of antiquity's most important monuments, has been a World Heritage Site since 1980, and the **Vatican**, technically a separate state but in reality located within Rome's city limits, has been on the Unesco list since 1984.

Of Rome's many ancient monuments, the most iconic is the **Colosseum** (parcocolosseo.it), the towering 1st-century-CE amphitheatre where

BEST FOR ART

Florence's Galleria degli Uffizi.

Roman Forum, Rome

gladiators met in mortal combat and condemned criminals fought off wild beasts. Nearby, the **Palatino** (Palatine Hill) was the ancient city's most exclusive neighbourhood, as well as its oldest – Romulus and Remus supposedly founded the city here in 753 BCE. From the Palatino, you can stroll down to the skeletal ruins of the **Roman Forum**, the once-beating heart of the ancient city. All three sights are covered by a single ticket.

To complete your tour of classical wonders search out the **Pantheon** (pantheonroma.com), the best preserved of Rome's ancient monuments. One of the most influential buildings in the world, this domed temple, now a church, is an extraordinary sight with its vast columned portico and soaring marble-clad interior.

 THE DRIVE
The easiest route to Siena, about three hours away, is via the A1 autostrada. Join this from the Rome ring road,

Photo Opportunity

The Roman Forum from the Palatino.

the GRA (Grande Raccordo Anulare), and head north, past Orvieto's dramatic clifftop cathedral, to the Valdichiano exit. Take this and follow signs onto the Raccordo Siena-Bettolle (E78) for the last leg into Siena.

02 **SIENA**
Siena is one of Italy's most enchanting medieval towns. Its walled centre, a beautifully preserved warren of dark lanes, Gothic *palazzi* (mansions) and pretty piazzas, is centred on **Piazza del Campo** (known as Il Campo), the sloping shell-shaped square that stages the city's annual horse race, Il Palio, on 2 July and 16 August.

On the piazza, the 102m-high **Torre del Mangia** (ticket@comune.siena.it) soars above the Gothic **Palazzo Pubblico** (Palazzo Comunale), home to the city's finest art museum, the **Museo Civico**. Of Siena's churches, the one to see is the 13th-century **Duomo** (Cattedrale di Santa Maria Assunta; operaduomo.siena.it), one of Italy's greatest Gothic churches. Highlights include the remarkable white, green and red facade, and, inside, the magnificent inlaid marble floor that illustrates historical and biblical stories.

ITALIAN ART & ARCHITECTURE

The Ancients
In pre-Roman times, the Greeks built theatres and proportionally perfect temples in their southern colonies at Agrigento, Syracuse and Paestum, while the Etruscans concentrated on funerary art, creating elaborate tombs at Tarquinia and Cerveteri. Coming in their wake, the Romans specialised in roads, aqueducts and monumental amphitheatres such as the Colosseum and Verona's Arena.

Romanesque
With the advent of Christianity in the 4th century, basilicas began to spring up, many with glittering Byzantine-style mosaics. The Romanesque period (c 1050–1200) saw the construction of fortified monasteries and robust, bulky churches such as Bari's Basilica di San Nicola and Modena's cathedral. Pisa's striking *duomo* (cathedral) displays a characteristic Tuscan variation on the style.

Gothic
Gothic architecture, epic in scale and typically embellished by gargoyles, pinnacles and statues, took on a more classical form in Italy. Assisi's Basilica di San Francesco is an outstanding early example, but for the full-blown Italian Gothic style check out the cathedrals in Florence, Venice, Siena and Orvieto.

Renaissance
From quiet beginnings in 14th-century Florence, the Renaissance erupted across Italy before spreading across Europe. In Italy, painters such as Giotto, Botticelli, Leonardo da Vinci and Raphael led the way, while architects Brunelleschi and Bramante rewrote the rule books with their beautifully proportioned basilicas. All-rounder Michelangelo worked his way into immortality, producing masterpieces such as *David* and the Sistine Chapel frescoes.

Baroque
Dominating the 17th century, the extravagant baroque style found fertile soil in Italy. Witness the Roman works of Gian Lorenzo Bernini and Francesco Borromini, Lecce's flamboyant *centro storico* (historic centre) and the magical baroque towns of southeastern Sicily.

Neoclassicism
Signalling a return to sober classical lines, neoclassicism majored in the late 18th and early 19th centuries. Signature works include Caserta's Palazzo Reale and La Scala opera house in Milan. In artistic terms, the most famous Italian exponent was Antonio Canova.

THE DRIVE
There are two alternatives to get to Florence. The quickest, which is via the fast RA3 Siena–Firenze Raccordo, takes about 1½ hours. But if you have the time, we recommend the scenic SR222, which snakes through the Chianti wine country, passing through quintessential hilltop towns and vine-laden slopes. Reckon on at least 2½ hours for this route.

DETOUR
San Gimignano
Start: 02 Siena

Dubbed the medieval Manhattan thanks to its 14 11th-century towers, San Gimignano is a classic hilltop town and an easy detour from Siena.

From the car park next to Porta San Giovanni, it's a short walk up to **Palazzo Comunale** (sangimignanomusei.it), which houses the town's art gallery, the **Pinacoteca**, and tallest tower, the **Torre Grossa**. Nearby, the Romanesque basilica, known as the **Collegiata** (duomosangimignano.it), has some remarkable Ghirlandaio frescoes.

Before leaving town, be sure to sample the local Vernaccia wine at the **Vernaccia di San Gimignano Wine Experience** (sangimignanomuseovernaccia.com) next to the Rocca (fortress).

San Gimignano is about 40km northwest of Siena. Head for Florence on the RA3 until Poggibonsi and then pick up the SS429.

03 FLORENCE
Cradle of the Renaissance and home of Michelangelo, Machiavelli and the Medici, Florence (Firenze) is magnetic, romantic, unique and busy. A couple of days is not long here but enough for a breathless introduction to the city's top sights, many of which can be enjoyed on foot.

Towering above the medieval skyline, the **Duomo** (Cattedrale

Cappella degli Scrovegni (p53), Padua

KAMIRA/SHUTTERSTOCK ©

Basilica di San Marco, Venice

WORLD HERITAGE SITES

With 58 World Heritage Sites, Italy has more than any other country. But what exactly is a World Heritage Site? Basically it's anywhere that Unesco's World Heritage Committee decides is of 'outstanding universal value' and inscribes on the World Heritage List. It could be a natural wonder such as the Great Barrier Reef in Australia or a human-made icon such as New York's Statue of Liberty, a historic city centre or a great work of art or architecture.

The list was set up in 1972 and has since grown to include 1157 sites from 167 countries. Italy first got in on the act in 1979 when it successfully nominated its first entry – the prehistoric rock drawings of the Valcamonica valley in northeastern Lombardy. The inscription process requires sites to be nominated by a country and then independently evaluated. If they pass scrutiny and meet at least one of 10 selection criteria, they get the green light at the World Heritage Committee's annual meeting. Once on the list, sites qualify for management support and access to the World Heritage Fund.

Italian nominations have generally fared well and since Rome's historic centre and the Chiesa di Santa Maria delle Grazie in Milan were inscribed in 1980, many of the nation's greatest attractions have made it onto the list – the historic centres of Florence, Naples, Siena and San Gimignano; the cities of Venice, Verona and Ferrara; the archaeological sites of Pompeii, Paestum and Agrigento; as well as natural beauties such as the Amalfi Coast, Aeolian Islands, Dolomites and Tuscany's Val d'Orcia.

di Santa Maria del Fiore; museum florence.com) dominates the city centre with its famous red-tiled dome and striking facade. A short hop away, **Piazza della Signoria** opens onto the sculpture-filled **Loggia dei Lanzi** and the **Torre d'Arnolfo** above **Palazzo Vecchio** (musefirenze.it), Florence's lavish City Hall.

Next to the *palazzo,* the **Galleria degli Uffizi** (uffizi.it) houses one of the world's great art collections, including works by Botticelli, Leonardo da Vinci, Michelangelo, Raphael and many other Renaissance maestros.

🚗 THE DRIVE

From Florence it's about 1½ hours to Pisa along the A11 autostrada or just over an hour using the speedy, toll-free FI-PI-LI (SS67) linking the two cities. At the end of either route, follow signs to Pisa *centro* (centre).

04 PISA

Once a maritime republic to rival Genoa and Venice, Pisa now owes its fame to an architectural project gone horribly wrong. The **Leaning Tower** (opapisa.it) is an extraordinary sight and one of Italy's most photographed monuments. The tower, originally erected as a *campanile* (bell tower) in the late 12th century, is one of three Romanesque buildings on the immaculate lawns of **Piazza dei Miracoli** (also known as Campo dei Miracoli or Piazza del Duomo).

The candy-striped **Duomo** (Duomo di Santa Maria Assunta; opapisa.it), begun in 1063, has a graceful tiered facade and cavernous interior, while to its west, the cupcake-like **Battistero** (opapisa.it) is something of an architectural hybrid, with a Pisan-Romanesque lower section and a Gothic upper level and dome. End your Piazza dei Miracoli foray with a saunter atop the city's old medieval walls, **Mura di Pisa** (muradipisa.it).

THE DRIVE
It's a 2½-hour drive up to Modena from Pisa. Head back towards Florence on the A11 and then pick up the A1 to Bologna. Continue as the road twists and falls through the wooded Apennines before flattening out near Bologna. Exit at Modena Sud (Modena South) and follow signs for the *centro*.

05 MODENA
One of Italy's top foodie towns, Modena has a stunning medieval centre and a trio of Unesco-listed sights. First up is the gorgeous **Duomo** (Cattedrale Metropolitana di Santa Maria Assunta e San Geminiano; duomodimodena.it), which is widely considered to be Italy's finest Romanesque church. Features to look out for include the Gothic rose window and a series of bas-reliefs depicting scenes from Genesis.

Nearby, the 13th-century **Torre Ghirlandina** (unesco.modena.it), an 87m-high tower topped by a Gothic spire, was named after Seville's Giralda bell tower by exiled Spanish Jews in the early 16th century. The last of the Unesco threesome is **Piazza Grande**, just south of the cathedral. The city's focal square, this is flanked by the porticoed **Palazzo Comunale**, Modena's elegant town hall.

THE DRIVE
From Modena reckon on about 1¼ hours to Verona, via the A22 and A4 autostradas. Follow the A22 as it traverses the flat Po valley plain, passing the medieval town of Mantua (Mantova; worth a quick break) before connecting with the A4. Turn off at Verona Sud and follow signs for the city centre.

06 VERONA

A World Heritage Site since 2000, Verona's historic centre is a beautiful mix of architectural styles and inspiring buildings. Chief among these is its stunning Roman amphitheatre, known as the **Arena**. Dating to the 1st century CE, this is Italy's third-largest amphitheatre after the Colosseum and Capua amphitheatre, and although it no longer seats 30,000, it still draws sizeable crowds for operas and concerts.

But Verona isn't simply a relic of the past. A thriving regional city, it also hosts a fantastic modern art gallery, **Galleria d'Arte Moderna Achille Forti** (gam.comune.verona.it), with a fabulous collection of under-appreciated Italian modernists such as Felice Casorati and Angelo Zamboni. It's also packed with excellent contemporary restaurants like **Locanda 4 Cuochi** (locanda4cuochi.it) and wine bars, such as **Antica Bottega del Vino** (bottegavini.it), showcasing regional wines.

THE DRIVE
To Padua it's about an hour from Verona on the A4 Venice autostrada. Exit at Padova Ovest (Padua West) and join the SP47 after the toll booth. Follow this until you see, after a road bridge, a turn-off signposted to the *centro*.

07 PADUA

Travellers to Padua (Padova) usually make a beeline for the city's main attraction, the **Cappella degli Scrovegni** (cappelladegliscrovegni.it), but there's more to Padua than Giotto frescoes and it's actually the **Orto Botanico** (ortobotanicopd.it) that represents Padua on Unesco's list of World Heritage Sites. The oldest botanical garden in the world, this dates to 1545 when a group

of medical students planted some rare plants in order to study their medicinal properties. Discover Padua's outsized contribution to science and, in particular, medicine at the fascinating **Museum of Medical History** (musme.it), housed in what was ostensibly the world's first hospital where medical students learnt clinical practice at a patient's bedside.

THE DRIVE
Traffic permitting, it's about 45 minutes to Venice along the A4. Pass through Mestre and over the Ponte della Libertà bridge to Interparking Venezia Tronchetto on the island of Tronchetto.

08 VENICE
The end of the road, quite literally, is Venice (Venezia). Of the city's many must-sees the most famous are on **Piazza San Marco**, including the **Basilica di San Marco** (basilicasanmarco.it), Venice's great showpiece church. Built originally to house the bones of St Mark, it's a truly awe-inspiring vision with its spangled spires, Byzantine domes, luminous mosaics and lavish marble work. For a bird's eye view, head to the nearby **Campanile**.

Adjacent to the basilica, the **Palazzo Ducale** (palazzoducale.visitmuve.it) was the residence of Venice's doges (ruling dukes) from the 9th century. Inside, its lavishly decorated chambers harbour some seriously heavyweight art, including Tintoretto's gigantic *Paradiso* in the Sala del Maggiore Consiglio. Connecting the palace to the city dungeons, the **Ponte dei Sospiri** (Bridge of Sighs) was named after the sighs that prisoners (including Casanova) emitted en route from court to cell. If you're hungry, hit the streets on foot to get a real taste of the city.

06

Wonders of Ancient Sicily

DURATION	DISTANCE	GREAT FOR
12–14 days	664km / 412 miles	Food and drink, history

BEST TIME TO GO	Spring and autumn are best. Avoid the heat and crowds of high summer.

Segesta

A Mediterranean crossroads for 25 centuries, Sicily is heir to an unparalleled cultural legacy, from the temples of Magna Graecia to Norman churches made kaleidoscopic by Byzantine and Arab artisans. This trip takes you from exotic, palm-fanned Palermo to the baroque splendours of Syracuse and Catania. On the way, you'll also experience Sicily's bucolic farmland, smouldering volcanoes and long stretches of aquamarine coastline.

Link your trip

01 Grand Tour

Head north to Naples where you can start your search for enlightenment and adventure.

04 Amalfi Coast

Don't miss this week-long adventure of hairpin turns and vertical landscapes amid the world's most glamorous stretch of coastline.

01 PALERMO

Palermo is a fascinating conglomeration of splendour and decay. Unlike Florence or Rome, many of its treasures are hidden rather than scrubbed up for endless streams of tourists. The city's cross-cultural history infuses its daily life, lending its dusty backstreet markets a distinct Middle Eastern feel and its architecture a unique East-meets-West look.

A trading port since Phoenician times, the city, which is best explored on foot, first came to prominence as the capital of Arab Sicily in the 9th century CE. When the Normans rode into

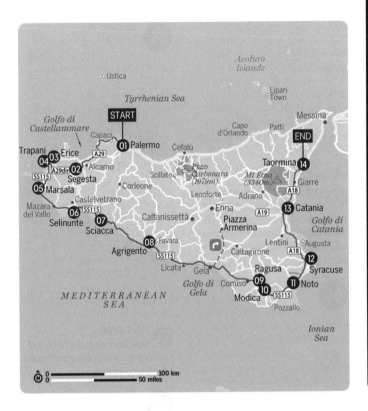

The 1693 Earthquake

On 11 January 1693, a devastating 7.4-magnitude earthquake hit southeastern Sicily, destroying buildings from Catania to Ragusa. The destruction was terrible, but it also created a blank palette for architects to rebuild the region's cities and towns out of whole cloth, in the latest style and according to rational urban planning – a phenomenon practically unheard of since ancient times. In fact, the earthquake ushered in an entirely new architectural style known as Sicilian baroque, defined by its seductive curves and elaborate detail, which you can see on display in Ragusa, Modica, Catania and many other cities in the region.

---

town in the 11th century, they used Arab know-how to turn it into Christendom's richest and most sophisticated city. The **Cappella Palatina** (Palatine Chapel; federicosecondo.org) is the perfect expression of this marriage, with its gold-inflected Byzantine mosaics crowned by a honeycomb *muqarnas* ceiling – a masterpiece of Arab craftsmanship.

For an insight into Sicily's long and turbulent past, the **Museo Archeologico Regionale Antonio Salinas** houses some of the island's most valuable Greek and Roman artefacts.

THE DRIVE
From Palermo the 82km trip to Segesta starts along the fast-moving A29 as it skirts the mountains west of Palermo, then runs along agricultural plains until you reach the hills of Segesta. The Greek ruins lie just off the A29dir.

02 SEGESTA
Set on the edge of a deep canyon in the midst of desolate mountains, the 5th-century-BCE ruins of Segesta are a magical sight. The city, founded by the ancient Elymians, was in constant conflict with Selinunte, whose destruction it sought with dogged

determination and singular success. Time, however, has done to Segesta what violence inflicted on Selinunte; little remains now, save the theatre and the never-completed Doric temple. The latter dates from around 430 BCE and is remarkably well preserved. On windy days its 36 giant columns are said to act like an organ, producing mysterious notes.

THE DRIVE
Keep heading along A29dir through a patchwork of green and ochre fields and follow signs for the 40km to Trapani. As you reach its outskirts, you'll head up the very windy SP31 to Erice, with great views of countryside and sea.

03 ERICE

A spectacular hill town, Erice combines medieval charm with astounding 360-degree views from atop the legendary **Mt Eryx** (750m) – on a clear day, you can see as far as Cape Bon in Tunisia. Wander the medieval streets interspersed with churches, forts and tiny cobbled piazzas. Little remains from its ancient past, though as a centre for the cult of Venus, it has a seductive history.

The best views can be had from the **Giardino del Balio**, which overlooks the rugged turrets and wooded hillsides down to the saltpans of Trapani and the sea. Adjacent to the gardens is the Norman **Castello di Venere** (fondazioneericearte.org/il-castello-di-venere), built in the 12th and 13th centuries over the ancient Temple of Venus. And while Venus may be the goddess of love, Erice's goddess of all things sweet is Maria Grammatico, whose eponymous **pasticceria** (mariagrammatico.it) is revered around the globe. Don't leave town without savouring one of her cannoli or lemon-flavoured *cuscinetti* (small fried pastries).

THE DRIVE
For the 12km to Trapani, it's back down the switchbacks of the SP31.

04 TRAPANI

Once a key link in a powerful trading network that stretched from Carthage to Venice, Trapani occupies a sickle-shaped spit of land that hugs its ancient harbour. Although Trapani's industrial outskirts are rather bleak, its historic centre is filled with atmospheric pedestrian streets and some lovely churches and baroque buildings. The narrow network of streets remains a Moorish labyrinth, although it takes much of its character from the fabulous 18th-century baroque of the Spanish period. Make time for the **Chiesa Anime Sante del Purgatorio**, home to the 18th-century *Misteri,* 20 life-sized effigies depicting the Passion of Christ.

THE DRIVE
For the 33km trip from Trapani to Marsala, head south on the SS115. Small towns alternate with farmland until you reach Marsala on Sicily's west coast.

05 MARSALA

Best known for its namesake sweet dessert wine, Marsala is an elegant town of stately baroque buildings within a perfect square of city walls. Founded by Phoenicians escaping Roman attacks, the city still has remnants of the 7m-thick ramparts they built, ensuring that it was the last Punic settlement to fall to the Romans.

Marsala's finest treasure is the partially reconstructed remains of a Carthaginian *liburna* (warship) – the only remaining physical evidence of the Phoenicians' seafaring superiority in the 3rd century BCE. You can visit it at the **Museo Archeologico Baglio Anselmi**.

THE DRIVE
For this 52km leg, once again head down the SS115, passing through farmland and scattered towns until you reach the A29. Continue on the autostrada to Castelvetrano, then follow the SS115 and SS115dir for the last leg through orchards and fields to seaside Selinunte.

06 SELINUNTE

Built on a promontory overlooking the sea, the Greek **ruins of Selinunte** (en.selinunte.com) are among the most impressive in Sicily, dating to around the 7th century BCE. There are few historical records of the city, which was once one of the world's most powerful, and even the names of the various temples have been forgotten and are now identified by letters. The most impressive, **Temple E**, has been partially rebuilt, its columns pieced together from their fragments with part of its tympanum. Many of the carvings, which are on a par with the Parthenon marbles, particularly those from **Temple C**, are now in Palermo's archaeological museum.

THE DRIVE
Head back up to the SS115 and past a series of hills and plains for the 37km trip to Sciacca.

07 SCIACCA

Seaside Sciacca was founded in the 5th century BCE as a thermal resort for nearby Selinunte. Until 2015, when financial woes forced the spa to shut down indefinitely, Sciacca's healing waters continued to be the big drawcard, attracting coachloads of Italian tourists who came to wallow in its sulphurous vapours and mineral-rich mud. Spas and thermal cures apart, it remains a laid-back town with an attractive medieval core and some excellent seafood restaurants.

THE DRIVE
Continue eastwards on the SS115 as it follows the southern coast onto Porto Empedocle and then, 10km inland, Agrigento's hilltop centre. In all, it's about 62km.

08 AGRIGENTO

Seen from a distance, Agrigento's unsightly apartment blocks loom incongruously on the hillside, distracting attention from the splendid **Valley of Temples** (parcovalledei templi.it) below. In the valley, the mesmerising ruins of ancient Akragras claim the best-preserved Doric temples outside of Greece.

The ruins are spread over a 13-sq-km site divided into eastern and western halves. Head first to the eastern zone, where you'll find the three best temples: the **Tempio di Hera**, the **Tempio di Ercole** and, most spectacularly, the **Tempio della Concordia** (Temple of Concord). This, the only temple to survive relatively intact, was built around 440 BCE and was converted into a Christian church in the 6th century.

Uphill from the ruins, Agrigento's **medieval centre** also has its charms, with a 14th-century cathedral and a number of medieval and baroque buildings.

🚗 THE DRIVE

For this 133km leg head back to the SS115, which veers from inland farmland to brief encounters with the sea. Past the town of Gela, you will head into more hilly country, including a steep climb past Comiso, followed by a straight shot along the SP52 to Ragusa.

📍 DETOUR
Villa Romana del Casale
Start: 08 Agrigento

Near the town of Piazza Armerina in central Sicily, the stunning 3rd-century Roman **Villa Romana del Casale** (villaromanadelcasale.it) is thought to have been the country retreat of Diocletian's co-emperor Marcus Aurelius

Maximianus. Buried under mud in a 12th-century flood, the villa remained hidden for 700 years before its floor mosaics – considered some of the finest in existence – were discovered in the 1950s. Covering almost the entire floor, they are thought unique for their range of hues and natural, narrative style.

09 RAGUSA

Set amid the rocky peaks northwest of Modica, Ragusa has two faces. Atop the hill sits **Ragusa Superiore**, a busy town with all the trappings of a modern provincial capital, while etched into the hillside is **Ragusa Ibla**. This sloping area of tangled alleyways, grey stone houses and baroque *palazzi* is Ragusa's magnificent historic centre.

Like other towns in the region, Ragusa Ibla collapsed after the 1693 earthquake. But the

Valley of Temples, Agrigento

aristocracy, ever impractical, rebuilt their homes on exactly the same spot. Grand baroque churches and *palazzi* line the twisting, narrow lanes, which then open suddenly onto sun-drenched piazzas. Piazza del Duomo, the centre of town, is dominated by the 18th-century baroque **Duomo di San Giorgio**, with its magnificent neoclassical dome and stained-glass windows.

THE DRIVE
Follow the SS115 for this winding, up-and-down 15km drive through rock-littered hilltops to Modica.

10 MODICA
Atmospheric Modica recalls a *presepe* (traditional nativity scene), its medieval buildings climbing steeply up either side of a deep gorge. But unlike

📷 Photo Opportunity
Mt Etna from Taormina's Greek theatre.

some of the other Unesco-listed cities in the area, it doesn't package its treasures into a single easy-to-see street or central piazza: rather, they are spread around the town and take some discovering. Its star attraction is the baroque **Duomo di San Giorgio**, which stands in isolated splendour atop a majestic 250-step staircase.

The city's nerve centre is **Corso Umberto**. A wide avenue flanked by graceful palaces, churches, restaurants and bars, the thoroughfare is where the locals

take their evening *passeggiata* (stroll). Originally a raging river flowed through town, but after major flood damage in 1902 it was dammed and Corso Umberto was built over it.

THE DRIVE
Head back onto the SS115, which becomes quite curvy as you close in on Noto, 40km away.

11 NOTO
Flattened by the 1693 earthquake, Noto was rebuilt quickly and grandly, and its sandstone buildings make it the finest baroque town in Sicily, especially impressive at night when illuminations accentuate its carved facades. The pièce de résistance is **Corso Vittorio Emanuele**, an elegantly manicured walkway flanked by thrilling baroque *palazzi* and churches.

Teatro Greco, Taormina

Just off Corso Vittorio Emanuele, the **Palazzo Castelluccio** (palazzocastelluccio.it) reveals the luxury to which local nobles were accustomed. Its suite of lavish rooms is awash with murals, evocative paintings, gilded settees, and worn glazed floors revealing the paths of long-gone servants.

🚗 THE DRIVE
The 39km drive to Syracuse from Noto takes you down the SP59 and then northeast on the A18/E45, past the majestic Riserva Naturale Cavagrande del Cassibile as you parallel Sicily's eastern coast.

12 SYRACUSE
Syracuse is a dense tapestry of overlapping cultures and civilisations. Ancient Greek ruins rise out of lush citrus orchards, cafe tables spill out onto baroque piazzas, and medieval lanes meander to the sea. Your visit, like the city itself, can be split into two easy parts: one dedicated to the archaeological site, the other to Ortygia, the ancient island neighbourhood connected to the modern town by bridge.

It's difficult to imagine now but in its heyday Syracuse was the largest city in the ancient world, bigger even than Athens and Corinth. The **Parco Archeologico della Neapolis** is home to well-preserved Greek (and Roman) remains, with the remarkably intact **Teatro Greco** – constructed in the 5th century BCE and rebuilt two centuries later – as the main attraction. In the grounds of **Villa Landolina**, about 500m east of the archaeological park, is the exceptional **Museo Archeologico Paolo Orsi** (regione.sicilia.it/beniculturali/museopaoloorsi).

Compact, labyrinthine **Ortygia** encompass 25 centuries of history. At its heart, the city's 7th-century **Duomo** looms over Piazza del Duomo, one of Italy's most magnificent squares. The cathedral was built over a pre-existing 5th-century-BCE Greek temple, incorporating most of the original Doric columns in its three-aisled structure. The sumptuous baroque facade was added in the 18th century.

🚗 THE DRIVE
From Syracuse to Catania, it is a 66km drive north along the A18/E45. This is orange-growing country and you will see many orchards, which can be gorgeously fragrant when in bloom.

13 CATANIA
Gritty, vibrant Catania is a true city of the volcano, much of it constructed from the lava that poured down on it during Mt Etna's 1669 eruption. The baroque centre is lava-black in colour, as if a fine dusting of soot permanently covers its elegant buildings, most of which are the work of Giovanni Battista Vaccarini. The 18th-century architect almost single-handedly rebuilt the civic centre into an elegant, modern city of spacious boulevards and set-piece piazzas.

Long buried under lava, the submerged stage of a 2nd-century Roman theatre and its small rehearsal theatre, part of the **Parco Archeologico Greco Romano**, remind you that Catania's history goes back much further. Picturesquely sited in a crumbling residential area, the ruins are occasionally brightened by laundry flapping on the rooftops of vine-covered buildings that appear to have sprouted organically from the half-submerged stage.

🚗 THE DRIVE
The 53km drive to Taormina along the A18/E45 is a coast-hugging northern run, taking in more orange groves as well as glimpses of the sparkling Ionian Sea.

14 TAORMINA
Over the centuries, Taormina has seduced an exhaustive line of writers and artists, from Goethe to DH Lawrence. The main reason for their infatuation? The perfect horseshoe-shaped **Teatro Greco**, a lofty ancient marvel looking out towards mighty Mt Etna and the Ionian Sea. Built in the 3rd century BCE, the *teatro* is the most dramatically situated Greek theatre in the world and the second largest in Sicily (after Syracuse).

The 9th-century capital of Byzantine Sicily, Taormina also has a well-preserved, if touristy, **medieval town**, its chi-chi streets dotted with fashionable cafes and bars perfect for a glamorous wrap-up toast to your journey.

07

Italian Riviera

BEST FOR FINE DINING

Purple San Remo prawns on the terrace of San Giorgio.

DURATION	DISTANCE	GREAT FOR
4 days	214km / 133 miles	Food and drink, family travel

BEST TIME TO GO	April, May and June for flowers and hiking; October for harvest.

Palazzo Borsa, Genoa

The Italian Riviera, backed by the Maritime Alps, curves west from Genoa to the French border at Ventimiglia. The contrast between sun-washed, sophisticated coastal towns and a mountainous hinterland full of heritage farms, olive oil producers and wineries gave rise to the Riviera's 19th-century fame, when European expatriates outnumbered locals. They amused themselves in lavish botanical gardens, gambled in the casino of San Remo and dined in style in fine art-nouveau villas, much as you will on this tour.

Link your trip

02 The Graceful Italian Lakes

Heading north from Genoa you're soon in the land of refreshing lakes and mountains.

13 Riviera Crossing

Roll right on into France for more beaches, glam cities and glittering seascapes.

01 GENOA

Like Dr Jekyll and Mr Hyde, Genoa is a city with a split personality. At its centre, medieval *caruggi* (narrow streets) untangle outwards to the **Porto Antico** and teem with hawkers, merchants and office workers. Along Via Garibaldi and Via XXV Aprile is another Genoa, one of Unesco-sponsored palaces, smart shops and grand architectural gestures like **Piazza de Ferrari** with its monumental fountain, art nouveau **Palazzo Borsa** (once the city's stock exchange) and the

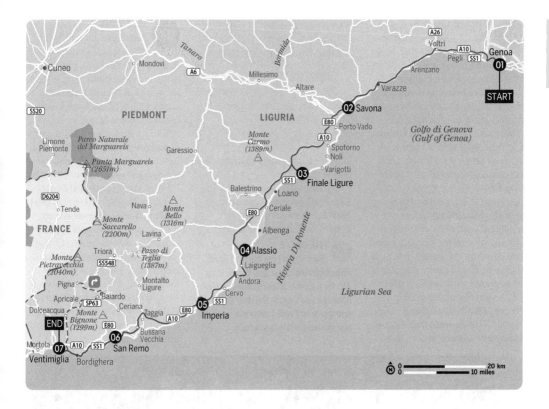

neoclassical **Teatro Carlo Felice** (operacarlofelicegenova.it).

Join the well-dressed *haute bourgeoisie* enjoying high-profile art exhibits in the grand Mannerist halls of the **Palazzo Ducale** (palazzoducale.genova.it), then retire to sip a spritz amid 17th-century frescoes at **Les Rouges** (lesrouges.it).

🚗 THE DRIVE
Exit Genoa westward, through a tangle of flyovers and tunnels, to access the A10 for the 56km drive to Savona. Once out of the suburbs the forested slopes of the Maritime Alps rise to your right and sea views peep out from the left as you duck through tunnels.

02 SAVONA
Don't be put off by Savona's horrifying industrial sprawl; the Savonesi were a powerful maritime people and the town centre is unexpectedly graceful. Standing near the port are three of the many medieval towers that once studded the cityscape. Genoa's greatest rival, the town was savagely sacked in 1528, the castle dismantled and most of the population slaughtered, but somehow the **Fortezza del Priamàr** (museoarcheosavona.it) and the **Cattedrale di Nostra Signora Assunta** survived.

But you're not here for the architecture – you're here for the food. The covered **market** is crammed with fruit-and-vegetable stalls and fish stands stacked with salt cod. **Grigiomar** salts its own local anchovies. Then there are the local specialities such as the addictive *farinata di grano* (wheat-flour flat bread) at **Vino e Farinata** (vinoefarinata.it).

🚗 THE DRIVE
Rejoin the A10 and leave the industrial chimneys of Savona behind you. For the first 13km the A10 continues with views of the sea, then at Spotorno it ducks inland for the final 15km to the Finale Ligure exit. Descend steeply for 3km to the Finale hamlets on the coast.

03 FINALE LIGURE

Finale Ligure comprises several seaside districts. The marina is narrow and charming, spreading along the sandy shore between two small rivers, the Porra and the Sciusa. A good place to pick up some picnic fare is **Salumeria Chiesa**, a delicatessen with a huge array of seafood salads, salamis, cheeses and gnocchi with pesto, of course.

Around 1.5km north of the seaside, **Finalborgo** is the old medieval centre. Its cobblestone streets are ripe for exploring, and you can stop for a meal or a pick-me-up at one of many charming restaurants with outdoor tables on the pavement. Each year in March, Finalborgo's cloisters are home to the **Salone dell'Agroalimentare Ligure**, where local

Photo Opportunity

Cascading terraces of exotic flowers at Giardini Botanici Hanbury in Ventimiglia.

farmers hawk seasonal delicacies and vintages.

On Thursday it's worth driving 9km up the coast to picturesque **Noli** for the weekly outdoor market on Corso d'Italia.

🚗 THE DRIVE

Once again take the high road away from the coast and follow the A10 for a further 35km to Alassio. Near Albenga you'll cross the river Centa and the broad valley where dozens of hothouses dot the landscape.

04 ALASSIO

Less than 100km from the French border, Alassio's popularity among the 18th- and 19th-century jet set has left it with an elegant colonial character. Its pastel-hued villas range around a broad, sandy beach, which stretches all the way to **Laigueglia** (4km to the south). American president Thomas Jefferson holidayed here in 1787 and Edward Elgar composed *In the South* inspired by his stay in 1904. **Il Muretto**, a ceramic-covered wall, records the names of 550 celebrities who've passed through.

Follow the local lead and promenade along Via XX Settembre or the unspoilt waterfront. Take coffee at **Antico Caffè Pasticceria Balzola** (balzola1902.com) and enjoy gelato on the beach beneath a stripy umbrella.

Giardini Botanici Hanbury, Ventimiglia

THE DRIVE
If you have time take the scenic coast road, SS1 (Via Roma), from Alassio through Laigueglia and Marina di Andora to Imperia. It is a shorter and more scenic jaunt when traffic is light. The alternative, when traffic is heavy, is to head back to the A10.

05 IMPERIA

Imperia consists of two small seaside towns, Oneglia and Porto Maurizio, on either side of the Impero river.

Oneglia, birthplace of Admiral Doria, the Genoese Republic's greatest naval hero, is the less attractive of the two, though **Piazza Dante**, with its arcaded walkways, is a pleasant place to grab a coffee. This is also where the great olive oil dynasties made their name. Visit the **Museo dell'Olivo** (museodellolivo.com), housed in an art-nouveau mansion belonging to the heritage Fratelli Carli factory. The museum is surprisingly extensive and details the history of the Italian Riviera industry from the 2nd century BC. Buy quality oil here or anywhere in town.

West of Oneglia is pirate haven **Porto Maurizio**, perched on a rocky spur that overlooks a yacht-filled harbour.

 THE DRIVE
Rejoining the A10 at Imperia, the landscape begins to change. The olive terraces are dense, spear-like cypresses and umbrella pines shade the hillsides, and the fragrant *maquis* (herbal scrubland) is prolific. Loop inland around Taggia and then descend slowly into San Remo.

06 SAN REMO

San Remo, Italy's wannabe Monte Carlo, is a sun-dappled Mediterranean resort with a grand belle-époque **casino**

(casinosanremo.it) and lashings of Riviera-style grandeur.

During the mid-19th century the city became a magnet for European exiles such as Czar Nicolas of Russia, who favoured the town's balmy winters. They built an onion-domed **Russian Orthodox church** reminiscent of Moscow's St Basil's Cathedral, which still turns heads down by the seafront. Swedish inventor Alfred Nobel also maintained a villa here, the **Villa Nobel**, which now houses a museum dedicated to him.

Beyond the waterfront, San Remo hides a little-visited old town, a labyrinth of twisting lanes that cascade down the Italian Riviera hillside. Curling around the base is the **Italian Cycling Riviera**, a path that tracks the coast as far as Imperia. For bike hire, enquire at the **tourist office** (visitriviera.info).

 THE DRIVE
For the final 17km stretch to Ventimiglia take the SS1 coastal road, which hugs the base of the mountains and offers uninterrupted sea views. In summer and at Easter, however, when traffic is heavy, your best bet is the A10.

07 VENTIMIGLIA

Despite its enviable position between the glitter of San Remo and the Côte d'Azur, Ventimiglia is a soulful but disorderly border town, its Roman past still evident in its bridges, amphitheatre and ruined baths. Now it's the huge **Friday market** that draws the crowds.

If you can't find a souvenir here then consider one of the prized artisanal honeys produced by **Marco Ballestra** (mieleballestra.it), which has hives in the hills above the Valle Roya. There are over a dozen different types.

SAN GIORGIO

Cult restaurant **San Giorgio** has been quietly wowing gourmets with its authentic Ligurian cooking since the 1950s when mother-and-son team Caterina and Alessandro opened the doors of their home in the *borgo* (medieval hamlet) of **Cervo Alta**. Dine out on the bougainvillea-draped terrace in summer, or in intimate dining rooms cluttered with family silverware and antiques in winter. Below the restaurant, in an old oil mill, is the less formal wine bar and deli **San Giorgino**.

To end the tour head over to the pretty western suburb of Ponte San Ludovico to the **Giardini Botanici Hanbury** (giardinihanbury.com), the 18-hectare estate of English businessman Sir Thomas Hanbury; he planted it with an extravagant 5800 botanical species from five continents.

DETOUR
L'Entroterra
Start: 07 **Ventimiglia**

The designation 'Riviera' omits the pleated, mountainous interior – *l'entroterra* – that makes up nine-tenths of the Italian Riviera. Harried by invasions, coast-dwellers took to these vertical landscapes over 1000 years ago, hewing their perched villages from the rock face of the Maritime Alps. You'll want to set aside two extra days to drive the coiling roads that rise up from Ventimiglia to **Dolceacqua**, **Apricale** and **Pigna**. If you do make the effort, book into gorgeous boutique hotel **Apricus Locanda** (apricuslocanda.com); it's worth it for the breakfast and see-forever panoramas.

DOPHOTO/SHUTTERSTOCK ©

Château de Langeais (p107)

France

Explore

France

Home to iconic monuments, celebrated masterpieces, fabulous food and world-class wines, France is made for road-tripping. Whether you want to cruise the *corniches* (coastal roads) of the Côte d'Azur, venture into the snowcapped peaks of the Pyrenees or taste your way around Champagne's hallowed vineyards, our driving routes promise magnificent scenery and unforgettable discoveries at every turn. All, of course, accompanied by long, leisurely lunches and relaxed coffees on sunny pavement terraces.

There are experiences for all ages and interests, for family travellers and history buffs, culinary connoisseurs and outdoor adventurers. So *bon voyage* – you're in for a thrilling ride.

Paris

As France's capital and largest city, Paris provides the country's *bienvenu* (welcome) to many travellers. Packed with historic buildings and cultural treasures, as well as restaurants, bars, cafes and hotels for every style and budget, it's the nation's main gateway and premier destination. There's an enormous amount to take in, and while you'll never be able to cover everything on a single visit, you should have time for its celebrated headline acts – the Eiffel Tower, the Centre Pompidou, and the Louvre and enigmatic *Mona Lisa*.

Transport-wise, the city has two international airports and excellent rail and road links, making it an obvious base for exploring northern France. It's the starting point for our countrywide Essential France tour and only three hours' drive from Normandy and the D-Day beaches.

Marseille

One of the Mediterranean's historic ports, the southern city of Marseille is well placed as a gateway for Provence and the French Riviera. Flights serve its international airport and the Gare de Marseille-Saint-Charles is a major rail hub. By car, Aix-en-Provence is within easy striking distance and Cannes is about two hours away.

The city, France's second largest, is exuberant and multicultural, full of noisy markets and gritty corners. Interest is

WHEN TO GO

For the best of all worlds – warm weather, blooming flowers and buzzing cafes – spring is hard to beat. Autumn is another top period with the *vendange* (grape harvest) fuelling many food and wine fairs. In summer you can expect sunshine, queues and heavy weekend traffic, as well as plenty of festival action. January is best for skiing.

focused on the Vieux Port, the original harbour and now a thriving marina flanked by cafes, bars and brasseries, as well as blockbuster sights such as Fort St-Jean and the Musée des Civilisations de l'Europe et de la Méditerranée. Weather permitting, you could also drop in on a *calanque,* one of the picturesque coves that pit the rocky coastline to the south of the city.

Bordeaux

An attractive riverside city, Bordeaux will whet your appetite for the road ahead. With its handsome 18th-century architecture, energetic vibe, and superlative food and wine, it makes a fine base for France's Atlantic coast. From the city you can head southwards to Biarritz, about 200km away, and beyond to the Pyrenees on the Spanish border. Alternatively, strike inland and the A89 leads on to the Dordogne, home to some of France's most celebrated prehistoric cave paintings.

TRANSPORT

France's two principal airports are Charles de Gaulle and Orly, both in Paris and both well connected to the city centre. For southern destinations, Nice is France's largest regional airport. There are also trains from neighbouring European countries and from the UK via the Channel Tunnel. Ferries sail to French ports from the UK, Ireland and Italy.

The city is well equipped with accommodation and, unsurprisingly, plenty of great places to eat and drink. It has its own international airport, otherwise you can get there by high-speed train from Paris in just under three hours.

 WHERE TO STAY

Be it a fairy-tale château, boutique hideaway, designer hostel or beachside campground, France has accommodation to suit every taste and pocket. Rates fluctuate throughout the year but top off in summer when demand skyrockets, particularly in coastal resorts and popular holiday destinations. In rural areas, *chambres d'hôtes* (B&Bs) are a popular choice, offering a personal touch and the chance to experience genuine local cooking. Self-catering cottages known as *gîtes* are another holiday favourite. Hikers and cyclists out in the wilds can bunk down in mountain refuges or basic hostel-like *gîtes d'étape.*

 WHAT'S ON

Festival de Cannes

(May; festival-cannes.com) Film stars sashay into Cannes for Europe's premier film festival.

Bastille Day

(14 July) France celebrates the storming of the Bastille with fireworks, balls, processions and parades.

Festival d'Avignon

(July; festival-avignon.com) Avignon's performing-arts festival turns the town into a stage for three weeks.

Fête des Lumières

(early December; fetedeslumieres. lyon.fr) Lyon's historic streets host France's biggest light show on and around 8 December.

Resources

Explore France *(france.fr)* Planning information, holiday ideas and sustainable travel tips from France's official tourism website.

France 24 *(france24.com/ en/france)* Get the lowdown on the latest French news.

Talking France *(thelocal. fr/podcasts/talking-france)* English-language podcast looking at French current affairs, talking points and national issues.

08

Essential France

BEST FOR FAMILIES

Braving the space-age rides and roller-coaster thrills of Futuroscope.

Château de Versailles

DURATION	DISTANCE	GREAT FOR
3 weeks	3060km / 1902 miles	History

BEST TIME TO GO	April to June for sunny weather, longer days and flowers.

City to city, coast to coast, this is the big one – an epic trek that travels all the way from the chilly waters of the English Channel to the gleaming blue Mediterranean. Along the way, you'll stop off at some of France's most unmissable sights: the palace of Versailles, the abbey of Mont St-Michel, the summit of Mont Blanc and the beaches of the French Riviera. *Allez-y!*

Link your trip

09 D-Day's Beaches

Take a side trip from Caen to follow the course of the WWII invasion on Normandy's beaches.

12 Riviera Crossing

Combine this journey with our jaunt down the French Riviera, which begins in Cannes.

01 **PARIS**

For that essentially Parisian experience, it's hard to beat **Montmartre** – the neighbourhood of cobbled lanes and cafe-lined squares beloved by writers and painters since the 19th century. This was once a notoriously ramshackle part of Paris, full of bordellos, brothels, dance halls and bars, as well as the city's first can-can clubs. Though its hedonistic heyday has long since passed, Montmartre still retains a villagey charm, despite the throngs of tourists.

The centre of Montmartre is **place du Tertre**, once the village's main square, now packed with buskers and portrait artists. You can get a sense of how the

Visiting Versailles

Versailles is one of the country's most popular destinations, so planning ahead will make your visit more enjoyable. Avoid the busiest days of Tuesday and Sunday, and remember that the château is closed on Monday. Save time by pre-purchasing tickets on the château's website, or arrive early if you're buying at the door – by noon queues spiral out of control.

You can also access off-limits areas (such as the Private Apartments of Louis XV and Louis XVI, the Opera House and the Royal Chapel) by taking a 90-minute **guided tour**.

---

area would once have looked at the **Musée de Montmartre** (museedemontmartre.fr), which details the area's bohemian past. It's inside Montmartre's oldest building, a 17th-century manor house once occupied by Renoir and Utrillo.

Nearby, Montmartre's finest view unfolds from the dome of the **Basilique du Sacré-Coeur** (sacre-coeur-montmartre.com). On a clear day, you can see for up to 30km.

THE DRIVE

From the centre of Paris, follow the A13 west from Porte d'Auteuil and take the exit marked 'Versailles Château'. Versailles is 28km southwest of the city.

02 VERSAILLES

Louis XIV transformed his father's hunting lodge into the **Château de Versailles** (chateauversailles.fr) in the mid-17th century, and it remains France's most majestic palace. The royal court was based here from 1682 until 1789, when revolutionaries massacred the palace guard and dragged Louis XVI and Marie Antoinette back to Paris, where they were ingloriously guillotined.

The architecture is truly eye-popping. Highlights include the **Grands Appartements du Roi et de la Reine** (State Apartments) and the famous **Galerie des Glaces** (Hall of Mirrors), a 75m-long ballroom filled with chandeliers and floor-to-ceiling mirrors. Outside, the vast park incorporates terraces, flower beds, paths and fountains, as well as the **Grand and Petit Canals**.

Northwest of the main palace is the **Domaine de Trianon** (Trianon Estate; chateauversailles.fr), where the royal family would have taken refuge from the intrigue and etiquette of court life.

THE DRIVE

The N10 runs southwest from Versailles through pleasant countryside and forest to Rambouillet, where you'll join the D906 to Chartres. All told, it's a journey of 76km.

03 CHARTRES

You'll know you're nearing Chartres long before you reach it thanks to the twin spires of the **Cathédrale Notre Dame** (cathedrale-chartres. org), considered to be one of the most important structures in Christendom.

The present cathedral was built during the late 12th century after the original was destroyed by fire. It's survived wars and revolutions remarkably intact, and the brilliant-blue stained-glass windows have even inspired their own shade of paint (Chartres blue). The cathedral also houses the Sainte Voile (Holy Veil), supposedly worn by the Virgin Mary while giving birth to Jesus.

The best views are from the 112m-high **Clocher Neuf** (North Tower).

FUTUROSCOPE

Halfway between Chambord and Bordeaux on the A10, 10km north of Poitiers, **Futuroscope** (futuroscope.com) is one of France's top theme parks. It's a futuristic experience that takes you whizzing through space, diving into the ocean depths, racing around city streets and on a close encounter with creatures of the future. Note that many rides have a minimum height of 120cm.

You'll need at least five hours to check out the major attractions, or two days to see everything. The park is in the suburb of Jaunay-Clan; take exit 28 off the A10.

 THE DRIVE

Follow the D939 northwest for 58km to Verneuil-sur-Avre, then take the D926 west for 78km to Argentan – both great roads through typical Norman countryside. Just west of Argentan, the D158/N158 heads north to Caen, then turns northwest on the N13 to Bayeux, 94km further.

04 BAYEUX

The **Bayeux Tapestry** (bayeuxmuseum.com) is without doubt the world's most celebrated (and ambitious) piece of embroidery. Over 58 panels, the tapestry recounts the invasion of England in 1066 by William I, or William the Conqueror, as he's now known.

Commissioned in 1077 by Bishop Odo of Bayeux, William's half-brother, the tapestry retells the battle in fascinating detail: look out for Norman horses getting stuck in the quicksands around Mont St-Michel, and the famous appearance of Halley's Comet in scene 32. The final showdown at the Battle of Hastings is particularly graphic, complete with severed limbs, decapitated heads, and the English King Harold getting an arrow in the eye.

 THE DRIVE

Mont St-Michel is 125km southwest of Bayeux; the fastest route is along the D6 and then the A84 motorway.

05 MONT ST-MICHEL

You've already seen it on a million postcards, but nothing prepares you for the real **Mont St-Michel** (abbaye-mont-saint-michel.fr). It's one of France's architectural marvels, an 11th-century island abbey marooned in the middle of a vast bay.

When you arrive, you'll be steered into one of the Mont's huge car parks. You then walk along the causeway (or catch a free shuttle bus) to the island itself. Guided tours are included, or you can explore solo with an audioguide.

The **Église Abbatiale** (Abbey Church) is reached via a steep climb along the **Grande Rue**. Around the church, the cluster of buildings known as **La Merveille** (The Marvel) includes the cloister, refectory, guest hall, ambulatory and various chapels.

For a different perspective, take a guided walk across the sands with **Découverte de la Baie du Mont-Saint-Michel** (decouverte baie.com) or **Chemins de la Baie** (cheminsdelabaie.com), both based in Genêts. Don't be tempted to do it on your own – the bay's tides are notoriously treacherous.

 THE DRIVE

Take the A84, N12 and A81 for 190km to Le Mans and the A28 for 102km to Tours, where you can follow a tour through the Loire Valley if you wish. Chambord is about 75km from Tours via the D952.

06 CHAMBORD

If you only have time to visit one château in the Loire, you might as well make it the grandest – and **Chambord** (chambord.org) is the most lavish of them all. It's a showpiece of Renaissance architecture, from the double-helix staircase up to the turret-covered rooftop. With 426 rooms, the sheer scale of the place is mindboggling – and in the Loire, that's really saying something. If you have time, detour to the richly furnished and

CLODIO/GETTY IMAGES ©

Cathédrale Notre Dame, Chartres

very elegant **Château de Chenonceau** (chenonceau.com).

THE DRIVE

It's 425km to Bordeaux via Blois and the A10 motorway. You could consider breaking the journey with stop-offs at Futuroscope and Poitiers, roughly halfway between the two.

07 BORDEAUX

When Unesco decided to protect Bordeaux's medieval architecture in 2007, it simply listed half the city in one fell swoop. Covering 18 sq km, this is the world's largest urban World Heritage Site, with grand buildings and architectural treasures galore.

Top of the heap is the **Cathédrale St-André** (cathedrale-bordeaux.fr), known for its stone carvings and generously gargoyled belfry, the **Tour Pey Berland**

Photo Opportunity

Mont Blanc from the top of the Aiguille du Midi.

(pey-berland.fr). But the whole old city rewards wandering, especially around the **Jardin Public** (cours de Verdun), the pretty squares of **Esplanade des Quinconces** and **place Gambetta**, and the city's 4km-long **riverfront esplanade**, with its playgrounds, paths and paddling pools. There's also the superb **La Cité du Vin** (laciteduvin.com), a must see for wine lovers.

THE DRIVE

It's a 194km drive to Sarlat-la-Canéda via the A89 motorway, or you can take a longer but more enjoyable route via the D936.

08 SARLAT-LA-CANÉDA

If you're looking for France's heart and soul, you'll find it among the forests and fields of the Dordogne. It's the stuff of French fantasies: riverbank châteaux, medieval villages, wooden-hulled *gabarres* (flat-bottomed barges), and market stalls groaning with truffles, walnuts and wines. The town of Sarlat-la-Canéda makes the perfect base, with a beautiful medieval centre and lots of lively markets.

It's also ideally placed for exploring the **Vézère Valley**, about 20km to the northwest, home to France's finest cave paintings. Most famous of all are the ones at the **Grotte de Lascaux**, although to prevent damage to the paintings, you now visit a replica of the cave's main sections in a nearby **grotto** (International Centre for Cave Art; lascaux.fr).

Aiguille du Midi cable car, Chamonix

THE DRIVE
The drive east to Lyon is a long one, covering well over 400km and travelling across the spine of the Massif Central. A good route is to follow the A89 all the way to exit 6, then turn off onto the N89/D89 to Lyon. This route should cover between 420km and 430km.

09 LYON
Fired up by French food? Then you'll love Lyon, with its *bouchons* (small bistros), bustling markets and fascinating food culture. Start in **Vieux Lyon** and the picturesque quarter of **Presqu'île**, then catch the funicular to the top of **Fourvière** to explore the city's Roman ruins and enjoy cross-town views.

Film buffs will also want to make time for the **Musée Lumière** (institut-lumiere.org), where the Lumière Brothers (Auguste and Louis) shot the first reels of the world's first motion picture, *La Sortie des Usines Lumières*, on 19 March 1895.

THE DRIVE
Take the A42 towards Lake Geneva, then the A40 towards St-Gervais-les-Bains. The motorway becomes the N205 as it nears Chamonix. It's a drive of at least 225km.

10 CHAMONIX
Snuggling among snow-clad mountains – including Europe's highest summit, Mont Blanc – adrenaline-fuelled Chamonix is an ideal springboard for the French Alps. In winter, it's a mecca for skiers and snowboarders, and in summer, once the snows thaw, the high-level trails become a trekkers' paradise.

There are two really essential Chamonix experiences. First,

catch the dizzying cable car to the top of the **Aiguille du Midi** to snap a shot of Mont Blanc.

Then take the combination mountain train and cable car from the **Gare du Montenvers** (montblancnaturalresort.com) to the **Mer de Glace** (Sea of Ice), France's largest glacier. Wrap up warmly if you want to visit the glacier's sculptures and ice caves.

THE DRIVE
The drive to the Riviera is full of scenic thrills. An attractive route is via the D1212 to Albertville, and then via the A43, which travels over the Italian border and through the Tunnel de Fréjus. From here, the N94 runs through Briançon, and a combination of the A51, N85 and D6085 carries you south to Nice. You'll cover at least 430km.

11 FRENCH RIVIERA
If there's one coast road in France you simply have to drive, it's the French Riviera, with its rocky cliffs, maquis-scented air and dazzling Mediterranean views. Sun-seekers have been flocking here since the 19th century, and its scenery still never fails to seduce.

Lively **Nice** and cinematic **Cannes** make natural starts, but for the Riviera's loveliest scenery, you'll want to drive down the gorgeous **Corniche de l'Estérel** to **St-Tropez**, still a watchword for seaside glamour. Crowds can make summer hellish, but come in spring or autumn and you'll have its winding lanes and fragrant hills practically to yourself. For maximum views, stick to the coast roads: the D6098 to Antibes and Cannes, the D559 around the Corniche de l'Estérel, and the D98A to St-Tropez. It's about 120km via this route.

THE DRIVE
From St-Tropez, take the fast A8 for about 125km west to Aix-en-Provence.

12 AIX-EN-PROVENCE
Sleepy Provence sums up the essence of *la douce vie* (the sweet life). Cloaked in lavender and spotted with hilltop villages, it's a region that sums up everything that's good about France.

Cruising the back roads and browsing the markets are the best ways to get acquainted with the region. Artistic Aix-en-Provence encapsulates the classic Provençal vibe, with its pastel buildings and Cézanne connections, while **Mont Ste-Victoire**, to the east, makes for a superb outing.

THE DRIVE
The gorges are 140km northeast of Aix-en-Provence, via the A51 and D952.

13 GORGES DU VERDON
Complete your cross-France adventure with an unforgettable expedition to the Gorges du Verdon – sometimes known as the Grand Canyon of Europe. This deep ravine slashes 25km through the plateaux of Haute-Provence; in places, its walls rise to a dizzying 700m, twice the height of the Eiffel Tower (321m).

The two main jumping-off points are the villages of **Moustiers Ste-Marie**, in the west, and **Castellane**, in the east. Drivers and bikers can take in the canyon panorama from two vertigo-inducing cliffside roads, but the base of the gorge is only accessible on foot or by raft.

09

D-Day's Beaches

Caen-Normandie Mémorial

DURATION	DISTANCE	GREAT FOR
3 days	142km / 88 miles	History

BEST TIME TO GO	April to July, to avoid summer-holiday traffic around the beaches.

The beaches and bluffs are quiet today, but on 6 June 1944 the Normandy shoreline witnessed the arrival of the largest armada the world has ever seen. This patch of the French coast will forever be synonymous with D-Day (known to the French as Jour-J), and the coastline is strewn with memorials, museums and cemeteries – reminders that though victory was won on the Longest Day, it came at a high price.

Link your trip

08 Essential France

The island abbey of Mont St-Michel is about 140km from the Normandy coastline, about two hours' drive via the A84 motorway.

13 Champagne Taster

For a change in focus head east, about four hours from Caen, to the cellars of Épernay for a fizz-fuelled tour.

01 CAEN

Situated 3km northwest of Caen, the award-winning **Caen-Normandie Mémorial** (memorial-caen.fr) is a brilliant place to begin with some background on the historic events of D-Day and the wider context of WWII. Housed in a purpose-designed building covering 14,000 sq metres, the memorial offers an immersive experience, using sound, lighting, film, animation and audio testimony to evoke the grim realities of war, the trials of occupation and the joy of liberation.

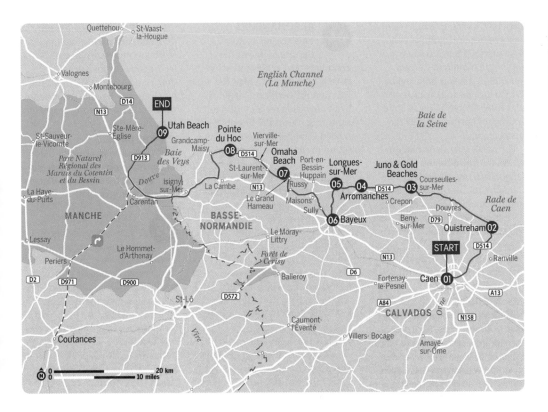

The visit begins with a whistle-stop overview of Europe's descent into total war, tracing events from the end of WWI through to the rise of fascism in Europe, the German occupation of France and the Battle of Normandy. A second section focuses on the Cold War. There's also the well-preserved original bunker used by German command in 1944.

On your way around, look out for a Hawker Typhoon fighter plane and a full-size Sherman tank.

🚗 THE DRIVE
From the museum, head north-east along Esplanade Brillaud de Laujardière, and follow signs to Ouistreham. You'll join the E46 ring road;

follow it to exit 3a (Porte d'Angleterre), and merge onto the D515 and D84 to Ouistreham. Park on the seafront on bd Aristide Briand. In all it's a trip of 18km.

02 OUISTREHAM
On D-Day, the sandy seafront around Ouistreham was code-named **Sword Beach** and was the focus of attack for the British 3rd Infantry Division.

There are precious few reminders of the battle now, but on D-Day the scene was very different: most of the surrounding buildings had been levelled by artillery fire, and German bunkers and artillery positions were strung out along the seafront. Sword Beach was the site of some

of the most famous images of D-Day – including the infamous ones of British troops landing with bicycles, and bagpiper Bill Millin piping troops ashore while under heavy fire.

🚗 THE DRIVE
Follow the seafront west onto rue de Lion, following signs for 'Overlord – L'Assaut' onto the D514 towards Courseulles-sur-Mer, 18km west. Drive through town onto rue de Ver, and follow signs to 'Centre Juno Beach'.

03 JUNO & GOLD BEACHES
On D-Day, Courseulles-sur-Mer was known as Juno Beach, and was stormed mainly by Canadian troops. It was here that the exiled French

General Charles de Gaulle came ashore after the landings – the first 'official' French soldier to set foot in mainland Europe since 1940. He was followed by Winston Churchill on 12 June and King George VI on 16 June. A Cross of Lorraine marks the historic spot.

The area's only Canadian museum, the **Juno Beach Centre** (junobeach.org) has exhibits on Canada's role in the war effort and the landings, and offers guided tours of Juno Beach, including the bunker there, from April to October.

A short way west is Gold Beach, attacked by the British 50th Infantry on D-Day.

THE DRIVE
Drive west along the D514 for 14km to Arromanches. You'll pass a car park and viewpoint marked with a statue of the Virgin Mary, which overlooks Port Winston and Gold Beach. Follow the road into town and signs to Musée du Débarquement.

04 ARROMANCHES

This seaside town was the site of one of the great logistical achievements of D-Day. In order to unload the vast quantities of cargo needed by the invasion forces without capturing one of the heavily defended Channel ports, the Allies set up prefabricated marinas off two landing beaches, code named **Mulberry Harbour**. These consisted of 146 massive cement caissons towed over from England and sunk to form a semicircular breakwater in which floating bridge spans were moored. In the three months after D-Day, the Mulberries facilitated the unloading of a mind-boggling 2.5 million men, four million tonnes of equipment and 500,000 vehicles.

At low tide, the stanchions of one of these artificial quays, **Port Winston** (named after Winston Churchill), can still be seen on the sands at Arromanches.

Beside the beach, the **Musée du Débarquement** (Landing Museum; musee-arromanches.fr) explains the logistics and importance of Port Winston; the museum was expanded and renovated for the 75th anniversary of D-Day in 2019.

THE DRIVE
Continue west along the D514 for 6km to the village of Longues-sur-Mer. You'll see the sign for the Batterie de Longues on your right.

05 LONGUES-SUR-MER

At Longues-sur-Mer you can get a glimpse of the awesome firepower available to the German defenders in the shape of a row of 150mm artillery guns, still housed in their concrete casements. On D-Day they were capable of hitting targets over 20km away – including Gold Beach (to the east) and Omaha Beach (to the west). Parts of the classic D-Day film *The Longest Day* (1962) were filmed here.

THE DRIVE
Backtrack to the crossroads and head straight over onto the D104, signed to Vaux-sur-Aure/Bayeux, for 8km. When you reach town, turn right onto the D613, and follow signs to the 'Musée de la Bataille de Normandie'.

06 BAYEUX

Though best known for its medieval tapestry, Bayeux has another claim to fame: it was the first town to be liberated after D-Day (on the morning of 7 June 1944).

It's also home to the largest of Normandy's 18 Commonwealth military cemeteries – the **Bayeux War Cemetery** (cwgc.org), situated on bd Fabien Ware. It contains 4848 graves of soldiers from the UK and 10 other

---

D-DAY IN FIGURES

Code named 'Operation Overlord', the D-Day landings were the largest military operation in history. On the morning of 6 June 1944, swarms of landing craft – part of an armada of over 6000 ships and 13,000 aeroplanes – hit the northern Normandy beaches, and tens of thousands of soldiers from the USA, the UK, Canada and elsewhere began pouring onto French soil. The initial landing force involved some 45,000 troops; 15 more divisions were to follow once successful beachheads had been established.

The majority of the 135,000 Allied troops stormed ashore along 80km of beaches north of Bayeux code named (from west to east) Utah, Omaha, Gold, Juno and Sword. The landings were followed by the 76-day Battle of Normandy, during which the Allies suffered 210,000 casualties, including 37,000 troops killed. German casualties are believed to have been around 200,000; another 200,000 German soldiers were taken prisoner. About 14,000 French civilians also died.

For more background and statistics, see normandie44lamemoire.com, dday.org and 6juin1944.com.

D-DAY DRIVING ROUTES

There are several signposted driving routes around the main battle sites – look for signs for 'D-Day-Le Choc' in the American sectors and 'Overlord – L'Assaut' in the British and Canadian sectors. A free booklet called *The D-Day Landings and the Battle of Normandy,* available from tourist offices, has details on the main routes.

Maps of the D-Day beaches are widely available in the region.

countries – including Germany. Across the road is a memorial for 1807 Commonwealth soldiers whose remains were never found. The Latin inscription reads: 'We, whom William once conquered, have now set free the conqueror's native land'.

Nearby, the **Musée Mémorial de la Bataille de Normandie** (bayeuxmuseum.com) explores the battle through photos, personal accounts, dioramas and film.

🕹 THE DRIVE

After overnighting in Bayeux, head northwest of town on the D6 towards Port-en-Bessin-Huppain. You'll reach a supermarket after about 10km. Go round the roundabout and turn onto the D514 for another 8km. You'll see signs to the 'Cimetière Americain' near the hamlet of Le Bray. Omaha Beach is another 4km further on, near Vierville-sur-Mer.

07 OMAHA BEACH

If anywhere symbolises the courage and sacrifice of D-Day, it's Omaha – still known as 'Bloody Omaha' to US veterans. It was here, on the 7km stretch of coastline between Vierville-sur-Mer, St-Laurent-sur-Mer and Colleville-sur-Mer, that the most brutal fighting on D-Day took place. US troops had to fight their way across the beach towards the heavily defended cliffs, exposed to underwater obstacles, hidden minefields and withering crossfire. The toll was heavy: of the 2500 casualties at Omaha on D-Day, more than 1000 were killed, most within the first hour of the landings.

High on the bluffs above Omaha, the **Normandy American**

DENNIS K. JOHNSON/GETTY IMAGES ©

Omaha Beach

Photo Opportunity

The forest of white marble crosses at the Normandy American Cemetery & Memorial.

Cemetery & Memorial (abmc. gov) provides a sobering reminder of the human cost of the battle. Featured in the opening scenes of *Saving Private Ryan,* this is the largest American cemetery in Europe, containing the graves of 9387 American soldiers, and a memorial to 1557 comrades 'known only unto God'.

Start off in the very thoughtfully designed visitor centre, which has moving portrayals of some of the soldiers buried here. Afterwards, take in the expanse of white marble crosses and Stars of David that stretch off in seemingly endless rows, surrounded by an immaculately tended expanse of lawn.

THE DRIVE

From the Vierville-sur-Mer seafront, follow the rural D514 through quiet countryside towards Grandcamp-Maisy. After about 10km you'll see signs to 'Pointe du Hoc'.

08 POINTE DU HOC

West of Omaha, this craggy promontory was the site of D-Day's most audacious military exploit. At 7.10am, 225 US Army Rangers commanded by Lt Col James Earl

Rudder scaled the sheer 30m cliffs, where the Germans had stationed a battery of artillery guns trained onto the beaches of Utah and Omaha. Unfortunately, the guns had already been moved inland, and Rudder and his men spent the next two days repelling counterattacks. By the time they were finally relieved on 8 June, 81 of the rangers had been killed and 58 more had been wounded.

Today the **Pointe du Hoc Ranger Memorial** (abmc. gov), which France turned over to the US government in 1979, looks much as it did on D-Day, complete with shell craters and crumbling gun emplacements.

THE DRIVE

Stay on the D514 to Grandcamp-Maisy, then continue south onto the D13. Stay on the road till you reach the turn-off for the D913, signed to St-Marie-du-Mont/Utah Beach. It's a drive of 44km.

09 UTAH BEACH

The D-Day tour ends at Ste-Marie-du-Mont, aka Utah Beach, assaulted by soldiers of the US 4th and 8th Infantry Divisions. The beach was relatively lightly defended, and by midday the landing force had linked with paratroopers from the 101st Airborne. By nightfall, some 20,000 men and 1700 vehicles had arrived on French soil, and the road to European liberation had begun.

Today the site is marked by military memorials and the

Musée du Débarquement (Utah Beach Landing Museum; utah-beach.com), a modern and impressive museum just inland from the beach.

DETOUR
Coutances
Start: 9 Utah Beach

The lovely old Norman town of Coutances makes a good detour when travelling between the D-Day beaches and Mont St-Michel. At the town's heart is its Gothic **Cathédrale Notre-Dame de Coutances** (cathe dralecoutances.free.fr). Interior highlights include several 13th-century windows, a 14th-century fresco of St Michael skewering the dragon, and an organ and high altar from the mid-1700s. You can climb the lantern tower on a tour.

Coutances is 50km south of Utah Beach by the most direct route via the D913 and D971.

10

Atlantic to Med

DURATION	DISTANCE	GREAT FOR
10 days	1498km / 931 miles	Food and drink, history

BEST TIME TO GO	Spring or autumn, for warm weather sans the crowds.

Tour de la Lanterne, La Rochelle

Atlantic ports, pristine mountain vistas, reminders of Rome and Hollywood glam: this sea-to-sea trip takes you through the best of southern France. In May the film stars of the world pour into Cannes to celebrate a year of movie-making. By the time you've finished scaling Pyrenean highs, chewing Basque tapas, acting like a knight in a castle and riding to the moon in a spaceship, you too will have the makings of a prize-winning film.

Link your trip

11 The Pyrenees

Take a side trip east or west from the A64 to further explore this majestic mountain landscape.

12 Riviera Crossing

Starting in Nice, this drive takes you through the glitzy, glam French Riviera.

01 LA ROCHELLE

Known as La Ville Blanche (the White City), La Rochelle is home to luminous limestone facades, arcaded walkways, half-timbered houses and gargoyles glowing in the coastal sunlight. A prominent French seaport from the 14th to the 17th centuries, it remains one of France's most attractive seafaring cities.

There are several defensive towers around the **Vieux Port** (Old Port), including the lacy **Tour de la Lanterne** (tours-la-rochelle.fr), that once served to protect the town at night in times of war. Scale

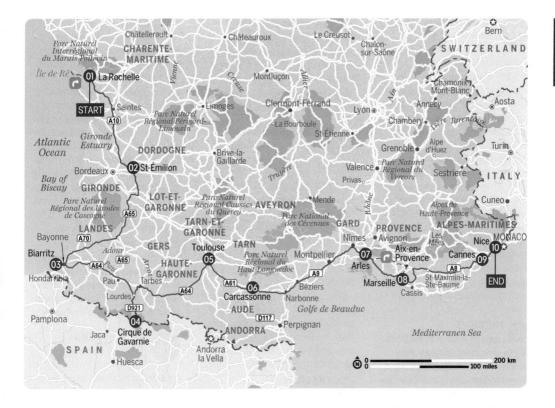

their sturdy stone heights for fabulous city and coastal views.

La Rochelle's number-one tourist attraction is its state-of-the-art **aquarium** (aquarium-larochelle. com). Equally fun for families is the **Musée Maritime** (musee maritimelarochelle.fr), with its fleet of boats to explore; and a trip out to sea with **Croisières Inter-Îles** (inter-iles.com) to admire the unusual iceberg of an island fortress, Fort Boyard.

THE DRIVE

Using the main A10 toll road it's 187km (about 2½ hours) to St-Émilion. Turn off the A10 at exit 39a, signed for Libourne. Skirt this industrial town and follow the D243 into St-Émilion.

DETOUR
Île de Ré
Start: **1** La Rochelle

Bathed in the southern sun, drenched in a languid atmosphere and scattered with villages of green-shuttered, whitewashed buildings with red Spanish-tile roofs, Île de Ré is one of the most delightful places on the west coast of France. The island spans just 30km from its most easterly and westerly points, and just 5km at its widest section. But take note: the secret's out and in high season it can be almost impossible to move around and even harder to find a place to stay.

On the northern coast, about 12km from the toll bridge that links the island to La Rochelle, is the quaint fishing

port of **St-Martin-de-Ré**, the island's main town. Surrounded by 17th-century fortifications (you can stroll along most of the ramparts) constructed by Vauban, the port town is a mesh of streets filled with craft shops, art galleries and sea-spray ocean views.

The island's best beaches are along the southern edge – including unofficial naturist beaches at **Rivedoux Plage** and **La Couarde-sur-Mer** – and around the western tip (northeast and southeast of Phare-des-Baleines). Many beaches are bordered by dunes that have been fenced off to protect the vegetation. From La Rochelle it's 24km and a half-hour drive to St-Martin-de-Ré via the toll bridge **Pont de l'Île de Ré** (pont-ile-de-re.com).

02 ST-ÉMILION

Built of soft honey-coloured rock, medieval St-Émilion produces some of the world's finest red wines. Visiting this pretty town, and partaking in some of the tours and activities on offer, is the easiest way to get under the (grape) skin of Bordeaux wine production. The **Maison du Vin de St-Émilion** (maisonduvinsaintemilion.com) runs wine-tasting classes and has a superb exhibition covering wine essentials.

Guided tours of the town and surrounding châteaux are run by the **tourist office** (saint-emilion-tourisme.com); reserve ahead in season. Several tours include tastings and vineyard visits.

THE DRIVE

Leave St-Émilion on the D243 to Libourne, cross the town, then pick up the D1089 signposted 'Agen, Bergerac, Bordeaux'. Continue on the N89 towards Bordeaux until you see signs for the A630 toll road – at which point sit back and hit cruise control for the remaining 226km to Biarritz. Count 240km and about 2½ hours in all.

03 BIARRITZ

This coastal town is as ritzy as its name makes out. Biarritz boomed as a resort in the mid-19th century due to the regular visits by Napoléon III and his Spanish-born wife, Eugénie. Along its rocky coastline are architectural hallmarks of this golden age, and the belle-époque and art-deco eras that followed.

Biarritz is all about its fashionable beaches, especially the central **Grande Plage** and **Plage Miramar**. In the heat of summer you'll find them packed end to end with sun-loving bathers.

THE DRIVE

It's 208km (2¾ hours) to the village of Gavarnie. Take the A63 and A64 toll roads to exit 11, then the D940 to Lourdes (worth a look for its religious Disneyland feel). Continue south along the D913 and D921.

04 CIRQUE DE GAVARNIE

The Pyrenees don't lack impressive scenery, but your first sight of the Cirque de Gavarnie is guaranteed to raise a gasp. This breathtaking mountain amphitheatre is one of the region's most famous sights, sliced by thunderous waterfalls and ringed by sawtooth peaks, many of which top out at over 3000m.

There are a couple of large car parks in the village of **Gavarnie**, from where it's about a two-hour walk to the amphitheatre. Wear proper shoes, as snow lingers along the trail into early summer.

THE DRIVE

Retrace your steps to Lourdes, then take the N21 towards Tarbes and veer onto the A64 to reach Toulouse. It takes nearly three hours to cover the 228km.

05 TOULOUSE

The vibrant southern city of Toulouse is dubbed 'La Ville Rose', a reference to the distinctive blushing-pink brickwork of its classic architecture. Its city centre is tough to navigate by car, but there's a paying car park right beneath Toulouse's magnificent central square, **place du Capitole**, the city's literal and metaphorical heart. South of the square, walk the tangle of lanes in the historic **Vieux Quartier** (Old Town). Then, of course, there are the soothing twists and turns of the nearby Garonne River and mighty Canal du Midi – laced with footpaths to stretch your legs.

Having a car is handy for visiting two out-of-town sights celebrating modern Toulouse's role as an aerospace hub: the gigantic museum of Airbus, **Aeroscopia** (musee-aeroscopia.fr), just north of the airport; and, across town, **Cite de l'Espace** (cite-espace.com), which brings this interstellar industry vividly to life through a shuttle simulator, a planetarium, a 3D cinema, a simulated observatory and so on. Both have free parking.

THE DRIVE

It's an easy 95km (one hour) down the fast A61 to Carcassonne. Notice how the vegetation becomes suddenly much more Mediterranean about 15 minutes out of Toulouse.

06 CARCASSONNE

Perched on a rocky hilltop and bristling with zigzagging battlements, stout walls and spiky turrets, from afar the fortified city of Carcassonne is most people's perfect idea of a medieval castle. Four million tourists a year stream through its city gates to explore La Cité, visit its **keep** (remparts-carcassonne.fr) and ogle at stunning views along the city's ancient ramparts.

THE DRIVE

Continue down the A61 to the Catalan-flavoured town of Narbonne, where you join the A9 (very busy in summer) and head east to Nîmes. From there the A54 will take you into Arles. Allow just over two hours to cover the 223km and expect lots of toll booths.

07 ARLES

Arles' poster boy is the celebrated impressionist painter Vincent van Gogh. If you're familiar with his work,

Photo Opportunity

Pose like a film star on the steps of Cannes' Palais des Festivals et des Congrès.

you'll be familiar with Arles: the light, the colours, the landmarks and the atmosphere, all faithfully captured. But long before Van Gogh rendered this grand Rhône River locale on canvas, the Romans valued its worth. Today it's the reminders of Rome that are probably the town's most memorable attractions. At **Les Arènes** (Amphithéâtre; arenes-arles.com) slaves, criminals and wild animals (including giraffes) met their dramatic demise before a jubilant 20,000-strong crowd during Roman gladiatorial displays.

 THE DRIVE
From Arles take the scenic N568 and A55 route into Marseille. It's 88km (an hour's drive) away.

DETOUR
Aix-en-Provence
Start: 7 Arles

Aix-en-Provence is to Provence what the Left Bank is to Paris: an enclave of bourgeois-bohemian chic. Art, culture and architecture abound here. A stroller's paradise, the highlight is the mostly pedestrian old city, **Vieil Aix**. South of cours Mirabeau, **Quartier Mazarin** was laid out in the 17th century, and is home to some of Aix's finest buildings. Central place des Quatre Dauphins, with its fish-spouting fountain (1667), is particularly enchanting. Further south locals play pétanque beneath plane trees in peaceful **Parc Jourdan**.

Les Arènes, Arles

From Arles it's a 77km (one-hour) drive down the A54 toll road to Aix-en-Provence. To rejoin the main route take the A51 and A7 for 32km (30 minutes) to Marseille.

08 MARSEILLE
With its history, fusion of cultures, souq-like markets, millennia-old port and *corniches* (coastal roads) along rocky inlets and sun-baked beaches, Marseille is a captivating and exotic city. Ships have docked for more than 26 centuries at the colourful **Vieux Port** (Old Port) and it remains a thriving harbour. Guarding the harbour are **Bas Fort St-Nicolas** and **Fort St-Jean**, founded in the 13th century by the Knights Hospitaller of St John of Jerusalem. A vertigo-inducing footbridge links the latter with the stunning **Musée des Civilisations de l'Europe et de la Méditerranée** (MuCEM; mucem.org), the icon of modern Marseille.

From the Vieux Port, hike up to the fantastic history-woven quarter of **Le Panier**, a mishmash of steep lanes hiding ateliers (workshops) and terraced houses strung with drying washing.

 THE DRIVE
To get from Marseille to Cannes, take the northbound A52 and join the A8 toll road just east of Aix-en-Provence. It's 181km and takes just under two hours.

09 CANNES
The eponymous film festival only lasts for two weeks in May, but thanks to regular visits from celebrities the buzz and glitz are in Cannes year-round. The imposing **Palais des Festivals et des Congrès** (palaisdesfestivals.com) is the

centre of the glamour. Stroll the red carpet, walk down the auditorium, tread the stage and learn about cinema's most prestigious event on a 1½-hour guided tour run by the **tourist office** (marseille-tourisme.com).

 THE DRIVE
Leave the motorways behind and weave along the D6007 to Nice, taking in cliffs framing turquoise Mediterranean waters and the yachties' town of Antibes. It's 31km and, on a good day, takes 45 minutes.

10 NICE
You don't need to be a painter or an artist to appreciate the extraordinary light in Nice. Matisse, Chagall et al spent years lapping up the city's startling luminosity, and for most visitors to Nice, it is this magical light that seduces. The city has several world-class sights, but the star attraction is the seafront **promenade des Anglais**. Stroll and watch the world go by.

11

The Pyrenees

BEST FOR OUTDOORS

Hiking to the Lac de Gaube or Refuge Wallon near Cauterets.

Lescun, Vallée d'Aspe

DURATION	DISTANCE	GREAT FOR
7 days	522km / 324 miles	Family travel, outdoors

BEST TIME TO GO	June to September, when roads are snow-free. October for autumn colours.

Traversing hair-raising roads, sky-top passes and snow-dusted peaks, this roller-coaster of a trip ventures deep into the sublime beauty of the Pyrenees mountains. With every valley and massif offering something new, it's a thrilling region to travel through and even the most hardened driver will feel the urge to get out of the car and take to a hiking trail.

Link your trip

08 Atlantic to Med

From Foix, head just over an hour northeast to Carcassone and then east for the balmy Med or west for the slower-paced Atlantic coast.

10 Essential France

From Foix, it's four hours' drive east to Aix-en-Provence, where you can commence the grand tour of France in reverse.

01 **PAU**

Palm trees might seem out of place in this mountainous region, but Pau (rhymes with 'so') has long been famed for its mild climate. In the 19th century this elegant town was a favourite wintering spot for the wealthy, and their legacy is visible in the town's grand villas and smart promenades.

Its main sight is the **Château de Pau** (chateau-pau.fr), built by the monarchs of Navarre and transformed into a Renaissance château in the 16th century. It's home to a fine collection of Gobelins tapestries and Sèvres porcelain.

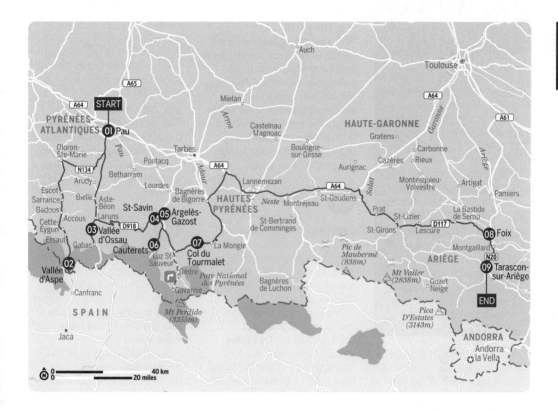

Pau's tiny old centre extends for around 500m around the château, and boasts many attractive medieval and Renaissance buildings.

Central street parking in Pau is mostly *payant* (chargeable), though there's limited free parking at the central Stadium de la Gare.

THE DRIVE

To reach the Vallée d'Aspe from Pau, take the N193 to Oloron-Ste-Marie. The first 30km are uneventful, but over the next 40km south of Oloron the mountain scenery unfolds in dramatic fashion, with towering peaks stacking up on either side of the road.

02 VALLÉE D'ASPE

The westernmost of the Pyrenean valleys makes a great day trip from Pau. Framed by mountains and bisected by the Aspe River, it's awash with classic Pyrenean scenery. Allow yourself plenty of time for photo stops, especially around pretty villages such as **Sarrance**, **Borcé** and **Etsaut**.

Near the quiet village of **Bedous**, it's worth detouring up the narrow road to **Lescun**, a tiny hamlet perched 5.5km above the valley, overlooking the peak of **Pic d'Anie** (2504m) and the **Cirque de Lescun**, a jagged ridge of mountain peaks that close out the head of the valley.

The return drive to Pau is just over 80km.

THE DRIVE

To reach the Vallée d'Ossau from Pau, take the N134 south of town, veering south onto the D934 towards Arudy/Laruns. From Pau to Laruns, it's about 42km.

03 VALLÉE D'OSSAU

More scenic splendour awaits in the Vallée d'Ossau, which tracks the course of its namesake river for a spectacular 60km. The first part of the valley as far as Laruns is broad, green and pastoral, but as you travel south the mountains really start to pile up, before broadening out again near Gabas.

The Transhumance

If you're travelling through the Pyrenees between late May and early June and find yourself stuck behind a livestock-shaped traffic jam, there's a good chance you may have just got caught up in the Transhumance, in which shepherds move their flocks from their winter pastures up to the high, grassy uplands.

This ancient custom has been a fixture on the Pyrenean calendar for centuries, and several valleys host festivals to mark the occasion. The spectacle is repeated in October, when the flocks are brought back down before the winter snows set in.

Halfway between Arudy and Laruns, you can spy on some of the mightiest birds of the western Pyrenees, griffon vultures, at the **Falaise aux Vautours** (Cliff of the Vultures; falaise-aux-vautours.com). Live CCTV images are beamed from their nests to the visitors centre in Aste-Béon. Griffon vultures are common throughout the western part of the Pyrenees. Much rarer cousins include the Egyptian vulture and the massive lammergeier.

The ski resort of **Artouste-Fabrèges**, 6km east of Gabas, is linked by cable car to the **Petit Train d'Artouste** (artouste.fr), a miniature mountain railway built for dam workers in the 1920s. The train is only open between June and September; reserve ahead and allow four hours for a visit.

THE DRIVE
The D918 between Laruns and Argelès-Gazost is one of the Pyrenees' most breathtaking roads, switchbacking over the lofty Col d'Aubisque. The road feels exposed, but it's a wonderfully scenic drive. You'll cover about 52km, but allow yourself at least 1½ hours. Once you reach Argelès-Gazost, head further south for 4km along the D101 to St-Savin.

04 ST-SAVIN
After the hair-raising drive over the Col d'Aubisque, St-Savin makes a welcome refuge. It's a classic Pyrenean village, with cobbled lanes, quiet cafes and timbered houses set around a fountain-filled main square.

It's also home to one of the Pyrenees' most respected hotel-restaurants, **Le Viscos** (hotel-leviscos.com), run by celeb chef Jean-Pierre St-Martin, known for his blend of Basque, Breton and Pyrenean flavours (as well as his passion for foie gras). After dinner, retire to one of the cosy country-style rooms and watch the sun set over the snowy mountains.

THE DRIVE
From St-Savin, travel back along the D101 to Argelès-Gazost. You'll see signs to the Parc Animalier des Pyrénées as you approach town.

05 ARGELÈS-GAZOST
The Pyrenees has a diverse collection of wildlife, but spotting it in the wild isn't always simple. Thankfully then, the **Parc Animalier des Pyrénées** (parc-animalier-pyrenees.com) does all the hard work for you. It's home to a menagerie of endangered

Pyrenean animals including wolves, marmots, lynxes, ravens, vultures, beavers and even a few brown bears (whose limited presence in the Pyrenees is highly controversial).

THE DRIVE
Take the D921 south of Argelès-Gazost for 6km to Pierrefitte-Nestalas. Here, the road forks; the southwest branch (the D920) climbs up a lush, forested valley for another 11km to Cauterets.

06 CAUTERETS
For Alpine scenery, the century-old ski and spa resort of Cauterets is perhaps the signature spot in the Pyrenees. Hemmed in by mountains and forests, it has clung on to much of its fin de siècle character, with a stately spa and grand 19th-century residences.

To see the scenery at its best, drive through town along the D920 (signed to the 'Pont d'Espagne'). The road is known locally as the **Chemins des Cascades** after the waterfalls that crash down the mountainside; it's 6.5km of nonstop hairpins, so take it steady.

At the top, you'll reach the giant car park at **Pont d'Espagne**. From here, a combination *télécabine* and *télésiege* ratchets up the mountainside allowing access to the area's trails, including the popular hike to the sapphire-tinted **Lac de Gaube** and the even more beautiful but longer walks to the **Refuge Wallon** (four hours return) and **Refuge Oulette de Gaube** (five to six hours return).

THE DRIVE
After staying overnight in Cauterets, backtrack to Pierrefitte-

Griffon vulture, Pyrenees

WHY I LOVE THIS TRIP

Stuart Butler, writer

The craggy peaks of the Pyrenees are home to some of France's rarest wildlife and most unspoilt landscapes, and every twist and turn in the road seems to reveal another knockout view. I've spent the past two decades living at the western foot of these mountains and still never tire of exploring them. For me, there is simply no more beautiful mountain range on earth. This west-to-east drive through the mountains showcases some of its finest, and most easily accessible, sights, views and experiences.

Nestalas and turn southeast onto the D921 for 12km to Luz-St-Sauveur. The next stretch on the D918 is another mountain stunner, climbing up through Barèges to the breathtaking Col du Tourmalet.

 DETOUR

Cirque de Gavarnie
Start: 6 Cauterets

For truly mind-blowing mountain scenery, it's well worth taking a side trip to see the Cirque de Gavarnie, a dramatic glacially formed amphitheatre of mountains 20km south of Luz-St-Sauveur. It's a return walk of about two hours from the village, and you'll need to bring sturdy footwear. There's another spectacular – and quieter – circle of mountains 6.5km to the east, the **Cirque de Troumouse**. It's reached via a hair-raising 8km toll road. There are no barriers and the drops are really dizzying, so drive carefully.

Photo Opportunity
Posing in the imposing Cirque de Gavarnie.

07 **COL DU TOURMALET**
At 2115m, Col du Tourmalet is the highest road pass in the Pyrenees, and it usually only opens between June and October. It's often used as a punishing mountain stage in the Tour de France, and you'll feel uncomfortably akin to a motorised ant as you crawl up towards the pass.

From the ski resort of La Mongie (1800m), a cable car climbs to the top of **Pic du Midi** (picdumidi.com). This high-altitude observatory commands otherworldly views – but it's often blanketed in cloud, so make sure you check the forecast before you go.

 THE DRIVE
The next stage to Foix is a long one. Follow the D918 and D935 to Bagnères de Bigorre, then the D938 and D20 to Tournay, a drive of 40km. Just before Tournay, head west onto the A64 for 82km. Exit onto the D117, signed to St-Girons. It's another 72km to Foix, but with twisting roads all the way and lots of 30km/h zones this last part takes at least 1½ hours.

08 **FOIX**
Looming above Foix is the triple-towered **Château de Foix**, constructed in the 10th century as a stronghold for the counts of the town. The view from the battlements is wonderful and a refurbishment has spruced

CHRISTOPHE FAUGERE/SHUTTERSTOCK ©

Cirque de Gavarnie

up the displays on medieval life. There's usually at least one daily tour in English in summer.

Afterwards, head 4.5km south to **Les Forges de Pyrène** (forges-de-pyrene.com), a fascinating 'living museum' that explores Ariège folk traditions. Spread over 5 hectares, it illustrates traditional trades such as glass-blowing, tanning, thatching and nail making, and even has its own blacksmith, baker and cobbler.

THE DRIVE
Spend the night in Foix, then head for Tarascon-sur-Ariège, 17km south of Foix on the N20. Look out for brown signs to the Parc de la Préhistoire.

09 TARASCON-SUR-ARIÈGE
Thousands of years ago, the Pyrenees were home to thriving communities of hunter-gatherers, who used the area's caves as shelters and left behind many stunning examples of prehistoric art.

Near Tarascon-sur-Ariège, the **Parc de la Préhistoire** provides a handy primer on the area's ancient past. It explores everything from prehistoric carving to the arts of animal-skin tent making and ancient spear-throwing.

About 6.5km further south, the **Grotte de Niaux** (sites-touristiques-ariege.fr) is home to the Pyrenees' most precious cave paintings. The centrepiece is the Salon Noir, reached after an 800m walk through the darkness and decorated with bison, horses and ibex. The cave can only be visited with a guide. From April to September there's usually one daily tour in English at 1.30pm. Bookings are advisable.

OLEG_MIT/SHUTTERSTOCK ©

View from the Col du Tourmalet

ROAD PASSES IN THE PYRENEES

The high passes between the Vallée d'Ossau, the Vallée d'Aspe and the Vallée de Gaves are often closed during winter. Signs are posted along the approach roads indicating whether they're *ouvert* (open) or *fermé* (closed). The dates given below are approximate and depend on seasonal snowfall.

Col d'Aubisque
(1709m, open May to October) The D918 links Laruns in the Vallée d'Ossau with Argelés-Gazost in the Vallée de Gaves. An alternative that's open year-round is the D35 between Louvie-Juzon and Nay.

Col de Marie-Blanque
(1035m, open most of the year) The shortest link between the Aspe and Ossau Valleys is the D294, which corkscrews for 21km between Escot and Bielle.

Col du Pourtalet
(1795m, open most of the year) The main crossing into Spain generally stays open year-round except during exceptional snowfall.

Col du Tourmalet
(2115m, open June to October) Between Barèges and La Mongie, this is the highest road pass in the Pyrenees. If you're travelling east to the Pic du Midi (for example, from Cauterets), the only alternative is a long detour north via Lourdes and Bagnères de Bigorre.

12

Riviera Crossing

BEST FOR GLAMOUR

☀

Strolling La Croisette in Cannes and fulfilling your film-star fantasies.

DURATION	DISTANCE	GREAT FOR
4 days	110km / 68 miles	History, food and drink

BEST TIME TO GO	Any time, but avoid July and August's crowds.

Cannes

Cruising the Côte d'Azur is as dazzling and chic as road trips get. From film town Cannes to sassy Nice via the corkscrew turns of the *corniches* and into millionaire's Monaco, it's a drive you'll remember forever. Filmmakers, writers, celebs and artists have all had their hearts stolen by this glittering stretch of coastline: by the end of this trip, you'll understand why.

Link your trip

08 Essential France

This trip makes a natural extension of our grand tour of France's unmissable sights.

10 Atlantic to Med

Cover the whole south of France by combining these coastal trips, which intersect at Cannes and Nice.

01 **CANNES**

What glitzier opening could there be to this Côte d'Azur cruise than Cannes, as cinematic as its reputation suggests. Come July during the film festival, the world's stars descend on **boulevard de la Croisette** (aka La Croisette) to stroll beneath the palms, plug their latest opus and hobnob with the media and movie moguls. Getting your picture snapped outside the **Palais des Festivals** (palaisdesfestivals.com) is a must-do, as is a night-time stroll along the boulevard, illuminated by coloured lights.

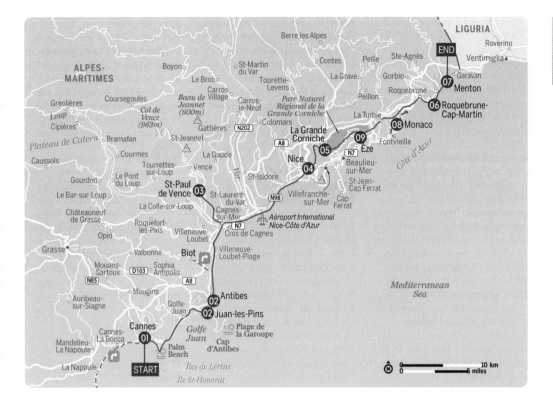

Outside festival time, Cannes still feels irresistibly ritzy. Private beaches and grand hotels line the seafront; further west lies old Cannes. Follow rue St-Antoine and snake your way up **Le Suquet**, Cannes' atmospheric original village. Pick up the region's best produce at **Marché Forville** (marche forville.com), a couple of blocks back from the port.

Need nature? Then head to the **Îles de Lérins**, two islands located a 20-minute boat ride away. Tiny and traffic-free, they're perfect for walks or a picnic. Boats for the islands leave from quai des Îles, on the western side of the harbour.

THE DRIVE

The most scenic route to Antibes is via the coastal D6007. Bear right onto av Frères Roustan before Golfe Juan. With luck and no traffic jams, you should hit Juan-les-Pins in 30 minutes or so.

DETOUR
Corniche de l'Estérel
Start: ① Cannes

West of Cannes, the winding coast road known as the Corniche de l'Estérel (sometimes known as the Corniche d'Or, the Golden Road) is well worth a side trip if you can spare the time. Opened in 1903 by the Touring Club de France, this twisting coast road is as much about driving pleasure as getting from A to B; it runs for 30 unforgettable coastal kilometres all the way to St-Raphael. En route you'll pass seaside villages, secluded coves (sandy, pebbled, nudist, you name it) and the rocky red hills of the Massif de l'Estérel, dotted with gnarly oaks, juniper and wild thyme. Wherever you go, the blue Mediterranean shimmers alongside, tempting you to stop for just one more swim. It's too much to resist.

02 ANTIBES & JUAN-LES-PINS

A century or so ago, Antibes and Juan-les-Pins were a refuge for artists, writers, aristocrats and hedonistic expats looking to escape the horrors of post-WWI Europe. They came in their droves – F Scott Fitzgerald wrote several books here, and

Picasso rented a miniature castle (it's now a museum dedicated to him).

First stop is the beach resort of Juan-les-Pins. It's a long way from the fashionable resort of Fitzgerald's day, but the beaches are still good for sun-lounging (even if you do have to pay).

Then it's on around the peninsula of **Cap d'Antibes**, where many of the greats had their holiday villas: the Hotel Cap du Eden Roc was one of their favourite fashionable haunts. Round the peninsula is pretty Antibes, with a harbour full of pleasure boats and an old town ringed by medieval ramparts. Aim to arrive before lunchtime, when the atmospheric **Marché Provençal** will still be in full swing, and then browse the nearby **Musée Picasso** (antibes-juanlespins.com/culture/musee-picasso) to see a few of the artist's Antibes-themed works.

🚗 THE DRIVE
Brave the traffic on the D6007 and avoid signs to turn onto the A8 motorway: it's the D2 you want, so follow signs for Villeneuve-Loubet. When you reach the town, cross the river. You'll pass through a tunnel into the outskirts of Cagnes-sur-Mer; now start following signs to St-Paul de Vence.

↩ DETOUR
Biot
Start: ② Antibes & Juan-les-Pins
About an 8km drive from Antibes along the coast road and the D4, this 15th-century hilltop village was once an important pottery-manufacturing centre. The advent of metal containers brought an end to this, but Biot is still active in handicraft production, especially glassmaking. At the foot of the village, the **Verrerie de Biot** (verreriebiot.

com) produces bubbled glass by rolling molten glass into baking soda; bubbles from the chemical reaction are then trapped by a second layer of glass. You can watch skilled glass-blowers at work and browse the adjacent art galleries and shop. There are also guided tours, during which you get the chance to try your hand at a spot of glass-blowing – and learn why it's probably best left to the professionals.

03 ST-PAUL DE VENCE
Once upon a time, hilltop St-Paul de Vence was just another village like countless others in Provence. But then the artists moved in: painters such as Marc Chagall and Pablo Picasso sought solitude here, painted the local scenery and traded canvases for room and board. This is how the hotel **La Colombe d'Or** (la-colombe-dor.com) came by its stellar art collection.

It's now one of the Riviera's most exclusive locations, a haven for artists, film stars and celebrities, not to mention hordes of sightseers, many of whom are here to marvel at the incredible art collection at the **Fondation Maeght** (fondation-maeght.com). Created in 1964 by collectors Aimé and Merguerite Maeght, it boasts works by all the big 20th-century names – including Miró sculptures, Chagall mosaics, Braque windows and canvases by Picasso, Matisse and others.

While you're here, it's worth taking a detour northwards to **Vence**, where the marvellous **Chapelle du Rosaire** (chapel lematisse.fr) was designed by an ailing Henri Matisse. He had a hand in everything here, from the stained-glass windows to the altar and candlesticks.

🚗 THE DRIVE
Return the way you came, only this time follow the blue signs onto the A8 motorway to Nice. Take exit 50 for promenade des Anglais, which will take you all 18km along the Baie des Anges. The views are great, but you'll hit nightmare traffic at rush hour.

04 NICE
With its mix of real-city grit, old-world opulence and year-round sunshine, Nice is the undisputed capital of the Côte d'Azur. Sure, the traffic is horrendous and the beach is made entirely of pebbles (not a patch of sand in sight!), but that doesn't detract from its charms. It's a great base, with loads of hotels and restaurants, and character in every nook and cranny.

Start with a morning stroll through the huge food and flower markets on **cours Saleya**, then delve into the winding alleyways of the old town, **Vieux Nice**, where there are many backstreet restaurants at which you can try local specialities such as *pissaladière* (onion tart topped with anchovies and olives) and *socca* (chickpea-flour pancake). Stop for an ice cream at famous **Fenocchio** (fenocchio. fr) – flavours include tomato, lavender, olive and fig – then spend the afternoon sunbathing on the beaches along the seafront **promenade des Anglais** before catching an epic sunset.

If you have the time, the city has some great museums too – you'll need at least an afternoon to explore all of the modern masterpieces at the **Musée d'Art Moderne et d'Art Contemporain** (MAMAC; mamac-nice.org).

THE DRIVE

Exit the city through Riquier on the D2564. You don't want the motorway – you want bd Bischoffsheim, which becomes bd de l'Observatoire as it climbs to the summit of Mont Gros. The next 12km are thrilling, twisting past the Parc Naturel Régional de la Grande Corniche. Stop for a picnic or a hilly hike, then continue towards La Turbie.

05 LA GRANDE CORNICHE

Remember that sexy scene from Hitchcock's *To Catch a Thief,* when Grace Kelly and Cary Grant cruised the hills in a convertible, enjoying sparkling banter and searing blue Mediterranean views? Well you're about to tackle the very same

Photo Opportunity

Standing by Augustus' monumental Trophée des Alpes, with Monaco and the Mediterranean far below.

drive – so don your shades, roll down the windows and hit the asphalt.

It's a roller-coaster of a road, veering through hairpins and switchbacks as it heads into the hills above Nice. There are countless picnic spots and photo opportunities along the way, including

the **Col d'Èze**, the road's highest point at 512m. Further on you'll pass the monumental Roman landmark known as the **Trophée des Alpes** (trophee-auguste.fr), a magnificent triumphal arch built to commemorate Augustus' victory over the last remaining Celtic-Ligurian tribes who had resisted conquest. The views from here are jaw-dropping, stretching all the way to Monaco and Italy beyond.

THE DRIVE

Monte Carlo may sparkle and beckon below, but keep your eyes on the road; the principality will keep for another day. Stay on the D2564 to skirt Monaco for another amazing 10km, then turn right into the D52 to Roquebrune.

Trophée des Alpes

06 ROQUEBRUNE-CAP-MARTIN

This village of two halves feels a world away from the glitz of nearby Monaco: the coastline around Cap Martin remains relatively unspoilt, as if Roquebrune had left its clock on medieval time. The historic half of the town, Roquebrune itself, sits 300m high on a pudding-shaped lump. It towers over the Cap, but they are, in fact, linked by innumerable, very steep steps.

The village is delightful and free of tack, and there are sensational views of the coast from the main village square, **place des Deux Frères**. Of all Roquebrune's steep streets, **rue Moncollet** – with its arcaded passages and stairways carved out of rock – is the most impressive. Scurry upwards to find architect Le Corbusier's grave at the cemetery at the top of the village (in section J, and yes, he did design his own tombstone).

🚗 THE DRIVE

Continue along the D52 towards the coast, following promenade du Cap-Martin all the way along the seafront to Menton. You'll be there in 10 minutes, traffic permitting.

07 MENTON

Last stop on the coast before Italy, the beautiful seaside town of Menton offers a glimpse of what the Riviera once looked like, before the high-rises, casinos and property developers moved in. It's ripe for wandering, with peaceful gardens and belle-époque mansions galore, as well as an attractive yacht-filled harbour. Meander the historic quarter all the way to the **Cimetière du Vieux Château** for the best views in town.

Parfumerie Fragonard, Grasse

PERFUME IN GRASSE

Up in the hills to the north of Cannes, the town of Grasse has been synonymous with perfumery since the 16th century, and the town is still home to around 30 makers – several of whom offer guided tours of their factories, and the chance to hone your olfactory skills.

It can take up to 10 years to train a perfumier, but since you probably don't have that much time to spare, you'll have to make do with a crash course. Renowned maker **Molinard** (molinard.com) runs workshops where sessions range from 30 minutes to two hours, during which you get to create your own custom perfume (sandalwood, vanilla, hyacinth, lily of the valley, civet, hare and rose petals are just a few of the potential notes you could include). At the end of the workshop, you'll receive a bottle of eau de parfum to take home. **Galimard** (galimard.com) and Fragonard's **Usine Historique** (fragonard.com/fr/usines/musee-du-parfum) offer similar workshops.

For background, make time to visit the excellent **Musée International de la Parfumerie** (museesdegrasse.com) and its nearby **gardens**, where you can see some of the many plants and flowers used in scent-making. Needless to say, the bouquet is overpowering.

With light that inspired Picasso and Matisse, history you can feel in your soul and a view over the Mediterranean at every hairpin turn, this drive takes in every dreamy hue of the Côte d'Azur. Each kilometre is special, from the glamour of Cannes and perfumeries of Grasse to the brassiness of Nice, audaciousness of Monaco and all the hilltop villages between.

Menton's miniature microclimate enables exotic plants to flourish here, many of which you can see at the **Jardin Botanique Exotique du Val Rahmeh** (mnhn.fr/fr/jardin-botanique-val-rahmeh-menton), where terraces overflow with fruit trees, and the beautiful, once-abandoned **Jardin de la Serre de la Madone** (menton.fr/Jardin-Serre-de-la-Madone.html), overgrown with rare plants. Spend your second night in town.

🚗 THE DRIVE

Leave Menton on the D6007, the Moyenne Corniche, skirting the upper perimeter of Monaco. When you're ready, turn off into Monaco. All the car parks charge the same rate.

Good options include the Chemin des Pêcheurs and Stade Louis II for old Monaco, or the huge underground Casino car park by allées des Boulingrins for central Monte Carlo.

08 MONACO

This pint-sized principality (covering barely 200 hectares) is ridiculous, absurd, ostentatious and fabulous all at once. A playground of the super-rich, with super-egos to match, it's the epitome of Riviera excess – especially at the famous **Casino de Monte Carlo** (casinomontecarlo.com), where cards turn, roulette wheels spin and eye-watering sums are won and lost.

For all its glam, Monaco is not all show. Up in the hilltop quarter of **Le Rocher**, shady streets surround the **Palais Princier de Monaco** (palais.mc), the wedding-cake castle of Monaco's royal family (time your visit for the pomptastic changing of the guard at 11.55am).

Nearby is the impressive **Musée Océanographique de Monaco** (oceano.mc), stocked with all kinds of deep-sea denizens. It even has a 6m-deep lagoon complete with circling sharks.

Round things off with a stroll around the cliffside **Jardin Exotique** (jardin-exotique.mc) and the obligatory photo of Monaco's harbour, bristling with over-the-top yachts.

🚗 THE DRIVE

Pick up where you left off on the Moyenne Corniche (D6007), and follow its circuitous route back up into the hills all the way to Èze.

09 ÈZE

This rocky little village perched on an impossible peak is outrageously romantic. The main attraction is technically the medieval village, with small higgledy-piggledy stone houses and winding lanes (and, yes, galleries and shops). It's undoubtedly delightful, but it's the ever-present views of the coast that are truly mesmerising. They just get more spectacular from the **Jardin Exotique d'Èze** (jardinexotique-eze.fr), a surreal cactus garden at the top of the village, so steep and rocky it may have been purpose-built for mountain goats. It's also where you'll find the old castle ruins; take time to sit and gaze, as few places on earth offer such a panorama.

Èze gets very crowded between 10am and 5pm; if you prefer a quiet wander, plan to be here early in the morning or before dinner. Or even better, treat yourself to a night and supper at the swish **Château Eza** (chateaueza.com), a fitting finish to this most memorable of road trips.

Jardin Exotique d'Èze

13

Champagne Taster

DURATION	DISTANCE	GREAT FOR
3 days	85km / 53 miles	Wine, history

BEST TIME TO GO	April to June for spring sunshine or September and October to see the harvest in Champagne.

Starting at the prestigious Champagne centre of Reims, passing through Épernay and ending in Le Mesnil-sur-Oger, this fizz-fuelled adventure whisks you through the heart of this Unesco World Heritage region and explores the world's favourite celebratory tipple – with ample time for tasting en route.

Link your trip

08 Essential France

Lying 150km west of Épernay, Paris marks the beginning of our epic journey around France's most essential sights.

09 D-Day's Beaches

From Épernay head west, skirting Paris, to Caen (four hours' drive) to follow the course of the Normandy invasion of WWII.

01 REIMS

There's nowhere better to start your Champagne tour than the regal city of Reims. Several big names have their *caves* (wine cellars) nearby. **Mumm** (mumm.com), pronounced 'moom', is the only *maison* in central Reims. Founded in 1827, it's the world's third- or fourth-largest Champagne producer, depending on the year. One-hour tours explore its enormous cellars, filled with 25 million bottles of bubbly, and include tastings of several vintages.

North of town, **Taittinger** (book-a-visit.taittinger.frr) provides an informative overview of how

DIRECTPHOTO COLLECTION/ALAMY STOCK PHOTO ©

Mumm Champange cellar

Champagne is actually made – you'll leave with a good understanding of the production process, from grape to bottle. Parts of the cellars occupy Roman stone quarries dug in the 4th century.

Before you leave town, don't forget to drop by **Waïda**, an old-fashioned confectioner which sells Reims' famous *biscuits roses* (pink biscuits), a sweet treat traditionally nibbled with a glass of Champagne.

 THE DRIVE
The countryside between Reims and Épernay is carpeted with vineyards, fields and back roads that are a dream to drive through. From Reims, head south along the D951 for 13km. Near Mont Chenot, turn onto

the D26, signposted to Rilly and the 'Route Touristique du Champagne'. The next 12km take you through the pretty villages of Rilly-la-Montagne and Mailly-Champagne en route to Verzenay.

02 VERZENAY
Reims marks the start of the 70km **Montagne de Reims Champagne Route**, the prettiest (and most prestigious) of the three signposted road routes

Photo Opportunity
Overlooking glossy vineyards from the Phare de Verzenay.

that wind their way through the Champagne vineyards. Of the 17 *grand cru* villages in Champagne, nine lie on and around the Montagne, a hilly area whose sheltered slopes and chalky soils provide the perfect environment for viticulture (grape growing). Most of the area's vineyards are devoted to the pinot noir grape. You'll pass plenty of producers offering *dégustation* (tasting) en route. It's up to you how many you visit – but whatever you do, don't miss the panorama of the vineyards of Verzenay from the top of the **Phare de Verzenay** (lepharedeverzenay.com), a lighthouse constructed as a publicity gimmick in 1909.

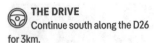

THE DRIVE
Continue south along the D26 for 3km.

03 VERZY

This village is home to several small vineyards that provide an interesting contrast to the big producers. **Étienne and Anne-Laure Lefevre** (champagne-etienne-lefevre. com) run group tours of their family-owned vineyards and cellars – if you're on your own, ring ahead to see if you can join a pre-arranged tour. There are no flashy videos or multimedia shows – the emphasis is firmly on the nitty-gritty of Champagne production.

For a glass of fizz high above the treetops, seek out the sleek **Perching Bar** (facebook.com/ perchingbar) deep in the forest.

 THE DRIVE
Stay on the D26 south of Verzy, and enjoy wide-open countryside views as you spin south to Ambonnay. Detour west onto the D19, signed to Bouzy, and bear right onto the D1 along the northern bank of the Marne River. When you reach the village of Dizy, follow signs onto the D386 to Hautvillers. It's a total drive of 32km or 45 minutes.

04 HAUTVILLERS

Next stop is the hilltop village of Hautvillers, a hallowed name among Champagne aficionados: it's where a Benedictine monk by the name of Dom Pierre Pérignon is popularly believed to have created Champagne in the late 16th century. The great man's tomb lies in front of the altar of the **Église Abbatiale**.

DANITA DELIMONT CREATIVE/ALAMY STOCK PHOTO ©

Vineyards, Hautvillers

The village itself is well worth a stroll, with a jumble of lanes, timbered houses and stone-walled vineyards. On place de la République, the **tourist office** (tourisme-hautvillers.com) hands out free maps detailing local vineyard walks; one-hour guided tours cost €7 (€9 with a tasting).

Steps away is **Au 36** (au36.net), a wine boutique with a 'wall' of Champagne quirkily arranged by aroma. There's a tasting room upstairs; a two-/three-glass session costs €13/17.

 THE DRIVE
From the centre of the village, take the rte de Cumières for grand views across the vine-cloaked slopes. Follow the road all the way to the D1, turn left and follow signs to Épernay's centre, 6km to the south.

05 **ÉPERNAY**
The prosperous town of Épernay is the self-proclaimed **capitale du Champagne** and is home to many of the most illustrious Champagne houses. Beneath the streets are an astonishing 110km of subterranean cellars, containing an estimated 200 million bottles of vintage bubbly.

Most of the big names are arranged along the grand av de Champagne. **Moët & Chandon** (moet.com) offers frequent and fascinating one-hour tours of its prestigious cellars, while at nearby **Mercier** (champagne mercier.fr) tours take place aboard a laser-guided underground train.

Finish with a climb up the 237-step tower at **De Castellane** (castellane.com), which offers knockout views over the town's rooftops and vine-clad hills.

Grape press, Hautvillers

THE SCIENCE OF CHAMPAGNE

Champagne is made from the red pinot noir (38%), the black pinot meunier (35%) or the white chardonnay (27%) grape. Each vine is vigorously pruned and trained to produce a small quantity of high-quality grapes. Indeed, to maintain exclusivity (and price), the designated areas where grapes used for Champagne can be grown and the amount of wine produced each year are limited.

Making Champagne according to the *méthode champenoise* (traditional method) is a complex procedure. There are two fermentation processes, the first in casks and the second after the wine has been bottled and had sugar and yeast added. Bottles are then aged in cellars for two to five years, depending on the *cuvée* (vintage).

For two months in early spring the bottles are aged in cellars kept at 12°C and the wine turns effervescent. The sediment that forms in the bottle is removed by *remuage*, a painstakingly slow process in which each bottle, stored horizontally, is rotated slightly every day for weeks until the sludge works its way to the cork. Next comes *dégorgement*: the neck of the bottle is frozen, creating a blob of solidified Champagne and sediment, which is then removed.

Moët & Chandon Champagne

CHAMPAGNE KNOW-HOW

Types of Champagne

Blanc de Blancs Champagne made using only chardonnay grapes. Fresh and elegant, with very small bubbles and a bouquet reminiscent of 'yellow fruits' such as pear and plum.

Blanc de Noirs A full-bodied, deep golden Champagne made solely with black grapes (despite the colour). Often rich and refined, with great complexity and a long finish.

Rosé Pink Champagne (mostly served as an aperitif) with a fresh character and summer-fruit flavours. Made by adding a small percentage of red pinot noir to white Champagne.

Prestige Cuvée The crème de la crème of Champagne. Usually made with grapes from *grand cru* vineyards and priced and bottled accordingly.

Millésimé Vintage Champagne produced from a single crop during an exceptional year. Most Champagne is nonvintage.

Sweetness

Brut Dry; most common style; pairs well with food.

Extra Sec Fairly dry but sweeter than Brut; nice as an aperitif.

Demi Sec Medium sweet; goes well with fruit and dessert.

Doux Very sweet; a dessert Champagne.

Serving & Tasting

Chilling Chill Champagne in a bucket of ice for 30 minutes before serving. The ideal serving temperature is 7°C to 9°C.

Opening Grip the bottle securely and tilt it at a 45-degree angle facing away from you. Rotate the bottle slowly to ease out the cork – it should sigh, not pop.

Pouring Hold the flute by the stem at an angle and let the Champagne trickle gently into the glass – less foam, more bubbles.

Tasting Admire the colour and bubbles. Swirl your glass to release the aroma and inhale slowly before tasting the Champagne.

THE DRIVE

Head south of town along av Maréchal Foch or av du 8 Mai 1945, following 'Autres Directions' signs across the roundabouts until you see signs for Cramant. The village is 10km southeast of Épernay via the D10.

06 CRAMANT

You'll find it hard to miss this quaint village, as the northern entrance is heralded by a two-storey-high Champagne bottle. From the ridge above the village, views stretch out in all directions across the Champagne countryside, taking in a patchwork of fields, farmhouses and rows upon rows of endless vines. Pack a picnic and your own bottle of bubbly for the perfect Champagne country lunch.

 THE DRIVE:

Continue southeast along the D10 for 7km, and follow signs to Le-Mesnil-sur-Oger.

07 LE MESNIL-SUR-OGER

Finish with a visit to the excellent **Musée de la Vigne et du Vin** (champagne-launois.fr), where a local wine-growing family has assembled a collection of century-old Champagne-making equipment. Among the highlights is a massive 16-tonne oak-beam grape press from 1630. Reservations must be made by phone or online; ask about the availability of English tours when you book.

Round off your trip with lunch at **La Gare** (lagarelemesnil.com), which prides itself on serving bistro-style grub prepared with seasonal produce, simple as pork tenderloin with cider and potatoes. There's a €9 menu for *les petits*.

WHY I LOVE THIS TRIP

Kerry Christiani, writer

You can sip Champagne anywhere, but a road trip really slips under the skin of these Unesco-listed vineyards. Begin with an eye-opening, palate-awakening tour and tasting at *grande maison* cellars in Épernay and Reims. I love the far-reaching view from Phare de Verzenay and touring the back roads in search of small producers, especially when the aroma of new wine hangs in the air and the vines are golden in autumn.

14

Châteaux of the Loire

BEST TWO DAYS

☑

The stretch between Chenonceau and Chambord takes in the true classics.

DURATION	DISTANCE	GREAT FOR
5 days	189km / 118 miles	Family travel

BEST TIME TO GO	May and June for good cycling weather; July for gardens and special events.

Château de Villandry

From warring medieval warlords to the kings and queens of Renaissance France, a parade of powerful men and women have left their mark on the Loire Valley. The result is France's most magnificent collection of castles. This itinerary visits nine of the Loire's most evocative châteaux, ranging from austere medieval fortresses to ostentatious royal pleasure palaces. Midway through, a side trip leads off the beaten track to four lesser-known châteaux.

Link your trip

08 Essential France

From Chambord either head north for Versailles and Paris, or south for a longer trip taking in wineries, the Alps and the Mediterranean.

10 Atlantic to Med

Head southeast to La Rochelle (a little over 200km) to begin a leisurely meander from coast to coast.

CHINON

01 Tucked between the medieval **Forteresse Royale de Chinon** (forteressechinon.fr) – a magnificent hilltop castle – and the Vienne River, Chinon is known to French schoolchildren as the venue of Joan of Arc's first meeting with Charles VII, future king of France, in 1429. Highlights include superb panoramas from the castle's ramparts and, down in the medieval part of town (along rue Voltaire), several fine buildings dating from the 15th to 17th centuries.

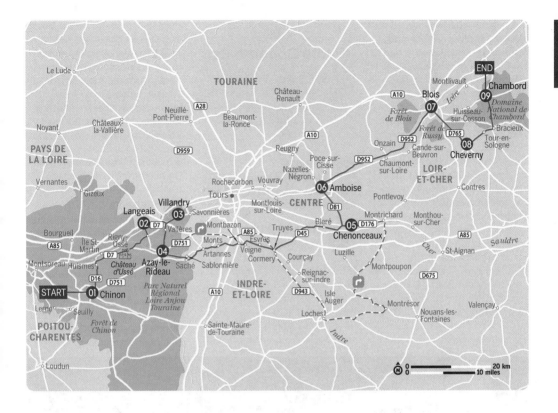

THE DRIVE

 Follow the D16 north of Chinon for 10km, then head 15km east on the riverside D7 past the fairy-tale Château d'Ussé (the inspiration for the fairy tale Sleeping Beauty) to Lignières, where you catch the D57 3km north into Langeais.

02 LANGEAIS

The most medieval of the Loire châteaux, the **Château de Langeais** (chateau-de-langeais.com) – built in the 1460s – is superbly preserved inside and out, looking much as it did at the tail end of the Middle Ages, with crenellated ramparts and massive towers dominating the surrounding village. Original 15th-century furniture and Flemish tapestries fill its flagstoned chambers. In one room, a life-size wax-figure tableau portrays the marriage of Charles VIII and Anne of Brittany, held here on 6 December 1491, which brought about the historic union of France and Brittany.

Langeais presents two faces to the world. From the town you see a fortified castle, nearly windowless, with machicolated walls rising forbiddingly from the drawbridge. But the newer sections facing the courtyard have large windows, ornate dormers and decorative stonework designed for more refined living.

Behind the château stands a ruined stone **keep** constructed in 994 by the warlord Foulques Nerra, France's first great château builder. It is the oldest such structure in France.

THE DRIVE

Backtrack south across the Loire River on the D57, then follow the riverbank east 10km on the D16 to Villandry.

03 VILLANDRY

The six glorious landscaped gardens at the **Château de Villandry** (chateau villandry.com) are among the finest in France, with over 6 hectares of cascading flowers, ornamental vines, manicured lime trees, razor-sharp box hedges and tinkling fountains. Try to visit when the gardens are blooming, between April and October; midsummer is most spectacular.

Wandering the pebbled walkways, you'll see the classical **Jardin d'Eau** (Water Garden), the **Labyrinthe** (Maze) and the **Jardin d'Ornement** (Ornamental Garden), which depicts various kinds of love (fickle, passionate, tender and tragic). But the highlight is the 16th-century-style **Potager Décoratif** (Decorative Kitchen Garden), where cabbages, leeks and carrots are laid out to create nine geometrical, colour-coordinated squares.

For bird's-eye views across the gardens and the nearby Loire and Cher Rivers, climb to the top of the **donjon** (keep), the only medieval remnant in this otherwise Renaissance-style château.

Photo Opportunity

Château de Chenonceau's graceful arches reflected in the Cher River.

THE DRIVE
Go southwest 4km on the D7, then turn south 7km on the D39 into Azay-le-Rideau.

04 AZAY-LE-RIDEAU
Romantic, moat-ringed **Azay-le-Rideau** (azay-le-rideau.fr), built in the early 1500s on a natural island in the middle of the Indre River, is wonderfully adorned with elegant turrets, Renaissance-style dormer windows, delicate stonework and

steep slate roofs. Its most famous feature is an Italian-style loggia staircase overlooking the central courtyard, decorated with the royal salamanders and ermines of François I and Queen Claude. The interior furnishings are mostly 19th century. Outside, the lovely English-style gardens are great for a stroll. A sound-and-light spectacular, **Les Nuits Fantastiques**, is usually projected on the château's walls in July and August.

THE DRIVE
Follow the D84 east 6km through the tranquil Indre Valley, then cross the river south into Saché, home to an attractive château and Balzac museum. From Saché continue 26km east on the D17, 11km northeast on the D45 and 9km east on the D976. Cross north over the Cher River and follow the D40 east 1.5km to Chenonceaux village and the Château de Chenonceau.

B&W AGENCJA FOTOGRAFICZNA SP. Z O.O./ALAMY STOCK PHOTO ©

Château de Chenonceau

DETOUR:

South of the Loire River

START: ❹ **AZAY-LE-RIDEAU**

Escape the crowds by detouring to four less-visited châteaux between Azay-le-Rideau and Chenonceaux.

First stop: Loches, where Joan of Arc, fresh from her victory at Orléans in 1429, famously persuaded Charles VII to march to Reims and claim the French crown. The undisputed highlight here is the walled **Cité Royale** (citeroyaleloches.fr), a vast citadel that spans 500 years of French château architecture in a single site, from Foulques Nerra's early-11th-century *donjon* (keep) to the Flamboyant Gothic and Renaissance styles of the Logis Royal. To get here from Azay-le-Rideau, head 55km east and then southeast along the D751, A85 and D943.

Next comes the quirky **Château de Montrésor** (chateaudemontresor.fr), 19km east of Loches on the D760, still furnished much as it was 160 years ago, when it belonged to Polish-born count, financier and railroad magnate Xavier Branicki. The eclectic Second Empire decor includes a Cuban mahogany spiral staircase, a piano once played by Chopin and a sumptuous library. Next, head 20km north on the D10 and D764 to the turreted **Château de Montpoupon** (montpoupon.com), idyllically situated in rolling countryside. Furnished in the late 19th and early 20th centuries by the family that still resides there, it has an intimate, lived-in feel.

Continue 12km north on the D764 to the ruins of the hilltop **Château de Montrichard,** another massive fortress constructed in the 11th century by Foulques Nerra. You can picnic in the park by the Cher River or taste sparkling wines at **Caves Monmousseau** (monmousseau.com). From Montrichard, head 10km west on the D176 and D40 to rejoin the main route at Chenonceaux.

05 CHENONCEAUX

Spanning the languid Cher River atop a supremely graceful arched bridge, the **Château de Chenonceau** (chenonceau.com) is one of France's most elegant castles. It's hard not to be moved and exhilarated by the glorious setting, the formal gardens, the magic of the architecture and the château's fascinating history. The interior is decorated with rare furnishings and a fabulous art collection.

This extraordinary complex is largely the work of several remarkable women (hence its nickname, Le Château des Dames). The distinctive arches and the eastern formal garden were added by Diane de Poitiers, mistress of King Henri II. Following Henri's death, Catherine de Médicis, the king's scheming widow, forced Diane (her 2nd cousin) to exchange Chenonceau for the rather less grand Château de Chaumont. Catherine completed the château's construction and added the yew-tree maze and the western rose garden. Chenonceau had an 18th-century heyday under the aristocratic Madame Dupin, who made it a centre of fashionable society; guests included Voltaire and Rousseau.

The château's pièce de résistance is the 60m-long, chequerboard-floored **Grande Gallerie** over the Cher. From 1940 to 1942 it served as an escape route for Jews and other refugees fleeing from German-occupied France (north of the Cher) to the Vichy-controlled south.

🚗 **THE DRIVE**

Follow the D81 north 13km into Amboise; 2km south of town, you'll pass the Mini-Châteaux theme park (parcminichateaux.com), whose intricate scale models of 41 Loire Valley châteaux are great fun for kids.

06 AMBOISE

Towering above town, the **Château Royal d'Amboise** (chateau-amboise.com) was a favoured retreat for all of France's Valois and Bourbon kings. The ramparts afford thrilling views of the town and river, and you can visit the furnished Logis (Lodge) and the Flamboyant Gothic **Chapelle St-Hubert** (1493), where Leonardo da Vinci's presumed remains have been buried since 1863.

Amboise's other main sight is **Le Clos Lucé** (vinci-closluce.com), the grand manor house where Leonardo da Vinci (1452–1519) took up residence in 1516 and spent the final years of his life at the invitation of François I.

Amboise's Sunday Food Market

Voted France's *marché préféré* (favourite market) a few years back, this riverfront extravaganza, 400m south-west of the château, hosts 200 to 300 open-air stalls selling everything you need for a scrumptious picnic. So delicious it's worth timing your visit around.

The most exciting Loire château to open to visitors in years, the **Château Gaillard** (chateau-gaillard-amboise.fr) is the earliest expression of the Italian Renaissance in France.

 THE DRIVE
Follow the D952 northeast along the Loire's northern bank, enjoying 35km of beautiful river views en route to Blois. The Château de Chaumont-sur-Loire, renowned for its world-class contemporary art and magnificent international garden festival (April to early November), makes a wonderful stop.

07 BLOIS
Seven French kings lived in the **Château Royal de Blois** (chateaudeblois.fr), whose four grand wings were built during four distinct periods in French architecture: Gothic (13th century), Flamboyant Gothic (1498–1501), early Renaissance (1515–20) and classical (1630s). You can easily spend a half-day immersing yourself in the

château's dramatic and bloody history and its extraordinary architecture.

In the Renaissance wing, the most remarkable feature is the spiral loggia staircase, decorated with fierce salamanders and curly Fs, heraldic symbols of François I. The **King's Chamber** was the setting for one of the bloodiest episodes in the château's history. In 1588 Henri III had his arch-rival, Duke Henri I de Guise, murdered by royal bodyguards. Dramatic and very graphic oil paintings illustrate these gruesome events next door in the **Council Chamber**.

 THE DRIVE
Cross the Loire and continue 16km southeast into Cheverny via the D765 and, for the final 1km, the D102.

08 CHEVERNY
Perhaps the Loire's most elegantly proportioned château, **Cheverny** (chateau-cheverny.fr) represents the zenith of French classical architecture: the perfect blend of symmetry, geometry and aesthetic order. Inside are some of the most elegantly furnished rooms anywhere in the Loire Valley. Highlights include the formal dining room, with panels depicting the story of Don Quixote; the king's bedchamber, with ceiling murals and tapestries illustrating stories from Greek mythology; and a children's playroom complete with toys from the time of Napoléon III.

Cheverny's kennels house about 100 pedigreed hunting dogs. Feeding time, known as the **Soupe des Chiens**, takes place on Monday, Wednesday, Thursday

and Friday at 11.30am (daily from April to mid-September). Behind the château, the 18th-century **orangerie**, which sheltered priceless artworks – including (apparently) the *Mona Lisa* – during WWII, is now a tearoom (open April to mid-November).

Fans of Tintin may recognise the château's facade as the model for Captain Haddock's ancestral home, Marlinspike Hall. **Les Secrets de Moulinsart** has interactive exhibits about the comics hero and his adventures.

 THE DRIVE
Take the D102 10km northeast into Bracieux, then turn north on the D112 for the final 8km run through the forested Domaine National de Chambord, the largest walled park in Europe. Catch your first dramatic glimpse of France's most famous château on the right as you arrive in Chambord.

09 CHAMBORD
One of the crowning achievements of French Renaissance architecture, the **Château de Chambord** (chambord.org) – with 426 rooms, 282 fireplaces and 77 staircases – is by far the largest, grandest and most visited château in the Loire Valley.

Rising through the centre of the structure, the world-famous double-helix staircase – very possibly designed by the king's chum Leonardo da Vinci – ascends to the great lantern tower and the rooftop, where you can marvel at a veritable skyline of cupolas, domes, turrets, chimneys and lightning rods, and gaze out across the vast grounds.

Château de Chambord

WHY I LOVE THIS TRIP

Daniel Robinson, writer

Travel doesn't get more splendidly French – or elegantly sumptuous – than this tour of the most famous Loire Valley châteaux, which bring together so many of the things I love most about France: supremely refined architecture, dramatic history, exquisite cuisine and delectable wines. My kids especially enjoy the forbidding medieval fortresses of Langeais and Loches, which conjure up a long-lost world of knights, counts and court intrigue.

PREMIER PHOTO/SHUTTERSTOCK ©

Cambridge (p125)

Great Britain

Explore

Great Britain

Britain packs an incredible amount of history, art and culture into its compact confines. Nature plays its part too, delivering Scottish lochs, rugged highlands, quaint English greens and dramatic Welsh coastlines. Travel through its three countries and you'll encounter wild, windswept moors, archetypal university towns and world-famous cities.

Our road trips run along bucolic country lanes and through remote valleys to reveal world-famous sights and hidden joys. They take in everything from contemporary landmarks and prehistoric stone circles to fast-paced cities and unspoiled national parks, paving the way for unforgettable experiences at every stop.

London

Few travellers visit England without spending at least a few days in London, the country's historic capital. A major business centre, transport hub and tourist hot spot, the city is a world unto itself with centuries' worth of museums, monuments and attractions, as well as more restaurants, pubs and clubs than you could visit in a lifetime. It's cosmopolitan and energetic, cutting-edge and fun.

It's also well connected. Situated in England's southeast, it's served by six airports, including four of Britain's busiest (Heathrow, Gatwick, Stansted and Luton), as well as local and long-distance trains and buses. For onward travel, car hire is widely available and major motorways run to/from the city. These include the main north-bound M1 and the westward M4, which traverses southern England as it courses on to Wales.

Manchester

England's northern powerhouse, Manchester makes an ideal base for the north of the country. Birthplace of the Industrial Revolution, the city has long been a hothouse of radical social thinking and a cultural cauldron – it gave rise to the 'Madchester' clubbing scene in the 1990s and is revered the world over for its two footballing giants, United and City. An exciting student city, it harbours a choice selection of museums and galleries as well as plenty of accommodation, eating and shopping options.

WHEN TO GO

Summer is best for the weather and for festivals, although it also means high-season prices and crowds in seaside resorts, national parks and big-draw cities. Spring and autumn are a good bet with fewer people around and often surprisingly good weather – no guarantees, though. Winter is the time for cosy pub nights and budget city breaks.

Flights serve its international airport, which is a 20-minute train ride from the centre, or there are regular trains and coaches from towns and cities across the country – London is about 2¼ hours away. By car, the city can be reached via the north–south M6 motorway or east–west M62.

Edinburgh

If you're travelling direct to Scotland, chances are you'll be arriving in Edinburgh. The city's airport is the country's largest, serving flights from around 150 worldwide destinations, and its central Waverley station welcomes trains from across the UK. From the city, it's 100 miles or so up to Balmoral Castle and the Cairngorms National Park, and 120 miles to Glencoe, starting point for the scenic drive up to Inverness.

Edinburgh is good looking and packed with historical sights ranging from its landmark castle

TRANSPORT

Most visitors fly into one of London's main airports, Heathrow, Gatwick or Stansted, all of which are well connected and offer car hire. Eurostar trains also run to London, as do long-distance coaches from European destinations. Cross-channel ferries sail to ports on the south coast while for northern destinations and Scotland there are airports at Manchester and Edinburgh.

to Scotland's national museum. You'll have no problem finding somewhere to stay – outside the August festival period, that is – and there's plenty of fun to be had in its world-class restaurants and brilliant pubs.

WHERE TO STAY

From luxury hotels to hostels, holiday cottages and self-catering apartments, Britain provides plenty of accommodation. B&Bs are a good choice, offering value for money and the chance to experience an authentic British breakfast (bacon, eggs, sausages etc). A similarly British experience is an evening in a pub, and with some pubs now offering accommodation you can really make a night of it. In rural parts, rental cottages are popular for family holidays. For shelter in the wilds of Scotland, you can bunk down in a bothy, a spartan refuge whose facilities often don't go much beyond a roof and four walls.

 WHAT'S ON

Glastonbury

(June; glastonburyfestivals.co.uk) This mammoth music fest draws huge crowds to a Somerset farm.

Edinburgh Festival

(August; edinburghfestivals.co.uk) Performers and artists swarm to Scotland's capital for this celebration of the arts.

Notting Hill Carnival

(August; nhcarnival.org) Sound systems and costumed carnival-goers take over London's Notting Hill neighbourhood.

Bonfire Night

(5 November) Bonfires light the night sky in memory of a failed plot to blow up parliament.

Resources

Visit Britain (*visitbritain. com*) Comprehensive site of Britain's tourist board with planning tips, ideas and up-to-date events info.

BBC (*bbc.co.uk*) News, entertainment and plenty more from Britain's national broadcaster.

Visit Scotland (*visitscotland.com*) Scotland's official tourist website is packed with ideas, suggestions and practical info.

15

The Best of Britain

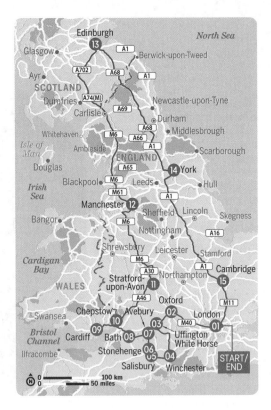

DURATION	DISTANCE	GREAT FOR
21 days	1815km / 1128 miles	History

BEST TIME TO GO	Myriad festivals take place between September and May.

London's bright lights, blockbuster attractions and stirring history bookend this epic expedition around the British mainland. In between, you'll explore ancient ruins and historic architecture, follow trails that lead from King Arthur to Shakespeare, and discover masterpiece-filled museums and galleries, all connected by quaint villages, patchworked farmland and glorious rolling green open countryside.

Link your trip

19 Royal Highlands & Cairngorms

Take a detour mid-trip to explore classic Scottish countryside: from Edinburgh head two hours north through Perthshire to the lovely village of Braemar.

18 Classic Lakes

Break up the long drive between Manchester and Edinburgh by turning west off the M6 onto the A590 to tour the charming Lake District.

01 LONDON

Prepare for your trip with at least a couple of days in Britain's most exhilarating city. Traversed by the serpentine River Thames, London is awash with instantly recognisable landmarks and open spaces, from **Trafalgar Square** to the **London Eye** (londoneye.com). Other unmissable sights include the **Houses of Parliament** (parliament. uk), topped by clock tower **Big Ben**; **Westminster Abbey** (westminster-abbey.org); **St James's Park** and **Palace**; **Buckingham Palace**; **Hyde Park**;

BEST FOR ARCHITECTURE

Trace centuries of architectural offerings in London, from classical to contemporary.

London Eye

Driving in London

Central London levies a congestion charge from 7am to 10pm daily. Entering the 'C'-marked zone costs £15. You can pay online, at petrol stations, or at some shops.

In addition, if your car is not a new, cleaner, greener model, the Ultra Low Emission Zone (ULEZ) charge (£12.50) needs to be paid in the same zone 24/7. You can pay online or over the phone. For full details, see the TFL website (www.tfl.gov.uk).

Kensington Gardens and **Palace**; and **Tower Bridge** (tower bridge.org.uk). World-leading and often-free museums and art galleries include the **Tate Modern** (tate.org.uk) and the **British Museum** (britishmuseum.org).

London's drinking, dining and nightlife options are limitless (Soho and Shoreditch make great starting points), as are its entertainment venues, not least grand

Photo Opportunity

Britain's biggest city spread below the London Eye.

theatre stages such as **Shakespeare's Globe** (shakespeares globe.com).

THE DRIVE
Take the M40 northwest through High Wycombe and the Chilterns Area of Outstanding Natural Beauty (AONB) to Oxford (59 miles in total).

02 OXFORD
The elegant honey-toned buildings of the university's colleges, scattered throughout the city, wrap around tranquil courtyards and along narrow cobbled lanes. The oldest colleges date back to the 13th century and little has changed inside since, although there's a busy, lively world beyond the

college walls. **Christ Church** (chch.ox.ac.uk) is the largest of all of Oxford's colleges, with the grandest quad. From the quad, you access 12th-century **Christ Church Cathedral** (chch.ox.ac.uk/cathedral), originally the abbey church and then the college chapel, before it was declared a cathedral by Henry VIII.

Other highlights include Oxford's **Bodleian Library** (bodleian.ox.ac.uk/bodley), one of the oldest public libraries in the world; and Britain's oldest public museum, the 1683-established **Ashmolean Museum** (ashmolean.org), second in repute only to London's British Museum.

THE DRIVE
Head southwest on the A420 to Pusey and continue southwest on the B4508. You'll reach the car park for the White Horse 2.3 miles southwest of Uffington off the B4507, a 24-mile journey altogether.

03 UFFINGTON WHITE HORSE
Just below Oxfordshire's highest point, the highly stylised **Uffington White Horse** (nationaltrust.org.uk) image is the oldest chalk figure in Britain, dating from the Bronze Age. It was created around 3000 years ago by cutting trenches out of the hill and filling them with blocks of chalk; local inhabitants have maintained the figure for centuries. Perhaps it was planned for the gods: it's best seen from the air above. It's a half-mile walk east through fields from the hillside car park.

THE DRIVE
It's a 49-mile trip to Winchester: return to the B4507 and drive southeast to Ashbury and take the B4000 southeast to join the southbound A34.

04 WINCHESTER
Set in a river valley, this ancient cathedral city was the capital of Saxon kings and a power base of bishops. It also evokes two of England's mightiest myth-makers: famous son Alfred the Great (commemorated by a statue) and King Arthur – a 700-year-old copy of the round table resides in Winchester's cavernous **Great Hall** (hants.gov.uk/greathall), the only part of 11th-century Winchester Castle that Oliver Cromwell spared from destruction.

Winchester's architecture is exquisite, from the handsome Elizabethan and Regency buildings in the narrow streets to the wondrous **Winchester Cathedral** (winchester-cathedral.org.uk) at its core. One of southern England's most awe-inspiring buildings, the 11th-century cathedral has a fine Gothic facade and one of the longest medieval naves in Europe (164m). Other highlights include intricately carved medieval choir stalls, Jane Austen's grave (near the entrance, in the northern aisle) and one of the UK's finest illuminated manuscripts, the dazzling, four-volume Winchester Bible dating from the 12th century. Book ahead for excellent tours of the ground floor, crypt and tower.

THE DRIVE
From Winchester, hop on the B3049 then the A30 for the 26-mile drive west to Salisbury.

05 SALISBURY
Salisbury has been an important provincial city for more than a thousand years, and its streets form an architectural timeline ranging from medieval walls and half-timbered Tudor town houses to Georgian mansions and Victorian villas. Its centrepiece is the majestic 13th-century **Salisbury Cathedral** (salisburycathedral.org.uk). This early-English Gothic-style structure has an elaborate exterior decorated with pointed arches and flying buttresses, and is topped by Britain's tallest spire at 123m, which was added in the mid-14th century. Beyond the cathedral's highly decorative West Front, a small passageway leads into the 70m-long nave. In the north aisle look out for a fascinating medieval clock dating from 1386, probably the oldest working timepiece in the world. Don't miss the cathedral's original, 13th-century copy of the Magna Carta in the chapter house, or, if they've resumed, a 90-minute tower tour, which sees you climbing 332 vertigo-inducing steps to the base of the spire for jaw-dropping views across the city and the surrounding countryside.

THE DRIVE
It's just 9.6 miles northwest from Salisbury via the A360 to other-worldly Stonehenge.

06 STONEHENGE
Stonehenge (englishheritage.org.uk) is one of Britain's most enduring archaeological mysteries: despite countless theories about the site's purpose, ranging from a sacrificial centre to a celestial timepiece, no one knows for sure what drove prehistoric Britons to expend so much time and effort on its construction. The first phase of building started around

Stonehenge

WHY I LOVE THIS TRIP

Anthony Ham, writer

Anything labelled 'Best of Britain' has a lot to live up to, which this trip certainly does. The classy contemporary cities you'll visit here provide a nice counterpoint to so many sites where history is writ large upon the land. Throw in castles, cathedrals and Shakespeare's home town and you really will enjoy Britain's finest.

3000 BCE, when the outer circular bank and ditch were erected. A thousand years later, an inner circle of granite stones, known as bluestones, was added.

An ultramodern makeover has brought an impressive visitor centre and the closure of an intrusive road (now restored to grassland). The result is a far stronger sense of historical context; dignity and mystery returned to an archaeological gem. A pathway frames the ring of massive stones. Although you can't walk in the circle, unless on a recommended **Stone Circle Access Visit** (english-heritage.org.uk), you can get close-up views. Admission is through timed tickets – secure a place well in advance.

🚗 THE DRIVE

Drive east to Durrington and take the A345 north, climbing over the grassy Pewsey Downs National Nature Reserve (home to another chalk figure, the Alton Barnes White Horse, dating from 1812), to reach Avebury (24 miles in total).

07 AVEBURY

With a diameter of 348m, **Avebury** (nationaltrust. org.uk) is the largest stone circle in the world. It is also one of the oldest, dating from 2500 to 2200 BCE. Though it lacks the dramatic trilithons of Stonehenge, the massive stone circle is just as rewarding to visit. Today, more than 30 stones are in place (pillars show where missing stones would have been) and a large section of the village is actually inside the stones – footpaths wind around them, allowing you to really soak up the extraordinary atmosphere. For a deeper understanding, join a volunteer-led guided walk (£5).

🚗 THE DRIVE

It's a 27-mile drive along the A4 past patchwork fields, country pubs and a smattering of villages to the Georgian streetscapes of Bath.

JUAN JIMENEZ/EYEEM/GETTY IMAGES ©

Roman Baths, Bath

08 BATH

World Heritage–listed Bath was founded on top of natural hot springs and has been a tourist draw for some 2000 years. Its 18th-century heyday saw the construction of magnificent Georgian architecture from the 18th century. The best way to explore the city's Roman Baths complex and beautiful neoclassical buildings is on foot.

Bath is known to many as a location in Jane Austen's novels, including *Persuasion* and *Northanger Abbey*. Although Austen lived in Bath for only five years, from 1801 to 1806, she remained a regular visitor and a keen student of the city's social scene. At the **Jane Austen Centre** (janeausten.co.uk), guides in Regency costumes regale you with Austenesque tales as you tour memorabilia relating to the writer's life in Bath.

THE DRIVE

It's 56.5 miles from Bath to the Welsh capital. Take the A46 north and join the westbound M4 over the Severn Estuary on the six-lane, cable-stayed Second Severn Crossing bridge.

09 CARDIFF

Between an ancient fort and ultramodern waterfront, Cardiff has been the capital of Wales since only 1955, but has embraced the role with vigour and is now one of Britain's leading urban centres, as you can see on a stroll through its compact streets.

Cardiff Castle (cardiffcastle. com) has a medieval keep at its heart, but it's the later additions that really capture the imagination. Explore, and you may wind

NATALIA VESTIGIO SERVICES/SHUTTERSTOCK ©

Chelsea Flower Show, London

BRITAIN'S BEST FESTIVALS

In London, see stunning blooms at the Royal Horticultural Society's **Chelsea Flower Show** (rhs.org.uk/chelsea); military bands and bear-skinned grenadiers during the martial pageant **Trooping the Colour** (householddivision.org.uk/trooping-the-colour); or steel drums, dancers and outrageous costumes at the famous multicultural Caribbean-style street festival **Notting Hill Carnival** (www.nhcarnival.org).

Wales' **National Eisteddfod** (Eisteddfod Genedlaethol Cymru; eisteddfod.cymru) is descended from ancient Bardic tournaments. It's conducted in Welsh, but welcomes all entrants and visitors. It moves about each year, attracting some 150,000 visitors.

Edinburgh's most famous happenings are the **International Festival** (eif.co.uk) and **Fringe** (edfringe.com), but the city also has events throughout the year. Check the full list at www.edinburghfestivals.co.uk.

up concurring with the fortress's claim to be the most fascinating castle in Wales. Devoted mainly to art and natural history, **National Museum Cardiff** (museum.wales/cardiff) fills a grand neoclassical building. It's both a part of the Welsh National Museum and one of Britain's best museums.

If you time it right, you can catch a fired-up rugby test at Cardiff's **Principality Stadium** (principalitystadium.wales).

 THE DRIVE
Take the A48 northeast for 32 miles, bypassing Newport, to riverside Chepstow.

10 **CHEPSTOW**
Nestled in an S-bend in the River Wye, Chepstow (Welsh: Cas-gwent) was first developed as a base for the Norman conquest of southeast Wales, later prospering as a port for the timber and wine trades. As river-borne commerce gave way to the railways, Chepstow's importance diminished to reflect its name, which means 'marketplace' in Old English.

One of Britain's oldest castles, imposing **Chepstow Castle** (cadw.gov.wales) perches atop a limestone cliff overhanging the river, guarding the main river crossing from England into South Wales. Building commenced in 1067, less than a year after William the Conqueror invaded England, and it was extended over the centuries. Today there are plenty of towers, battlements and wall walks to explore. A cave in the cliff below the castle is one of many places where legend says King Arthur and his knights

are napping until the day they're needed to save Britain.

 THE DRIVE
Farmland makes up most of this 68-mile drive. Head northeast on the A48 along the River Severn to Gloucester, then continue northeast on the A46 to Stratford-upon-Avon.

11 **STRATFORD-UPON-AVON**
Experiences linked to the life of Stratford's fêted son William Shakespeare range from the touristy (medieval recreations and Bard-themed tearooms) to the humbling – Shakespeare's modest grave in **Holy Trinity Church** (stratford-upon-avon.org) – and the sublime: a play by the **Royal Shakespeare Company** (rsc.org.uk). One of the best ways to get a feel for the town's Tudor streets and willow-lined riverbanks is on foot.

Combination tickets are available for the three houses associated with Shakespeare in town – **Shakespeare's Birthplace** (shakespeare.org.uk), **Shakespeare's New Place** and **Hall's Croft**. If you also plan to visit the childhood home of Shakespeare's wife, **Anne Hathaway's Cottage**, and his mother's farm, **Mary Arden's Farm**, you can buy a combination ticket covering all five properties.

Don't miss a pint with the locals at Stratford's oldest and most atmospheric pub, the 1470-built **Old Thatch Tavern** (oldthatchtavernstratford.co.uk).

 THE DRIVE
The fastest route from Stratford-upon-Avon to Manchester is to head northwest on Birmingham

Rd and pick up the northbound M42, which becomes the M6. You'll see the hilly Peak District National Park to your east. It's a 116-mile journey; this stretch incurs road tolls that vary according to the time of day.

12 **MANCHESTER**
A rich blend of history and culture is on show in this northern powerhouse's museums, galleries and innovative, multigenre art centres, such as **HOME** (homemcr.org).

The **Manchester Art Gallery** (manchesterartgallery.org) has a superb collection of British art and a hefty number of European masters. The older wing has an impressive selection that includes 37 Turner watercolours, as well as the country's best assemblage of Pre-Raphaelite art, while the newer gallery is home to 20th-century British art starring Lucien Freud, Francis Bacon, Stanley Spencer, Henry Moore and David Hockney. A wonderful collection of British watercolours is also displayed at Manchester's **Whitworth Art Gallery** (whitworth.manchester.ac.uk), which has an exceptional collection of historic textiles.

Manchester is famed for its rival football teams **Manchester United** (www.manutd.com) and **Manchester City** (www.mancity.com), and its **National Football Museum** (nationalfootballmuseum.com) charts British football's evolution from its earliest days to the multibillion-pound phenomenon it is today.

The city is also world renowned for its live-music scene, with gigs in all genres most nights of the week.

National Football Museum, Manchester

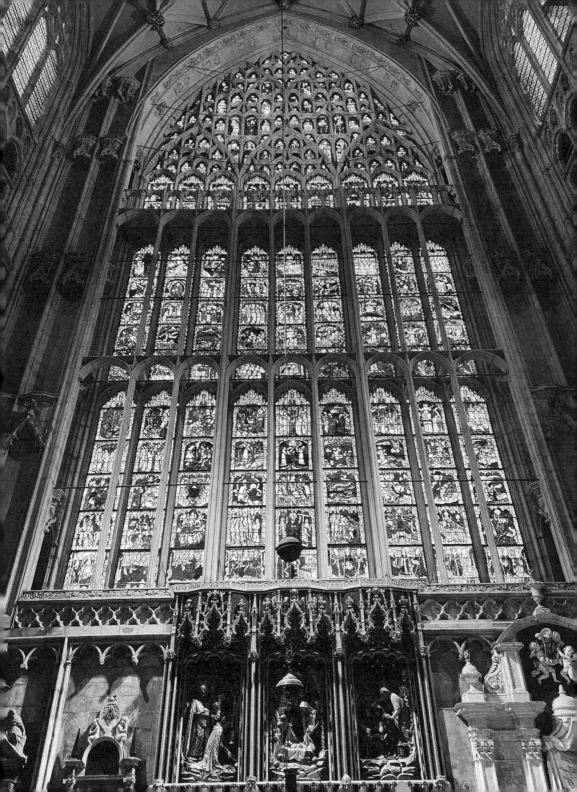

SCOTLAND'S CRAFT GIN

Scotland is famed around the world for its whisky, but Scottish craft gin (thescottishginsociety.com) is also hugely popular. Over 70% of gin consumed in the UK is produced in Scotland – there are more than 90 gin distilleries in the country, and nearly a dozen in the Edinburgh area. Bars all over the capital are offering cocktails based on brands such as Pickering's, 56 North, Edinburgh Gin and Holyrood.

THE DRIVE
This trip's longest drive, at 216 miles, takes you northwest via the M61 and M6, passing between the Yorkshire Dales National Park to your east and the Lake District National Park to your west. Once you cross into Scotland, the road becomes the A74 and climbs into the Southern Uplands, then becomes the A702 as it leads into Edinburgh.

13 EDINBURGH
The Scottish capital is entwined with its landscape, with buildings and monuments perched atop crags and overshadowed by cliffs. From the Old Town's picturesque jumble of medieval tenements along the Royal Mile, its turreted skyline strung between the black, bull-nosed Castle Rock and the russet palisade of Salisbury Crags, to the New Town's neat neoclassical grid, the city offers a constantly changing perspective.

Along with a walk through the Old Town, unmissable experiences here include visiting **Edinburgh Castle** (edinburghcastle.scot), which has played a pivotal role in Scottish history, both as a royal residence – King Malcolm Canmore (r 1058–93) and Queen

Margaret first made their home here in the 11th century – and as a military stronghold; and climbing to the hilltop **Arthur's Seat** for city panoramas.

Edinburgh has 700-plus pubs, more per square mile than any other UK city. Sample a dram of Scottish whisky at icons like the **Malt Shovel** (belhavenpubs.co.uk), with over 100 single malts behind the bar.

THE DRIVE
Drive southeast on the A68, passing through the Scottish Borders, and enter Northumberland National Park at the English border. Join the southbound A1 at Darlington, then take the eastbound A59 to York (191 miles altogether).

14 YORK
A magnificent ring of 13th-century walls encloses York's medieval spider's web of streets. At its heart lies the immense, awe-inspiring **York Minster** (yorkminster.org). Constructed mainly between 1220 and 1480, it encompasses all the major stages of Gothic architecture. The transepts (1220–55) were built in Early English style; the octagonal chapter house (1260–90) and nave (1291–1340)

in the Decorated style; and the west towers, west front and central (or lantern) tower (1470–72) in Perpendicular style.

Don't miss a walk on York's City Walls, which follow the line of the original Roman walls and give a whole new perspective on the city. Cover just the highlights or allow 1½ to two hours for the full circuit of 4.5 miles.

THE DRIVE
From York, it's 156 miles to Cambridge. Take the A64 southwest to join onto the A1 heading southeast.

15 CAMBRIDGE
Surrounded by meadows, Cambridge is a university town extraordinaire, with a tightly packed core of ancient colleges and picturesque riverside 'Backs' (college gardens), which you can stroll around.

The colossal neoclassical pile containing the **Fitzwilliam Museum** (fitzmuseum.cam.ac.uk), locally dubbed 'the Fitz', was built to house the treasures that the seventh Viscount Fitzwilliam bequeathed to his old university. Standout exhibits include Roman and Egyptian grave goods, artworks by many of the great masters and some quirkier collections such as banknotes, literary autographs, watches and armour.

For the full Cambridge experience, rent a river boat from operators such as **Scudamore's Punting** (scudamores.com).

THE DRIVE
Hop on the M11 for the 55-mile zip back south to London.

York Minster

16

Britain's Wild Side

DURATION	DISTANCE	GREAT FOR
21 days	2310km / 1435 miles	Outdoors

BEST TIME TO GO	June to September offers the best conditions for outdoor activities.

Immerse yourself in wild Britain on this tricountry trip through glorious national parks and protected Areas of Outstanding Natural Beauty. Get up close to soaring mountain peaks, desolate moorland, sea-sprayed beaches, scalloped bays, lush hills, green dales, high, barren fells, and glassy lakes, some of which teem with wildlife. Along the way, get out and explore the breathtaking countryside on foot, bicycle, horseback and kayak.

Link your trip

17 The Historic South

Soak up some of England's rich heritage before starting your wild trip – it's an hour and a half south on the A34 from Oxford to the New Forest.

20 Great Glen

Do this lake-and-mountain themed ramble through the Scottish Highlands in reverse from Inverness.

NEW FOREST

01 With typical, accidental, English irony, the New Forest is anything but new – it was first proclaimed a royal hunting preserve in 1079. It's also not much of a forest, being mostly heathland ('forest' is from the Old French for 'hunting ground'). For an overview of New Forest, which was designated a national park in 2005, stop by the **New Forest Museum** (newforestcentre.org.uk). Wild ponies mooch around pretty scrubland, deer flicker in the distance and rare birds flit among

BEST FOR WILDLIFE

Spot wild red deer, especially in autumn, at Exmoor National Park.

New Forest pony

the foliage. Genteel villages dot the landscape, connected by a web of walking and cycling trails. **Lyndhurst tourist office** (thenewforest.co.uk) stocks maps and guides; they're also available from its website. New Forest is also a popular spot for horse riding; **Burley Villa** (Western Riding; burleyvilla.co.uk) organises rides using traditional English and also Western saddle styles (per 90 minutes £54).

THE DRIVE
Take the A31 then the A35 south-west to Weymouth and Chesil Beach. Follow the Jurassic Coast northwest along the B3157 to Lyme Regis (81 miles in total).

02 LYME REGIS
Fossils regularly emerge from the unstable cliffs surrounding Lyme Regis, exposed by the landslides of a retreating shoreline, making this a key stop along the Unesco-listed **Jurassic Coast**.

For an overview, **Dinosaurland** (dinosaurland.co.uk) overflows with fossilised remains; look out for belemnites, a plesiosaurus and an impressive locally found ichthyosaur. Kids love the lifelike dinosaur models, rock-hard tyrannosaur eggs and 73kg dinosaur dung.

Three miles east of Lyme, the **Charmouth Heritage Coast Centre** (charmouth.org) runs

one to seven fossil-hunting trips a week (adult/child £8/4). In Lyme itself, **Lyme Regis Museum** (lymeregismuseum.co.uk) organises three to seven walks a week (up to six people £125). Book walks ahead.

THE DRIVE
Drive west on the A3052 through the dazzling East Devon AONB to Exeter and take the B3212 up into Postbridge, a small village in the middle of Dartmoor National Park (52 miles all up).

03 DARTMOOR NATIONAL PARK
Covering 368 sq miles, this vast **national park** (dartmoor.gov.uk) feels like it's tumbled straight out of a Tolkien

tome, with its honey-coloured heaths, moss-covered boulders, meandering streams and eerie granite tors (hills). It's one of Britain's most wildly beautiful corners.

On sunny days Dartmoor is idyllic: ponies wander and sheep graze beside the road, as seen in Steven Spielberg's WWI epic *War Horse.* But Dartmoor is also the setting for Sir Arthur Conan Doyle's *The Hound of the Baskervilles,* and in sleeting rain and swirling mists the moor morphs into a bleak wilderness where tales of a phantom hound can seem very real. Be aware too that the military uses live ammunition in its training ranges.

Dartmoor is a haven for outdoor activities, including hiking, cycling, riding, climbing and white-water kayaking; the **Dartmoor National Park Authority** (dartmoor.gov.uk) has detailed information. And there are plenty of rustic pubs to cosy up in when the fog rolls in.

 THE DRIVE
Head west through Tavistock to pass through the Tamar Valley, another AONB, on the A390. At Dobwalls, pick up the A38 and drive west along the forested River Fowey to join the southwest-bound A30. Take the Victoria turn-off and travel northwest past Newquay Cornwall Airport to Carnewas at Bedruthan (62 miles altogether).

Photo Opportunity

Cornwall's Carnewas at Bedruthan at sunset.

04 **CARNEWAS AT BEDRUTHAN**
On Cornwall's surf-pounded coast loom the stately rock stacks of **Bedruthan** (nationaltrust.org.uk). These mighty granite pillars have been carved out by thousands of years of wind and waves, and the area is now owned by the National Trust (NT). The beach itself is accessed via a steep staircase and is submerged at high tide. Towards the north end is a rocky shelf known as Diggory's Island, which separates the main beach from another little-known cove.

 THE DRIVE
Drive east to join the northeast-bound A39, which runs parallel to the Cornish coast, to the town of Lynmouth in Exmoor National Park (94 miles in total).

05 **EXMOOR NATIONAL PARK**
In the middle of Exmoor National Park is the higher moor, an empty, expansive, other-worldly landscape of tawny grasses and huge skies.

Exmoor supports one of England's largest wild red deer populations, best experienced in autumn when the annual 'rutting' season sees stags bellowing, charging at each other and clashing horns in an attempt to impress prospective mates. The **Exmoor National Park Authority** (exmoor-nationalpark.gov. uk) runs regular wildlife-themed guided walks (free), which include evening deer-spotting hikes. Alternatively, head out on an organised jeep safari.

The open moors and a profusion of marked bridleways offer excellent hiking. Cycling is also popular; **Exmoor Adventures** (exmooradventures.co.uk) runs a mountain-biking skills course (from £30) and also rents out bikes (per day £25).

THE DRIVE
From Lynmouth to Libanus in the Brecon Beacons National Park it's 143 miles. Take the A39 east along the coast to join the M5 at Bridgwater. Take the Second Severn Crossing bridge and head west towards Cardiff to join the northwest-bound A470.

06 **BRECON BEACONS NATIONAL PARK**
Brecon Beacons National Park (Parc Cenedlaethol Bannau Brycheiniog) ripples for 45 miles from the English border to near Llandeilo in the west. High mountain plateaus of grass and heather, their northern rims scalloped with glacier-scoured hollows, rise above wooded, waterfall-splashed valleys and green, rural landscapes.

Within the park there are four distinct regions: the wild, lonely **Black Mountain** (Mynydd Du) in the west, with its high moors and glacial lakes; **Great Forest**

WARNING: DARTMOOR MILITARY RANGES

Live ammunition is used on Dartmoor's training ranges. Check locations with the Firing Information Service (mod.uk/access) or tourist offices. Red flags fly at the edges of in-use ranges by day; red flares burn at night. Beware unidentified metal objects lying in the grass. Don't touch anything; report finds to the Dartmoor Training Safety Officer on 01837-657210.

South West Coast Path, Exmoor National Park

Hiking Exmoor

The open moors and a profusion of marked bridleways make Exmoor an excellent area for hiking. The best-known routes are the **Somerset & North Devon Coast Path**, which is part of the **South West Coast Path** (southwestcoastpath.org. uk), and the Exmoor section of the **Two Moors Way** (two moorsway.org), which starts in Lynmouth and travels 102 miles south over Dartmoor to Ivybridge. From there a 15-mile extension leads to the south Devon coast at Wembury.

Another superb route is the **Coleridge Way** (www.cole ridgeway.co.uk), which winds for 51 miles from Lynmouth to Nether Stowey, crossing Exmoor, the Brendon Hills and the Quantocks. Part of the 180-mile **Tarka Trail** (tarkatrail. org.uk) cuts through the park. The coastal section sweeps from Lynton to Bideford, before heading down into north Devon.

Check to see if walks run by the **Exmoor National Park Authority** (exmoor-national park.gov.uk) are running. Past events include deer safaris, nightjar birdwatching walks and dark-sky strolls.

ENPA tourist offices also sell a great range of day-walk leaflets.

Seeing Stars in the Brecon Beacons

The Brecon Beacons is just one of a handful of places in the world to be awarded 'Dark-Sky Reserve' status. With almost zero light pollution, this is one of the UK's finest places for stargazing. Meteor showers, nebulae, strings of constellations and the Milky Way twinkle brightly in the night sky when the weather is clear. Among the 10 best spots are **Carreg Cennen** (cadw.gov.wales), **Sugar Loaf** (Mynydd Pen-y-Fâl) and **Llanthony Priory** (cadw.gov.wales).

Visitor centres throughout the park can give you information about stargazing events, or check out breconbeacons. org/stargazing.

(Fforest Fawr), whose rushing streams and spectacular waterfalls form the headwaters of the Rivers Tawe and Neath; the **Brecon Beacons** (Bannau Brycheiniog) proper, a group of very distinctive, flat-topped hills that includes Pen-y-Fan (886m), the park's highest peak; and the rolling heathland ridges of the **Black Mountains** (Y Mynyd-doedd Duon) – not to be confused with the Black Mountain (singular) in the west. The park's main **visitor centre** (breconbeacons.org) has details of walks, hiking and biking trails, outdoor activities, wildlife and geology (call first to check it's open).

THE DRIVE

Drive north along the A470 to reach the southern boundary of Snowdonia National Park at Mallwyd (79 miles altogether).

07 SNOWDONIA NATIONAL PARK

Wales' best-known and most-visited slice of nature, Snowdonia National Park (Parc Cenedlaethol Eryri) became the country's first national park in 1951. Every year more than 350,000 people walk, climb or take the rack-and-pinion **railway** (snowdonrailway.co.uk) to the 1085m summit of Snowdon. The park's 823 sq miles embrace stunning coastline, forests, valleys, rivers, bird-filled estuaries and Wales' biggest natural lake. The **Snowdonia National Park Information Centre** (eryri-npa. gov.uk) is an invaluable source of information about walking trails, mountain conditions and more.

THE DRIVE

Continue north on the A470 and take the A5 northwest to Bangor.

Snowdon Mountain Railway, Snowdonia National Park

Cross Robert Stephenson's 1850-built Britannia Bridge over the Menai Strait and take the A545 northwest to Beaumaris (a 72-mile trip).

08 ISLE OF ANGLESEY

The 276-sq-mile Isle of Anglesey (Ynys Môn) offers miles of inspiring coastline, hidden beaches and the country's greatest concentration of ancient sites.

Almost all of the Anglesey coast has been designated as an AONB (Area of Outstanding Natural Beauty). Beyond the handsome Georgian town of Beaumaris (Biwmares), there are hidden gems scattered all over the island. It's very much a living centre of Welsh culture, too, as you can see for yourself at **Oriel Ynys Môn** (orielmon.org). A great, introductory day walk from Beaumaris takes in the ancient monastic site of **Penmon Priory** (cadw.gov. wales), Penmon Point with views across to Puffin Island, and Blue Flag beach Llanddona.

🚗 THE DRIVE

Return to the mainland and take the A55 northeast, crossing the border into England where the road becomes the M56. Continue northeast towards Manchester before turning off on the southeast-bound M6. At Sandbach turn east on the A534 and follow the signs to Leek, then take the A53 northeast before turning east towards Longnor and then Bakewell (138 miles all up).

09 PEAK DISTRICT NATIONAL PARK

Founded in 1951, the Peak District was England's first national park and is Europe's busiest. But even at peak times, there are 555 sq miles of open countryside in which to soak up the scenery. Caving and climbing, cycling and, above all, walking (including numerous short walks) are the most popular activities. The **Peak District National Park Authority** (peakdistrict.gov.uk) has reams of information about the park and also operates several cycle-hire centres. The charming town of Bakewell also has a helpful **tourist office** (visitpeakdistrict.com).

🚗 THE DRIVE

From Bakewell take the A623 northwest towards Manchester and pick up the northbound M66, then at Burnley take the northeast-bound M65 to Skipton. Enter the Yorkshire Dales National Park on the B6265 to Grassington and head northwest on the B6265 to Aysgarth. Then take the A684 along the River Ure to Hawes (a total of 118 miles).

10 YORKSHIRE DALES NATIONAL PARK

Protected as a national park since the 1950s, the glacial valleys of the Yorkshire Dales (named from the old Norse word

---

---

dalr, meaning 'valleys') are characterised by a distinctive landscape of high heather moorland, stepped skylines and flat-topped hills above valleys patchworked with drystone dykes and little barns. Hawes is home to the **Wensleydale Creamery** (wensleydale. co.uk), producing famous Wensleydale cheese. In the limestone country of the southern Dales you'll encounter extraordinary examples of karst scenery (created by rainwater dissolving the underlying limestone bedrock).

🚗 THE DRIVE

Head southwest on the B6255 to Ingleton. Take the A65 northwest to Sizergh then the A590 southwest to the Lake District's southern reaches at Newby Bridge. Drive north along Lake Windermere before veering northwest to Hawkshead (53 miles all up).

11 LAKE DISTRICT NATIONAL PARK

The Lake District (or Lakeland, as it's commonly known round these parts) is by far the UK's most popular national park. Ever since the Romantic poets arrived in the 19th century, its postcard panorama of craggy hilltops, mountain tarns and glittering lakes has stirred visitors' imaginations. It's awash with outdoor opportunities, from lake cruises to mountain walks.

Many people visit for the region's literary connections: among the many writers who found inspiration here are William Wordsworth, Samuel Taylor Coleridge, Arthur Ransome and, of course, Beatrix Potter, a lifelong lover of the Lakes, whose delightful former farmhouse, **Hill Top** (nationaltrust.org.uk/hill-top), inspired many of her tales, including *Peter Rabbit.*

WHY I LOVE THIS TRIP

Anthony Ham, writer

This classic journey through wild Britain will leave you wondering how such diversity can possibly be within reach on one relatively short trip. Forests and cliffs, mountains and moors – Great Britain is one beautiful place, and this stirring exploration of lakes and national parks showcases the best that Britain's natural world has to offer.

THE DRIVE
Drive northwest on the A591 to join the A595 to Carlisle. Then take the A689 and A69 northeast to Walltown along Hadrian's Wall (72 miles altogether).

12 HADRIAN'S WALL

Hadrian's Wall is one of Britain's most revealing and dramatic Roman ruins, its 2000-year-old procession of abandoned forts, garrisons, towers and milecastles marching across the wild and lonely landscape of northern England. The wall was about defence and control, but this edge-of-empire barrier also symbolised the boundary of civilised order – to the north lay the unruly land of the marauding Celts, while to the south was the Roman world of orderly taxpaying, underfloor heating and bathrooms. There's an excellent visitor centre at **Walltown** (Northumberland National Park Visitor Centre; northumberland nationalpark.org.uk). The finest sections of the wall run along the southern edge of remote **Northumberland National Park**

(northumberlandnationalpark. org.uk), one of Britain's finest wilderness areas.

THE DRIVE
Follow the B6318 northeast along Hadrian's Wall. Turn north on the B6320 to Bellingham. Continue northwest alongside the North Tyne river and Kielder Water lake to the village of Kielder (a 43-mile journey).

13 KIELDER WATER & FOREST PARK

Adjacent to Northumberland National Park, the Kielder Water & Forest Park is home to the vast artificial lake Kielder Water, holding 200 billion litres. Surrounding its 27-mile-long shoreline is England's largest plantation forest, with 150 million spruce and pine trees. Kielder Water is a water-sports playground (and midge magnet; bring insect repellent), and also has walking and cycling as well as great birdwatching. Comprehensive information is available at visitkielder.com.

The lack of population here helped see the area awarded dark-sky status by the International Dark Skies Association in 2013 (the largest such designation in Europe), with controls to prevent light pollution. For the best views of the Northumberland International Dark Sky Park, attend a stargazing session at state-of-the-art, 2008-built **Kielder Observatory** (kielderobservatory.org). Book ahead and dress warmly as it's seriously chilly here at night.

THE DRIVE
It's a 139-mile drive from Kielder to Balloch on the southern shore of Loch Lomond. Head north into Scotland and join the A68 towards Edinburgh. Take the M8 to Glasgow and then the A82 northwest to Balloch.

14 LOCH LOMOND

Loch Lomond is mainland Britain's largest lake and, after Loch Ness, the most famous of Scotland's lochs. It's part of **Loch Lomond & the Trossachs National Park** (lochlomond-trossachs.org), which extends over a sizeable area, from Balloch north to Tyndrum and Killin, and from Callander west to the forests of Cowal.

From Balloch, **Sweeney's Cruises** (sweeneyscruiseco.com) offers, among other trips, a popular one-hour return cruise to the island of Inchmurrin (adult/child £12.50/8, nine times daily April to September, twice daily October to March). The quay is directly opposite Balloch train station. With departures from Tarbet and Luss on the loch's western shore, **Cruise Loch Lomond** (cruiselochlomond.co.uk) runs short cruises and two-hour trips to Arklet Falls and Rob Roy's Cave (adult/child £15/9.50). There are also several options that involve drop-offs and pick-ups with a hike in between.

THE DRIVE
Follow the A82 along Loch Lomond's western shoreline and pick up the northeast-bound A85 at Crianlarich, then the A827. Then take the northwest-bound A9 to Aviemore (a total of 141 miles).

15 CAIRNGORMS NATIONAL PARK

The vast Cairngorms National Park (cairngorms. co.uk) stretches from Aviemore in the north – which has a handy **tourist office** (visitaviemore. com) – to the Angus Glens in the south, and from Dalwhinnie in the west to Ballater and Royal Deeside in the east.

The park encompasses the highest landmass in Britain – a broad mountain plateau, riven only by the deep valleys of the Lairig Ghru and Loch Avon, with an average altitude of over 1000m and including five of the six highest summits in the UK. This wild mountain landscape of granite and heather has a sub-Arctic climate and supports rare alpine tundra vegetation and high-altitude bird species, such as snow bunting, ptarmigan and dotterel. Lower down, scenic glens are softened by beautiful open forests of native Scots pine, home to rare animals and birds such as pine martens, Scottish wildcats, red squirrels, ospreys, capercaillies and crossbills.

🚗 THE DRIVE
Take the A9 northwest to Inverness, then the southwest-bound A82 along Loch Ness. At Invermoriston join the westbound A887, which becomes the A87, and continue to Kyle of Lochalsh, where you'll cross the Skye Bridge to the Isle of Skye. Continue along the A87 to reach Portree (145 miles all up).

16 ISLE OF SKYE
The Isle of Skye (an t-Eilean Sgiathanach in Gaelic) takes its name from the old Norse *sky-a,* meaning 'cloud island', a Viking reference to the often-mist-enshrouded Cuillin Hills. It's a 50-mile-long patchwork of velvet moors, jagged mountains, sparkling lochs and towering sea cliffs. Lively Portree (Port Righ) has the island's only **tourist office** (visitscotland.com/destinations-maps/isle-skye).

Skye offers some of the finest walking in Scotland, including short, low-level routes. The sheltered coves and sea lochs around

Black house, Lewis

OUTER HEBRIDES
If you're not ready to return to the mainland after visiting the Isle of Skye, consider a trip to the Outer Hebrides (aka the Western Isles; Na h-Eileanan an Iar in Gaelic) – a 130-mile-long string of islands west of Skye. More than a third of Scotland's registered crofts are here, and no less than 60% of the population are Gaelic speakers. With limited time, head straight for the west coast of **Lewis** with its prehistoric sites, preserved black houses, beautiful beaches, and arts and crafts studios – the **Stornoway Tourist Office** (visitouterhebrides.co.uk) can provide a list. Ferries (car £31.65, driver and passenger £6.50 each) run once or twice daily from Uig on Skye to Lochmaddy (1¾ hours) and Tarbert (1½ hours).

the coast of Skye provide magnificent sea-kayaking. **Whitewave Outdoor Centre** (white-wave.co.uk) runs expeditions and courses for beginners and experienced paddlers to otherwise inaccessible places.

Skye's stunning scenery is the main attraction, but there are castles, crofting museums and cosy pubs and restaurants, along with dozens of art galleries and craft studios.

17

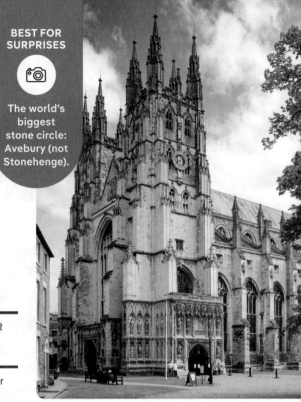

The Historic South

DURATION	DISTANCE	GREAT FOR
9–11 days	720km / 450 miles	History, outdoors

BEST TIME TO GO	Spring and autumn. Plus summer if you don't mind more crowds.

Canterbury Cathedral

Stand by to tour some of the world's most beautiful castles and most memorable archaeological sites. Take in impressive cathedrals, Georgian cityscapes, Churchill's palace and Oxford's spires. Discover art and England's fine tradition of seaside kitsch. Motor to a car museum, explore unspoiled villages and encounter 14th-century fellow travellers' tales. And in doing so, take a road trip through the very best of Britain's past.

Link your trip

21 West Wales: Swansea to St Davids

From Oxford, head west on the M4 to Swansea for the sweeping beaches and vast sand dunes of the Welsh coast.

16 Britain's Wild Side

It's an hour and a half south from Oxford to the New Forest to pick up this exploration of Britain's glorious national parks.

01 LONDON

Vibrant London is so packed with historic sights, it can be difficult to know where to start. Try the cathedral that is the capital's touchstone: **St Paul's** (stpauls.co.uk). Designed by Sir Christopher Wren in 1675 after the Great Fire, its vast dome is famed for avoiding Luftwaffe raids during the Blitz. Head inside and up 257 steps to the walkway called the Whispering Gallery, then to the Golden Gallery at the top for unforgettable London views. Next, walk north to the **Museum of London** (museumoflondon.org.uk), where the capital's rich

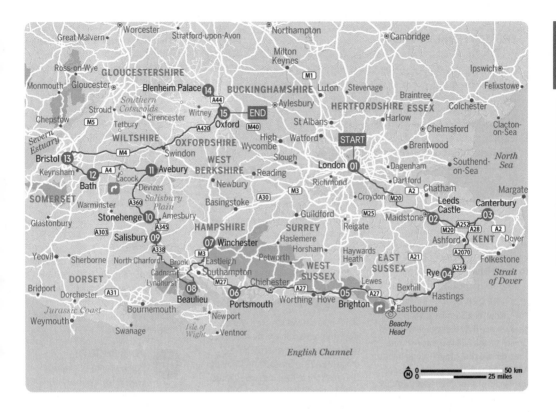

past is explored in riveting style. Then head east to elegant **Tower Bridge** (towerbridge.org.uk) to learn in its exhibition just how they raise the arms – and the road – to let ships through.

 THE DRIVE
London's streets and suburbs meet bursts of the Kent countryside; you're heading for the A20 towards Sidcup, then the M20 towards Dover. Shortly after Maidstone leave the motorway behind, picking up A20 signs for Lenham and then Leeds Castle, some 40 miles from the capital.

02 **LEEDS CASTLE**
Immense and moat-ringed, for many **Leeds Castle** (leeds-castle.com) is one

of the world's most romantic, and is certainly one of Britain's most visited. The formidable, intricate structure balancing on two islands is known as something of a 'ladies castle'. This stems from the fact that in its more than 1000 years of history, it has been home to a who's who of medieval queens, most famously Henry VIII's first wife, Catherine of Aragon.

THE DRIVE
Next up is a 25-mile cruise, high up over the vast chalk ridge of the North Downs. Behind you stretch the villages and fields of the Weald of Kent. But you're headed northeast, largely along the A252/A28 – the Canterbury Rd which echoes the old pilgrim footpath to the cathedral city.

03 **CANTERBURY**
Canterbury tops the charts for English cathedral cities – and no wonder. Here medieval alleyways frame exquisite architecture, with **Canterbury Cathedral** (canterbury-cathedral.org) as the centrepiece. This towering Gothic masterpiece features fine stonework, a cavernous crypt and the site of English history's most famous murder: Archbishop Thomas Becket was killed here in 1170 after 'hints' from King Henry II, and the site has drawn pilgrims for more than 800 years since. Knowledgeable guides double up as energetic oarsmen at **Canterbury Historic River Tours**

THE CANTERBURY TALES

The Canterbury Tales is the best-known work of English literature's father figure: Geoffrey Chaucer (1342–1400). Chaucer was the first English writer to introduce characters – rather than 'types' – into fiction. They feature strongly in *The Canterbury Tales*, an unfinished series of 24 vivid stories told by a party of pilgrims travelling between London and Canterbury. The text remains a pillar of the literary canon. But more than that, it's a collection of rollicking good yarns of adultery, debauchery, crime and edgy romance, and is filled with Chaucer's witty observations about human nature.

(canterburyrivertours.co.uk) for fascinating, multi-award-winning River Stour minicruises. For a taste of even older Canterbury, head to the mosaics of the **Roman Museum** (canterbury museums.co.uk).

THE DRIVE

Now for a 35-mile drive. Head back up and over those creamy North Downs on the A28 towards Ashford. Then plunge down to roll along the A2070, through the verdant valley of the Weald of Kent, then take the A259. Soon you're edging the flat-lands of Romney Marsh and arriving at Rye.

04 RYE

Welcome to one of England's prettiest sea-side towns. Here cobbled lanes, wonky Tudor buildings and tales of smugglers abound. The best place to start stretching your legs is **Mermaid Street**. It bristles with 15th-century timber-framed houses with quirky names such as 'The House with Two Front Doors' and 'The House Opposite'. The **Rye Heritage Centre** (rye heritage.co.uk) offers themed walking tours.

THE DRIVE

The next 50-mile leg sees you taking a string of A roads west. They lead past the woods and farms of the High Weald AONB and up another chalk ridge, this time the amphitheatre of hills known as the South Downs. Eventually, it's time to descend to Brighton on the shore.

◆ DETOUR
Beachy Head
Start: ❹ Rye

An 8-mile detour off your route leads to a truly remarkable view. Around 25 miles west of Rye, peel off the A27 onto the A22 to Eastbourne. Head to the seafront to take the signed route that climbs to Beachy Head. Pick from several parking spots and follow the footpaths to the cliffs themselves. These 162m-tall sheer chalk faces are the highest point of cliffs that slice across the rugged coastline at the southern end of the South Downs. Far below sits a squat red-and-white-striped lighthouse. Appealing walks include the 1.5-mile hike west to the beach at Birling Gap.

05 BRIGHTON

Famously hedonistic, exuberant and home to the UK's biggest gay scene, Brighton rocks the south. The bright and breezy seafront boasts the grand, century-old **Brighton Pier** (brightonpier. co.uk), complete with fairground rides, amusement arcades and candy-floss stalls. Stroll inland to the magnificent **Royal Pavilion** (brightonmuseums.org.uk/royal pavilion), the glittering palace of Prince George (later King George IV). It's one of the most opulent buildings in England, and Europe's finest example of early-19th-century chinoiserie. Take in the Salvador Dalí sofa modelled on Mae West's lips at the **Brighton Museum & Art Gallery** (brightonmuseums. org.uk), then gear up for a lively night out by shopping amid the boutiques of the tightly packed Brighton Lanes.

THE DRIVE

Next is a 50-mile blast due west, largely along A roads, to the historic port of Portsmouth. As the 170m-high Spinnaker Tower gets closer on the horizon, pick up signs for the Historic Dockyard Car Park.

06 PORTSMOUTH

For a world-class collection of maritime heritage, head to **Portsmouth Historic Dockyard** (historic dockyard.co.uk). The blockbuster draw is Henry VIII's favour-ite flagship, the **Mary Rose**. A £35-million, boat-shaped museum has now been built around her, giving uninterrupted views of the preserved timbers of her massive hull. Equally impressive is **HMS Victory**. Other nautical sights include the Victorian **HMS Warrior** and a wealth of imaginative museums. Round it all off by strolling around the defences in the his-toric **Point district**.

THE DRIVE

Time to head inland; a 30-mile motorway cruise (the M27 then the M3) takes you to Winchester.

HMS Warrior, Portsmouth

07 WINCHESTER

Calm, collegiate Winchester is a mellow must-see. One of southern England's most awe-inspiring buildings, 11th-century **Winchester Cathedral** (winchester-cathedral.org.uk) adorns its core. It boasts a fine Gothic facade, one of the longest medieval naves in Europe (164m) and intricately carved medieval choir stalls, sporting everything from mythical beasts to a mischievous green man. Jane Austen's grave is near the entrance, in the northern aisle. The fantastical crumbling remains of **Wolvesey Castle** (english-heritage.org.uk) sit nearby, as does one of England's most prestigious private schools: **Winchester College** (winchester college.org), which you can visit on a tour.

THE DRIVE

Leave Winchester's ancient streets to take the motorways towards Southampton (initially the M3). After 14 miles turn off onto the A35 towards Lyndhurst. From here it's a 9-mile drive to Beaulieu through the New Forest's increasingly wooded roads.

08 BEAULIEU

The vintage car museum and stately home at **Beaulieu** (beaulieu.co.uk) is centred on a 13th-century Cistercian monastery that passed to the ancestors of the current proprietors, the Montague family, after Henry VIII's 1536 monastic land-grab. Today its **motor museum** includes F1 cars and jet-powered land-speed record-breakers, as well as wheels driven by James Bond and Mr Bean. The **palace** began life as a 14th-century Gothic abbey gatehouse, and received a 19th-century Scottish baronial makeover from Baron Montague in the 1860s.

THE DRIVE

The SatNav may want to start this 28-mile leg by routing you onto the A326. Resist! Opt for the A and B roads that wind through the villages of Lyndhurst, Cadnam, Brook and North Charford, revealing the New Forest's blend of woods and open heath. Eventually join the A338 to Salisbury. Soon an immense cathedral spire rises over the town.

09 SALISBURY

Salisbury's skyline is dominated by the tallest spire in England, which soars from its central, majestic 13th-century **cathedral** (salisburycathedral.org.uk).

TRAVELLIGHT/SHUTTERSTOCK ©

Avebury

This early-English Gothic–style structure's elaborate exterior is decorated with pointed arches and flying buttresses, while its statuary and tombs are outstanding. Don't miss the daily tower tours and the cathedral's original, 13th-century copy of the Magna Carta. The surrounding **Cathedral Close** has a hushed, otherworldly feel. Nearby, the hugely important finds at **Salisbury Museum** (salisburymuseum.org.uk) include Iron Age gold coins, a Bronze Age gold necklace and the Stonehenge Archer, the bones of a man found in the ditch surrounding the stone circle.

 THE DRIVE
Next: a 10-mile drive taking you back 5000 years. The A345 heads north. Soon after joining the A303, detail a passenger to watch the right windows – the world's most famous stone circle will soon pop into view. The entry to the site is just beyond.

10 STONEHENGE
Welcome to Britain's best-known archaeological site: **Stonehenge** (english-heritage.org.uk), a compelling ring of monolithic stones that dates, in parts, back to 3000 BCE. Head into the **Visitor Centre** to see 300 finds from the site and experience an impressive 360-degree projection of the stone circle through the ages and seasons. Next hop on a trolley bus (or walk; it's 1.5 miles) to the monument. There, as you stroll around it, play 'spot-the-stone': look out for the **bluestone horseshoe** (an inner semicircle), the **trilithon horseshoe** (sets of two vertical stones topped by a horizontal one) and the **Slaughter Stone** and **Heel Stone** (set apart, on the northeast side). Then try to

Stonehenge's Ritual Landscape

As you drive the roads around Stonehenge it's worth registering that the site forms part of a huge complex of ancient monuments. North of Stonehenge and running roughly east–west is the **Cursus**, an elongated embanked oval; the smaller **Lesser Cursus** is nearby. Two clusters of burial mounds, the **Old Barrow** and the **New Kings Barrow**, sit beside the ceremonial pathway **The Avenue**. This routeway cuts northeast of Stonehenge's **Heel Stone** and originally linked the site with the River Avon, 2 miles away. Theories abound as to what these sites were used for, ranging from ancient sporting arenas to processional avenues for the dead.

work out what on earth it all means. Note that entrance is by timed ticket; secure yours well in advance.

 THE DRIVE
Now for a 24-mile, A-road meander through rural England. After dodging through Devizes, it's not long before signs point left to Avebury's main car park.

11 AVEBURY
A two-minute stroll from the car park (£7 per day) leads to a ring of stones that's so big an entire village sits inside. Fringed by a massive bank and ditch and with a diameter of 348m, **Avebury** (nationaltrust.org.uk) is the largest stone circle in the world. Dating from 2500 to 2200

BCE, more than 30 stones are still in place and you can wander between them and clusters of other stones at will. Houses, the **Henge Shop** (hengeshop.com) and a pub, the **Red Lion** (chefandbrewer.com/pubs/wiltshire/red-lion), also nestle inside the circle.

 THE DRIVE
Next, a cruise due west, as the A4 winds for 30 miles past fields and through villages to the city of Bath.

DETOUR
Lacock
Start: **11** Avebury
Around 16 miles into your Avebury-to-Bath cruise, consider a detour south. Because a drive of just 4 extra miles leads to a real rarity: a medieval village that's been preserved in time. In Lacock, the sweet streets framed by stone cottages, higgledy-piggledy rooftops and mullioned windows are a delight to stroll around. Unsurprisingly, it's a popular movie location – it's popped up in the Harry Potter films, *The Other Boleyn Girl* and a BBC adaptation of *Pride and Prejudice*. The 13th-century former Augustinian nunnery of **Lacock Abbey** (nationaltrust.org.uk) is a must-see: its deeply atmospheric rooms and stunning Gothic entrance hall are lined with bizarre terracotta figures – spot the scapegoat with a lump of sugar on its nose. The **Fox Talbot Museum** (nationaltrust.org.uk) features an intriguing display on early photography, while the **Sign of the Angel** (signoftheangel.co.uk) is a gorgeous, 15th-century restaurant-with-rooms.

12 BATH
Sophisticated, stately and ever-so-slightly snooty, Bath is graced with some of the finest Georgian architecture anywhere in Britain. Wandering around the streets here is a real joy. For an insight into how the

WHY I LOVE THIS TRIP

Anthony Ham, writer

It doesn't get more classically British than this journey through the south. Quintessentially British seaside towns, at once quaint and kitsch, vie for attention with the cathedrals of Canterbury, Salisbury and Winchester. There's everyone's favourite archaeological ruin, and two towns – Bath and Bristol – that get that whole history-meets-modern-Britain cachet down perfectly.

city came to look like it does, head to the **Museum of Bath Architecture** (museumofbath architecture.org.uk). The **Bath Assembly Rooms** (nationaltrust. org.uk), where socialites once gathered, gives an insight into the Georgian world. To discover the city's culinary heritage head for **Sally Lunn's** (sallylunns.co.uk), which bakes the famous Bath Bunn (a brioche-meets-bread treat). For a free glass of the spring water that made the city rich, stop by the **Pump Room** (romanbaths.co.uk). Then perhaps soak yourself at **Thermae Bath Spa** (thermaebathspa.com), with its steam rooms, waterfall showers and a choice of swimming pools (including a gorgeous rooftop one).

 THE DRIVE
It's a 13-mile blast from Bath to Bristol along the A36/A4.

13 **BRISTOL**
In Bristol a fascinating seafaring heritage meets an edgy, contemporary vibe.

The mighty **SS Great Britain** (ssgreatbritain.org) sits on the city's waterfront. Designed in 1843 by engineering genius Isambard Kingdom Brunel, its interior has been impeccably refurbished, including the galley, the surgeon's quarters and a working model of the original steam engine. The whole vessel is contained in an air-tight dry dock, dubbed a 'glass sea'.

At the **Bristol Museum & Art Gallery** (bristolmuseums.org. uk) take in the *Paint-Pot Angel* by world-famous street artist Banksy. In the suburb of Clifton explore Georgian architecture, especially in Cornwallis and Royal York Crescents. The **Clifton Observatory** (cliftonobservatory. com), meanwhile, features a rare camera obscura which offers incredible views of the deep fissure that is the Avon Gorge.

 THE DRIVE
Travelling partly on the M4 and partly on A roads, the next 80-mile leg sees you skirting Oxford (for now) and arriving at the tree-lined avenue that leads to one of Britain's finest stately homes.

14 **BLENHEIM PALACE**
Blenheim Palace (blenheimpalace.com), a monumental baroque fantasy designed by Sir John Vanbrugh and Nicholas Hawksmoor, was built between 1705 and 1722. The house is filled with statues, tapestries, ostentatious furniture, priceless china and giant oil paintings. Highlights include the Great Hall, a soaring space topped by a 20m-high ceiling adorned with images of the first duke. Britain's legendary WWII prime minister, Sir Winston

Churchill, was born here in 1874 – the **Churchill Exhibition** is dedicated to his life, work, paintings and writings. The house is encircled by vast, lavish gardens and parklands, parts of which were landscaped by the great Lancelot 'Capability' Brown. A minitrain (£1) whisks you to the Pleasure Gardens, which feature a yew maze, adventure playground, lavender garden and butterfly house.

 THE DRIVE
From Blenheim's grandeur, it's a 10-mile trip down the A44/A34/A4144 to Oxford's dreaming spires.

15 **OXFORD**
One of the world's most famous university towns, the centre of Oxford is rich in history and studded with august buildings. The city has 38 colleges – **Christ Church** (chch.ox.ac.uk) is the largest, with 650 students, and has the grandest quad. Christ Church was founded in 1524 by Cardinal Thomas Wolsey, and alumni include Albert Einstein and 13 British prime ministers. It's also famous as a location for the Harry Potter films. At the **Ashmolean** (ashmolean.org), Britain's oldest public museum has had a modern makeover; interactive displays and glass walls revealing multilevel galleries help showcase treasures that include Egyptian mummies, Indian textiles and Islamic art. Beautiful **Magdalen College** (magd.ox.ac. uk) is worth a visit for its medieval chapel, 15th-century cloisters and 40-hectare grounds. Nearby, head to **Magdalen Bridge Boathouse** (oxfordpunting.co.uk) for a ride on a chauffeured punt.

Photo opportunity

Lounging in a punt with a backdrop of Oxford's divine buildings.

18

Classic Lakes

BEST FOR FAMILIES

Bike trails, sculptures and zip lines at Grizedale Forest.

Windermere Jetty Museum

DURATION	DISTANCE	GREAT FOR
5 days	260km / 162 miles	History, family travel

BEST TIME TO GO	Summer and Easter can be hectic in the Lakes; spring and autumn are best.

William Wordsworth, Samuel Taylor Coleridge and Beatrix Potter are just a few of the literary luminaries who have fallen in love with the Lake District. It's been a national park since 1951, and is studded by England's highest hills (fells), including the highest of all, Scafell Pike. This drive takes in lakes, forests, hills and valleys, with country houses, hill walks and cosy pubs thrown in for good measure.

Link your trip

15 The Best of Britain

Start this circuit of Britain's greatest hits by picking up the M6 at Penrith between Manchester and Edinburgh.

16 Britain's Wild Side

Head north or south along the A591 to visit more of Britain's glorious natural beauty spots.

01 **BOWNESS-ON-WINDERMERE**

At 10.5 miles long, Windermere is the largest body of water in England: more a loch than a lake. It's also one of the most popular places in the Lake District, and has been a tourist centre since the late 19th century, especially for lake cruises.

Windermere gets its name from the old Norse, 'Vinandr mere' (Vinandr's lake; so 'Lake Windermere' is actually tautologous). Encompassing 5.7 sq miles between Ambleside and Newby Bridge, the lake is a mile wide at its broadest point, with a maximum depth of about 220m. There are 18 islands on Windermere: the largest is Belle Isle, encompassing 16 hectares and an

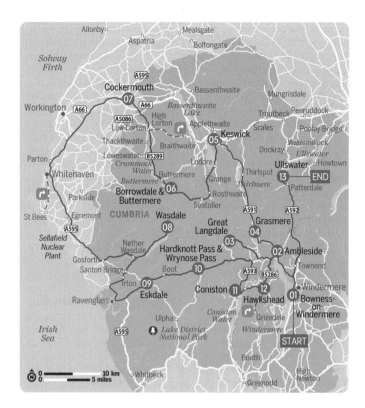

TOP TIP:

National Trust Membership

Being a member of the National Trust (nationaltrust. org.uk) comes in very handy in the Lake District. The Trust owns several key attractions, including Hill Top and the Beatrix Potter Gallery near Hawkshead, Wordsworth House in Cockermouth and Fell Foot and Wray Castle near Windermere. Best of all, you get to park for free at all the NT's car parks – handy in celebrated beauty spots like Buttermere, Borrowdale, Wasdale, Gowbarrow Park and Tarn Hows.

18th-century Italianate mansion, while the smallest is Maiden Holme, little more than a patch of soil and a solitary tree.

The wonderful **Windermere Jetty Museum** (lakelandarts.org. uk/windermere-jetty-museum), finally opened after years of development, explores the history of cruising with a glorious collection of vintage boats, punts and steam yachts – including the *Esperance,* which provided the inspiration for Captain Flint's houseboat in Arthur Ransome's *Swallows and Amazons.* Best of all, you can take your own trip aboard the 1902 *Osprey* or the 1930 *Penelope II.* There's simply no more stylish way to see Windermere.

Alternatively, **Windermere Lake Cruises** (windermere-lake cruises.co.uk) offers sightseeing trips departing from Bowness Pier.

THE DRIVE
From Bowness, follow Rayrigg Rd north until it joins the A591, which rolls all the way to Ambleside, 6 miles north.

02 AMBLESIDE
At the northern end of Windermere lies the old mill town of Ambleside. It's a pretty place, well stocked with outdoors shops and some excellent restaurants: don't miss a meal at the fabulous **Lake Road Kitchen** (lakeroadkitchen.co.uk),

run by an imaginative chef who trained at the legendary Noma in Copenhagen.

Afterwards, work off some calories with a half-hour walk up to the waterfall of **Stock Ghyll Force**, a clattering 18m-high cascade on the edge of town. The trail is signposted behind the old Market Hall at the bottom of Stock Ghyll Lane. If you feel energetic, you can follow the trail beyond the falls up **Wansfell Pike** (482m), a reasonably steep walk of about two hours.

THE DRIVE
Take the A593 west towards Skelwith Bridge, and follow signs to Elterwater and Great Langdale. It's a wonderful 8-mile drive that gets

wilder and wilder the deeper you head into the valley. There's a large car park beside the Old Dungeon Ghyll Hotel, but it gets busy in summer; there's usually overflow parking available in a nearby field.

03 GREAT LANGDALE

The Lake District has some truly stunning valleys, but Great Langdale definitely ranks near the top. As you pass through the pretty village of **Elterwater** and its village green, the scenery gets really wild and empty. Fells stack up like dominoes along the horizon, looming over a patchwork of barns and fields.

If you're up for a hike, then you might consider tackling the multi-peak circuit around the **Langdale Pikes** – a tough, full-day hike into the wild fells above Langdale, which allows you to pick off between three and five summits depending on your route, including the four main 'Pikes' of Pike O' Stickle (709m), Loft Crag (682m), Harrison Stickle (736m) and Pavey Ark (700m). You'll need proper boots, hiking gear and an Ordnance Survey map.

Alternatively, the more sedentary option is to just admire the views over a pint of locally brewed ale from the cosy bar of the **Old Dungeon Ghyll** (odg. co.uk), a classic hikers' haunt.

THE DRIVE
Retrace the road to Ambleside and head north to Grasmere on the A591 for 5 miles.

04 GRASMERE

The lovely little village of Grasmere is inextricably linked with the poet William Wordsworth, who made it his home in the late 18th century and never left unless he really had to. Two of his houses are now open to the public. The most famous is **Dove Cottage** (wordsworth.org.uk), a tiny house where he lived with his sister Dorothy, wife Mary and three children between 1798 and 1808. Guided tours explore the house, and next door the **Jerwood Museum** has lots of memorabilia and original manuscripts relating to the Romantic poets.

A little way south of Grasmere is the house where Wordsworth spent most of his adult life, **Rydal Mount** (rydalmount. co.uk). It's still owned by the poet's descendants, and is a much grander affair than Dove Cottage: you can have a look around the library, visit the poet's attic study and wander around the gardens he designed. Below the house, **Dora's Field** is filled with daffodils in springtime; it was planted in memory of Wordsworth's daughter, who died of tuberculosis.

If you have a sweet tooth, you'll also want to pick up a souvenir at **Sarah Nelson's Gingerbread Shop** (grasmeregingerbread. co.uk), which still makes its gingerbread to a recipe formulated in 1854.

THE DRIVE
From Grasmere, continue north on the A591. You'll pass through the dramatic pass known as Dunmail Raise, where a great battle is said to have taken place between the Saxons and the Celtic king Dunmail, who was slain near the pass. Stay on the road past the lake of Thirlmere all the way to Keswick (13 miles).

05 KESWICK

Another of the Lake District's classic market towns, Keswick is a place that revolves around the great outdoors. Several big fells lie on its doorstep, including the imposing lump of **Skiddaw** and the dramatic ridge of **Blencathra**, but it's the lake of **Derwentwater** that really draws the eye: it was said to be Beatrix Potter's favourite, and she supposedly got the idea for Squirrel Nutkin while watching red squirrels frolicking on its shores.

The **Keswick Launch** (keswick-launch.co.uk) travels out around the lake year-round: you could combine it with an easy hike up to the top of **Catbells** (451m), a favourite first-time fell for many walkers. The views of the lake and the distant hills are absolutely breathtaking.

Back in town, don't miss a visit to **George Fisher** (georgefisher. co.uk), the most famous outdoors shop in the Lake District: if you need a new pair of hiking boots, this is the place to come.

THE DRIVE
The drive into Borrowdale on the B5289 is a beauty, passing several pretty villages as it travels through the valley. You can't get lost en route to Honister Pass (10 miles from Keswick) – there's only one road to take; Buttermere lies on the other side of the pass. You'll want to stop for numerous photos on the way.

06 BORROWDALE & BUTTERMERE

South of Keswick, the B5289 tracks along the eastern side of Derwentwater and enters the bucolic valley of Borrowdale,

Derwentwater, Keswick

a classic Lakeland canvas of fields, fells, streams and endless drystone walls. It's worth stopping off to see the geological oddity of the **Bowder Stone**, a huge boulder deposited by a glacier, and for a quick hike up to the top of **Castle Crag**, which has the best views of the valley.

Then it's up and over the perilously steep **Honister Pass**, where the Lake District's last working **slate mine** (honister. com) is still doing a thriving trade. You can take a guided tour down into the mine or brave the heights along the stomach-upsetting via ferrata, and pick up slate souvenirs in the shop.

Nearby Buttermere has a sparkling twinset of lakes, **Buttermere** and **Crummock Water**, and is backed by a string of impressive fells. The summit

of **Haystacks** is a popular route: it was the favourite fell of Alfred Wainwright, who penned the definitive seven-volume set of guidebooks of the Lake District's fells between the 1950s and '70s. It's a two- to three-hour return walk from Buttermere.

THE DRIVE

From Buttermere village, bear left on the B5289 signed towards Loweswater and Crummock Water, which continues into the Lorton Valley. At Low Lorton, stay on the B5289, which continues 4 miles to Cockermouth. (Total distance: 11 miles.)

DETOUR

Whinlatter Forest Park
Start: **6** **Buttermere**

Encompassing 4.6 sq miles of pine, larch and spruce, **Whinlatter** (forestry. gov.uk/whinlatter) is England's only true mountain forest, rising sharply

to 790m about 5 miles from Keswick. The forest is a designated red squirrel reserve; you can check out live video feeds from squirrel cams at the visitor centre. It's also home to two exciting mountain-bike trails and a treetop assault course. You can hire bikes next to the visitor centre.

To get to Whinlatter Forest Park from Buttermere, look out for the right turn onto the B5292 at Low Lorton, which climbs up to Whinlatter Pass.

07 COCKERMOUTH

Grasmere might be Wordsworth central, but completists will want to visit the poet's **childhood home** (national trust.org.uk/wordsworth-house) in Cockermouth. Now owned by the National Trust, it's been redecorated in period style according to details published in Wordsworth's own father's

Climbing Scafell Pike, Wasdale

accounts: you can wander round the drawing room, kitchen, pantry and garden, and see the rooms where little Willie and his brother John slept. Costumed guides wander around the house for added period authenticity. Outside is the walled kitchen garden mentioned in Wordsworth's autobiographical epic *The Prelude*.

 **THE DRIVE**
Head west on the A66 and detour onto the A595, which tracks the coast all the way to Whitehaven. To reach Wasdale (35 miles all up), turn off at Gosforth, and then follow signs to Nether Wasdale and Wasdale Head. It's quite easy to miss the turning, so keep your eyes peeled; satnavs can be very unreliable here.

DETOUR
St Bees Head
Start: 7 Cockermouth

Cumbria's coastline might not have the white sandy beaches of Wales or the epic grandeur of the Scottish coast, but it has a bleak beauty all of its own – not to mention a renowned seabird reserve at **St Bees Head** (stbees. head@rspb.org.uk), where you can spot species including fulmars, herring gulls, kittiwakes and razorbills – as well as England's only nesting black guillemots at nearby Fleswick Bay. Just try and forget the fact that one of the UK's largest nuclear reactors, Sellafield, is round the corner.

The village of **St Bees** lies 5 miles south of Whitehaven, and the headland is signposted from there.

 08 WASDALE
Wild Wasdale is arguably the most dramatic valley in the national park. Carving its way for 5 miles from the coast, it was gouged out by a long-extinct glacier during the last Ice Age; if you look closely you can still see glacial marks on the scree-strewn

Photo opportunity
Striking a pose in Wasdale, surrounded by England's highest hills.

slopes above Wastwater. It's a truly dramatic drive that feels rather like heading into the depths of a remote Scottish glen: in terms of mountain scenery, it's probably the most impressive stretch of road this side of the Highlands.

Most people come for the chance to reach the summit of **Scafell Pike**, England's highest point (978m); it's a tough six- to seven-hour slog, but the views from the top are quite literally as good as they get (assuming the weather plays ball, of course).

Afterwards, reward yourself with a meal at the **Wasdale Head Inn** (wasdale.com), a gloriously olde-worlde hostelry with lashings of mountain heritage: it was here that the sport of rock climbing was pioneered in the mid-19th century.

 THE DRIVE
Retrace your route to Gosforth, and take the coast road (A595) south to Ravenglass and follow signs to Eskdale (22 miles). Alternatively, there's a shortcut into Eskdale via Nether Wasdale and Santon Bridge, but it's easy to get lost, especially if you're relying on satnav; a good road map is really handy here.

 09 ESKDALE
The valley of Eskdale was once a centre for mineral mining, and a miniature steam train was built to carry ore down from the hillsides to the coast.

Now known as the **Ravenglass & Eskdale Railway** (ravenglass-railway.co.uk), or La'al Ratty to locals, its miniature choo-choos are a beloved Lakeland attraction. They chuff for 7 miles along the valley from the station at Ravenglass to the final terminus at Dalegarth, stopping at several stations in between. Nearby, the **Boot Inn** (thebooteskdale.co.uk) makes a pleasant stop for lunch.

 THE DRIVE
Since you're driving, the most sensible idea is to park near Dalegarth Station, ride the train to Ravenglass and back, and then set off for Hardknott Pass. There's only one road east. Take it and get ready for a hair-raising, white-knuckle drive. It's 6 (very steep!) miles from Eskdale to Hardknott Pass.

10 HARDKNOTT PASS & WRYNOSE PASS
At the eastern end of Eskdale lie England's two steepest road passes, Hardknott and Wrynose. Reaching 30% gradient in some places, and with precious few passing places on the narrow, single-file road, they're absolutely

not for the faint-hearted or for nervous drivers – but the views are amazing, and they're doable if you take things slow (although it's probably best to leave the caravan or motor home in the garage). Make sure your car has plenty of oil and water, as you'll do much of the road in 1st gear, and the strain on the engine can be taxing. Take it slow, and take breaks – you need to keep your focus on the road ahead.

From Eskdale, the road ascends via a series of very sharp, steep switchbacks to the remains of **Hardknott Fort**, a Roman outpost where you can still see the remains of some of the walls. Soon after you reach Hardknott Pass at 393m (1289ft). The vistas here are magnificent: you'll be able to see all the way to the coast on a clear day. Next you'll

drop down into Cockley Beck before continuing the climb up to Wrynose Pass (393m/1289ft). Near the summit is a small car park containing the **Three Shire Stone**, where the counties of Cumberland, Westmorland and Lancashire historically met. Then it's a slow descent down through hairpins and corners to the packhorse Slaters Bridge and on into the valley of **Little Langdale**. Phew! You made it.

THE DRIVE
Once you reach Little Langdale, follow the road east until you reach the A593, the main road between Skelwith Bridge and Coniston. Turn right and follow it for 5 miles.

11 **CONISTON**
South of Ambleside, the old mining village of Coniston is dominated by its

hulking fell, the **Old Man of Coniston**, an ever-popular objective for hikers, but it's perhaps best known for the world speed record attempts made here by father and son Malcolm and Donald Campbell between the 1930s and 1960s. Though they jointly broke many records, in 1967 Donald was tragically killed during an attempt in his jetboat *Bluebird;* the little **Ruskin Museum** (ruskinmuseum.com) has the full story.

Coniston Water is also said to have been the inspiration for Arthur Ransome's classic children's tale, *Swallows and Amazons*. The best way to explore is aboard the **Steam Yacht Gondola** (nationaltrust.org.uk/steam-yacht-gondola), a beautifully restored steam yacht built in 1859. It travels over the lake to the stately home of

Hawkshead

Brantwood (brantwood.org.uk), owned by the Victorian polymath, critic, painter and inveterate collector John Ruskin. The house is packed with furniture and crafts, and the gardens are glorious.

THE DRIVE
Heading north from Coniston, turn right onto the B5285 up Hawkshead Hill. You'll pass Tarn Hows and the Drunken Duck en route to Hawkshead, about 4 miles east.

12   HAWKSHEAD
If you're searching for the perfect chocolate-box lakeland village, look no further – you've found it in Hawkshead, an improbably pretty confection of whitewashed cottages, winding lanes and slate roofs. It's car-free, so you can wander at will: don't miss the **Beatrix Potter Gallery**, which has a collection of the artist's original watercolours and botanical paintings (she had a particular fascination with fungi).

Nearby, it's worth making a detour to have a stroll around the lake of **Tarn Hows** (national trust.org.uk/coniston-and-tarn-hows) – a bucolic place, but one that's artificially created (it was made by joining three neighbouring tarns in the 19th century).

After your walk, pop in for lunch at the Lake District's finest dining pub, the wonderfully named **Drunken Duck** (drunkenduckinn.co.uk).

THE DRIVE
Head back to Ambleside and then follow the A591 back towards Windermere. Just before you reach it, take the turn-off onto the A592 to Troutbeck Bridge, which climbs up to the lofty Kirkstone Pass – at 454m this is the highest mountain pass in Cumbria that's open to road traffic. It's

steep, but it's a main A road so it's well maintained.

DETOUR
Forest Wander
Start: 12 Hawkshead
Stretching for more than 2400 hectares across the hilltops between Coniston Water and Esthwaite Water, **Grizedale Forest** (forestry.gov.uk/grizedale) is a wonderful place for a wander. It's criss-crossed by cycling trails, and is also home to more than 40 outdoor sculptures created by artists since 1977, including a xylophone and a man of the forest. There's an online guide at www.grizedalesculpture.org.

As you leave the Hawkshead car park, you'll immediately see a brown sign for Grizedale, heading right onto North Lonsdale Rd. Just follow the brown signs from here – it's 3 miles' drive from the village.

13   ULLSWATER
From the windlashed heights of Kirkstone Pass, the A592 loops down towards the last stop on this jaunt around the Lake District: stately Ullswater, the national park's second-largest lake (after Windermere). It's an impressive sight, with its silvery surface framed by jagged fells and plied by the puttering **Ullswater 'Steamers'** (ullswater-steamers.co.uk); you can also hire your own vessels from the **Glenridding Sailing Centre** (glenridding sailingcentre.co.uk).

As you skirt up the lake's western edge, it's worth stopping for a walk around **Gowbarrow Park** (nationaltrust.org.uk), where there's a clattering waterfall to admire called **Aira Force**, and impressive displays of daffodils in springtime (Wordsworth dreamt up his most famous poem while walking nearby).

Hill Top

Two miles from Hawkshead in the tiny village of Near Sawrey, the idyllic cottage at **Hill Top** (nationaltrust.org.uk/hill-top) is the most famous house in the whole of the Lake District. It belonged to Beatrix Potter, and was used as inspiration for many of her tales: the house features directly in Samuel Whiskers, Tom Kitten, Pigling Bland and Jemima Puddle-Duck, and you will doubtless recognise the kitchen garden from Peter Rabbit.

Following her death in 1943, Beatrix bequeathed Hill Top (along with more than 1600 hectares of land) to the National Trust, with the proviso that the house be left with her belongings and decor untouched. The house formed the centrepiece for celebrations to mark the author's 150th birthday in 2016.

It's probably the Lake District's most popular attraction, however, so don't expect to have it all to yourself...

For an epic end to the trip, strap on your hiking boots and tackle the famous ridge climb via Striding Edge to the summit of **Helvellyn**, the Lake District's third-highest mountain at 950m. You'll need a head for heights, but you'll feel a real sense of achievement: you've just conquered perhaps the finest hill walk in all of England.

19

BEST FOR WILDLIFE

Watching the nesting osprey at Loch Garten.

Royal Highlands & Cairngorms

DURATION	DISTANCE	GREAT FOR
4–5 days	238km / 149 miles	History, outdoors

BEST TIME TO GO	July and August mean good weather and all attractions are open.

Balmoral Castle

The heart of the Scottish Highlands features a feast of castles and mountains, wild roller-coaster roads, ancient Caledonian pine forest, and the chance to see Highland wildlife up close and personal. You'll tick off the highlights of Royal Deeside and the central Highlands as you make this circuit around Cairngorms National Park.

Link your trip

20 Great Glen

The stirring wilderness of the northwest Highlands awaits – it's an hour and three-quarters west to Glen Coe.

15 The Best of Britain

Head an hour and a half south to Edinburgh to begin our epic loop of Britain's greatest hits at its midpoint.

01 BRAEMAR

Braemar is a pretty little village with a grand location on a broad plain ringed by mountains where the Dee valley and Glen Clunie meet. In winter this is one of the coldest places in the country – temperatures as low as -29°C have been recorded.

Just north of the village, turreted **Braemar Castle** (braemarcastle.co.uk) dates from 1628 and served as a government garrison after the 1745 Jacobite rebellion. It was taken over by the local community in 2007, and now offers guided tours of the historic castle apartments.

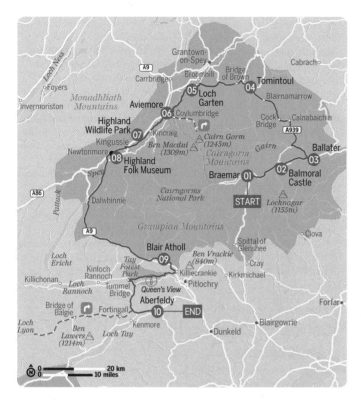

There are Highland games in many towns throughout the summer, but the best known is the **Braemar Gathering** (braemar gathering.org), which takes place on the first Saturday in September.

THE DRIVE
The upper valley of the River Dee stretches east from Braemar to Aboyne. Made famous by its long association with the monarchy, the region is often called Royal Deeside. Head east from Braemar on the A93 for 9 miles to the car park at the entrance to Balmoral Castle.

02 BALMORAL CASTLE
Built for Queen Victoria in 1855 as a private residence for the royal family,

Balmoral Castle (balmoral castle.com) kicked off the revival of the Scottish Baronial style of architecture that characterises so many of Scotland's 19th-century country houses. Admission is by guided tour (book ahead); the tour is interesting and well thought out, but very much an outdoor one through garden and grounds.

As for the castle itself, only the ballroom, which displays a collection of Landseer paintings and royal silver, is open to the public. Don't expect to see the Queen's private quarters! The main attraction is learning about Highland estate management, rather than royal revelations.

You can buy a booklet that details several waymarked walks within Balmoral Estate; the best is the climb to **Prince Albert's Cairn**.

THE DRIVE
Continue east on the A93 for another 8 miles to Ballater.

03 BALLATER
The attractive village of Ballater owes its 18th-century origins to the curative waters of nearby Pannanich Springs (now bottled commercially as Deeside Natural Mineral Water), and its prosperity to nearby Balmoral Castle.

After the original station was destroyed by fire in 2015, the **Old Royal Station** building – newly restored to exactly replicate the one built in 1866 to receive Queen Victoria when she visited Balmoral by train – reopened in 2018. It houses a tourist office, a tearoom and a cafe-bistro. Behind the tourist office is a replica of Queen Victoria's carriage.

There are many pleasant walks in the surrounding area. The steep woodland walk up **Craigendarroch** (400m) takes just over one hour; ask at the tourist office for more info. You can hire bikes from **CycleHighlands** (cyclehighlands. com) and **Bike Station** (bike stationballater.co.uk), which also offer guided bike rides and advice on local trails.

THE DRIVE
The A939 strikes north through the mountains from Ballater to Tomintoul (25 miles). The section beyond Cock Bridge is a magnificent roller-coaster of a road, much loved by motorcyclists, summiting at the Lecht pass (637m) where there's a small skiing area (it's usually the first road in Scotland to be blocked by snow when winter closes in).

04 TOMINTOUL

Tomintoul (tom-in-towel) is a pretty, stone-built village with a grassy, tree-lined main square. It was built by the Duke of Gordon in 1775 on the old military road that leads over the Lecht pass from Corgarff, a route now followed by the A939. The **Tomintoul & Glenlivet Discovery Centre** (discovery@ tgdt.org.uk) celebrates local history, with reconstructions of a crofter's kitchen and a blacksmith's forge.

There's excellent mountain biking at the **BikeGlenlivet** (glenlivetestate.co.uk) trail centre, 4.5 miles north of Tomintoul, off the B9136 road.

THE DRIVE

Continue northwest from Tomintoul on the A939 for 8.5 miles before turning left on a minor road to the village of Nethy Bridge. In the village, turn left towards Aviemore on the B970; then, after 600m, turn left again on a minor road to Loch Garten (total 17 miles).

05 LOCH GARTEN

A car park on the shores of Loch Garten, amid beautiful open forest of Scots pine, gives access to the **RSPB Loch Garten Osprey Centre** (rspb.org.uk/lochgarten). Ospreys nest in a tall pine tree on the reserve – you can watch from a hide as the birds feed their young, and see live CCTV feeds from the nest. These rare and beautiful birds – the only bird of prey in the world that eats only fish – migrate here each spring from Africa, arriving in April and leaving in August (check the website to see if they're in residence).

THE DRIVE

The minor road leads back to the B970, where you turn left along the banks of the River Spey to Coylumbridge; turn right here to reach Aviemore (11 miles).

06 AVIEMORE

The gateway to the Cairngorms, Aviemore may not be the prettiest town in Scotland – the main attractions are in the surrounding area – but when bad weather puts the hills off limits, Aviemore fills up with hikers, cyclists and climbers (plus skiers and snowboarders in winter) cruising the outdoor-equipment shops or recounting their latest adventures in the cafes and bars.

Strathspey Steam Railway (strathspeyrailway.co.uk) runs steam trains on a section of restored line between Aviemore and Broomhill, 10 miles to the northeast, via **Boat of Garten**. There are four or five trains daily from June to August, and a more limited service in April, May, September, October and December, with the option of eating afternoon tea, Sunday lunch or a three-course dinner on board.

THE DRIVE

From Aviemore, drive south on the B9152, which follows the valley of the River Spey; after 8.5 miles, soon

---

DETOUR:
Cairngorm Mountain

START: 6 AVIEMORE

Cairngorm Mountain (1245m), 10 miles southeast of Aviemore, is the sixth-highest summit in the UK and home to Scotland's biggest ski area. From Aviemore, it's a 10-mile drive to Coire Cas car park at the end of Ski Rd; from here the climb to the summit is 2 miles and takes about two hours to the top (a challenging climb that requires a map and compass; beware of changeable weather conditions). The old funicular railway here closed in 2018.

From Aviemore, the road to Cairngorm Mountain passes through the **Rothiemurchus Estate**, famous for having one of Scotland's largest remnants of Caledonian forest, the ancient forest of Scots pine that once covered most of the country. The **Rothiemurchus Centre** (rothie murchus.net) has maps detailing more than 50 miles of footpaths and cycling trails, including the 4-mile trail around **Loch an Eilein**, with its ruined castle and peaceful pine woods.

Six miles east of Aviemore, the road passes **Loch Morlich**, surrounded by some 8 sq miles of pine and spruce forest that make up the **Glenmore Forest Park**. Its attractions include a sandy beach (at the east end) and a water-sports centre.

Nearby, the **Cairngorm Reindeer Centre** (cairngormreindeer.co.uk) runs guided walks to see and feed Britain's only herd of reindeer, which are free-ranging but very tame. Walks take place at 11am daily (weather-dependent), plus another at 2.30pm from May to September. Book tickets in advance by phone.

Steam train, Boat of Garten

after passing through the village of Kincraig, you'll see a sign on the right for the Highland Wildlife Park.

07 HIGHLAND WILDLIFE PARK

The **Highland Wildlife Park** (highlandwildlifepark.org) features a drive-through safari park and animal enclosures that offer the chance to view rarely seen native wildlife, such as Scottish wildcats, capercaillies, pine martens and red squirrels. It is also home to species that once roamed the Scottish hills but have long since disappeared, including wolves, lynx, wild boars, beavers and European bison. Last entry is two hours before closing.

THE DRIVE

Continue southwest on the B9152 through Kingussie to the Highland Folk Museum (6.5 miles).

Photo Opportunity

Happy snaps of how the other half used to live in Blair Castle.

08 HIGHLAND FOLK MUSEUM

The old Speyside towns of **Kingussie** (kin-yew-see) and **Newtonmore** sit at the foot of the great heather-clad humps known as the Monadhliath Mountains. Newtonmore is best known as the home of the excellent **Highland Folk Museum** (highlandfolk.com), an open-air collection of historical buildings and artefacts revealing many aspects of Highland culture and

lifestyle. Laid out like a farming township, it has a community of traditional thatch-roofed cottages, a sawmill, a schoolhouse, a shepherd's bothy (hut) and a rural post office.

THE DRIVE

Join the main A9 Inverness to Perth road and follow it south for 35 miles to Blair Atholl, passing through bleak mountain scenery and climbing to a high point of 460m at the Pass of Drumochter.

09 BLAIR ATHOLL

The picturesque village of Blair Atholl dates only from the early 19th century, built by the Duke of Atholl, head of the Murray clan, whose seat – magnificent **Blair Castle** (blair-castle.co.uk) – is one of the most popular tourist attractions in Scotland.

Blair Castle

Thirty rooms are open to the public and they present a wonderful picture of upper-class Highland life from the 16th century on. The original tower was built in 1269, but the castle underwent significant remodelling in the 18th and 19th centuries. Highlights include the 2nd-floor Drawing Room with its ornate Georgian plasterwork and Zoffany portrait of the 4th duke's family, complete with a pet lemur called Tommy; and the Tapestry Room draped with 17th-century wall hangings created for Charles I. The dining room is sumptuous – check out the 9-pint wine glasses.

There are more than 50 miles of cycling trails through the estate; hire a bike from **Blair Atholl Bike Hire** (segway-ecosse.com/bike-hire).

THE DRIVE

Follow the B8079 southeast out of Blair Atholl for a few miles, past the historic battle site of

DETOUR:
Glen Lyon

START: ⑩ ABERFELDY

The 'longest, loneliest and loveliest glen in Scotland', according to Sir Walter Scott, stretches for 32 unforgettable miles of rickety stone bridges, native woodland and heather-clad hills, becoming wilder and more uninhabited as it snakes its way west. The ancients believed it to be a gateway to Faerieland, and even the most sceptical of visitors will be entranced by the valley's magic.

There are no villages in the glen – the majestic scenery is the main reason to be here – just a cluster of houses at Bridge of Balgie, where the **Glenlyon Tearoom**, with a suntrap of a terrace overlooking the river, serves as a hub for walkers, cyclists and motorists. The owner is a fount of knowledge about the glen, and her pistachio and almond cake is legendary.

There are several waymarked woodland walks beginning from a car park a short distance beyond Bridge of Balgie, and more challenging hill walks into the surrounding mountains (see walkhighlands.co.uk/perthshire).

From Aberfeldy, the B846 leads to the pretty village Fortingall, famous for its ancient yew tree, where a narrow minor road strikes west up the glen; another steep and spectacular route from Loch Tay crosses the hills to meet it at Bridge of Balgie. The road continues west as far as the dam on Loch Lyon, passing a memorial to Robert Campbell (1808–94), a Canadian explorer and fur trader who was born in the glen.

Killiecrankie, and turn right on the B8019 Strathtummel road. This gloriously scenic road leads along Loch Tummel (stop for photographs at Queen's View) to Tummel Bridge; turn left here on the B846 over the hills to Aberfeldy (29 miles).

⑩ ABERFELDY

Aberfeldy is the gateway to Breadalbane (the historic region surrounding Loch Tay), and a good base: adventure sports, angling, art and castles all feature on the menu here. It's a peaceful, pretty place on the banks of the Tay, but if it's moody lochs and glens that steal your heart, you may want to push further west into Glen Lyon.

You arrive in the town by crossing the River Tay via the elegant Wade's Bridge, built in 1733 as part of the network of military roads designed to tame the Highlands. At the eastern end of town is **Aberfeldy Distillery** (dewars aberfeldydistillery.com), home of the famous Dewar's whisky; entertaining tours of the whisky-making process are followed by a tasting of venerable Aberfeldy single malts and others.

20

BEST FOR FAMILIES

Taking a Nessie-hunting cruise from Fort Augustus.

Great Glen

Glen Coe

DURATION	DISTANCE	GREAT FOR
2–3 days	235km / 147 miles	History, family travel

BEST TIME TO GO	April to see snow on the mountains; October for autumn colour in the forests.

The Great Glen is a geological fault running in an arrow-straight line across Scotland, filled by a series of lochs including Loch Ness. This trip follows the A82 road along the glen (completed in 1933 – a date that coincides with the first sightings of the Loch Ness monster!) and links two areas of outstanding natural beauty – Glen Coe to the south, and Glen Affric to the north.

Link your trip

16 Britain's Wild Side

Explore more of Britain's natural beauty spots by taking this trip in reverse from Inverness.

19 Royal Highlands & Cairngorms

Get your fill of Scottish splendour by beginning with this tour of castles and mountains before heading west to Glen Coe.

01 **GLEN COE**
Scotland's most famous glen is also one of its grandest. The A82 road leads over the **Pass of Glencoe** and into the narrow upper glen. The southern side is dominated by three massive, brooding spurs, known as the **Three Sisters**, while the northern side is enclosed by the continuous steep wall of the knife-edged **Aonach Eagach** ridge, a classic mountaineering challenge.

Glencoe Visitor Centre (nts.org.uk) provides comprehensive information on the geological, environmental and cultural history of Glencoe, charts the

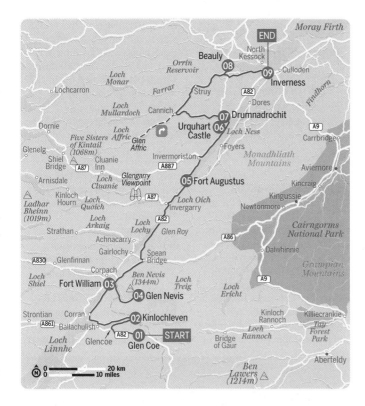

03 FORT WILLIAM

Basking on the shores of **Loch Linnhe** amid magnificent mountain scenery, Fort William has one of the most enviable settings in the whole of Scotland. If it wasn't for the busy dual carriageway crammed between the less-than-attractive town centre and the loch, and one of the highest rainfall records in the country, it would be almost idyllic. Even so, the Fort has carved out a reputation as **Outdoor Capital of the UK** (outdoorcapital.co.uk).

The small but fascinating **West Highland Museum** (westhighlandmuseum.org.uk) is packed with all manner of Highland memorabilia. Look out for the secret portrait of Bonnie Prince Charlie – after the Jacobite rebellions, all things Highland were banned, including pictures of the exiled leader, and this tiny painting looks like nothing more than a smear of paint until viewed in a cylindrical mirror.

THE DRIVE

At the roundabout on the northern edge of Fort William, take the minor road that runs into Glen Nevis; it leads to a car park at the far end of the glen, 6.5 miles away.

04 GLEN NEVIS

Scenic Glen Nevis – used as a filming location for *Braveheart* and the Harry Potter movies – wraps around the base of Ben Nevis, Britain's highest mountain. The **Glen Nevis Visitor Centre** is situated 1.5 miles up the glen, and provides information on hiking, weather forecasts, and specific advice on climbing **Ben Nevis**.

development of mountaineering in the glen, and tells the story of the Glencoe Massacre in all its gory detail.

THE DRIVE

From Glencoe village at the foot of the glen, head east on the B863 for 7 miles along the southern shore of Loch Leven to Kinlochleven.

02 KINLOCHLEVEN

Kinlochleven is hemmed in by high mountains at the head of beautiful **Loch Leven**, where the West Highland Way brings a steady stream of hikers through the village. It is also the starting point for walks up the glen of the River Leven, through pleasant woods to the **Grey Mare's Tail** waterfall, and harder mountain hikes into the Mamores.

Scotland's first **Via Ferrata** (verticaldescents.com) – a 500m climbing route equipped with steel ladders, cables and bridges – snakes through the crags around the Grey Mare's Tail, allowing non-climbers to experience the thrill of climbing (you'll need a head for heights, though!).

THE DRIVE

Return west along the north side of Loch Leven, perhaps stopping for lunch at the excellent Lochleven Seafood Cafe, then head north on the A82 to Fort William (22 miles).

From the car park at the end of the road, 5 miles beyond the visitor centre, there is an excellent 1.5-mile walk through the spectacular, verdant **Nevis Gorge** valley to **Steall Falls**, a 100m-high bridal-veil waterfall. You can reach the foot of the falls by crossing the river on a wobbly, three-cable wire bridge – one cable for your feet and one for each hand – a real test of balance!

THE DRIVE
Return down Glen Nevis and head north on the A82. At Invergarry, turn left onto the A87 which climbs high above Loch Garry; stop at the famous Glengarry Viewpoint (layby on left). By a quirk of perspective, the lochs to the west appear to form the map outline of Scotland. Return to the A87 and continue to Fort Augustus (44 miles).

Photo Opportunity

Failing a shot of the Loch Ness monster, the atmospheric ruins of Urquhart Castle.

05 **FORT AUGUSTUS**
Fort Augustus, at the junction of four old military roads, was originally a government garrison and the headquarters of General George Wade's road-building operations in the early 18th century. Today, it's a neat and picturesque little place bisected by the Caledonian Canal.

Boats using the canal are raised and lowered 13m by a 'ladder' of five consecutive locks. It's fun to watch, and the neatly landscaped canal banks are a great place to soak up the sun. The **Caledonian Canal Centre**, beside the lowest lock, has information on the history of the canal.

Cruise Loch Ness (cruiseloch ness.com), at the jetty beside the canal bridge, operates one-hour cruises on Loch Ness accompanied by the latest high-tech sonar equipment so you can keep an underwater eye open for the Loch Ness monster.

THE DRIVE
It's a straightforward but scenic 17-mile drive along the shores of Loch Ness to Urquhart Castle.

06 **URQUHART CASTLE**
Commanding a superb location with outstanding views over Loch Ness, **Urquhart**

JAROSLAV MORAVCIK/SHUTTERSTOCK ©

Urquhart Castle

Castle (historicenvironment. scot) is a popular Nessie-hunting hotspot. The castle was repeatedly sacked and rebuilt (and sacked and rebuilt) over the centuries; in 1692 it was blown up to prevent the Jacobites from using it. The five-storey tower house at the northern point is the most impressive remaining fragment and offers wonderful views across the water.

The **visitor centre** includes displays of medieval items discovered in the castle and a video theatre: the film, with a dramatic 'reveal' of the castle at the end, can be downloaded onto your phone using a QR code if the visitor centre is closed.

THE DRIVE
A short hop of 2 miles leads to Drumnadrochit.

07 DRUMNADROCHIT
Deep, dark and narrow, Loch Ness stretches for 23 miles between Inverness and Fort Augustus. Its bitterly cold waters have been extensively explored in search of Nessie, the elusive Loch Ness monster, but most visitors see her only in the form of a cardboard cut-out at Drumnadrochit's monster exhibitions.

The **Loch Ness Centre** (loch ness.com) adopts a scientific approach that allows you to weigh the evidence for yourself. Exhibits include the original equipment – sonar survey vessels, miniature submarines, cameras and sediment coring tools – used in various monster hunts, as well as original photographs and film footage of sightings. You'll find

out about hoaxes and optical illusions, as well as learning a lot about the ecology of Loch Ness – is there enough food in the loch to support even one 'monster', let alone a breeding population?

THE DRIVE
Head west on the A831 which leads to the village of Cannich – jumping-off point for the Glen Affric detour – before turning north along lovely Strathglass to reach Beauly (30 miles).

DETOUR
Glen Affric
Start: **7 Drumnadrochit**

Glen Affric, one of the most beautiful glens in Scotland, extends deep into the hills beyond Cannich, halfway between Drumnadrochit and Beauly. The upper reaches of the glen, now designated as **Glen Affric Nature Reserve**, are a scenic wonderland of shimmering lochs, rugged mountains and native Scots pine forest, home to pine martens, wildcats, otters, red squirrels and golden eagles.

A narrow, dead-end road leads southwest from Cannich; about 4 miles along is **Dog Falls**, a scenic spot where the River Affric squeezes through a narrow, rocky gorge. A circular walking trail (red waymarks) leads from Dog Falls car park to a footbridge below the falls and back on the far side of the river (2 miles, allow one hour). The road continues beyond Dog Falls to a parking area and picnic site at the eastern end of **Loch Affric**, where there are several short walks along the river and the loch shore. The circuit of Loch Affric (10 miles, allow five hours walking, two hours by mountain bike) follows good paths right around the loch and takes you deep into the heart of some very wild scenery.

08 BEAULY
Mary, Queen of Scots, is said to have given this village its name in 1564 when she visited, exclaiming in French: 'Quel beau lieu!' (What a beautiful place!) Founded in 1230, the red-sandstone **Beauty Priory** is now an impressive ruin, haunted by the cries of rooks nesting in a magnificent centuries-old sycamore tree.

Corner on the Square makes a good place to break your journey; it's well worth the stop.

THE DRIVE
Drive east on the A862 for 12 miles to Inverness.

09 INVERNESS
Inverness has a great location astride the River Ness at the northern end of the Great Glen. In summer it overflows with visitors intent on monster hunting at nearby Loch Ness, but it's worth a visit in its own right for a stroll along the picturesque River Ness, a cruise on Loch Ness, and a meal in one of the city's excellent restaurants.

The main attraction in Inverness is a leisurely stroll along the river to the **Ness Islands**. Planted with mature Scots pine, fir, beech and sycamore, and linked to the riverbanks and each other by elegant Victorian footbridges, the islands make an appealing picnic spot. They're a 20-minute walk south of the castle – head upstream on either side of the river (the start of the Great Glen Way), and return on the opposite bank.

21

BEST FOR FAMILIES

Splashing about on the beach at Tenby.

West Wales: Swansea to St Davids

DURATION	DISTANCE	GREAT FOR
4 days	207km / 129 miles	History, family travel

BEST TIME TO GO	June, July and August offer the best beach weather.

Oystermouth Castle, Mumbles

The broad sandy arc of Swansea Bay is only a teaser for what is to come. Escape the city sprawl, and the majesty of the Welsh coast immediately begins to assert itself. Waves crash against sheer cliffs painted from a rapidly changing palate of grey, purple and inky black. In between are some of Britain's very best beaches: glorious sandy stretches and remote coves alike.

Link your trip

15 The Best of Britain

The Welsh coast tour is an obvious side trip from our grand tour of the best sights of Britain – it's an hour's drive between Swansea and Cardiff.

17 The Historic South

Sample some heritage and culture before hitting the wild coast: from Oxford, it's 2½ hours west on the M4 to Swansea.

01 **SWANSEA**
Wales' second city has its own workaday charm and an enviable setting on 5-mile-long, sandy Swansea Bay. An active bar scene is enthusiastically supported by a large student population, while a new brace of affordable ethnic eateries and swimmingly good seafood restaurants have improved the city's once drab dining options no end. Literature lovers will relish the handsome Uplands area where the country's best-known writer, Dylan Thomas, was born, bred, inspired and inebriated.

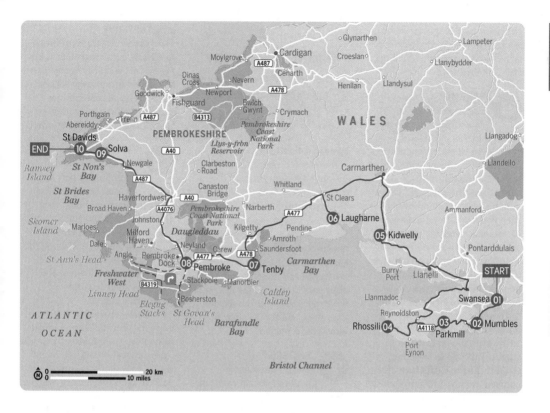

Fuel up on everything from wondrous Welsh cakes to tantalising Thai food at one of the nation's best markets, **Swansea Market** (swanseaindoormarket. co.uk), then dive into the whizz-bang **National Waterfront Museum** (museum.wales/ swansea). Dylan Thomas fans can tour the district surrounding his **birthplace** (dylanthomas birthplace.com), explore his legacy at the **Dylan Thomas Centre** (dylanthomas.com) and visit some of the (many!) pubs he famously frequented.

🚗 **THE DRIVE**
Broad Oystermouth Rd traces the edge of Swansea Bay, changing its

name to Mumbles Rd halfway along. It's only 4 miles from central Swansea to the heart of The Mumbles strip.

02 **MUMBLES**
Swansea's swanky seaside suburb sprawls along the western curve of Swansea Bay and terminates in the pair of rounded hills which may have gifted the area its unusual name (from the French Les Mamelles – 'the breasts'). The Norman fortress of **Oystermouth Castle** (swansea. gov.uk/oystermouthcastle) stands guard over the fashionable Newton Rd and seafronting Mumbles Rd with their spread of tempting restaurants and bars.

Pick up an ice cream at **Joe's** (joes-icecream.com), a Swansea institution founded by an Italian immigrant in 1922, and take a stroll along the waterside promenade to the Victorian **pier** (mumbles-pier.co.uk). There's a pretty little sandy beach tucked just beneath it. If you're peckish, there are some good cafes and restaurants spread along the waterfront, some serving the region's highly regarded seafood, and plenty of pubs and bars too.

🚗 **THE DRIVE**
From the Mumbles it's 6 miles to Parkmill on the Gower Peninsula. Head uphill on Newton Rd, following the Gower signs. Eventually the houses

give way to fields and, at the village of Murton, a sharp right-hand turn leads to the B4436 and on to the A4118, the main Gower road.

03 **PARKMILL**

The spectacular coastal landscape of the **Gower Peninsula** was recognised by officialdom when it was declared the UK's first Area of Outstanding Natural Beauty in 1956.

In the gateway village of Parkmill, historic mill buildings have been converted into the **Gower Heritage Centre** (gowerheritage centre.co.uk). Despite its worthy-sounding name, it's a great place to take kids, incorporating a petting zoo and a puppet theatre. Nearby **Parc-le-Breos** contains the remains of a 5500-year-old burial chamber.

However, the real reason to stop in Parkmill is to take a stroll to **Three Cliffs Bay**. Recognised as one of Britain's most beautiful sandy beaches, Three Cliffs has a memorable setting, with the ruined 13th-century

WHY I LOVE THIS TRIP

Luke Waterson, writer

Traversing two of Wales' most acclaimed beauty spots (the Gower Peninsula and the Pembrokeshire Coast), this journey also offers up a couple of urban extremes in the form of a large post-industrial city (Swansea) and its near antithesis, an ancient settlement that is Britain's smallest and most westerly city (St Davids). Meander there via time-lost fishing villages, thickset fortresses and serendipitous sandy beaches.

Photo opportunity

The view of Three Cliffs Bay from Pennard Castle.

Pennard Castle above and a triple-pointed rock formation framing a natural arch at its eastern end.

 THE DRIVE

From Parkmill, head west along the A4118, following the signs to Rhossili. Eventually the road turns left towards the village of Scurlage and the Rhossili turn-off. All up, it's a distance of 10 miles along good roads, but it's quite likely you'll be sporadically stuck behind a slow-moving campervan or tractor.

04 **RHOSSILI**

The 3 miles of surf-battered golden sands of **Rhossili Bay** make it the Gower Peninsula's most spectacular strand. Rhossili village at the southern end of the beach makes the best casual stop. There's a National Trust **visitor centre** (nationaltrust.org.uk/rhosili-and-south-gower-coast) here, and the excellent **Bay Bistro & Coffee House** (thebaybistro.co.uk). Beware of swimming here: tides can make it dangerous.

This end of the beach is abutted by **Worms Head**, a dragon-shaped promontory which turns into an island at high tide and is home to seals and many seabirds. It's safe to explore on foot for 2½ hours either side of low tide. Don't get cut off by incoming tides! Surfers tend to prefer Llangennith, near the north end of the beach, as a base.

 THE DRIVE

It's only 31 miles from Rhossili to Kidwelly, but allow an hour as the first part of the journey zigzags along tiny byways on the Gower Peninsula's northern edge. Before and after navigating the scraggly outskirts of Llanelli, it's a pleasantly rural drive.

05 **KIDWELLY**

Castles are a dime a dozen in this part of Wales – a legacy of a time when Norman 'Marcher' lords were given authority and a large degree of autonomy to subjugate the Welsh in the south and along the English border. The cute little Carmarthenshire town of Kidwelly has a particularly well-preserved example.

Originally erected in 1106, only 40 years after the Norman invasion of England, **Kidwelly Castle** (cadw.gov.wales) got its current configuration of imposing stone walls in the 13th century. Wander around and explore its remaining towers and battlements, or just stop by to take a photo of the grey walls looming above the peaceful river far below.

Extensive **Pembrey Country Park** (pembreycountrypark. wales) is 5 miles south of Kidwelly. With 200 hectares of trail-crossed woods abutting one of Wales' longest sandy beaches, you could spend hours mooching about here.

THE DRIVE

From Kidwelly, motor north along the A484 through the green fields of Carmarthenshire. At Carmarthen, a pleasant but unremarkable county town, switch to the A40 dual carriageway to St Clears, and then follow the A4066 south to the becalmed estuary town of Laugharne: 21 miles in total.

Pennard Castle

06 LAUGHARNE

While shooting down the highway between Carmarthen and Tenby, it's worth considering taking a left at St Clears to visit the town of Laugharne (pronounced *'larn'*) on the Taf estuary. Perched picturesquely above the reed-lined shore, **Laugharne Castle** (cadw.gov.wales) is a hefty 13th-century fortress, converted into a mansion in the 16th century.

Swansea may have been Dylan Thomas' birthplace, but Laugharne is where he lived out his final years, getting inspiration for his classic play for voices *Under Milk Wood*. Many fans make the pilgrimage here to visit the **boathouse** (dylanthomasboathouse.com) where he lived, the shed where he wrote and his final resting place in the graveyard of St Martin's Church. Also worth a visit is cosy **Brown's Hotel**, one of his favourite watering holes. Then there is the **Dylan Thomas Birthday Walk** (laugharnetownship-wcc.gov.uk), taking you on a trail around the town and nearby estuary to spots associated with the poet.

Laugharne is situated 4 miles off the highway: allocate a few hours to explore it properly. Although you can continue southwest from here on narrow roads, you're better off backtracking to the A477 to get to Tenby.

THE DRIVE

Twenty miles of verdant farmland separate Laugharne from Tenby via the A477 and then, once you hit Kilgetty, the A478.

07 TENBY

Sandy, family-friendly beaches spread out in either direction from this pretty pastel-hued resort town tumbling over the headland above. Pembrokeshire's (if not Wales') premier seaside resort it is, but Tenby's eclectic blend of architecture and steep twisty streets, still part-wrapped by Norman walls, almost evoking Greek island towns at times, impress most.

Tenby

KEVIN EAVES/SHUTTERSTOCK ©

The beaches are the major attraction here, plus the variety of eateries stashed away amid the sinuous cobbled streets. The other big draws – the sea-bashed crag of **St Catherine's Island** (saintcatherinesisland.co.uk) topped by its bombastic fort, along with the **Tenby Boat Trips** (tenbyboattrips.co.uk) out to **Caldey Island**, home to seals, seabirds, beaches and a community of Cistercian monks – are lovely additional strings to Tenby's bow.

THE DRIVE

From Tenby, it's a short, sweet 10-mile hop to Pembroke. From the town centre, head west on Greenhill Rd, go under the railway bridge and turn right at the roundabout. Follow Hayward Lane (the B4318) through a patchwork of fields until you reach the Sageston roundabout. Turn left onto the A477, and then veer left on the A4075 (or plump for the equally distanced but quieter A4139 via Jameston, where enticing lanes shoot off to the likes of Manorbier and Freshwater East beaches).

08 PEMBROKE

Pembroke is dominated by hulking **Pembroke Castle** (pembroke-castle.co.uk), which looms over the end of the town's main street. The fortress is best viewed from the Mill Pond, a pretty lake which forms a moat on three sides of the headland from which the castle rises. Pembroke played a leading role in British history as the birthplace of the first Tudor king, Henry VII. The castle is in extremely good condition, with lots of well-preserved towers, dungeons and wall walks to explore.

A strip of mainly Georgian and Victorian buildings leads down

Barafundle Bay

DETOUR:

West of Pembroke

START: 8 PEMBROKE

The remote peninsula that forms the bottom lip of the long, deep-sea harbour of Milford Haven has some of the Pembrokeshire Coast's most dramatic geological features and blissful little beaches. An especially lovely area includes the golden sands of **Barafundle Bay** and **Broad Haven South**, and a network of walking tracks around **Bosherston Lily Ponds**.

The B4319 winds south from Pembroke to Bosherston. Continue past Bosherston to the coast and a short, steep path leads to the photogenic shell of **St Govan's Chapel**, wedged into a slot in the cliffs just above the pounding waves. Sadly, the coast here and just west is part of a military firing range: when red flags are flying there's no public access to some of the Pembrokeshire Coast's most arresting natural sights – neither the chapel, nor **Elegug Stacks**, nor the gigantic arch known as the **Green Bridge of Wales**.

After sidestepping the firing range, the road continues on to **Freshwater West** – a moody, wave-battered stretch of coast that has provided a brooding backdrop for movies such as *Harry Potter and the Deathly Hallows* and Ridley Scott's *Robin Hood*. It's widely held to be Wales' best surf beach, but also one of the most dangerous for swimmers.

From Pembroke, it's just over 6 miles to Barafundle Bay (heading southeast) or 8 miles to Freshwater West (heading west). For all these sights, you could easily make a day of it. Best is to take the B4319 heading south from Pembroke; Bosherston and the Elegug Stack Rocks are reached from narrow country lanes branching off it. The B4319 continues past Freshwater West and terminates at the B4320, where you can turn right to return to Pembroke.

St David's Day

St David's Day is to the Welsh what St Patrick's Day is to the Irish – a day to celebrate one's essential Welshness, albeit somewhat more soberly than Ireland does. If you're in Wales on 1 March, there's no better place to be than the saint's own city, St Davids. Around the cathedral, a host of golden daffodils flower seemingly right on cue; people pin leek, daffodil or red dragon badges to their lapels; streets are strung with flags bearing the black-and-gold St David's cross; and cawl (a traditional soupy stew) is consumed in industrial quantities. You should also visit the cathedral, where the saint's remains lie (year-round) in a recently restored shrine.

a vast sandy surf beach backed by a high bank of pebbles. From here the road more or less shadows the coast.

09 SOLVA

Clustered around a long, hook-shaped harbour, Solva is the classic Welsh fishing village straight out of central casting. Pastel-hued cottages line the gurgling stream running through its lower reaches, while Georgian town houses cling to the cliffs above. When the tide's out, the water disappears completely from the harbour, leaving the sailing fleet striking angular poses on the sand.

Lower Solva is the part of interest to travellers. Amble about antique shops and galleries, settle in somewhere cosy for a meal or walk a section of the Pembrokeshire Coast Path, which approaches its most exquisite around Solva. Our favourite eatery for its sheer novelty is **MamGu Welshcakes** (mamguwelshcakes.com), a lively cafe specialising in wacky takes on the typical Welsh sweet snack of Welsh cakes.

If you need to shed some calories afterwards, a 1-mile walk will take you upstream to the **Solva Woollen Mill** (solvawoollenmill.co.uk), the oldest working mill of its kind in Pembrokeshire.

🚗 THE DRIVE

You really can't go wrong on the 3-mile drive to St Davids. Just continue west.

10 ST DAVIDS

A city only by dint of its prestigious cathedral, pretty St Davids feels more like an oversized village. Yet this little settlement looms large in the Welsh consciousness as the hometown of its patron saint and has a very special vibe as a result.

Mesmeric **St David's Cathedral** (stdavidscathedral.org.uk) stands on the site of the saint's own 6th-century religious settlement. Wonderful stone and wooden carvings decorate the interior, and there's a treasury and historic library hidden within.

St David was born at **St Non's Bay**, a ruggedly attractive section of coast with a holy well and a cute little chapel, a short walk from the centre of town. If it's a swim or surf you covet, head to broad, beautiful **Whitesands Bay** (Porth Mawr), although there are other, quieter beaches dotted between the headlands hereabouts.

Also not to be missed are the city's distinguished cafes and restaurants, which are ever-ready to sate weary travellers' bellies.

But do not just dally in St Davids now that you have come this far west. Get out and roam the emerald-green, undulating landscape around as it bows to sandy and stony bays where you will truly feel the significance of the Welsh word *'Penfro',* which explains how Pembrokeshire gets its name. The meaning? 'Land's end.'

from the castle, including some good pubs and the excellent **Food at Williams** cafe.

🚗 THE DRIVE

The 24-mile journey to Solva heads through the port town of Pembroke Dock, crosses the Daugleddau estuary and then traverses Pembrokeshire's nondescript county town Haverfordwest. Exit Haverfordwest on the A487, trundling through farmland before reaching the coast at Newgale,

St David's Cathedral

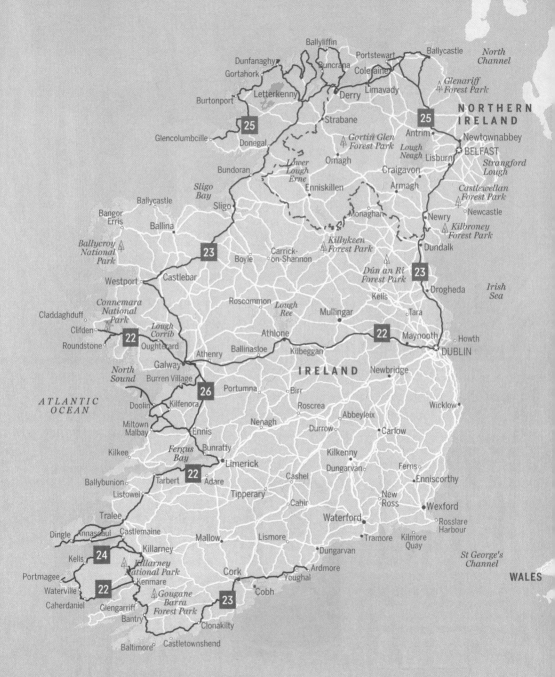

Gap of Dunloe (p191)

Ireland

Explore

Ireland

Captivating Atlantic seascapes, vertiginous cliffs, windswept wilds and undulating emerald-green hills – a trip to Ireland means all this and so much more. There's history and culture in its cool, cosmopolitan cities, stirring scenery to admire, and fun to be had in its much-imitated but never-bettered pubs.

Distances are not huge and with your own wheels (and designated driver) you'll be able to take in much of what the island – divided into the Republic of Ireland and smaller Northern Ireland (part of the UK) – has to offer. So whether you want to drive through the wildest terrain or sample great food while hopping between spa treatments, we've got you covered.

Dublin

Ireland's capital and showcase city, Dublin is the first stop on many travellers' Irish itinerary. Located on the east coast, it's served by the country's largest airport and regular ferries from the UK and France. And with a ready supply of museums, galleries, monuments and sights, as well as a wide choice of accommodation, restaurants, pubs and clubs, it's a fabulous destination in its own right. A few days will give you time to enjoy a Guinness or two and take in top sights such as Trinity College and the extraordinary Book of Kells.

As a base, Dublin is well placed and well connected: to the north, Belfast is just under two hours' drive along the M1 and A1; to the west, Galway is over on the Atlantic coast, two and a half hours away via the M6 motorway.

Belfast

For a base in Northern Ireland, Belfast is the obvious choice. The country's capital and main east coast port has two airports and a port operating direct ferries to/from Liverpool (England) and Cairnryan (Scotland). For onward travel, the M2 leads north from the city to connect with the A26, which runs up to Ballycastle, the second stop on our The North in a Nutshell trip.

The city has had a troubled past but in recent years it has pulled off a remarkable transformation, polishing off its historic and cultural sights and emerging as a vibrant city packed with

WHEN TO GO

You'll catch the best weather between June and mid-September. This is high season, and tourist hot spots and the coasts are busy. Crowds – and prices – drop off in late September when it's often still warm. May is another good month, though the weather can be variable. Winter brings the cold and wet, as well as reduced hours in coastal areas.

hotels, cool restaurants and brimming pubs. For a taster, take a day or two to visit star attractions, such as the multi-media Titanic Belfast museum and the impressive City Hall.

Cork

Many trips to southern Ireland pass through Cork, the country's second-largest city. An energetic, cosmopolitan place full of charming streets and exciting restaurants, it's centred on a compact island in the River Lee. Here you can wander grand Georgian avenues and cramped 17th-century alleyways, stopping for artisanal coffees in hip cafes and taking in trad music jams in snug pubs.

To reach the city, you can fly directly to its airport, one of Ireland's busiest, or take a bus or train from within Ireland.

TRANSPORT

Ireland has several airports: Belfast (Northern Ireland), Cork, Shannon (about 25km west of Limerick) and Dublin. The latter is Ireland's main international gateway with direct flights to/from the UK, Europe and North America. For a more sedate passage, ferries sail to Belfast, Cork, Dublin, Larne and Rosslare from ports in England, Scotland, Wales and France.

And when the time comes to move on, you can hire a car and join The Long Way Round tour.

 WHAT'S ON

St Patrick's Day

(17 March; stpatricksday.ie) Ireland erupts into one giant party as St Patrick is celebrated across the country.

Galway International Arts Festival

(July; giaf.ie) Ireland's most important arts festival takes over Galway in the last two weeks of July.

Féile An Phobail

(early August; feilebelfast.com) Irelands' largest community arts festival hosts events in and around west Belfast.

Resources

Entertainment Ireland *(entertainment.ie)* Countrywide listings for every kind of entertainment.

Discover Ireland *(discover ireland.ie)* Official tourist website for the Republic – practical info, holiday ideas, up-to-date listings and a huge accommodation database.

Discover Northern Ireland *(discovernorthernireland. com)* Official tourist-board site covering things to do, places to go, activities and trip planning.

 WHERE TO STAY

From hotels and hostels to B&Bs, self-catering cottages and beachside campsites, you'll find every kind of accommodation in Ireland. Advance bookings are recommended and absolutely necessary in the peak holiday months of July and August. B&Bs are ubiquitous and while standards vary, the best offer a homey alternative to hotels. They come in all shapes and sizes, from elegant townhouses to traditional thatched farmhouses. Cottages are also available to rent as self-catering accommodation, often on a weekly basis. For something a bit different, Ireland excels at alternative accommodation, offering nights in historic castles, lighthouses and even stone towers.

22

Iconic Ireland

BEST TWO DAYS

☑

The Connemara peninsula and the Ring of Kerry.

DURATION	DISTANCE	GREAT FOR
7 days	959km / 596 miles	Food and drink, history, outdoors

BEST TIME TO GO	April to September for the long days and best weather.

Old Library, Trinity College, Dublin

Every time-worn truth about Ireland will be found on this trip: the breathtaking scenery of stone-walled fields and wave-dashed cliffs; the picture-postcard villages and bustling towns; the ancient ruins that have stood since before history was written. The trip begins in Ireland's storied, fascinating capital and transports you to the wild west of Galway and Connemara before taking you south to the even wilder folds of County Kerry.

Link your trip

23 The Long Way Round

For comprehensive coverage of the best of the south and north, combine these two trips making a loop from Galway.

26 Musical Landscapes

Take a detour from Galway through County Clare's hottest trad music spots, picking up the trail again in Lisdoonvarna.

01 **DUBLIN**

World-class museums, superb restaurants and the best collection of entertainment in the country – there are plenty of good reasons why the capital is the ideal place to start your trip. Get some sightseeing in on a walking tour before 'exploring' at least one of the city's storied – if not historic – pubs.

Your top stop should be the grounds of **Trinity College** (tcd.ie), home to the gloriously illuminated **Book of Kells**. It's kept in the stunning 65m Long Room of the **Old Library**.

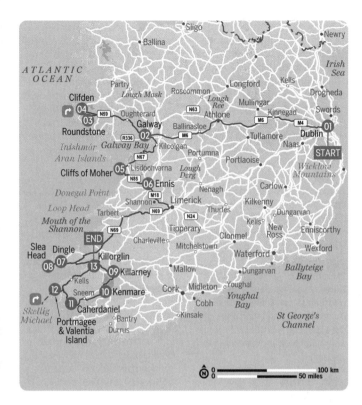

WHY I LOVE THIS TRIP

Fionn Davenport, writer

The loop from Dublin west to Galway and then south through Kerry into Cork explores all of Ireland's scenic heavy hitters. It's the kind of trip I'd make if I was introducing visiting friends to Ireland at its very best, a taster trip that would entice them to come back and explore the country in greater depth.

THE DRIVE

It's a 208km trip to Galway city across the country along the M6 motorway, which has little in terms of visual highlights beyond green fields, which get greener and a little more wild the further west you go. Twenty-two kilometres south of Athlone (about halfway) is a worthwhile detour to Clonmacnoise.

02 GALWAY CITY

The best way to appreciate Galway is to amble – around Eyre Sq and down Shop St towards the Spanish Arch and the River Corrib, stopping off for a little liquid sustenance in one of the city's classic old pubs. Top

of our list is **Tig Cóilí** (facebook. com/tig.choili), a fire-engine-red pub that draws them in with its two live *céilidh* (traditional music and dancing sessions) each day. A close second is **Tigh Neachtain** (tighneachtain.com), known simply as Neachtain's (*nock*-tans) or Naughtons – stop and join the locals for a pint.

THE DRIVE

The most direct route to Roundstone is to cut through Connemara along the N59, turning left on the Clifden Rd – a total of 76km. Alternatively, the 103km coastal route, via the R336 and R340, winds its way around small bays, coves and lovely seaside hamlets.

03 ROUNDSTONE

Huddled on a boat-filled harbour, Roundstone (Cloch na Rón) is one of Connemara's gems. Colourful terrace houses and inviting pubs overlook the dark recess of Bertraghboy Bay, which is home to lobster trawlers and traditional *currachs* (rowing boats) with tarred canvas bottoms stretched over wicker frames.

Just south of the village, in the remains of an old Franciscan monastery, is Malachy Kearns' **Roundstone Musical Instruments** (bodhran.com). Kearns is Ireland's only full-time maker of traditional bodhráns (hand-held goatskin drums). Watch him work and buy a tin whistle, harp or booklet filled with Irish ballads; there's also a small free folk museum and a cafe.

THE DRIVE

The 22km inland route from Roundstone to Clifden is a little longer, but the road is better (especially the N59) and the brown, barren beauty of Connemara is yours to behold. The 18km coastal route along the R341 brings you through more speckled landscape; to the south you'll have glimpses of the ocean.

04 CLIFDEN

Connemara's 'capital', Clifden (An Clochán) is an appealing Victorian-era country town with an amoeba-shaped oval of streets offering evocative strolls. It presides over the head of the narrow bay where the River Owenglin tumbles into the sea. The surrounding countryside beckons you to walk through woods and above the shoreline.

THE DRIVE
It's 154km to the Cliffs of Moher; you'll have to backtrack through Galway city (take the N59) before turning south along the N67. This will take you through the unique striated landscape of the Burren, a moody, rocky and at times fearsome space accented with ancient burial chambers and medieval ruins.

DETOUR
The Sky Road
Start: 4 Clifden

From the N59 heading north out of Clifden, signs point towards the Sky Road, a 12km route tracing a spectacular loop out to the township of Kingston and back to Clifden, taking in some rugged, stunningly beautiful coastal scenery en route. It's a cinch to drive, but you can also easily walk or cycle it.

05 CLIFFS OF MOHER

Star of a million tourist brochures, the Cliffs of Moher (Aillte an Mothair, or Ailltreacha Mothair) are one of the most popular sights in Ireland.

The entirely vertical cliffs rise to a height of 214m, their edge falling away abruptly into the constantly churning sea. A series

of heads, the dark limestone seems to march in a rigid formation that amazes, no matter how many times you look.

Such appeal comes at a price: crowds. This is check-off tourism big time and bus loads come and go constantly in summer. A vast **visitor centre** (cliffsofmoher.ie) handles the hordes.

Like so many overpopular natural wonders, there's relief and joy if you're willing to walk for 10 minutes. Past the end of the 'Moher Wall', a 5km trail leads south along the cliffs to **Hag's Head** – few venture this far.

THE DRIVE
The 39km drive to Ennis goes inland at Lahinch (famous for its world-class golf links); it's then 24km to your destination, through flat south Clare. Dotted with stone walls and fields, it's the classic Irish landscape.

06 ENNIS

As the capital of a renowned music county, Ennis (Inis) is filled with pubs featuring trad music. In fact, this is the best reason to stay here. Where's best changes often; stroll the streets pub-hopping to find what's on any given night.

If you want to buy an authentic (and well-made) Irish instrument, pop into **Custy's Music Shop** (custysmusic.com), which sells fiddles and other musical items, as well as giving general info about the local scene.

THE DRIVE

It's 186km to Dingle if you go via Limerick city, but only 142km if you go via the N68 to Killimer for the ferry across the Shannon estuary to Tarbert. The views are fabulous beyond Tralee, especially if you take the 456m Connor Pass, Ireland's highest.

07 DINGLE TOWN

In summer, Dingle's hilly streets can be clogged with visitors, there's no way around it; in other seasons, its authentic charms are yours to savour. Many pubs double as shops, so you can enjoy Guinness and a singalong among screws and nails, wellies and horseshoes.

ENNIS' BEST TRAD SESSION PUBS

Cíaran's Bar
Slip into this small place by day and you can be just another geezer pondering a pint. At night there's usually trad music. Bet you wish you had a copy of the Guinness mural out front!

Brogan's
On the corner of Cooke's Lane, Brogan's (brogansbarandrestaurant.com) sees a fine bunch of musicians rattling even the stone floors from about 9pm Monday to Thursday, plus even more nights in summer.

Cruises Pub
There are trad-music sessions most nights at Cruises (queenshotel ennis.com) from 9.30pm.

Poet's Corner Bar
This old pub (oldgroundhotelennis.com/poets-corner-bar.html) often has massive trad sessions on Fridays.

THE DRIVE

It's only 17km to Slea Head along the R559. The views – of the mountains to the north and the wild ocean to the south and west – are a big chunk of the reason you came to Ireland in the first place.

08 SLEA HEAD

Overlooking the mouth of Dingle Bay, Mt Eagle and the Blasket Islands, Slea Head has fine beaches, good walks and superbly preserved structures from Dingle's ancient past, including beehive huts, forts, inscribed stones and church sites. Dunmore Head is the westernmost point on the Irish mainland and the site of the wreckage in 1588 of two Spanish Armada ships.

The Iron Age **Dunbeg Fort** is a dramatic example of a promontory fortification, perched atop a sheer sea cliff about 7km southwest of Ventry on the road to Slea Head. The fort has four outer walls of stone. Inside are the remains of a house and a beehive hut, as well as an underground passage.

THE DRIVE

The 88km to Killarney will take you through Annascaul (home to a pub once owned by Antarctic explorer Tom Crean) and Inch (whose beach is seen in Ryan's Daughter). At Castlemaine, turn south towards Miltown, then take the R563 to Killarney.

09 KILLARNEY

Beyond its proximity to lakes, waterfalls, woodland and moors dwarfed by 1000m-plus peaks, Killarney has many charms of its own as well as being the gateway to the Ring of Kerry, perhaps the outstanding highlight of many a visit to Ireland.

Photo Opportunity

The Lakes of Killarney from Ladies' View on the Ring of Kerry.

Besides the breathtaking views of the mountains and glacial lakes, highlights of the 102-sq-km **Killarney National Park** include Ireland's only wild herd of native red deer, the country's largest area of ancient oak woods and 19th-century **Muckross House**.

THE DRIVE

It's 27km along the narrow and winding N71 to Kenmare, much of it through magnificent scenery, especially at Ladies' View (much loved by Queen Victoria's ladies-in-waiting) and, 5km further on, Moll's Gap, a popular stop for photos and food.

10 KENMARE

Picturesque Kenmare carries its romantic reputation more stylishly than does Killarney, and there is an elegance about its handsome central square and attractive buildings. It still gets very busy in summer, all the same. The town stands where the delightfully named Finnihy, Roughty and Sheen Rivers empty into Kenmare River. Kenmare makes a pleasant alternative to Killarney as a base for visiting the Ring of Kerry and the Beara Peninsula.

THE DRIVE

The 47km to Caherdaniel along the southern stretch of the Ring of Kerry duck in and out of view of Kenmare River, with the marvellous Beara Peninsula to the south. Just before

you reach Caherdaniel, a 4km detour north takes you to the rarely visited Staigue Fort, which dates from the 3rd or 4th century.

11 CAHERDANIEL

The big attraction here is **Derrynane National Historic Park** (derrynanehouse. ie), the family home of Daniel O'Connell, the campaigner for Catholic emancipation. His ancestors bought the house and surrounding parkland, having grown rich on smuggling with France and Spain. It's largely furnished with O'Connell memorabilia, including the restored triumphal chariot in which he lapped Dublin after his release from prison in 1844.

THE DRIVE

Follow the N70 for about 18km and then turn left onto the Skellig Ring (roads R567 and R566), cutting through some of the wildest and most beautiful scenery on the peninsula, with the ragged outline of Skellig Michael never far from view. The whole drive is 35km long.

12 PORTMAGEE & VALENTIA ISLAND

Portmagee's single street is a rainbow of colourful houses, and is much photographed. On summer mornings, the small pier comes to life with boats embarking on the choppy crossing to the Skellig Islands.

A bridge links Portmagee to 11km-long Valentia Island (Oileán Dairbhre), an altogether homier isle than the brooding Skelligs to the southwest. Like the Skellig Ring it leads to, Valentia is an essential, coach-free detour from the Ring of Kerry. Some lonely ruins are worth exploring.

Valentia was chosen as the site for the first transatlantic telegraph cable. When the connection was made in 1858, it put Caherciveen in direct contact with New York. The link worked for 27 days before failing, but went back into action years later.

The island makes an ideal driving loop. From April to October, there's a frequent, quick ferry trip at one end, as well as the bridge to Portmagee on the mainland at the other end.

THE DRIVE

The 55km between Portmagee and Killorglin keep the mountains to your right (south) and the sea – when you're near it – to your left (north). Twenty-four kilometres along is the unusual Glenbeigh Strand, a tendril of sand protruding into Dingle Bay with views of Inch Point and the Dingle Peninsula.

13 KILLORGLIN

Killorglin (Cill Orglan) is a quiet enough town, but that all changes in mid-August, when it erupts in celebration for **Puck Fair**, Ireland's best-known extant pagan festival. First recorded in 1603, with hazy origins, this lively (read: boozy) festival is based around the custom of installing a billy goat (a poc, or puck), the symbol of mountainous Kerry, on a pedestal in the town, its horns festooned with ribbons. Other entertainment ranges from a horse fair and bonny baby competition to street theatre, concerts and fireworks; the pubs stay open until 3am.

Author Blake Morrison documents his mother's childhood here in *Things My Mother Never Told Me* (2002).

Skellig Michael

DETOUR:
Skellig Michael

START: 12 PORTMAGEE & VALENTIA ISLAND

The jagged, 217m-high rock of **Skellig Michael** (heritageireland.ie) – Archangel Michael's Rock – is the larger of the two Skellig Islands and a Unesco World Heritage Site. Early Christian monks survived here from the 6th until the 12th or 13th century; their determined quest for ultimate solitude led them to this remote, wind-blown edge of Europe.

Skellig Michael featured as Luke Skywalker's secret retreat in the Star Wars movies *The Force Awakens* (2015) and *The Last Jedi* (2017), attracting a whole new audience to the island's dramatic beauty.

It's a tough place to get to, and requires care to visit, but it's worth every effort. The 12km sea crossing can be rough, and there are no toilets or shelter, so bring something to eat and drink, and wear stout shoes and weatherproof clothing. Due to the steep (and often slippery) terrain and sudden wind gusts, it's unsuitable for young children or people with limited mobility.

Note that the island's fragility requires limits on the number of daily visitors. The 15 boats are licensed to carry no more than 12 passengers each, for a maximum of 180 people at any one time. It's wise to book ahead in July and August, bearing in mind that if the weather is bad, the boats may not sail (about two days out of seven). Trips usually run from Easter until September, depending, again, on weather.

Boats (about €100 per person) leave Portmagee, Ballinskelligs and Derrynane at around 10am, returning at 3pm. Boat owners generally restrict you to two hours on the island, which is the bare minimum to see the monastery, look at the birds and have a picnic. The crossing takes about 1½ hours from Portmagee, 35 minutes to one hour from Ballinskelligs and 1¾ hours from Derrynane.

23

The Long Way Round

DURATION	DISTANCE	GREAT FOR
14 days	1300km / 807 miles	Food and drink, history, outdoors

BEST TIME TO GO	June and August have the best weather (and the crowds); September is ideal.

There's a strong case to be made that the very best Ireland has to offer is closest to its jagged, dramatic coastlines: the splendid scenery, the best mountain ranges (geographically, Ireland is akin to a bowl, with raised edges) and most of its major towns and cities – Dublin, Belfast, Galway, Sligo and Cork. The western edge – between Donegal and Cork – corresponds to the Wild Atlantic Way driving route.

Link your trip

22 Iconic Ireland

For comprehensive coverage of the best of north and south, combine these two trips making a loop from Galway.

26 Musical Landscapes

Take a detour from Galway through County Clare's hottest trad music spots, picking up the trail again in Ennis.

01 DUBLIN

From its music, art and literature to the legendary nightlife that has inspired those same musicians, artists and writers, Dublin has always known how to have fun, and it does it with deadly seriousness.

Should you tire of the city's more highbrow offerings, the **Guinness Storehouse** (guinness-store house.com) is the most popular place to visit in town. It's a beer-lover's Disneyland and multimedia bells-and-whistles homage to the country's most famous export and the city's most enduring symbol. The old

BEST FOR HISTORY

Delve into the maritime past in Belfast's Titanic Quarter.

Guinness Storehouse, Dublin

grain storehouse is a suitable cathedral in which to worship the black gold; shaped like a giant pint of Guinness, it rises seven impressive storeys high around a stunning central atrium.

THE DRIVE

It's 165km of dual carriageway to Belfast – M1 in the Republic, A1 in Northern Ireland – but remember that the speed limit changes from kilometres to miles as you cross into the North.

02 BELFAST

Belfast is in many ways a brand-new city. Once lumped with Beirut, Baghdad and Bosnia as one of the four 'Bs' for travellers to avoid, it has pulled off a remarkable transformation from bombs-and-bullets pariah to a hip-hotels-and-hedonism party town.

The old shipyards on the Lagan continue to give way to the luxury apartments of the Titanic Quarter, whose centrepiece, the stunning, star-shaped edifice housing the **Titanic Belfast centre** (titanicbelfast.com), covering the ill-fated liner's construction here, has become the city's number-one tourist draw.

New venues keep popping up – historic **Crumlin Road Gaol** (crumlinroadgaol.com) and **SS Nomadic** are now open to the public, and WWI warship **HMS Caroline** is a floating museum. They all add to a list of attractions that includes beautifully restored Victorian architecture, a glittering waterfront lined with modern art, a fantastic foodie scene and music-filled pubs.

THE DRIVE

The fastest way to the causeway is to take the A26 north, through Ballymena, before turning off at Ballymoney – a total of 100km – but the longer (by 16km), more scenic route is to take the A8 to Larne and follow the coast through handsome Cushendall and popular Ballycastle.

03 GIANT'S CAUSEWAY

When you first see it you'll understand why the ancients believed the causeway was not a natural feature. The vast expanse of regular, closely packed, hexagonal stone columns dipping gently beneath the waves looks for all the world like the handiwork of giants.

This spectacular rock formation – a national nature reserve and Northern Ireland's only Unesco World Heritage Site – is one of Ireland's most impressive and atmospheric landscape features, but it can get very crowded. If you can, try to visit midweek or out of season to experience it at its most evocative. Sunset in spring and autumn is the best time for photographs.

Visiting the Giant's Causeway itself is free of charge, but you pay to use the car park on a combined ticket with the **Giant's Causeway Visitor Experience** (nationaltrust.org.uk); parking-only tickets aren't available.

THE DRIVE
Follow the A29 and A37 as far as Derry, then cross the invisible border into the Republic and take the N13 to Letterkenny before turning northwest along the N56 to Dunfanaghy. It's a total of 136km.

04 DUNFANAGHY
Huddled around the waterfront beneath the headland of Horn Head, Dunfanaghy's small, attractive town centre has a surprisingly wide range of accommodation and some of the finest dining options in the county's northwest. Glistening beaches, dramatic coastal cliffs, mountain trails and forests are all within a few kilometres.

THE DRIVE
The 145km south to Sligo town will take you back through Letterkenny (this stretch is the most scenic), after

Photo Opportunity
Wave-hewn steps of the Giant's Causeway.

which you'll follow the N13 as far as Ballyshannon and then, as you cross into County Sligo, the N15 to Sligo town.

DETOUR
Horn Head
Start: **Dunfanaghy**

Horn Head has some of Donegal's most spectacular coastal scenery and plenty of birdlife. Its dramatic quartzite cliffs, covered with bog and heather, rear over 180m high, and the view from their tops is heart-pounding.

The road circles the headland; the best approach by car is in a clockwise direction from the Falcarragh end of Dunfanaghy. On a fine day, you'll encounter tremendous views of Tory, Inishbofin, Inishdooey and tiny Inishbeg islands to the west; Sheep Haven Bay and the Rosguill Peninsula to the east; Malin Head to the northeast; and the coast of Scotland beyond. Take care in bad weather as the route can be perilous.

05 SLIGO TOWN
Sligo is in no hurry to shed its cultural traditions but it doesn't sell them out either. Pedestrian streets lined with inviting shopfronts, stone bridges spanning the River Garavogue and *céilidh* sessions spilling from pubs contrast with genre-bending contemporary art and glass towers rising from prominent corners of the compact town.

THE DRIVE
It's 100km to Westport, as you follow the N17 (and the N5 once you leave Charlestown); the landscape is flat, the road flanked by fields, hedge

---

DETOUR:
Giant's Causeway to Ballycastle

START: 3 GIANT'S CAUSEWAY

Between the Giant's Causeway and Ballycastle lies the most scenic stretch of the Causeway Coast, with sea cliffs of contrasting black basalt and white chalk, rocky islands, picturesque little harbours and broad sweeps of sandy beach. It's best enjoyed on foot, following the 16.5km of waymarked **Causeway Coast Way** (walkni.com) between the Carrick-a-Rede car park and the Giant's Causeway, although the main attractions can also be reached by car or bus.

About 8km east of the Giant's Causeway is the meagre ruin of 16th-century **Dunseverick Castle**, spectacularly sited on a grassy bluff. Another 1.5km on is the tiny seaside hamlet of **Portbradden**, with half a dozen harbourside houses. Visible from Portbradden and accessible via the next junction off the A2 is the spectacular **White Park Bay**, with its wide, sweeping sandy beach.

The main attraction on this stretch of coast is the famous – or notorious, depending on your head for heights – **Carrick-a-Rede Rope Bridge.** The 20m-long, 1m-wide bridge of wire rope spans the chasm between the sea cliffs and the little island of Carrick-a-Rede, swaying gently 30m above the rock-strewn water.

rows and clusters of farmhouses. Castlebar, 15km before Westport, is a busy county town.

06 WESTPORT

There's a lot to be said for town planning, especially if 18th-century architect James Wyatt was the brain behind the job. Westport (Cathair na Mairt), positioned on the River Carrowbeg and the shores of Clew Bay, is easily Mayo's most beautiful town and a major tourist destination for visitors to this part of the country.

It's a Georgian classic, its octagonal square and tidy streets lined with trees and handsome buildings, most of which date from the late 18th century.

THE DRIVE

Follow the N5, then the N84 as far as the outskirts of Galway city – a trip of about 100km. Take the N67

south into County Clare. Ballyvaughan provides a good base to explore the heart of the Burren.

07 THE BURREN

The karst landscape of the Burren is not the green Ireland of postcards. But there are wildflowers in spring, giving the 560-sq-km Burren brilliant, if ephemeral, colour amid its austere beauty. Soil may be scarce, but the small amount that gathers in the cracks and faults is well drained and nutrient-rich. This, together with the mild Atlantic climate, supports an extraordinary mix of Mediterranean, Arctic and alpine plants. Of Ireland's native wildflowers, 75% are found here, including 24 species of beautiful orchids, the creamy-white burnet rose, the little starry flowers of

An Ancient Fort

For a look at a well-preserved *caher* (walled fort) of the late Iron Age to early Christian period, stop at **Caherconnell Fort** (caherconnell.com), a privately run heritage attraction in the heart of the Burren that's more serious than sideshow. Exhibits detail how the evolution of these defensive settlements may have reflected territorialism and competition for land among a growing, settling population. The drystone walling of the fort is in excellent condition. The top-notch visitor centre also has information on many other monuments in the area. It's about 1km south of Poulnabrone Dolmen on the R480.

ESSEVU/SHUTTERSTOCK ©

Inishmore

mossy saxifrage and the magenta-coloured bloody cranesbill.

 THE DRIVE
It's some 40km to Doolin, heading south first via the N67, then onto the R480, which corkscrews over the lunar, limestone landscape of the Burren's exposed hills. Next, curve west onto the R476 to meander towards Doolin via more familiar Irish landscapes of green fields, and the villages of Kilfenora and Lisdoonvarna – great for pit stops and trad-music sessions.

 08 DOOLIN
Doolin is renowned as a centre of Irish traditional music, but it's also known for its setting, 6km north of the Cliffs of Moher. Down near the ever-unsettled sea, the land is wind-blown, with huge rocks exposed by the long-vanished topsoil.

Many musicians live in the area, and they have a symbiotic relationship with the tourists: each desires the other and each year things grow a little larger. But given the heavy concentration of visitors, it's inevitable that standards don't always hold up to those in some of the less-trampled villages in Clare.

 THE DRIVE
Ferries from Doolin to Inishmore take about 1½ hours to make the crossing.

 09 INISHMORE
A step (and boat or plane ride) beyond the desolate beauty of the Burren are the **Aran Islands**. Most visitors are satisfied to explore only Inishmore (Inis Mór) and its main attraction, **Dun Aengus** (Dún Aonghasa; heritageireland.ie), the stunning stone fort perched

perilously on the island's towering cliffs. Powerful swells pound the 87m-high cliff face. A complete lack of rails or other modern additions that would spoil this amazing ancient site means that you can not only go right up to the cliff's edge but also potentially fall to your doom below quite easily. When it's uncrowded, you can't help but feel the extraordinary energy that must have been harnessed to build this vast site.

The arid landscape west of **Kilronan** (Cill Rónáin), Inishmór's main settlement, is dominated by stone walls, boulders, scattered buildings and the odd patch of deep-green grass and potato plants.

 THE DRIVE
Once you're back on terra firma at Doolin, it's 223km to Dingle via the N85 to Ennis, then the M18 to Limerick city. The N69 will take you into County Kerry as far as Tralee, beyond which it's 50km on the N86 to Dingle.

 10 DINGLE
Unlike the Ring of Kerry, where the cliffs tend to dominate the ocean, it's the ocean that dominates the smaller Dingle Peninsula. The opal-blue

waters surrounding the promontory's multihued landscape of green hills and golden sands give rise to aquatic adventures and to fishing fleets that haul in fresh seafood that appears on the menus of some of the county's finest restaurants.

Centred on charming Dingle town, there's an alternative way of life here, lived by artisans and idiosyncratic characters and found at trad sessions and folkloric festivals across Dingle's tiny settlements.

The classic loop drive around Slea Head from Dingle town is 47km, but allow a day to take it all in – longer if you have time to stay overnight in Dingle town.

 THE DRIVE
Take the N86 as far as Annascaul and then the coastal R561 as far as Castlemaine. Then head southwest on the N70 to Killorglin and the Ring of Kerry. From Dingle, it's 53km.

 11 RING OF KERRY
The Ring of Kerry is the longest and the most diverse of Ireland's big circle drives, combining jaw-dropping coastal scenery with emerald pastures and villages.

The 179km circuit usually begins in Killarney and winds past pristine beaches, the island-dotted Atlantic, medieval ruins, mountains and loughs (lakes). The coastline is at its most rugged between Waterville and Caherdaniel in the southwest of the peninsula. It can get crowded in summer, but even then, the remote Skellig Ring can be uncrowded and serene – and starkly beautiful.

The Ring of Kerry can easily be done as a day trip, but if you want to stretch it out, places to stay are scattered along the route. Killorglin and Kenmare have the best dining options, with some excellent restaurants; elsewhere, basic (sometimes very basic) pub fare is the norm. The Ring's most popular diversion is the **Gap of Dunloe**, an awe-inspiring mountain pass at the western edge of Killarney National Park. It's signposted off the N72 between Killarney and Killorglin. The incredibly popular 19th-century **Kate Kearney's Cottage** is a pub where most visitors park their cars before walking up to the gap.

 KENMARE

If you've done the Ring in an anticlockwise fashion (or cut through the Gap of Dunloe), you'll end up in handsome Kenmare, a largely 18th-century town and the ideal alternative to Killarney as a place to stay overnight.

THE DRIVE
Picturesque villages, a fine stone circle and calming coastal scenery mark the less-taken 143km route from Kenmare to Cork city. When you get to Leap, turn right onto the R597 and go as far as Rosscarbery; or, even better, take twice as long (even though it's only 24km more) and make your way along narrow roads near the water the entire way.

 CORK CITY

Ireland's second city is first in every important respect, at least according to the locals, who cheerfully refer to it as the 'real capital of Ireland'. The compact city centre is surrounded by interesting waterways and is chock-full of great restaurants fed by arguably the best foodie scene in the country.

THE DRIVE
It's only 60km to Ardmore, but stop off in Midleton, 24km east of Cork along the N25, and visit the whiskey museum. Just beyond Youghal, turn right onto the R673 for Ardmore.

THE HEALY PASS

Instead of going directly into County Cork along the N71 from Kenmare, veer west onto the R571 and drive for 16km along the northern edge of the Beara Peninsula. At Lauragh, turn onto the R574 and take the breathtaking **Healy Pass Road**, which cuts through the peninsula and brings you from County Kerry into County Cork. At Adrigole, turn left onto the R572 and rejoin the N71 at Glengarriff, 17km east.

ARDMORE

Due to its location off the main drag, Ardmore is a sleepy seaside village and one of the southeast's loveliest spots – the ideal destination for those looking for a little waterside R&R.

St Declan reputedly set up shop here sometime between 350 and 420 CE, which would make Ardmore the first Christian bastion in Ireland – long before St Patrick landed. The village's 12th-century **round tower**, one of the best examples of these structures in Ireland, is the town's most distinctive architectural feature, but you should also check out the ruins of St Declan's church and holy well, 1km east on a bluff on Ardmore's signposted 5km cliff walk.

Ardmore Round Tower

24

Ring of Kerry

BEST FOR WILDLIFE

Killarney National Park, home to Ireland's only wild herd of native red deer.

DURATION	DISTANCE	GREAT FOR
4 days	202km / 125 miles	History, outdoors

BEST TIME TO GO	May and September for temperate weather free of summer crowds.

Driving the Ring of Kerry

You can drive the Ring of Kerry in a day, but the longer you spend here, the more you'll enjoy it. The circuit winds past pristine beaches, medieval ruins, mountains, loughs and the island-dotted Atlantic, with the coastline at its most rugged between Waterville and Caherdaniel in the peninsula's southwest. You'll also find plenty of opportunities for serene, starkly beautiful detours, such as the Skellig Ring and the Cromane Peninsula.

Link your trip

22 Iconic Ireland

From Killarney, pick up the trail north to complete in reverse this tour of the very best of Ireland's attractions.

26 Musical Landscapes

Drive about three hours north from Killarney to Galway to start a quest for County Clare's hottest trad music spots.

01 KILLARNEY

A town that's been in the business of welcoming visitors for more than 250 years, Killarney is a well-oiled tourism machine fuelled by the sublime scenery of its namesake national park, and competition keeps standards high. Killarney nights are lively and most pubs put on live music.

Killarney and its surrounds have likely been inhabited since the Neolithic period, but it wasn't until the 17th century that Viscount Kenmare developed the region as an Irish version of England's Lake District; among its notable 19th-century tourists were Queen Victoria and Romantic poet Percy

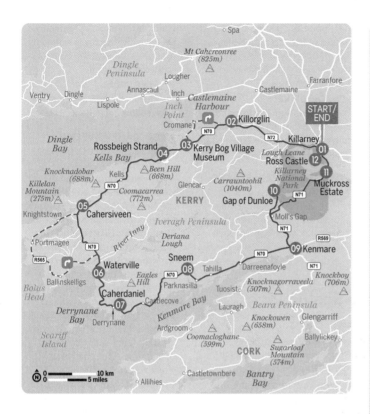

DETOUR:

Cromane Peninsula

START: ❷ KILLORGLIN

Open fields give way to spectacular water vistas and multihued sunsets on the Cromane Peninsula, with its tiny namesake village sitting at the base of a narrow shingle spit.

Cromane's exceptional eating place, **Jacks' Coastguard Restaurant** (jackscromane.com), is a local secret and justifies the trip. Entering this 1866-built coastguard station feels like arriving at a low-key village pub, but a narrow doorway at the back of the bar leads to a striking, whitewashed contemporary space with lights glittering from midnight-blue ceiling panels, stained glass and metallic fish sculptures, and huge picture windows looking out across the water. Seafood is the standout, but there's also steak, roast lamb and a veggie dish of the day.

Cromane is 9km from Killorglin. Heading southwest from Killorglin along the N70, take the second right and continue straight ahead until you get to the crossroads. Turn right; Jack's Coastguard Restaurant is on your left.

Bysshe Shelley. The town itself lacks major attractions, but the landscaped grounds of nearby Killarney House and Muckross House frame photo-worthy panoramas of lake and mountain, while former carriage drives around these aristocratic estates now serve as scenic hiking and biking trails open to all.

The town can easily be explored on foot in an hour or two, or you can get around by horse-drawn jaunting car.

🚗 THE DRIVE

From Killarney, head 22km west to Killorglin along the N72, with views south to Ireland's highest mountain range, Macgillycuddy's Reeks. The mountains' elegant forms were carved by glaciers, with summits buttressed by ridges of purplish rock. The name derives from the ancient Mac Gilla Muchudas clan; reek means 'pointed hill'. In Irish, they're known as Na Crucha Dubha (the Black Tops).

❷ KILLORGLIN

Killorglin (Cill Orglan) is quieter than the waters of the River Laune that lap against its 1885-built eight-arched bridge – except in mid-August, when there's an explosion of time-honoured ceremonies at the famous **Puck Fair** (Aonach an Phuic; puckfair. ie), a pagan festival first recorded in 1603. A statue of King Puck (a goat) peers out from the Killarney end of the bridge.

Killorglin has some of the finest eateries along the Ring – **Bianconi** (bianconi.ie) and **Jack's Bakery** are both good spots for a late breakfast or early lunch.

THE DRIVE
Killorglin sits at the junction of the N72 and the N70; continue 13km along the N70 to the Kerry Bog Village Museum.

03 KERRY BOG VILLAGE MUSEUM
Between Killorglin and Glenbeigh, the **Kerry Bog Village Museum** (kerrybog village.ie) recreates a 19th-century settlement typical of the small communities that carved out a precarious living in the harsh environment of Ireland's ubiquitous peat bogs. You'll see the thatched homes of the turf cutter, blacksmith, thatcher and labourer, as well as a dairy, and meet rare Kerry Bog ponies.

THE DRIVE
It's less than 1km from the museum to the village of Glenbeigh; turn off here and drive 2km west to unique Rossbeigh Strand.

04 ROSSBEIGH STRAND
This unusual beach is a 3km-long finger of shingle and sand protruding into Dingle Bay, with views of Inch Point and the Dingle Peninsula. On one side, the sea is ruffled by Atlantic winds; on the other, it's sheltered and calm.

THE DRIVE
Rejoin the N70 and continue 25km southwest to Cahersiveen.

05 CAHERSIVEEN
Cahersiveen's population – over 30,000 in 1841 – was decimated by the Great Famine and emigration to the New World. A sleepy outpost remains, overshadowed by the 688m peak of **Knocknadobar**. It looks rather dour compared with the peninsula's other settlements, but the atmospheric remains of 16th-century **Ballycarbery Castle**, 2.4km along the road to White Strand Beach from the town centre, are worth a look.

Along the same road are two stone ring forts. The larger, **Cahergall**, dates from the 10th century and has stairways on the inside walls, a *clochán* (circular stone building shaped like an old-fashioned beehive) and the remains of a house. The smaller, 9th-century **Leacanabuile** has an entrance to an underground passage. Their inner walls and chambers give a strong sense of what life was like in a ring fort. Leave your car in the parking area next to a stone wall and walk up the footpaths.

THE DRIVE
From Cahersiveen you can continue 17km along the classic Ring of Kerry on the N70 to Waterville, or take the ultrascenic route via Valentia Island and the Skellig Ring, and rejoin the N70 at Waterville.

DETOUR:
Valentia Island & the Skellig Ring

START: 5 CAHERSIVEEN

Crowned by Geokaun Mountain, 11km-long Valentia Island (Oileán Dairbhre) makes an ideal driving loop, with some lonely ruins that are worth exploring. Knightstown, the only town, has pubs, food and walks.

The **Skellig Experience** (skelligexperience.com) heritage centre, in a distinctive building with turf-covered barrel roofs, has informative exhibits on the Skellig Islands offshore. From April to October, it also runs two-hour cruises around the Skelligs.

If you're here between April and October, and you're detouring via Valentia Island and the Skellig Ring, a ferry service from Reenard Point, 5km southwest of Cahersiveen, provides a handy shortcut to Valentia Island. The five-minute crossing departs every 10 minutes. Alternatively, there's a bridge between Portmagee and the far end of the island.

Immediately across the bridge on the mainland, the single street of **Portmagee** is a rainbow of colourful houses. On summer mornings the small pier comes to life, with boats embarking on the choppy crossing to the Skellig Islands.

Portmagee holds **set-dancing workshops** (www.moorings.ie) over the May bank holiday weekend, with plenty of stomping practice sessions in the town's **Bridge Bar** (moorings.ie), a friendly local gathering point that's also good for impromptu music year-round and more formal sessions in summer.

The wild and beautiful 18km-long Skellig Ring road links Portmagee and Waterville via a Gaeltacht (Irish-speaking) area centred on Ballinskelligs (Baile an Sceilg), with the ragged outline of Skellig Michael never far from view.

Ballycarbery Castle

06 WATERVILLE

A line of colourful houses on the N70 between Lough Currane and Ballinskelligs Bay, Waterville is charm-challenged in the way of many mass-consumption beach resorts. A statue of its most famous guest, Charlie Chaplin, beams from the seafront. The **Charlie Chaplin Comedy Film Festival** (chaplin filmfestival.com) is held in August.

Waterville is home to a famous **links golf course**. At the north end of Lough Currane, **Church Island** has the ruins of a medieval church and beehive cell reputedly founded as a monastic settlement by St Finian in the 6th century.

THE DRIVE
Squiggle your way for 14km along the Ring's most tortuous stretch, past cliffs, craggy hills and stunning views, to Caherdaniel.

07 CAHERDANIEL

The scattered hamlet of Caherdaniel counts two of the Ring of Kerry's highlights: Derrynane National Historic Park, the childhood home of the 19th-century hero of Catholic emancipation, Daniel O'Connell; and what is plausibly claimed as 'Ireland's finest view' over rugged cliffs and islands, as you crest the hill at Beenarourke (there's a large car park here).

Most activity here centres on the Blue Flag beach. **Derrynane Sea Sports** (derrynaneseasports. com) organises sailing, canoeing, surfing, windsurfing and water-skiing (from €40 per person), as well as equipment hire (around €20 per hour).

THE DRIVE
Wind your way east along the N70 for 21km to Sneem.

08 SNEEM

Sneem's Irish name, An tSnaidhm, translates as 'the knot', which is thought to re-fer to the River Sneem that twists and turns, knot-like, into nearby Kenmare Bay. Take a gander at the town's two cute squares, then pop into the **Blue Bull**, a perfect little old stone pub, for a pint.

THE DRIVE
Along the 27km drive to Kenmare, the N70 drifts away from the water to take in views towards the Kerry mountains.

09 KENMARE

The copper-covered limestone spire of **Holy Cross Church**, drawing the eye to the wooded hills above town, may make you forget for a split second that Kenmare is a seaside town. With rivers named Finnihy,

LENA STEINMEIER/SHUTTERSTOCK ©

Kenmare Stone Circle

Roughty and Sheen emptying into Kenmare Bay, you couldn't be anywhere other than southwest Ireland.

In the 18th century, Kenmare was laid out on an X-shaped plan, with a triangular market square in the centre. Today the inverted V to the south is the focus. Kenmare River (actually an inlet of the sea) stretches out to the southwest, and there are glorious mountain views.

Signposted southwest of the square is an early Bronze Age **stone circle**, one of the biggest in southwest Ireland. Fifteen stones ring a boulder dolmen, a burial monument rarely found outside this part of the country.

🚗 THE DRIVE

The coastal scenery might be finished but, if anything, the next 23km are even more stunning as you head north from Kenmare to the Gap of Dunloe. The narrow, vista-crazy N71 winds between crag and lake, with plenty of lay-bys to stop and admire the views (and recover from the switchback bends).

10 GAP OF DUNLOE

Just west of Killarney National Park, the Gap of Dunloe is ruggedly beautiful. In the winter it's an awe-inspiring mountain pass, squeezed between Purple Mountain and Macgillycuddy's Reeks.

In high summer it's a magnet for the tourist trade, with buses ferrying countless visitors here for horse-and-trap rides through the Gap.

On the southern side, surrounded by lush, green pastures, is **Lord Brandon's Cottage**, accessed by turning left at Moll's Gap on the R568, then taking the first right, another right at

Red deer, Killarney National Park

KILLARNEY NATIONAL PARK

Designated a Unesco Biosphere Reserve in 1982, **Killarney National Park** (killarneynationalpark.ie) is among the finest of Ireland's national parks. And while its proximity to one of the southwest's largest and liveliest urban centres (including pedestrian entrances right in Killarney's town centre) encourages high visitor numbers, it's an important conservation area for many rare species. Within its 102 sq km is Ireland's only wild herd of native red deer, which has lived here continuously for 12,000 years, as well as the country's largest area of ancient oak woods and views of most of its major mountains.

Glacier-gouged Lough Leane (the Lower Lake or 'Lake of Learning'), Muckross Lake and the Upper Lake make up about a quarter of the park. Their crystal waters are as rich in wildlife as the surrounding land: great crested grebes and tufted ducks cruise the lake margins, deer swim out to graze on islands, and salmon, trout and perch prosper in a pike-free environment.

With a bit of luck, you might see white-tailed sea eagles, with their 2.5m wingspan, soaring overhead. The eagles were reintroduced here in 2007 after an absence of more than 100 years. There are now more than 50 in the park and they're starting to settle in Ireland's rivers, lakes and coastal regions. And like Killarney itself, the park is also home to plenty of summer visitors, including migratory cuckoos, swallows and swifts.

Keep your eyes peeled, too, for the park's smallest residents – its insects, including the northern emerald dragonfly, which isn't normally found this far south in Europe and is believed to have been marooned here after the last ice age.

GABRIEL12/SHUTTERSTOCK ©

WHY I LOVE THIS TRIP

Neil Wilson, writer

In a land criss-crossed with classic drives, the Ring of Kerry is perhaps the most classic of all. Now a key stretch of the Wild Atlantic Way, this trip showcases Ireland's most spectacular coastal scenery, its ancient and recent history, and its traditional pubs with crackling turf fires and spontaneous, high-spirited trad music sessions. Here you'll also encounter the Emerald Isle's most engaging asset: its welcoming, warm-hearted locals.

the bottom of the hill, then right again at the crossroads (about 13km from the N71 all up).

A simple 19th-century hunting lodge, it has an open-air cafe and a dock for boats from Ross Castle near Killarney. From here a (very) narrow road weaves up the hill to the Gap – theoretically you can drive this 8km route to the 19th-century pub **Kate Kearney's Cottage** and back, but only outside summer.

Even then, walkers and cyclists have right of way and the precipitous hairpin bends are nerve-testing. It's worth walking or taking a jaunting car (or, if you're carrying two wheels, cycling) through the Gap: the scenery is a fantasy of rocky bridges over clear mountain streams and lakes. Alternatively, there are various options for exploring the Gap from Killarney.

 THE DRIVE
Continue on the N71 north through Killarney National Park to Muckross Estate (32km).

11 MUCKROSS ESTATE

The core of Killarney National Park is Muckross Estate, donated to the state by Arthur Bourn Vincent in 1932. **Muckross House** (muckross-house.ie) is a 19th-century mansion, restored to its former glory and packed with period fittings. Entrance is by guided tour.

The beautiful **gardens** slope down, and a building behind the house contains a restaurant, craft shop and studios where you can see potters, weavers and bookbinders at work.

Jaunting cars wait to run you through deer parks and woodland to **Torc Waterfall** and **Muckross Abbey** (about €20 each, return; haggling can reap discounts). The visitor centre has an excellent cafe.

Adjacent to Muckross House are the **Muckross Traditional Farms**. These reproductions of 1930s Kerry farms, complete with chickens, pigs, cattle and horses, recreate farming and living conditions when people had to live off the land.

 THE DRIVE
Continuing a further 2km north through the national park brings you to historic Ross Castle.

12 ROSS CASTLE

Restored **Ross Castle** (heritageireland.ie) dates back to the 15th century, when it was a residence of the O'Donoghues. It was the last place in Munster to succumb to Cromwell's forces, thanks partly to its cunning spiral staircase, every step of which is a different height in order to break an attacker's stride. Access is by guided tour only.

TOP TIP:
Around & Across the Ring

Tour buses travel anticlockwise around the Ring, and authorities generally encourage visitors to drive in the same direction to avoid traffic congestion and accidents. If you travel clockwise, watch out on blind corners, especially on the section between Moll's Gap and Killarney. There's little traffic on the Ballaghbeama Gap, which cuts across the peninsula's central highlands, with some spectacular views.

You can take a motorboat trip (around €10 per person) from Ross Castle to **Inisfallen**, the largest of Killarney National Park's 26 islands. The first monastery on Inisfallen is said to have been founded by St Finian the Leper in the 7th century. The island's fame dates from the early 13th century when the Annals of Inisfallen were written here. Now in the Bodleian Library at Oxford, they remain a vital source of information on early Munster history. Inisfallen shelters the ruins of a 12th-century oratory with a carved Romanesque doorway and a monastery on the site of St Finian's original.

 THE DRIVE
It's just 3km north from Ross Castle back to Killarney.

Ross Castle

25

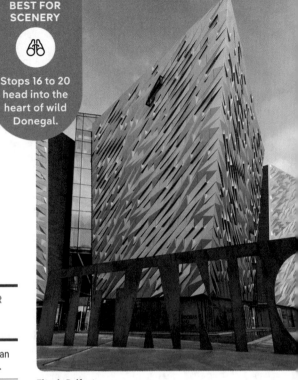

The North in a Nutshell

DURATION	DISTANCE	GREAT FOR
10 days	470km / 292 miles	History, outdoors

BEST TIME TO GO	March to June and September mean good weather but fewer crowds.

Titanic Belfast

On this road-trip-to-remember, you'll drive routes that cling to cliffs, cross borders and head high onto mountain passes. You'll witness Ireland's turbulent past and its inspiring path to peace. And you'll also explore rich faith, folk and music traditions, ride a horse across a sandy beach, cross a swaying rope bridge and spend a night on a castaway island. Not bad for a 10-day drive.

Link your trip

22 Iconic Ireland

Trip down to Dublin (four hours via the N3) to add the best of the south's attractions to your northern jaunt.

23 The Long Way Round

From Glencolumbcille head 53km west to Donegal to complete the west and south legs of this coastal tour of vibrant port cities and island treasures.

01 **BELFAST**
In bustling, big-city Belfast, the past is palpably present – walk the city's former sectarian battlegrounds for a profound way to start exploring the North's story. Next, cross the River Lagan and head to the Titanic Quarter. Dominated by the towering yellow Harland and Wolff (H&W) cranes, it's where RMS Titanic was built. **Titanic Belfast** (titanicbelfast.com) is a stunning multisensory experience: see bustling shipyards, join crowds at Titanic's launch, feel temperatures drop as it strikes that iceberg, and look through a glass floor at

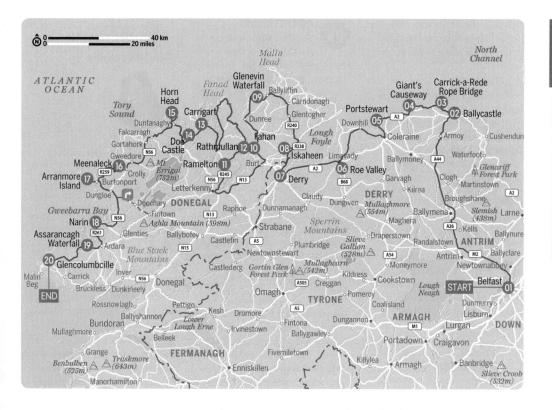

watery footage of the vessel today. Slightly to the west, don't miss the **Thompson Graving Dock** (titanicsdock.com), where you descend into the immense dry dock where the liner was fitted out.

THE DRIVE
As you drive the M3/M2 north, the now-familiar H&W cranes recede. Take the A26 through Ballymena; soon the Antrim Mountains loom large to the right. Skirt them, following the A26 and then the A44 into Ballycastle, 96km from Belfast.

02 BALLYCASTLE
Head beyond the sandy beach to the harbour at the appealing resort of Ballycastle. From here, daily **ferries**

(rathlinballycastleferry.com) depart for **Rathlin Island**, where you'll see sea stacks and thousands of guillemots, kittiwakes, razorbills and puffins.

THE DRIVE
Pick up the B15 towards Ballintoy, which meanders up to a gorse-dotted coastal plateau where hills part to reveal bursts of the sea. As the road plunges downwards, take the

Photo Opportunity

Crossing the Carrick-a-Rede Rope Bridge as it swings above the waves.

right turn to the Carrick-a-Rede Rope Bridge (10km).

03 CARRICK-A-REDE ROPE BRIDGE
The **Carrick-a-Rede Rope Bridge** (nationaltrust.org.uk/carrick-a-rede) loops across a surging sea to a tiny island 20m offshore. This walkway of planks and wire rope sways some 30m above the waves, testing your nerve and head for heights. The bridge was originally put up each year by salmon fishers to help them set their nets, and signs along the 1km clifftop hike to the bridge detail the fascinating process. Declining stocks have put an end to fishing,

however. If you want to cross the bridge, it's best to book a ticket online in advance, as numbers are limited.

THE DRIVE
The B15 and then the A2 snake west along clifftops and past views of White Park Bay's sandy expanse. Swing right onto the B146, passing Dunseverick Castle's fairy-tale tumblings, en route to the Giant's Causeway (11km).

04 GIANT'S CAUSEWAY

Stretching elegantly out from a rugged shore, the **Giant's Causeway** (nationaltrust.org.uk) is one of the world's true geological wonders. Clambering around this jetty of fused geometric rock chunks, it's hard to believe it's not human-made. Legend says Irish giant Finn McCool built the Causeway to cross the sea to fight Scottish giant Benandonner. More prosaically, scientists tell us the 60-million-year-old rocks were formed when a flow of molten basaltic lava cooled and hardened from the top and bottom inwards. It contracted and the hexagonal cracks spread as the rock solidified.

Entry to the Causeway site is free, but to use the National Trust car park you'll need to buy a ticket that includes the **Giant's Causeway Visitor Experience** (nationaltrust.org.uk).

THE DRIVE
Continue west, through Bushmills, with its famous distillery, picking up the A2 Coastal Causeway route, signed to Portrush. You'll pass wind-pruned trees, crumbling Dunluce Castle and Portrush's long sandy beaches before arriving at Portstewart (16km).

05 PORTSTEWART

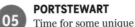

Time for some unique parking. Head through resort-town Portstewart, following signs for the **Strand** (beach). Ever-sandier roads descend to an immense shoreline that doubles as a car park for 1000 vehicles. It's a decidedly weird experience to drive and park (£7) on an apparently endless expanse of hard-packed sand. It's also at your own risk, which doesn't deter the locals (but do stick to central, compacted areas). Nearby, a 1km **walking trail** meanders up a sand ladder, through huge dunes and past marram grass and occasional orchids.

THE DRIVE
Take the A2 west, through Coleraine towards Downhill. About 1km after the Mussenden Temple's dome appears, take Bishop's Rd left up steep hills with spectacular Lough Foyle views. Descend, go through Limavady and onto the B68 (signed Dungiven). Soon a brown Country Park sign points to Roe Valley (42km).

06 ROE VALLEY

This beguiling country park is packed with rich reminders of a key Irish industry: linen production. The damp valley was ideal for growing the flax that made the cloth; the fast-flowing water powered the machinery. The **Green Lane Museum**, near the car park, features sowing fiddles, flax breakers

and spinning wheels. Look out for nearby watchtowers, built to guard linen spread out to bleach in the fields, and Scutch Mills, where the flax was pounded.

THE DRIVE
Head back into Limavady to take the A2 west to Derry (28km). Green fields give way to suburbs and then city streets.

07 DERRY

Northern Ireland's second city offers another powerful insight into the North's troubled past and the remarkable steps towards peace. It's best experienced on foot by walking the old city walls. Partway round, drop into the **Tower Museum** (derrystrabane.com/towermuseum). Its imaginative Story of Derry exhibit leads you

THE BORDER

Driving 20 minutes north out of Derry will see you entering another country: the Republic of Ireland. On road signs, be aware speed limits will suddenly change from mph to km/h, while wording switches from English to Irish and English. Stock up on euros in Derry or visit the first post-border ATM.

Carrick-a-Rede Rope Bridge (p195)

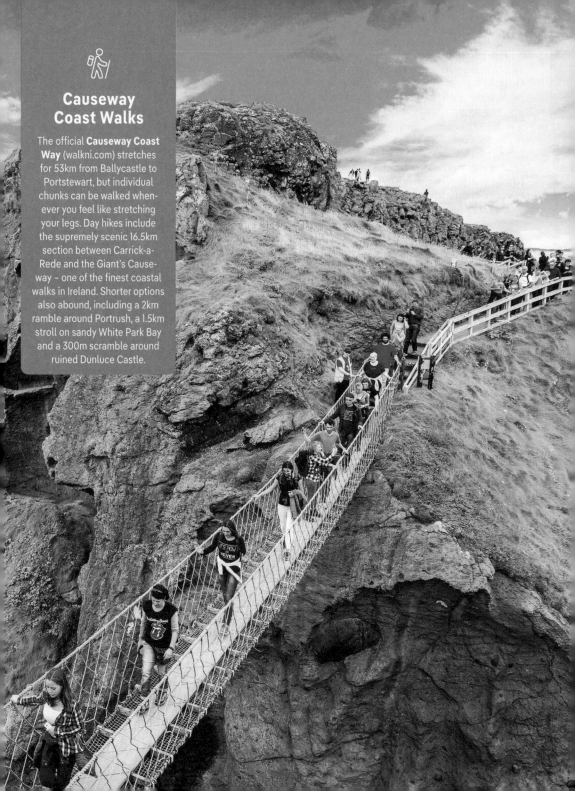

Causeway Coast Walks

The official **Causeway Coast Way** (walkni.com) stretches for 53km from Ballycastle to Portstewart, but individual chunks can be walked whenever you feel like stretching your legs. Day hikes include the supremely scenic 16.5km section between Carrick-a-Rede and the Giant's Causeway – one of the finest coastal walks in Ireland. Shorter options also abound, including a 2km ramble around Portrush, a 1.5km stroll on sandy White Park Bay and a 300m scramble around ruined Dunluce Castle.

through the city's history, from the 6th-century monastery of St Colmcille (Columba) to the 1960s Battle of the Bogside.

 THE DRIVE
The A2 heads north towards Moville. Soon speed-limit signs switch from mph to km/h: welcome to the Republic of Ireland. Shortly after Muff take the small left turn, signed Iskaheen, up the hill. Park beside Iskaheen church (11km).

08 ISKAHEEN

It's completely off the tourist trail, but Iskaheen church's tiny **graveyard** offers evidence of two of Ireland's most significant historical themes: the poverty that led to mass migration and the consequences of sectarian violence. One gravestone among many is to the McKinney family, recording a string of children dying young: at 13 years, 11 months, nine months and six

weeks. It also bears the name of 34-year-old James Gerard McKinney, one of 13 unarmed civilians shot dead when British troops opened fire on demonstrators on Bloody Sunday, 1972.

 THE DRIVE
Rejoin the R238 north, turning onto the R240 to Carndonagh, climbing steeply into rounded summits. After quaint Ballyliffin and Clonmany, pick up the Inis Eoghain Scenic Route signs towards Mamore's Gap, and park at the Glenevin Waterfall car park.

09 GLENEVIN WATERFALL

Welcome to Butler's Bridge – from here a 1km trail winds beside a stream through a wooded glen to Glenevin Waterfall, which cascades 10m down the rock face. It's an utterly picturesque, gentle, waymarked route – the perfect leg stretch.

 THE DRIVE
The Inis Eoghain snakes south up to Mamore's Gap, a high-altitude, white-knuckle mountain pass that climbs 260m on single-lane, twisting roads, past shrines to the saints. After a supremely steep descent (and glorious views) go south through Buncrana, and on to Fahan (37km), parking beside the village church.

10 FAHAN

St Colmcille founded a monastery in Fahan in the 6th century. Its creeper-clad ruins sit beside the church. Among them, hunt out the beautifully carved **St Mura Cross**. Each face of this 7th-century stone slab is decorated with a cross in intricate Celtic weave. The barely discernible Greek inscription is the only one known in Ireland from this early Christian period and is thought to be part of a prayer dating from 633.

LUKASEK/SHUTTERSTOCK ©

Doe Castle

THE DRIVE
Take the N13 to Letterkenny, before picking up the R245 to Ramelton (aka Rathmelton), a 10km sweep north through the River Swilly valley. Turn off for the village, heading downhill to park beside the water in front of you (50km).

11 RAMELTON

In this picture-perfect town, rows of Georgian houses and rough-walled stone warehouses curve along the River Lennon. Strolling right takes you to a string of three-storey, three-bay Victorian warehouses; walking back and left up Church Rd leads to the ruined **Tully-aughnish Church** with its Romanesque carvings in the eastern wall. Walking left beside the river leads past Victorian shops to the three-arched, late-18th-century **Ramelton Bridge**.

THE DRIVE
Cross the town bridge, turning right (north) for Rathmullan. The hills of the Inishowen Peninsula rise ahead and Lough Swilly swings into view – soon you're driving right beside the shore. At Rathmullan (11km), make for the harbour car park.

12 RATHMULLAN

Refined, tranquil Rathmullan was the setting for an event that shaped modern Ireland. In 1607 a band of nobles boarded a ship here, leaving with the intention of raising an army to fight the occupying English. But they never returned. Known as the Flight of the Earls, it marked the end of the Irish (Catholic) chieftains' power. Their estates were confiscated, paving the way for the Plantation of Ulster with British (Protestant) settlers. Beside the sandy beach,

NORTH WEST 200 ROAD RACE

Driving this delightful coast can have its challenges, so imagine doing it at high speed. Each May, the world's best motorcyclists do just that, going as fast as 300km/h in the **North West 200** (northwest200. org), which is run on a road circuit taking in Portrush, Portstewart and Coleraine. This classic race is Ireland's biggest outdoor sporting event and one of the last to take place on closed public roads anywhere in Europe. It attracts up to 150,000 spectators; if you're not one of them, it's best to avoid the area on the race weekend.

look for the striking modern **sculpture**, depicting the earls' departure, waving to their distressed people as they left.

THE DRIVE
Head straight on from the harbour, picking up Fanad/Atlantic Dr, a roller-coaster road that surges up Lough Swilly's shore, round huge Knockalla, past the exquisite beach at Ballymastocker Bay and around Fanad Head.

13 CARRIGART

Most visitors scoot straight through laid-back Carrigart, heading for the swimming beach at Downings. But they miss a real treat: a horse ride on a vast beach. The **Carri-gart Riding Centre** is just across the main street from sandy, hill-ringed Mulroy Bay, meaning you can head straight onto the beach for an hour-long ride amid the shallows and the dunes. Trips go on the hour, but it's best to book.

THE DRIVE
Head south for Creeslough. An inlet with a creamy, single-towered castle soon pops into view. The turn-off comes on the plain, where brown signs point through narrow lanes and past farms to Doe Castle (12km) itself.

14 DOE CASTLE

The best way to appreciate the charm of early-16th-century **Doe Castle**

(heritageireland.ie) is to wander the peaceful grounds, admiring its slender tower and crenellated battlements. The castle was the stronghold of the Scottish MacSweeney family until it fell into English hands in the 17th century. It's a deeply picturesque spot: a low, water-fringed promontory with a moat hewn out of the rock.

THE DRIVE
Near Creeslough, the bulk of Muckish Mountain rears up before the N56 to Dunfanaghy undulates past homesteads, loughs and sandy bays. Once in Dunfanaghy, with its gently kooky vibe, welcoming pubs and great places to sleep, look out for the signpost pointing right to Horn Head (25km).

15 HORN HEAD

This headland provides one of Donegal's best clifftop drives, along sheer, heather-clad quartzite cliffs with views of an island-dotted sea. A circular road bears left to the coastguard station – park to take the 20-minute walk due north to the signal tower. Hop back in the car, continuing east – around 1km later a viewpoint tops cliffs 180m high. There's another superb vantage point 1km further round – on a fine day you'll see Ireland's most northerly point, Malin Head.

THE DRIVE

The N56 continues west. Settlements thin out, the road climbs and the pointed peak of Mt Errigal fills more and more of your windscreen before the road swings away. At tiny Crolly follow the R259 towards the airport, then turn right, picking up signs for Leo's Tavern (35km) in Meenaleck.

16 MEENALECK

You never know who'll drop by for one of the legendary singalongs at **Leo's Tavern** (leostavern.com) in Meenaleck. It's owned by Bartley Brennan, brother of Enya and her siblings Máire, Ciaran and Pól (aka the group Clannad). The pub glitters with gold, silver and platinum discs and is packed with musical mementos – there's **live music** nightly in summer.

THE DRIVE

Continue west on the R259 as it bobbles and twists besides scattered communities and an at-first-boggy, then sandy, shore. Head on to the pocket-sized port of Burtonport, following ferry signs right, to embark for Arranmore Island (25km).

17 ARRANMORE ISLAND

Arranmore (Árainn Mhór) offers a true taste of Ireland. Framed by dramatic cliff faces, cavernous sea caves and clear sandy beaches, this 9km-by-5km island sits 5km offshore. Here you'll discover a prehistoric triangular fort and an offshore bird sanctuary fluttering with corncrakes, snipes and seabirds. Irish is the main language spoken, pubs put on turf fires and traditional-music sessions run late into the night. The **Arranmore Island Ferry** (arranmoreferry.com) takes 20 minutes and runs up to eight times a day.

THE DRIVE

The R259 bounces down to Dungloe, where you take the N56 south into a rock-strewn landscape that's backed by the Blue Stack Mountains. After a stretch of rally-circuit-esque road, the sweep of Gweebarra Bay emerges. Take the sharp right towards Narin (R261), following signs to the beach *(trá)*, 45km from Burtonport.

⟳ DETOUR

Fintown Railway
Start: 17 **Arranmore Island**

You've been driving for days now – time to let the train take the strain. The charming **Fintown Railway** (antraen.com) runs along a rebuilt 5km section of the former County Donegal Railway track beside picturesque Lough Finn. It's been lovingly restored to its original condition and a return trip in the red-and-white 1940s diesel railcar takes around 40 minutes. From Burtonport head south on the R259 to Dungloe, then east on the N56 and R252 to reach the railway. Then settle back to enjoy the ride.

18 NARIN

You've now entered the beautiful Loughrea Peninsula, which glistens with tiny lakes cupped by undulating hills. Narin boasts a spectacular 4km-long, wishbone-shaped Blue Flag beach, the sandy tip of which points towards **Iniskeel Island**. You can walk to the island at low tide along a 500m sandy causeway. Your reward? An intimate island studded with early Christian remains: St Connell, a cousin of St Colmcille, founded a monastery here in the 6th century.

THE DRIVE

Continue south on the R261 through tweed-producing Ardara. Shortly after leaving town, take the second turning (the first turning after

the John Malloy factory outlet), marked by a hand-painted sign to 'Maghera', following a road wedged between craggy hills and an increasingly sandy shore. In time the Assarancagh Waterfall (14km) comes into view.

19 ASSARANCAGH WATERFALL

Stepping out of the car reveals just what an enchanting spot this is. As the waterfall streams down the sheer hillside, walk along the road towards the sea. This 1.5km route leads past time-warp farms – sheep bleat and the tang of peat smoke scents the air. At tiny Maghera head through the car park, down a track, over a boardwalk and onto a truly stunning expanse of pure-white sand. This exquisite place belies a bloody past. Some 100 villagers hid from Cromwell's forces in nearby caves – all except one were discovered and massacred.

THE DRIVE

Drive west through Maghera on a dramatic route that makes straight for the gap in the towering hills. At the fork, turn right, heading deeper into the remote headland, making for Glencolumbcille (20km).

20 GLENCOLUMBCILLE

The welcome in the scattered, pub-dotted, bayside village of Glencolumbcille (Gleann Cholm Cille) is warm. This remote settlement also offers a glimpse of a disappearing way of life. **Father McDyer's Folk Village** (glenfolkvillage.com) took traditional life of the 1960s and froze it in time. Its thatched cottages recreate daily life with genuine period fittings, while the Craft Shop sells local crafts, marmalade and whiskey truffles – a few treats at your journey's end.

26

Musical Landscapes

BEST FOR TUNES

♫

Ennis, on summer nights, where local musicians showcase their skills.

Galway

DURATION	DISTANCE	GREAT FOR
5–6 days	155km / 96 miles	History, food and drink, outdoors

BEST TIME TO GO	The summer months for outdoor *céilidh* and music festivals

Prepare for an embarrassment of musical riches. Join the big bawdy get-togethers of Galway's always-on music scene and Ennis' rollicking urban boozers. Then take a seat at the atmospheric small pub sessions in crossroad villages like Kilfenora and Kilronan on the Aran Islands, where pretty much everyone joins in. Whatever way you like it, this region is undeniably one of Ireland's hottest for toe-tapping tunes.

Link your trip

23 The Long Way Round

From Galway, pick up this trip north or south for crenellated coastlines, vibrant port cities and island treasures.

24 Ring of Kerry

Head south to Killarney via Limerick to encounter jaw-dropping scenery around the Iveragh Peninsula.

01 **GALWAY CITY**

Galway (Gaillimh) has a young student population and a largely creative community that give a palpable energy to the place. Walk its colourful medieval streets, packed with heritage shops, street-side cafes and pubs, all ensuring there's never a dull moment. Galway's pub selection is second to none and some swing to tunes every night of the week. **Crane Bar** (thecranebar.com), an atmospheric old pub west of the River Corrib, is the best spot in Galway to catch an informal *céilidh* most nights. Or for something more contemporary, **Róisín Dubh**

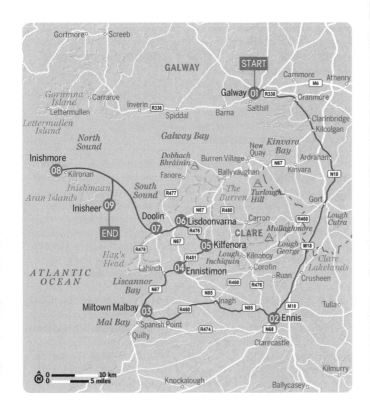

The Pied Piper

Half the population of Miltown Malbay seems to be part of the annual **Willie Clancy Summer School** (scoilsamhraidhwillie clancy.com), a tribute to a native son and one of Ireland's greatest pipers. The eight-day festival, now in its fourth decade, begins on the first Saturday in July, when impromptu sessions occur day and night, the pubs are packed and Guinness is consumed by the barrel – up to 10,000 enthusiasts from around the globe turn up for the event. Specialist workshops and classes underpin the event; don't be surprised to attend a recital with 40 noted fiddlers.

(roisindubh.net) is the place to hear emerging international and local singer-songwriters.

THE DRIVE

From Galway city centre, follow the coast road (R338) east out of town as far as the M18 and then cruise south to Ennis (65km), where your great musical tour of Clare begins.

02 ENNIS

Ennis (Inis), a medieval town in origin, is packed with pubs featuring trad music. **Brogan's** (brogansbarand restaurant.com), on the corner of Cook's Lane, sees a fine bunch of musicians rattling even the stone floors almost every night in

summer, while the wood-panelled **Poet's Corner Bar** (oldground hotelennis.com/poets-corner-bar. html) is a hideout for local musicians serious about their trad sessions. The tourist office collates weekly live music listings for the town's pubs. **Cois na hAbhna** (coisnahabhna.ie), a pilgrimage point for traditional music and culture, has frequent performances and a full range of classes in dance and music; it's also an archive and library of Irish traditional music, song, dance and folklore. Traditional music aficionados might like to time a visit with **Fleadh Nua** (fleadhnua.com), a lively festival held in late May.

THE DRIVE

From the N85, which runs south of the Burren, you'll arrive at the blink-and-you'll-miss-it village of Inagh. Swing right on to the smaller R460 for the run into Miltown Malbay – some 32km in all.

03 MILTOWN MALBAY

Miltown Malbay was a resort favoured by well-to-do Victorians, though the beach itself is 2km southwest at **Spanish Point**. To the north of Spanish Point there are beautiful walks amid the low cliffs, coves and isolated beaches. A classically friendly place in the chatty Irish way, Miltown Malbay hosts the annual Willie Clancy Summer School, one of Ireland's great trad music events. In town, one of a couple of genuine old-style places with occasional trad sessions is **Friel's Bar** – don't be confused by the much bigger sign on the front proclaiming 'Lynch's'. Another top music pub is the dapper **Hillery's**.

THE DRIVE
Hugging the coast, continue north on the N67 until you come to the small seaside resort of Lahinch. Just a few streets backing a wide beach, it's renowned for surfing. From here, it's only 4km up the road to the lovely heritage town of Ennistimon.

04 ENNISTIMON
Ennistimon (Inis Díomáin) is one of those charming market towns where people go about their business barely noticing the characterful buildings lining Main St. Behind this bustling facade there's a surprise: the roaring **Cascades**, the stepped falls of the River Inagh. After heavy rain they surge, beer-brown and foaming, and you risk getting drenched on windy days in the flying drizzle. Not to be missed, **Cooley's House** is a great trad pub, with music most

---

WHY I LOVE THIS TRIP

Belinda Dixon, writer

To witness a proper traditional session in one of the music houses of Clare or the fine old pubs of Galway can be a transcendent experience, especially if it's appropriately lubricated with a pint (or few) of stout. Sure, there'll be plenty of tourists about, but this is authentic, traditional Ireland at its most evocative.

---

nights in summer and several evenings a week in winter.

THE DRIVE
Heading north through a patchwork of green fields and stony walls on the R481, you'll land at the tiny village of Kilfenora, some 9km later. Despite its diminutive size, the pulse of Clare's music scene beats strongly in this area.

05 KILFENORA
Underappreciated Kilfenora (Cill Fhionnúrach) lies on the southern fringe of the Burren. It's a small place, with a diminutive 12th-century **cathedral** that is best known for its high crosses. The town has a strong music tradition that rivals that of Doolin, but without the crowds. The celebrated **Kilfenora Céili Band** (kilfenora ceiliband.com) has been playing for more than a century. Its traditional music features fiddles, banjos, squeeze boxes and more, and can be enjoyed most Wednesday evenings at **Linnane's Pub**. A short stroll away, **Vaughan's** (vaughanspub.ie) has music in the bar every night during the summer and terrific set-dancing sessions in the neighbouring barn on Sunday nights.

THE DRIVE
From Kilfenora the R476 meanders northwest 8km to Lisdoonvarna, home of the international matchmaking festival. Posh during Victorian times, the town is a little less classy today, but friendly, good-looking and far less overrun than Doolin.

06 LISDOONVARNA
Lisdoonvarna (Lios Dún Bhearna), often just called 'Lisdoon', is well known for its mineral springs. For centuries

---

Photo Opportunity
Set-dancing at the crossroads, in Vaughan's of Kilfenora.

people have been visiting the local spa to swallow its waters. Down by the river at **Roadside Tavern** (burrenexperiences.ie/the-roadside-tavern), third-generation owner Peter Curtin knows every story worth telling. There are trad sessions nightly in summer and on Friday and Saturday evenings in winter. Look for a trail beside the pub that runs 400m down to two wells by the river. A few paces from the tavern, the **Burren Smokehouse** (burrensmokehouse.ie) is where you can learn about the ancient Irish art of oak-smoking salmon.

THE DRIVE
Just under 10 minutes' drive west, via the R478/479, you'll reach the epicentre of Clare's trad music scene, Doolin. Also known for its setting – 6km north of the Cliffs of Moher – Doolin is really three small neighbouring villages. First comes Roadford, then 1km west sits Doolin itself, then another 1km west comes pretty Fisherstreet, nearest the water.

07 DOOLIN
Doolin gets plenty of press as a centre of Irish traditional music, owing to a trio of pubs that have sessions through the year. **McGann's** (mcgannspubdoolin.com) has all the classic touches of a full-on Irish music pub; the action often spills out onto the street. Right

on the water, **Gus O'Connor's** (gusoconnorsdoolin.com), a sprawling favourite, has a rollicking atmosphere. It easily gets the most crowded and has the highest tourist quotient. **McDermott's** (MacDiarmada's; mcdermottspub.com) is a simple and sometimes rowdy old pub popular with locals. When the fiddles get going, it can seem like a scene out of a John Ford movie.

🚘 THE DRIVE
This 'drive' is really a sail – you'll need to leave your car at one of Doolin's many car parks to board the ferry (doolin2aranferries.com or doolinferry.com) to the Aran Islands.

08 **INISHMORE**
The Aran Islands sing their own siren song to thousands of travellers each year, who find their desolate beauty beguiling. The largest and most accessible Aran, Inishmore (Inis Mór), is home to ancient fort **Dun Aengus** (Dún Aonghasa; heritageireland.ie), one of the oldest archaeological remains in Ireland, as well as some lively pubs and restaurants in the only town, **Kilronan**. Irish remains the local tongue, but most locals speak English with visitors. **Tí Joe Watty's Bar** (joewattys.ie) is the best pub in Kilronan, with traditional sessions most summer nights. Turf fires warm the air on the 50 weeks a year when this is needed. Informal music sessions, glowing fires and a broad terrace with harbour views make **Tí Joe Mac's** another local favourite, as is **The Bar**

(inismorbar.com), which has nightly live music from May to mid-October, and weekends the rest of the year.

🚘 THE DRIVE
In the summer, passenger ferries run regularly between the Aran Islands. They cost €10 to €15; schedules can be a little complex – book in advance.

09 **INISHEER**
On Inisheer (Inis Oírr), the smallest of the Aran Islands, the breathtakingly beautiful end-of-the-earth landscape adds to the island's distinctly mystical aura. Steeped in mythology, traditional rituals are

very much respected here. Locals still carry out a pilgrimage with potential healing powers, known as the *Turas*, to the Well of Enda, an ever-burbling spring in the southwest. For a week in late June the island reverberates to the thunder of traditional drums during **Craiceann** (craiceann.com). Bodhrán masterclasses, workshops and pub sessions are held, as well as Irish dancing. Rory Conneely's atmospheric inn **Tigh Ruairí** (Rory's) hosts live music sessions and, here since 1897, **Tigh Ned** (tighned.com) is a welcoming, unpretentious place, with harbour views and lively traditional music.

Gus O'Connor's, Doolin

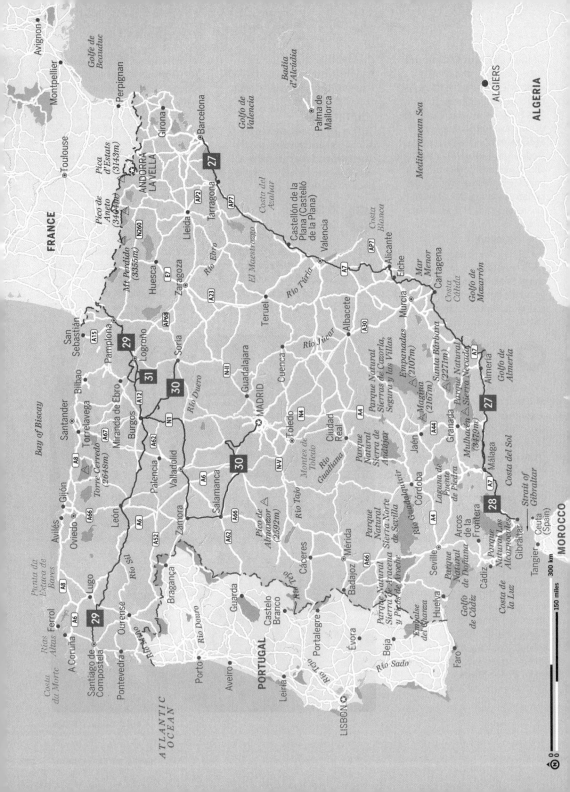

JON CHICA/SHUTTERSTOCK ©

Vineyards, La Rioja (p242)

Spain

Explore

Spain

Spectacular beaches, surreal architecture, medieval villages and some of the most celebrated restaurants on the planet – Spain has an allure that few destinations can match. There's much to see and do amid the ancient cities and enchanting landscapes that inspired Picasso and Velàzquez. You can admire fairy-tale palaces and breathtaking cathedrals, feast on the world's best tapas, and give yourself up to fiery passions at fiestas and flamenco shows.

Our drives offer something for everyone: beach lovers, outdoor adventurers, family travellers, music fiends, foodies and those simply wanting to dip into Spain's extraordinary historical and cultural legacy.

Madrid

Spain's capital and largest city, Madrid is Spain's principal gateway. Its airport is the country's busiest, serving flights from across the world, and its central position makes it convenient for heading either north or south. Motorways spear off the city in all directions, including the A6, which runs up to Segovia, the second stop in our Historic Castilla y León tour.

As one of Spain's top destinations, Madrid is well supplied with cultural and historic sites, as well as accommodation options and no end of bars, restaurants and clubs. It's home to world-class art museums, including the Prado and world-class Thyssen-Bornemisza, and it's renowned for its magnificent tapas bars and never-ending nightlife. In fact, once you've hit your stride in Madrid, you'll find leaving is far harder than getting there.

Barcelona

On Spain's northeastern coast, Barcelona is one of the country's most popular destinations, as well as a major commercial and transport hub. Most visitors fly into El Prat airport, though you can also reach it from Girona-Costa Brava and Reus airports. By land, there are trains from Paris and other major European cities, as well as long-haul bus services. For onward travel, you can hire a car and hook up with our Mediterranean Meander trip by driving down to Tarragona, about 1¼ hours away via the C32 and AP7.

WHEN TO GO

Spring and autumn are ideal for road-tripping and outdoor activities with warm, clear weather and some major festivals. Summer heralds high season prices on the coast and crowds on the beach, as well as reliably high temperatures. Winter can be wet, particularly in the north, but you can still find sunshine down south.

Of course, Barcelona merits an exploration of a few days. The soaring cathedrals and shadowy lanes of the Barri Gòtic, Gaudí's modernist masterpieces, the city's sandy beach and superb restaurant scene will get your Spanish adventure off to a memorable start.

Málaga

Andalucía's main international gateway and the starting point for the weeklong Mediterranean Meander drive, Málaga is your ideal southern base. It's easy to get to – its airport is Spain's fourth busiest and there are regular high-speed trains from Madrid – and it has an ample array of hotels, hostels and guesthouses. It's also fun, boasting a buzzing bar scene and a food culture that encompasses Michelin-starred restaurants and tatty-cool fish shacks. To warm up your sightseeing muscles you can take in its landmark cathedral, Moorish fortress,

and selection of fine museums, including the excellent Museo Picasso Málaga.

When the time comes to leave, strike east on the A7 coastal motorway and push on to Almuñécar and Almería.

TRANSPORT

Spain is well linked to other European countries by air, rail, sea and road. The main intercontinental airports are Madrid-Barajas and Barcelona's El Prat but you can also fly to airports across the country, including Málaga, a major southern hub. Trains and buses link Spain with France and Portugal while ferries sail in from north Africa, the UK and Italy.

WHAT'S ON

Las Fallas de San José

(15 to 19 March) Valencia's fiery annual bash culminates in the burning of giant papier-mâché figures.

Semana Santa

Easter is celebrated across Spain with parades, hooded penitents and giant crowds.

Feria de Abril

(April) Festival-goers don traditional costume for Seville's weeklong party.

Fiesta de San Fermín

(6 to 14 July) Pamplona's world-famous festivities centre on the controversial running of the bulls.

Resources

Fiestas *(fiestas.net)* Lists festivals and major events around the country; in Spanish but simple to navigate.

Paradores *(parador.es)* For information and booking of Spain's historic *paradores*.

Turespaña *(spain.info)* Spain's multilingual tourist website with plenty of suggestions, ideas and practical information.

WHERE TO STAY

Accommodation is plentiful in Spain and often excellent value by European standards. Options run the gamut, ranging from urban design hotels to family-run guesthouses, self-catering apartment rentals, villas and campgrounds. Booking ahead is generally a good idea and essential in high season, especially on the coast and for major festivals when prices skyrocket. For a memorable stay, Spain's *paradores* are state-funded hotels housed in historic buildings such as renovated castles or medieval convents. Away from the bright lights, *casas rurales* are a good option, offering modest rural accommodation in restored village houses or farmsteads.

27

Mediterranean Meander

Centre Pompidou Málaga

DURATION	DISTANCE	GREAT FOR
7 days	1107km / 688 miles	History, outdoors

BEST TIME TO GO	March to June is sunny, but not too hot, and there are plenty of festivals.

From the Costa Daurada to the Costa del Sol, from Catalan pride to Andalucian passion, from Roman ruins in Tarragona to Barcelona's flamboyant Modernisme buildings: this drive provides technicolour proof that not all southern Spain is a beach bucket of cheesy tourist clichés. The full 1107km trajectory passes through four regions, two languages, Spain's second, third and sixth largest cities, and beaches too numerous to count.

Link your trip

28 Costa del Sol Beyond the Beaches

Can't get enough of the Mediterranean? Jump on this trip in Málaga and hug the coast all the way to Gibraltar.

30 Historic Castilla y León

From Barcelona it's nearly six hours west to Madrid, but you'll encounter some of Spain's most captivating historic towns and villages.

01 MÁLAGA

The Costa del Sol can seem a pretty soulless place until you hit Málaga, the Andalucian city everyone is talking about. For decades the city was overlooked by the millions of tourists who crowded the Costa's seaside resorts, but in recent years it has transformed itself into a hip, stylish metropolis brimming with youthful vigour. It boasts 30-odd museums and an edgy urban art scene as well as contemporary restaurants, boutique hotels and stylish shopping.

Art lovers are spoiled for choice at museums such as the **Museo Ruso de Málaga** (coleccionmuseoruso.es) and **Centre Pompidou Málaga** (centrepompidou.es), while the **Museo de Málaga** (museosdeandalucia.es/museodemalaga) houses an extensive archaeology collection. The city's premier museum is the unmissable **Museo Picasso Málaga** (museopicassomalaga.org), dedicated to the Málaga-born artist.

For an edgier, urban scene, head to the Soho neighbourhood near the port where you'll find giant murals, arty cafes, ethnic restaurants and street markets.

THE DRIVE

Head east out of Málaga on the A7. This is southern Spain's main coastal road (also known as the E15) and will be your companion for much of this trip. The coast gets ever more precipitous as you move east into Granada province. After 68km turn south on the N340 and follow for 8km into Almuñécar.

02 ALMUÑÉCAR

There's a hint of Italy's Amalfi Coast about the Costa Tropical, Granada province's 80km coastline. Named for its subtropical microclimate, it's often dramatically beautiful, with dun-brown mountains and whitewashed villages huddled into coves and bays. The area's main resort is the popular summer destination of Almuñécar.

Summer action is focused on Almuñécar's long seafront, the two beaches of which are divided by a rocky outcrop, the **Peñón del Santo**. To the west of this stretches the pebbly **Playa de San Cristóbal**, while to the east the grey-sanded **Playa Puerta del Mar** fronts the old town.

Up in the *casco antiguo*, the small **Museo Arqueológico Cueva de Siete Palacios** displays ancient finds in a series of underground stone cellars. Tickets also include entry to the hilltop **Castillo de San Miguel**.

THE DRIVE

Continue eastwards on the A7, skirting around Motril and passing increasing numbers of unsightly plastic greenhouses as the landscape becomes ever more arid. Almería beckons. All told, it's about 130km to Almería.

03 ALMERÍA

Don't overlook Almería, an energetic waterfront city with an illustrious past. Once the main port for the 10th-century Córdoba caliphate, the sun-baked city has a handsome centre, punctuated by palm-fringed plazas and old churches, as well as several museums and plenty of fantastic tapas bars. Its main draw is its spectacular **Alcazaba**, once one of the most powerful Moorish fortresses in Spain.

At the foot of the hilltop fort sprawls the maze-like Almedina, the old Moorish quarter. Continue through this to the city's six-towered **cathedral** (catedralalmeria.com), another formidable structure with an impressive Gothic interior.

Nearby, the **Museo de la Guitarra** charts Almería's role in the development of the iconic instrument.

Round off your sightseeing with a soak at the **Hammam Aire de Almería** (beaire.com), a modern-day version of an Arabic bathhouse.

THE DRIVE

Head east out of Almería on the N340a to join up with the AL12 airport road and its continuation, the N344. Continue on this, following signs to San José through a series of small roundabouts near Retamar. Eventually you should emerge onto the AL3108, which runs through low hills to Cabo de Gata (total distance 40km).

04 CABO DE GATA

Covering Spain's southeastern tip, the **Parque Natural de Cabo de Gata-Níjar** boasts some of Andalucía's most flawless and least crowded beaches. These glorious *playas* lie strung along the area's dramatic cliff-bound coastline while inland remote white villages dot the stark, semi-desert hinterland.

On the park's east coast, the low-key resort of **San José** makes an ideal base. It's well set up with hotels and restaurants and the surrounding coastline hides several sublime beaches. The most beautiful, including **Playa de los Genoveses** and **Playa de Mónsul**, are accessible by a dirt road signposted 'Playas' and/or 'Genoveses/Mónsul.'

For more active pursuits, you can walk the park's coastal paths or organise diving, kayaking, bike hire and guided tours at agencies across town – try **MedialunAventura** (medialun aventura.com).

THE DRIVE

Follow the AL3108 inland from San José until you hit the A7 just shy of Níjar. Head northeast towards Valencia for 43km to exit 520. Come off here and follow signs to Mojácar along the A370 and AL6111.

05 MOJÁCAR

Tucked away in an isolated corner of Almería province, Mojácar is both a seaside resort and a charming hill town. Mojácar Pueblo, a picturesque jumble of white-cube houses, sits atop a hillside 3km inland from Mojácar Playa, a modern low-rise resort fronting 7km of sandy beach.

Exploring Mojácar Pueblo is mainly a matter of wandering its maze-like streets, stopping off at craft shops, galleries and boutiques. You can see how life in the town once was at the **Casa La Canana**, and admire sweeping views from the lofty **Mirador del Castillo**.

Down at Mojácar Playa, you'll find the best sands at the southern end of town, which also has a pleasant seafront promenade.

Legacy of the Romans

What did the Romans ever do for us? Well, quite a lot actually, as you'll discover as you drive up Spain's Mediterranean coast.

The Roman colonies in Hispania (their name for the Iberian peninsula) lasted from around 200 BCE to 470 CE, and reminders of their existence lie dotted along the coast, from Andalucía to Catalonia.

In **Málaga** you can admire an **amphitheatre**, dating from the 1st century CE when the settlement was called Malaca. An adjacent interpretive centre outlines its history and displays a few artefacts unearthed on the site.

Cartagena (Carthago Nova to the Romans) boasts several Roman sites, including the Museo del Teatro Romano, centred on a 1st-century BCE Roman theatre.

Further north, **Tarragona** (Tarraco) was once capital of Rome's Spanish provinces and has ruins to prove it, including an amphitheatre, a forum, street foundations and the two-tiered **Aqüeducte de les Ferreres**. Ocean-themed mosaics can be seen in the nearby **Museu Nacional Arqueològic de Tarragona** (mnat.cat).

THE DRIVE
Retrace your steps from Mojácar back onto the northbound A7. After 10km merge onto the toll-charging AP7 near Vera and continue to the exit for Cartagena Oeste. Take this and follow the signposted route along the N332 into the city. Mojácar to Cartagena is 134km.

06 CARTAGENA
Cartagena's fabulous natural harbour has been used for thousands of years. Stand on the battlements of the castle that overlooks the city and you can literally see layer upon layer of history spread below you, from the wharf where Phoenician traders docked their ships to the streets where Roman legionaries once marched, from the factories of the industrial age to the contemporary warships of what is still an important naval base.

As archaeologists continue to unearth the city's ancient roots, it is finally starting to get the recognition it deserves. Highlights include the **Museo Nacional de Arqueología Subacuática** (Arqua; museoarqua.mcu.es), an excellent museum dedicated to underwater archaeology and maritime history, and the **Museo del Teatro Romano** (teatro romanocartagena.org), centred on a 1st-century BCE Roman theatre.

THE DRIVE
Double back to the AP7 and head north towards Alicante. After 75km, the autopista rejoins the A7. Follow this for 32km before taking exit 17A signposted for Alicante.

DETOUR
Orihuela
Start: 6 Cartagena

Beside the Río Segura and flush with the base of a barren mountain of

Teatro Romano, Cartagena

rock, Orihuela harbours some superb Gothic, Renaissance and baroque buildings. Its old town, once the second city of the kingdom of Valencia, is strung out between the river and the castle-capped mountain.

Standout sights include the 14th-century Catalan Gothic **Catedral de San Salvador**, which features three finely carved portals and an exquisite two-level cloister. Nearby, the **Museo Diocesano de Arte Sacro** (museode artesacro.es) has a fine display of religious art, culminating in Velázquez' *Temptation of St Thomas*. Also worth searching out is the **Colegio de Santo Domingo** (colegio.cdsantodomingo.com), a 16th-century convent with two fine Renaissance cloisters.

To reach Orihuela, branch west off the AP7 around 60km north of Cartagena and continue on the CV945 and CV95.

07 ALICANTE
Of all mainland Spain's provincial capitals, Alicante is the most tourist-driven. Nevertheless, it's a dynamic, attractive city with a castle, old quarter and long waterfront. The eating scene is exciting and the nightlife is legendary.

There are sweeping views over the city from the large 16th-century **Castillo de Santa Bárbara** (castillodesantabar bara.com), which also houses a museum recounting the history of Alicante. Further historical artefacts await in the **Museo Arqueológico de Alicante** (MARQ; marqalicante.com) which has a strong collection of ceramics and Iberian art. For a more contemporary outlook, the free **Museo de Arte Contemporáneo de Alicante** (MACA; maca-alicante.es) impresses with its displays of works by the likes of Dalí, Miró, Picasso and others.

Las Fallas de San José, Valencia

FESTIVAL SEASON

If you're undertaking this trip in February, March or August, look out for the following festivals.

Sitges Carnaval

Carnaval in Sitges (visitsitges.com) is a sparkly week-long booze-soaked riot, complete with masked balls and capped by extravagant gay parades on the Sunday and Tuesday, featuring flamboyantly dressed drag queens, giant sound systems and a wild all-night party.

Las Fallas de San José

The exuberant, anarchic swirl of Las Fallas de San José (fallas.com) – fireworks, music, festive bonfires and all-night partying – is a must if you're visiting Valencia in mid-March. The *fallas* themselves are huge papier mâché sculptures satirising celebrities, current affairs and local customs. After midnight on the final day, each *falla* goes up in flames.

Feria de Malaga

(feria.malaga.eu) Málaga's nine-day *feria* (fair), launched by a huge fireworks display, is the most ebullient of Andalucía's summer *ferias*. Head for the city centre to be in the thick of it. At night, festivities switch to large fairgrounds and nightly rock and flamenco shows at Cortijo de Torres, 3km southwest of the city centre.

THE DRIVE

Leave Alicante on the A77 signposted Valencia and continue on to the A7. The autovia proceeds north, passing through a couple of tunnels and heading progressively downhill as it forges inland towards Valencia. After almost 90km, exit on the CV645 signposted Xàtiva. From here it's about 5km to the town.

08 XÀTIVA

Xàtiva (Spanish: Játiva) is often visited on a day trip from Valencia or, as in this case, as a stop on the way north from Alicante. It has an intriguing historic quarter and a mighty castle strung along the crest of the Serra Vernissa, with the town snuggled at its base.

The Muslims established Europe's first paper manufacturing plant in Xàtiva, which is also famous as the birthplace of the Borgia Popes Calixtus III and Alexander VI. The town's glory days ended in 1707 when Felipe V's troops torched most of the town.

Xàtiva's **castle** (xativaturismo. com), which clasps the summit of a double-peaked hill overlooking the old town, is one of the most evocative in the Valencia region. Behind its crumbling battlements you'll find flower gardens (bring a picnic), tumbledown turrets, towers and other buildings. The walk up to the castle is a long one (2km), but the views are sensational.

THE DRIVE

Use the N340 to rejoin the A7 and head north to Valencia. Just outside the city, where the A7 merges with the AP7, take the V31, Valencia's main southern access road for the final push into the city centre. All told, the 63km journey should take around 50 minutes.

09 VALENCIA

Valencia, Spain's third-largest city, exudes confidence. Content for Madrid and Barcelona to grab the headlines, it quietly gets on with being a wonderfully liveable spot, hosting thriving cultural, eating and nightlife scenes. Its star attraction is the strikingly futuristic **Ciudad de las Artes y las Ciencias** (City of Arts & Sciences; cac.es) on the old Turia riverbed. Counting an opera house, science museum, 3D cinema and aquarium, the complex was largely the work of local-born starchitect Santiago Calatrava.

Other brilliant contemporary buildings grace the city, which also has a fistful of fabulous Modernista buildings, great museums, a long stretch of beach and a large, characterful old quarter. Look out for **La Lonja** (valencia. es), Valencia's late-15th-century silk and commodity exchange, and the **Mercado Central** (mercadocentralvalencia.es), the vast Modernista market.

The city also enjoys premiership foodie credentials as the home of paella, but its buzzing dining scene offers plenty more besides.

THE DRIVE

Leave Valencia on the V21 signposted Puçol. After 23km or so you'll rejoin your old friend, the AP7, which will whisk you 200km up the coast into Catalonia. Come off at exit 38 and continue on the A7 for the final 35km into Tarragona. Reckon on 257km for the entire leg.

DETOUR
Delta de l'Ebre
Start: 9 Valencia

Near Catalonia's southern border, the Delta de l'Ebre is a remote, exposed place of reed-fringed lagoons, dune-backed beaches and mirror-smooth marshes. Some 78 sq km are protected in the **Parc Natural del Delta de l'Ebre**, northern Spain's most important waterbird habitat. Migration season (October and November) sees bird populations peak, but birds are also numerous in winter and spring. Even if you're not a twitcher, the park is worth a visit. The landscape, with its whitewashed farmhouses and electric-green rice paddies, is hauntingly beautiful and the flat waterside trails are ideal for cyclists and ramblers.

Scruffy **Deltebre** sits at the centre of the delta but smaller villages like **Riumar** or **Poblenou del Delta** are more appealing.

To reach Deltebre, branch off the AP7 at exit 41, 180km north of Valencia. Take the N340 to connect with the TV3454, which leads to the town some 13km to the east.

10 TARRAGONA

In the effervescent port city of Tarragona, Roman history collides with beaches, bars and a food scene that perfumes the air with freshly grilled seafood. The main drawcard is the city's collection of ancient ruins, including those housed in a mosaic-packed museum and a seaside amphitheatre where gladiators once faced each other (or wild animals) in mortal combat. The Unesco-listed Roman sites are scattered around town but you can get a combined ticket at the **Museu d'Historia de Tarragona** (tarragona.cat/patrimoni/museu-historia).

A roll call of fantastic places to eat and drink is a good reason to linger in the attractive medieval centre. This maze of cobbled lanes is encircled by steep walls

and crowned by a towering **cathedral** (catedraldetarragona.com) with Romanesque and Gothic flourishes.

THE DRIVE
From Tarragona use the N240 to get back on the AP7 and head east towards Barcelona. After about 11km take exit 31 onto the C32. Follow this for just over 30km, crossing one viaduct and burrowing through two tunnels, to Sitges.

SITGES
Just 40km shy of Barcelona, Sitges has been a favourite beach resort since the 19th century. The former fishing village, which was a key location for the Modernisme art movement and is now one of Spain's premier gay destinations, is renowned for its party beach life, riotous carnival celebrations and hedonistic nightlife – at its most bacchanalian in July and August. Despite this, it remains a classy destination with a good array of galleries and museums and plenty of restaurants in its boutique-laden historic centre.

Sunseekers will enjoy its long sandy beach, which is flanked by

Photo Opportunity
The chameleonic Sagrada Familia changes every time you visit.

the seafront **Passeig Maritim**. The cultural highlight is the **Museu del Cau Ferrat** (museus desitges.cat), built in the 1890s as a house-studio by artist Santiago Rusiñol – a pioneer of the Modernisme movement. The whitewashed mansion is full of his own art and that of his contemporaries, including his friend Picasso.

THE DRIVE
It's only 40km to Barcelona. Get back onto the toll-charging C32 and fly through a multitude of tunnels. After about 30km, exit at junction 16B and follow signs for Barcelona, Gran Vía and Centre Ciutat.

BARCELONA
Barcelona is a guidebook in itself and a cultural colossus to rival Paris or Rome. The city's ever-evolving symbol

is Gaudí's **La Sagrada Família** (sagradafamilia.org), which rises like an unfinished symphony over L'Eixample district. The surrounding neighbourhood is renowned for its Modernisme architecture, which appears in buildings such as **La Pedrera** (Casa Milà; lapedrera.com), a madcap Unesco-listed masterpiece with a rippling grey-stone facade and chimney pots resembling medieval knights. For more conventional, historical sights, head to the Barri Gótic, home to the city's vast Gothic **cathedral** (catedralbcn.org), and the medieval La Ribera quarter where you'll find the excellent **Museu Picasso** (museupicasso.bcn.cat).

A good orientation point in this complex city is **La Rambla**, whose tree-lined pedestrian promenade was made with the evening *paseo* (stroll) in mind. La Rambla divides the Barri Gòtic and La Ribera from the bohemian, multicultural El Raval neighbourhood. To the northeast lies the Modernisme-inspired L'Eixample quarter; to the south are the steep parks and gardens of Montjuic, site of the 1992 Olympics.

La Sagrada Família, Barcelona

28

BEST FOR FAMILIES

Beaches, theme parks, and the Andalucian love for kids.

Costa del Sol Beyond the Beaches

DURATION	DISTANCE	GREAT FOR
3–4 days	208km / 129 miles	Food and drink, family travel

BEST TIME TO GO	March to June or September to November when temperatures are cooler.

View from Balcón de Europa, Nerja

This drive from Nerja in the east to Gibraltar in the west leads through a constantly shifting landscape, taking you from orchards of subtropical fruit trees to shimmering white resorts, from a culture-loving metropolis to the cobbled backstreets of a former fishing village. Be prepared for a trip that challenges any preconceived ideas you may have about this, Spain's most famous, tourist-driven coastline.

Link your trip

27 Mediterranean Meander

Málaga is the start of this east-coast adventure that takes in several of Spain's most stunning cities, including its final destination: Barcelona.

32 Alentejo & Algarve Beaches

For more stunning coast, head west via Seville to the Portuguese border, then on to Cacela Velha to do the Algarve trip in reverse.

01 NERJA

Sitting in a charmed spot at the base of the Sierra Almijara mountains, this former fishing village has retained its low-rise village charm, despite the proliferation of souvenir shops and the large number of visitors it sees. At its heart is the **Balcón de Europa**, a seafront balcony built over the site of a Moorish castle. Grab a coffee at one of the terraced cafes before heading north of town to the extraordinary **Cueva de Nerja** (cuevadenerja. es). This 4km-long cave complex, which dates back a

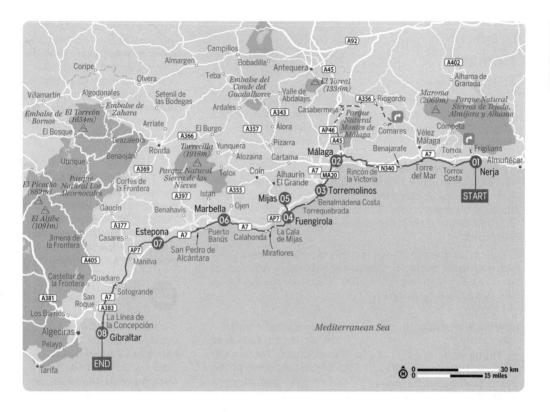

cool five million years, is a wonderland of extraordinary rock formations, subtle shifting colours, stalactites and stalagmites.

🚗 THE DRIVE

The quickest route to Málaga is via the main A7 (E15). More scenic, if slower, is the N340, which meanders along the coast, traversing pretty agricultural land and bypassing centuries-old watchtowers. At Rincón de la Victoria join the A7 for the last few kilometres into Málaga. It's a total drive of 58km (1¼ hours).

🧭 DETOUR

Frigiliana

Start: ① Nerja

After the cavernous gloom of the Cueva de Nerja, consider heading inland to

Frigiliana, a *pueblo blanco* once voted Andalucía's prettiest by the Spanish tourism authority. It's an enchanting place with a tangible Moroccan feel and a steeply banked old town of pretty, whitewashed houses. Wander its quaint streets and pick up some of its famous sweet wine and honey in the small village shops.

It's a straightforward 7km drive from Nerja: take the M5105 inland, passing groves of mango and avocado trees, and follow signs to the *casco historico* (old town) and car park.

02 MÁLAGA

Book a night or two to get the best out of Málaga. The city positively crackles with energy, hosting a buzzing bar life and vibrant restaurant scene.

It also boasts genuine cultural credentials and its art museums are seriously impressive – check out the **Museo Carmen Thyssen** (carmenthyssenmalaga.org), the **Museo Ruso** (coleccionmuseoruso. es) and the unmissable **Museo Picasso** (museopicassomalaga. org), dedicated to the city's most famous son. A short walk away, the 16th-century **Catedral de Málaga** (malagacatedral.com) offers fabulous rooftop views and an interior bedecked with gorgeous retables (a raised shelf above an altar) and 18th-century religious art. Travel further back in time at the **Roman Amphitheatre** and adjacent **Alcazaba** (alcazabaygibralfaro.malaga.eu), a

DETOUR:

Comares

START: 2 MÁLAGA

Heading northeast from Málaga brings you to La Axarquía, an area of rugged hiking country stippled with pretty, unspoiled *pueblos* (villages). A highlight, quite literally, is Comares which sits like a snowdrift on a lofty mountain (739m), commanding spectacular views over the surrounding mountains. Stroll its steep winding lanes and don't miss the remarkable summit cemetery. There are also several walking trails that start here, as well as a 436m-long zip line, the **Tirolina de Comares** (1/2 rides €15/20), which provides a 50-second ride over to the opposite slopes. This is generally open on an appointment-only basis so it's best to book a ride through an activity company like **Vive Aventura** (viveaventura.es).

To get to Comares from Málaga, take the A45 towards Granada, Córdoba and Seville, then exit for Casabermeja and continue onto Comares via the A356 (through Riogordo) and MA3107. The journey is about 60km and should take about 70 minutes.

fascinating 11th-century Moorish palace-fortress.

THE DRIVE

Leaving Málaga, take the A7 in the direction of Algecíras, Torremolinos and Cádiz, then follow the MA20 signposted to Torremolinos. This is a busy stretch of autovía that passes the airport. It's a drive of about 18km or 25 minutes.

03 TORREMOLINOS

Torremolinos, once the poster child of industrial-scale package tourism, now attracts a wide cross-section of people, including trendy clubbers, beach-loving families, gay visitors and, yes, even some Spanish tourists. The centre of town revolves around the pedestrian shopping street **Calle San Miguel**, from where steps lead down to the main beach at **Playamar**. To the southwest, round a small rocky outcrop (La Punta), **La Carihuela** is a former fishing *barrio* which is now, fittingly, home to

some hugely popular seafood restaurants such as **Casa Juan** (losmellizos.net). The beachfront *paseo* continues to Benalmádena, Torre's western twin, where you'll find a large marina designed as a kind of homage to Gaudí and a giant **Buddhist stupa** (stupa benalmadena.org).

THE DRIVE

It's a straightforward 17km drive to Fuengirola on the N340, which hugs the coast and passes through the busy coastal resort of Benalmádena Costa. Note that there's a 50km speed limit on this scenic stretch.

04 FUENGIROLA

Fuengirola's appeal, apart from its 7km of beaches, lies in the fact that it is a genuine Spanish working town, as well as a popular resort. It has a large population of foreign residents, many of whom arrived in the '60s and stayed long after their ponytails had gone grey. Stop by **Plaza de la Constitucíon**, a

pretty square overlooked by the baroque-style facade of Fuengirola's main church, then explore the surrounding streets lined with idiosyncratic shops and tapas bars. A five-minute walk away, the **Bioparc** (bioparcfuengirola.es) is the Costa's best zoo with spacious enclosures and conservation and breeding programmes.

THE DRIVE

From Fuengirola, take Avenida Alcalde Clemente Díaz Ruiz, then the Carretera de Mijas to join the A387. This crosses the A7 and continues up to Mijas about 9km (20 minutes) away. In Mijas follow signs to the underground car park (€1 for 24 hours).

05 MIJAS

The *pueblo blanco* (white village) of Mijas has retained its sugar-cube cuteness despite being on the coach-tour circuit. Art buffs should check out the **Centro de Arte Contemporáneo de Mijas** (cacmijas.info), a contemporary art museum that houses the world's second-largest collection of Picasso ceramics. Otherwise the village is all about strolling the narrow cobbled streets, dipping into tapas bars and shopping for souvenirs. Be sure to walk up to the **Plaza de Toros**, an unusual square-shaped bullring at the top of the village, surrounded by lush ornamental gardens with spectacular coastal views. For more exercise, there are numerous trails leading out from the village, including a tough, well-marked route up to **Pico Mijas** (1151m) – allow about five hours to get there and back.

THE DRIVE

Return to the A7 autovia. This dual carriageway traverses the most densely built-up stretch of the Costa,

WHY I LOVE THIS TRIP

Duncan Garwood, writer

Loud, brash and always fun, Spain's famous Costa makes for a wonderfully entertaining trip. Our route reveals the sunshine coast in all its gaudy glory, taking in Malaga's cultural hits, a giant Buddhist stupa in party-loving Torremolinos, and Marbella's star-studded seafront. Providing the grand finale is Gibraltar, the legendary Rock that guards the gateway to the Mediterranean.

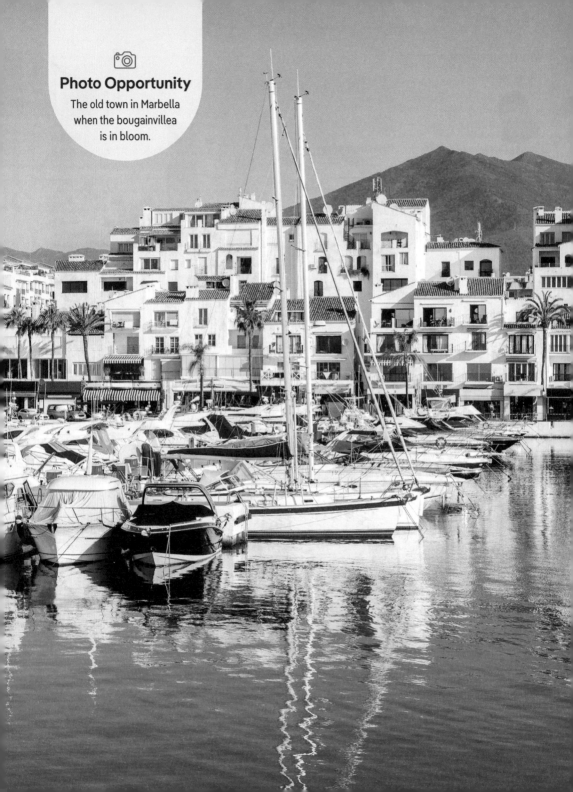

Photo Opportunity

The old town in Marbella
when the bougainvillea
is in bloom.

passing through resorts like Calahonda and Miraflores, which were developed during the Costa's 1980s boom period. Continue west along the A7 until you reach the exit for Marbella; a total drive of 33km or 25 minutes.

06 MARBELLA

Marbella is the Costa del Sol's most high-profile resort town and a good choice for an overnight stop. Well known for its star-studded clubs, shiny restaurants and expensive hotels, it also has other, less ostentatious charms: a magnificent natural setting, sheltered by the beautiful Sierra Blanca mountains, and a gorgeous old town replete with pristine white houses, narrow traffic-free lanes and well-tended flower boxes. At its heart is picturesque **Plaza de los Naranjos**, dating back to 1485 with tropical plants, palms and orange trees. From here you can walk down to the seafront via the lush **Parque de la Alameda** gardens. Follow along the so-called **Golden Mile** (actually, it's about 6km) and you'll eventually reach the luxurious marina of **Puerto Banús**. En route, take time to check out the **Museo Ralli** (museoralli.es), a wonderful private museum displaying works by primarily Latin American and European artists in bright, well-lit galleries.

THE DRIVE

Continue west on the A7 autovia, following signs to Algeciras and Cádiz. This stretch of highway is less built up and passes by San Pedro de Alcántara, as well as five golf courses (they don't nickname this the Costa del Golf for nothing!). It's a snappy 20 minutes or just 24km to your next stop: Estepona.

07 ESTEPONA

Estepona was one of the first resorts to attract tourists almost 50 years ago and, despite the surrounding development, it retains a charming historic centre of narrow cobbled streets, simple *pueblo* houses and well-tended pots of geraniums. Make a beeline for Plaza de las Flores with its fountain centrepoint, orange trees and handy **tourist office** (estepona.es). A 10-minute walk from here, Estepona's fabulous **Orchidarium** (orchidariumestepona.com) houses 1500 species of orchid – the largest collection in Europe – as well as 5000 subtropical plants, flowers and trees, and a 17m-high artificial waterfall. To the southwest of the town centre, Puerto Deportivo is the focal point of the town's nightlife, especially at weekends, and is also excellent for water sports.

Toll Road AP7

If you're travelling in July and August, consider taking the AP7 toll road, at least between Fuengirola and Marbella, as the A7 can become horribly congested. This particular A7 stretch (formerly part of the N340) used to be notorious for accidents, but the situation has improved since the introduction of an 80km/h speed limit in former trouble spots.

THE DRIVE

For the final leg, consider taking the AP7 toll road for the first 20km (€3.35 in peak summer months) as the N340 here is very slow, with numerous roundabouts. At Guadiaro the AP7 merges with the A7 for the rest of the 49km journey. Consider a refreshment stop at swanky Sotogrande harbour, home to Spain's leading golf course, the Real Club Valderrama.

08 GIBRALTAR

Red pillar boxes, fish-and-chip shops and creaky 1970s seaside hotels – there's no getting away from Gibraltar's Britishness. Poised strategically at the jaws of Europe and Africa, Gibraltar, with its Palladian architecture and camera-hogging Barbary apes, makes an interesting finale to your trip. The Rock is one of the most dramatic landforms in southern Europe and most of its upper sections (but not the main lookouts) fall within the **Upper Rock Nature Reserve**. Entry to this includes admission to **St Michael's Cave**, the **Apes' Den**, the **Great Siege Tunnels**, the **Military Heritage Centre** and **Nelson's Anchorage**. The Rock's most famous residents are the 160 or so tailless Barbary macaques that hang around the top cable-car station and Apes' Den. Most Gibraltar visits start in Grand Casemates Sq, once the sight of public executions but now a jolly square surrounded by bars and restaurants. Learn more about the Rock's history at the fine **Gibraltar Museum** (gibmuseum.gi), which displays exhibits ranging from prehistoric and Phoenician Gibraltar to the infamous Great Siege (1779–83).

Puerto Banús, Marbella

29

BEST FOR A SENSE OF ACHIEVEMENT

Reaching Santiago de Compostela.

Northern Spain Pilgrimage

DURATION	DISTANCE	GREAT FOR
5–7 days	786km / 488 miles	History, outdoors

BEST TIME TO GO	April to June for fields of poppies, September and October for golden leaves.

Catedral, Pamplona

For over a thousand years pilgrims have marched across the top of Spain on the Camino de Santiago (Way of St James) to the tomb of St James the Apostle in Santiago de Compostela. Real pilgrims walk, but by driving you'll enjoy religious treasures, grand cathedrals, big skies and wide open landscapes – and no blisters.

Link your trip

30 Historic Castilla y León

From Burgos you can head south to discover the rich heritage of the cities of the Spanish plain.

31 Roving La Rioja Wine Region

With the Camino de Santiago ticked off, carry on to Fisterra and a spectacular trip along Galicia's awe-inspiring coast.

01 RONCESVALLES

History hangs thick in the air of the Roncesvalles **monastery complex** (roncesvalles. es), where pilgrims give thanks for a successful crossing of the Pyrenees. The monastery contains a number of different buildings of interest, including the 13th-century Gothic **Real Colegiata de Santa María**, which houses a much-revered, silver-covered statue of the Virgin beneath a modernist-looking canopy. Also of interest is the cloister, containing the tomb of King Sancho VII (El Fuerte) of Navarra, leader of one of the victorious Christian armies in

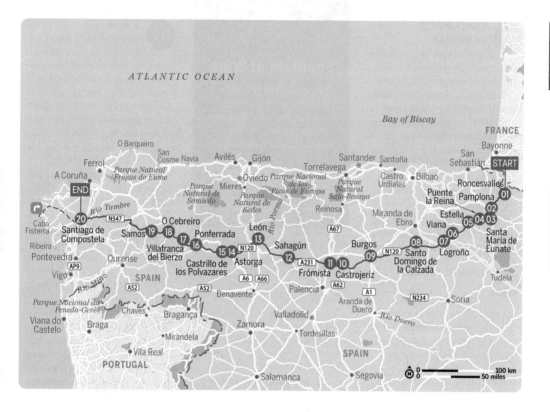

the battle of Las Navas de Tolosa, fought against the Muslims in 1212.

THE DRIVE

It's 49km (one hour) basically downhill to Pamplona – a pretty drive along the N135 through mountain-scapes, forests and gentle farmland. Innumerable hamlets and villages are painted in the red and white Basque colours and centred on old stone churches, many of them crammed with religious treasures.

02 PAMPLONA

Renowned across the world for the **Sanfermines festival** (6 to 14 July), when bulls tear through the streets at 8am, causing chaos as they go (and alcohol-fuelled revellers cause chaos for the remainder of the day – and night), Pamplona (Iruña in Basque) is a quiet, low-key city at any other time of the year. Animal welfare groups condemn the bullrunning as a cruel tradition. Pamplona's history stretches back to Roman times, and is best traced in the fantastic **Museo de Navarra** (navarra.es), whose highlights include huge Roman mosaics. Another Pamplona highlight is the tour of the **Catedral** (catedraldepamplona.com), a late-medieval Gothic gem with a neoclassical facade. The tour

takes you into the cloisters and a museum displaying the remains of a Roman-era house and the tiny skeleton of a seven-month-old baby found there. The 11.15am tour also goes up the bell tower to see (and possibly hear) the second-largest church bell in Spain.

THE DRIVE

Take the A12 southwestward. After about 10 minutes take exit 9 onto the driver-friendly NA1110. Drive through Astraín and continue along this peaceful country road for 15 minutes to Legarda and Muruzábal, then it's 2km southeast to Santa María de Eunate. Total 22km; about 40 minutes.

03 SANTA MARÍA DE EUNATE

Surrounded by cornfields and brushed by wildflowers, the near-perfect octagonal Romanesque chapel of **Santa María de Eunate** (santamariadeeunate.es) is one of the most picturesque churches along the Camino. It dates from around the 12th century but its origins – and the reason why it's located in the middle of nowhere – are a mystery.

THE DRIVE
From the chapel it's just a 5km drive along the NA6064 and NA1110 to gorgeous Puente la Reina.

04 PUENTE LA REINA

The chief calling card of Puente la Reina (Basque: Gares) is the spectacular six-arched **medieval bridge** dominating the western end of town, but Puente la Reina rewards on many other levels. A key stop on the Camino de Santiago, the town's pretty streets throng with the ghosts of a multitude of pilgrims. Pilgrims' first stop here is the late-Romanesque Iglesia del Crucifijo. Erected by the Knights Templar, it contains one of the finest Gothic crucifixes in existence.

THE DRIVE
The fastest way between Puente la Reina and Estella is on the A12 (20km, 20 minutes), but the more enjoyable drive is along the slower, more rural NA1110, taking about half an hour. You'll probably spy a few Camino pilgrims striding along.

05 ESTELLA

Estella (Basque: Lizarra) was known as 'La Bella' in medieval times because of the splendour of its monuments and buildings, and though the old

Fountain of Wine

Opposite Estella's Monasterio de Iratxe is the well-known local wine producer, **Bodegas Irache** (irache.com). For the benefit of Camino de Santiago pilgrims, the winery has installed two taps providing free liquid. From one flows water; from the other, wine – 100L per day.

dear has lost some of its beauty to modern suburbs, it still has charm. During the 11th century Estella became a main reception point for the growing flood of pilgrims along the Camino. Today most visitors are continuing that same tradition. The attractive old quarter has a couple of notable churches, including the 12th-century **Iglesia de San Pedro de la Rúa**, whose cloisters are a fine example of Romanesque sculptural work. Across the river and overlooking the town is the **Iglesia de San Miguel**, with a fine Romanesque north portal. The countryside around Estella is littered with monasteries. Two of the most impressive are **Monasterio de Iratxe**, 2.5km southwest near Ayegui, and **Monasterio de Irantzu**, 11km north near Abárzuza.

THE DRIVE
It's a 40km (50 minute) drive to Viana. Take the A12 westward and turn onto the NA1110 at junction 58. Follow the NA1110 through the sleepy villages of Los Arcos, Sansol and Torres del Río. In hillside Torres, you'll find a remarkably intact eight-sided Romanesque chapel, the Iglesia del Santo Sepulcro.

06 VIANA

Overlooked by many non-pilgrim tourists, Viana, the last town in Navarra, started life as a garrison town defending the kingdom of Navarra from Castilla. The old part of the town, which sits atop a hill, is still largely walled and is an interesting place to wander about for a couple of hours. Work started on the **Iglesia de Santa María** in the 13th century and it's one of the more impressive religious structures on this eastern part of the Camino. Viana's former bullring is now a plaza in the middle of town, where children booting footballs are considerably more common than bulls.

THE DRIVE
It's 10km to Logroño. The first half of the drive is through open, big-sky countryside; the last part through the city suburbs. There's a large car park under Paseo del Espolón on the south edge of Logroño's old town.

07 LOGROÑO

Logroño, capital of La Rioja – Spain's wine-growing region par excellence – doesn't feel the need to be loud and brash. Instead it's a stately town with a heart of tree-studded squares, narrow streets and a monumentally good selection of *pintxos* (tapas) bars. It's the sort of place where you can't help feeling contented. And it's not just the wine. The superb **Museo de la Rioja** (museodelarioja.es) in the centre takes you on a wild romp through Riojan history and culture, from the days when dinner was killed with arrows to recreations of the kitchens that many a Spanish granny grew up using. The other major attraction

is the **Catedral de Santa María de la Redonda** (laredonda.org); it started life as a Gothic church before maturing into a full-blown cathedral in the 16th century.

THE DRIVE

For the 45km (35-minute) hop to Santo Domingo de la Calzada, the Camino walking trail parallels – mostly at a respectful distance – the fast, and dull, A12. There's not much reason for you to veer off the motorway (none of the quieter roads really follow the Camino).

08 SANTO DOMINGO DE LA CALZADA

Santo Domingo is small-town Spain at its very best. A large number of the inhabitants still live in the partly-walled old quarter, a labyrinth of medieval streets where the past is alive and the sense of community is strong. The **Catedral de Santo Domingo de la Calzada** (catedralsantodomingo.com) and its attached museum glitter with the gold that attests to the great wealth the Camino has bestowed on otherwise backwater towns. The cathedral's most eccentric feature is the white rooster and hen that forage in a glass-fronted cage opposite the entrance to the crypt. Their presence celebrates a long-standing legend, the Miracle of the Rooster, which tells of a young man who was unfairly executed only to recover miraculously, while the broiled cock and hen on the plate of his judge suddenly leapt up and chickened off, fully fledged.

THE DRIVE

It's 68km (one hour) to Burgos. Again you're sort of stuck with using the main road, the N120.

09 BURGOS

On the surface, conservative Burgos seems to embody all the stereotypes of a north-central Spanish town, with sombre grey stone architecture, the fortifying cuisine of the high *meseta* (plateau) and a climate of extremes. But Burgos is a city that rewards. The historic centre is austerely elegant, guarded by monumental gates and with the **cathedral** (catedraldeburgos.es) as its centrepiece – a World Heritage–listed masterpiece that started life as a modest Romanesque church, but over time became one of the most impressive cathedrals in a land of impressive cathedrals.

THE DRIVE

It's 48km (45 minutes) to castle-topped Castrojeriz. Head southwest on the A62 to junction 32 and turn off northwest along the minor BU400.

MILOSK50/SHUTTERSTOCK ©

Catedral de Burgos

10 CASTROJERIZ

With its mix of old and new buildings huddled around the base of a hill that's topped with what's left of a crumbling **castle**, Castrojeriz is a typical small *meseta* town. It's worth a climb up to the castle if only for the views. The town's church, **Iglesia de San Juan**, is worth a look as well.

🚗 THE DRIVE

From Castrojeriz it's 26km (30 minutes) along the BU403 and P432 to Frómista. The scenery is classic *meseta* and if you're lucky you'll catch a glimpse of such evocative sights as a flock of sheep being led over the alternately burning or freezing plateau by a shepherd.

11 FRÓMISTA

The main (and some would say only) reason for stopping here is the village's exceptional **Iglesia de San Martín**. Dating from 1066 and restored in the early 20th century, this harmoniously proportioned church is one of the premier Romanesque churches in rural Spain, adorned with human and animal forms below the eaves. The capitals within are also richly decorated.

🚗 THE DRIVE

Take the P980 (the Camino runs alongside it) to Carrión de los Condes, then the more major A231 west to Sahagún (56km; 45 minutes).

12 SAHAGÚN

Despite appearances, Sahagún was an immensely powerful and wealthy Benedictine centre by the 12th century. The brick Romanesque churches, some with later Mudéjar additions, merit a visit.

Route marker, Camino de Santiago

WHAT IS THE CAMINO DE SANTIAGO?

The Camino de Santiago (Way of St James) originated as a medieval pilgrimage. For more than a millennium, people have taken up the challenge of the Camino and walked to Santiago de Compostela. It all began in the 9th century when a remarkable event occurred in the poor Iberian hinterlands: following a shining star, a religious hermit named Pelayo unearthed the tomb of St James the Apostle (Santiago in Spanish). The news was confirmed by the local bishop, the Asturian king and later the pope.

Compostela became the most important destination for Christians after Rome and Jerusalem. Its popularity increased with an 11th-century papal decree granting it Holy Year status: pilgrims could receive a plenary indulgence (a full remission of your life's sins) during a Holy Year. These occur when Santiago's feast day (25 July) falls on a Sunday: 2021 is such a year and the next is 2027 – but driving there doesn't count...

The 11th and 12th centuries marked the heyday of the pilgrimage. The Reformation was devastating for Catholic pilgrimages and by the 19th century the Camino had nearly died out. In its startling late-20th-century reanimation, which continues today, it's equally popular as a personal and spiritual journey of discovery as for primarily religious motives. These days over 350,000 people a year arrive in Santiago on foot, or sometimes bicycle and occasionally horseback, having completed one of the many Camino routes that lead to the city from all points of the Iberian Peninsula and beyond. The most popular route has always been the Camino Francés, which in its full extent crosses some 770km of northern Spain from the Pyrenees, and attracts walkers of all backgrounds and ages from across the world. For pilgrims, it's equal to visiting Jerusalem, and by finishing it, you can expect a healthy chunk of time off purgatory.

THE DRIVE

The 60km (50-minute) stretch from Sahagún to León along the A231 and A60 isn't a memorable drive. Still, you have to feel for those walking the Camino: some pilgrims bus between Burgos and León because so much of the route is next to busy roads.

13 LEÓN

León is a wonderful city, combining stunning historical architecture with an irresistible energy. Its standout attraction is the 13th-century **Catedral** (catedraldeleon.org), one of the most beautiful cathedrals in Spain and arguably the country's premier Gothic masterpiece. Whether spotlit at night or bathed in glorious sunshine, it exudes an almost luminous quality. The showstopping facade has a radiant rose window, three richly sculpted doorways and two muscular towers. Inside, an extraordinary gallery of stained-glass windows awaits. The even older **Real Basílica de San Isidoro** provides a stunning Romanesque counterpoint to the cathedral's Gothic strains. Fernando I and Doña

Sancha founded this church in 1063 to house the remains of San Isidoro, and of themselves and 21 other early Leonese and Castilian monarchs. The main basilica is a hotchpotch of styles, but the two main portals on the southern facade are pure Romanesque. The attached **Real Colegiata de San Isidoro** (Panteón Real; museo sanisidorodeleon.com) houses royal sarcophagi, which rest with quiet dignity beneath a canopy of some of the finest Romanesque frescoes in Spain. Motif after colourful motif of biblical scenes drench the vaults and arches of this extraordinary hall.

THE DRIVE

Taking the N120 to Astorga will keep you on the route of the Camino, which runs alongside the road for long stretches. It's a 50km (one-hour) drive. The AP71 is much faster, but what's the point in coming all this way to drive on a road like that?

14 ASTORGA

Perched on a hilltop on the frontier between the bleak plains of northern Castilla and the mountains that rise

west towards Galicia, Astorga is a fascinating small town with a wealth of attractions way out of proportion to its size. The most eye-catching sight is the **Palacio Episcopal**, a rare flight of fancy in this part of the country, designed by Antoni Gaudí. There's also a smattering of Roman ruins (Astorga was once an important Roman settlement called Astúrica Augusta), a fine Gothic and plateresque **cathedral** and even a **Museo del Chocolate**, dedicated to the town's long chocolate-making tradition. Less sinfully, the town sees a steady stream of pilgrims passing through along the Camino de Santiago.

THE DRIVE

It's just 8km (15 minutes) along the rural LE142 to Castrillo de los Polvazares. Non-residents are not allowed to drive into Castrillo, so park in one of the parking areas on the edge of the village.

15 CASTRILLO DE LOS POLVAZARES

One of the prettiest villages along the Camino – if a little twee – is Castrillo de los Polvazares. It consists of little but one main cobbled street, a small church and an array of well-preserved 18th-century stone houses. If you can be here before the tour buses arrive, or after they have left, then it's an absolute delight of a place and one in which the spirit of the Camino can be strongly felt.

THE DRIVE

Continue along the LE142 to Ponferrada (53km; 1¼ hours). It runs pretty much beside the Camino and you'll pass through attractive stone villages, most of which have churches topped with storks' nests. Rabanal del Camino, with its 18th-century church

---

WHO WAS ST JAMES THE APOSTLE?

St James, or James the Greater, was one of the 12 disciples of Jesus. He may even have been the first disciple. He was also probably the first to be martyred, by King Herod in 44 CE. So, if St James was living in the Holy Lands 2000 years ago, an obvious question persists: what were his remains doing in northwest Spain 800 years later? The legend (and we're not standing by its historical accuracy) suggests that two of St James' own disciples secreted his remains on a stone boat which sailed across the Mediterranean and passed into the Atlantic to moor at present-day Padrón (Galicia). After various trials and tribulations, they buried his body in a forest named Libredón (present-day Santiago de Compostela). All was then forgotten until about 820 CE, when a religious hermit found the remains. Further legends attest that during his lifetime St James preached in various parts of Spain including Galicia, which might explain why his remains were brought here.

Catedral de Santa María de Astorga

Ermita del Bendito Cristo de la Vera Cruz, is worth a quick stop.

16 PONFERRADA

Ponferrada is not the region's most enticing town, but its castle and remnants of the old town centre (around the stone clock tower) make it worth a brief stop. Built by the Knights Templar in the 13th century, the walls of the fortress-monastery **Castillo Templario** rise high over the Río Sil with a lonely and impregnable air, and its square, crenellated towers ooze romance and history.

 THE DRIVE
If you're not in a huge hurry, take the NVI to Villafranca del Bierzo (24km, 30 minutes). It's slower but gentler than the A6 motorway.

17 VILLAFRANCA DEL BIERZO

Villafranca del Bierzo has a very well-preserved old core and a number of interesting churches and other religious buildings. Chief among these are **San Nicolás El Real**, a 17th-century convent with a baroque altarpiece, and the 12th-century **Iglesia de Santiago**. The northern doorway of this church is called the 'door of forgiveness'. Pilgrims who were sick, or otherwise unable to continue to Santiago de Compostela, were granted the same godly favours as if they'd made it all the way.

 THE DRIVE
It's 32km (45 minutes) uphill to O Cebreiro using the NVI, or a bit quicker via the A6. On the NVI you can admire or pity the pilgrims making the Camino's longest, hardest climb, right beside the road on several stretches. Turn off at Pedrafita do Cebreiro and take the LU633 for the last 4km.

18 O CEBREIRO

 O Cebreiro, 1300m high, is the first village in Galicia on the Camino. It's an atmospheric and picturesque little place, busy with pilgrims happy to have completed the climb from Villafranca. O Cebreiro contains several *pallozas* (circular, thatched dwellings known in Galicia since pre-Roman times). A former village priest here, Elías Valiño (1929–1989), is considered to have been the driving force behind the revival of the Camino de Santiago in the late 20th century.

 THE DRIVE
The marvellous 33km drive to Samos winds down the LU633 through refreshingly green countryside with great long-distance views, frequently criss-crossing the Camino.

19 SAMOS

 A pretty village in the Río Sarria valley, Samos is built around the very fine Benedictine **Mosteiro de Samos** (abadiadesamos.com). This monastery has two beautiful big cloisters – one Gothic, with distinctly unmonastic Greek nymphs adorning its fountain, the other neoclassical and filled with roses.

 THE DRIVE
Follow the LU633 and N547 to stay fairly close to the Camino and pass through attractive villages and small towns such as Portomarín. There's no avoiding the A54 motorway to get past Santiago airport. Follow 'Centro Histórico' signs towards the city centre (137km, 2¾ hours from Samos). Private vehicles are barred from the Old Town; underground car parks around its fringes charge around €15 per 24 hours. Cheaper are Aparcadoiro Xoan XXIII (€11) and open-air Aparcadoiro Belvís (€7.50).

20 SANTIAGO DE COMPOSTELA

This, then, is it. The end of the Way. And what a spectacular finish. Santiago de Compostela, with its granite buildings and frequent drizzle, is one of the most beautiful and fascinating cities in Spain. With over 350,000 pilgrims arriving here annually,

---

THE PORTICO DE LA GLORIA

Santiago cathedral's artistically unparalleled Pórtico de la Gloria features 200 Romanesque sculptures by Maestro Mateo, who was placed in charge of the cathedral-building programme in the late 12th century. These detailed and remarkably lifelike sculptures add up to a comprehensive review of major figures and scenes from the Bible. The Old Testament and its prophets (including a famously smiling Daniel) are on the north side; the New Testament, Apostles and Last Judgement are on the south; and glory and resurrection are depicted in the central archway.

Visits are limited to 25 people at a time. Spanish-language guided visits are conducted several times daily, with tickets sold up to 90 days ahead through the cathedral website or on the same day (if available) at the Pazo de Xelmírez adjoining the cathedral, where the visit starts. Fifteen-minute unguided visits happen from 7pm to 8pm Monday to Saturday; 50 tickets for these (free) are given out between 7pm and 8pm the day before at the Fundación Catedral office in the Casa do Deán. For Monday visits go on Saturday. Take your ID document.

Santiago has a busy, festive atmosphere throughout the warmer half of the year (May to October). The magnificent **Catedral de Santiago de Compostela** (cate draldesantiago.es) soars above the city centre in a splendid jumble of spires and statues. Its beauty is a mix of the original Romanesque structure (built between 1075 and 1211) and later Gothic and baroque flourishes. The tomb of Santiago beneath the main altar is a magnet for all who arrive here. The artistic high point is the **Pórtico de la Gloria** inside the west entrance.

Grand **Praza do Obradoiro**, in front of the cathedral's west facade, is traffic- and cafe-free and has a unique atmosphere. From here you can start exploring Santiago's other fine squares and

Photo Opportunity

Standing outside the cathedral of Santiago de Compostela.

churches. At the square's northern end, the **Hostal dos Reis Católicos** (parador.es) was built in the 16th century as a refuge for exhausted pilgrims. Today it's a *parador* (luxurious state-owned hotel), but its four courtyards are open to visitors.

DETOUR
Cabo Fisterra
Start: 20 Santiago de Compostela

This spectacular, cliff-girt, wave-lashed cape has, in popular imagination, long been considered the western edge of Spain, and in days way before satnav it was believed to be the very end of the world. The name Fisterra (Finisterre in Castilian Spanish) means 'Land's End'. In fact, Spain's real westernmost point is Cabo Touriñán, 20km north, but that doesn't lessen Fisterra's magnetic appeal. The end point of a highly popular extension to the Camino de Santiago, the cape is an 82km, 1½-hour drive west from Santiago. Camino pilgrims ritually burn smelly socks, T-shirts and the like on the rocks just past the lighthouse. Many people come for sunset but it's a magnificent spot at any time (unless shrouded in fog or rain).

Fisterra town, 3.5km before the cape, is a fishing port with a picturesque harbour and some beautiful beaches within a few kilometres.

NATURSPORTS/SHUTTERSTOCK ©

Catedral de Santiago de Compostela

30

Historic Castilla y León

BEST FOR CULTURE

Irresistible Salamanca street life against a glorious architectural backdrop.

Acueducto, Segovia

DURATION	DISTANCE	GREAT FOR
7 days	764km / 475 miles	History

BEST TIME TO GO	March to May and September to October to avoid extremes of heat and cold.

From Segovia to Soria, the towns of Castilla y León rank among Spain's most appealing historic centres. Architecture may be central to their attraction, but these are no museum pieces. Instead, the relentless energy of life lived Spanish-style courses through the streets, all set against a backdrop of grand cathedrals and animating stately squares. Out in the countryside, postcard-perfect villages complement the clamour of city life.

Link your trip

29 Northern Spain Pilgrimage

Criss-cross the Camino de Santiago pilgrim route, two-and-a-half hours' north from Soria.

31 Roving La Rioja Wine Region

Discover the wealth of the grape on this peaceful countryside drive, just an hour-and-a-half-north from Soria.

01 **MADRID**

Madrid is the most Spanish of all of Spain's cities. Its food culture, drawn from the best the country has to offer, makes it one of Europe's more underrated culinary capitals, while its nightlife and irresistible *alegría* (joy) exist like some Spanish stereotype given form. But there is more to Madrid than just nonstop colour and movement. This is one of the premier art cities on the continent, with three world-class galleries – the **Museo del Prado** (museodelprado.es), **Museo Thyssen-Bornemisza** (museothyssen.org) and **Centro de Arte Reina Sofía** (museoreinasofia.es) – all clustered close to one of

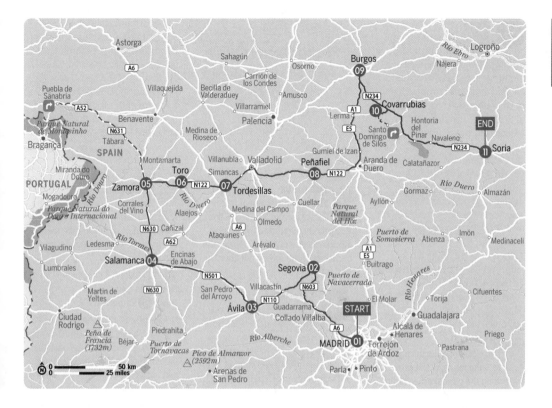

the city's main boulevards and a short walk from the **Parque del Buen Retiro**, one of the loveliest and most expansive monumental parks in Europe. In short, this is a city that rewards those who linger and long to immerse themselves in all things Spanish.

THE DRIVE
Getting out of Madrid can be a challenge, with a complicated system of numbered motorways radiating out from the city. Drive north along the Paseo de la Castellana, turn west along the M50 ring road, then take the A6, direction A Coruña. Of the two main roads to Segovia from the A6, the N603 is the prettier (92km).

02 SEGOVIA
Unesco World Heritage–listed Segovia is a stunning confluence of everything that's good about the beautiful towns of Castilla. There are historic landmarks in abundance, among them the Roman **Acueducto**, the fairy-tale **Alcázar** (alcazardesegovia.com), which is said to have inspired Walt Disney, and Romanesque gems such as the **Catedral** (turismodesegovia.com) or the **Iglesia de San Martín**. This is also one of the most dynamic towns in the country, a winning mix of students and international visitors filling the city's bars and public spaces with

an agreeable crescendo of noise. To cap it all, the setting is simply superb – a city strung out along a ridge, its warm terracotta and sandstone hues arrayed against a backdrop of Castilla's rolling hills and the often snow-capped Sierra de Guadarrama. There are many vantage points to take in the full effect, but our favourite can be found anywhere in the gardens near the entrance to the Alcázar.

THE DRIVE
It's 66km from Segovia to Ávila along the N110. The road runs southwest, parallel to the Sierra de Guadarrama, with some pretty views en route. Around halfway, you'll cross the A6 motorway.

03 ÁVILA

Ávila's old city, surrounded by 12th-century *murallas* (walls) with eight monumental gates, 88 watchtowers and over 2500 turrets, is one of the best-preserved walled cities in Spain. Two sections of the **Murallas** (muralladeavila.com) can be climbed – a 300m stretch accessed from just inside the Puerta del Alcázar, and a longer 1300m stretch that runs along the old city's northern perimeter. The best views are those at night from **Los Cuatro Postes**, a short distance northwest of the city. Ávila is also the home city of Santa Teresa, with the **Convento de Santa Teresa** (teresadejesus.com) as its centrepiece and plenty of other important religious buildings nearby.

🚗 THE DRIVE

The N501 runs northwest of Ávila to Salamanca, in the process traversing the pancake-flat high *meseta* (plateau) of central Spain and covering 109km en route.

04 SALAMANCA

Whether floodlit by night or bathed in the sunset, there's something magical about Salamanca. This is a city of rare beauty, awash with golden sandstone overlaid with ochre-tinted Latin inscriptions; an extraordinary virtuosity of plateresque and Renaissance styles. The monumental highlights are many, with the exceptional **Plaza Mayor** (illuminated to stunning effect at night) an unforgettable highlight. Built between 1729 and 1755, it is widely considered to be Spain's most beautiful central plaza. But this is also Castilla's liveliest city: home to a massive Spanish and international student population

Photo Opportunity

Salamanca's Plaza Mayor lit up at night.

that throngs the streets at night and provides the city with so much youth and vitality.

🚗 THE DRIVE

The N630 runs due north from Salamanca to Zamora (67km), a relatively quiet road by Spanish standards and one that follows the contours of the rolling hill country of Castilla y León's west.

05 ZAMORA

If you're arriving by road, first appearances can be deceiving and, as in so many Spanish towns, your introduction to provincial Zamora is likely to be nondescript apartment blocks. But persevere as the *casco historico* is hauntingly beautiful, with sumptuous medieval monuments that have earned Zamora the popular sobriquet 'Romanesque Museum'. Much of the old town is closed to motorised

transport and walking is easily the best way to explore this subdued encore to the monumental splendour of Salamanca. Zamora is also one of the best places to be during Semana Santa, with haunting processions of hooded penitents parading through the streets. Whatever time of year you're here, don't miss the **Museo de Semana Santa** (semanasantadezamora.com).

🚗 THE DRIVE

The A11 tracks east of Zamora – not far out along the sweeping plains that bake in summer, take the turn-off to Toro. Total distance: 40km.

⟳ DETOUR
Puebla de Sanabria
Start: **5** Zamora

Northwest of Zamora, close to the Portuguese border, this captivating village is a tangle of medieval alleyways that unfold around a 15th-century castle and trickle down the hill. This is one of Spain's loveliest hamlets and it's well worth the detour, or even stopping overnight: the quiet cobblestone lanes make it feel like you've stepped back centuries. Wandering the village is alone worth the trip here but a few attractions are worth tracking

FROG-SPOTTING IN SALAMANCA

A compulsory task facing all visitors to Salamanca is to search out the frog sculpted into the facade of the **Universidad Civil** (salamanca.es). Once pointed out, it's easily enough seen, but the uninitiated can spend considerable time searching. Why bother? Well, they say that those who detect it without help can be assured of good luck and even marriage within a year. Some hopeful students see a guaranteed examination's victory in it. If you believe all this, stop reading now. If you need help, look at the busts of the Reyes Católicos (Catholic Monarchs) Fernando and Isabel. From there, turn your gaze to the largest column on the extreme right of the front. Slightly above the level of the busts is a series of skulls, atop the leftmost of which sits our little amphibious friend (or what's left of his eroded self).

Plaza Mayor, Salamanca

WHY I LOVE THIS TRIP

Anthony Ham, writer

The towns north and west of Madrid are windows on the Spanish soul, each with their own distinctive appeal. Segovia, Ávila, Salamanca, Zamora and Burgos are all Spanish classics, dynamic cities with extraordinary architectural backdrops. Throw in some beautiful villages along the way and you've captured the essence of this remarkable country in just a week.

down. Crowning the village's high point and dominating its skyline for kilometres around, the **Castillo** has some interesting displays on local history, flora and fauna and superb views from the ramparts. Also at the top of the village, the striking **Plaza Mayor** is surrounded by some fine historical buildings. The 17th-century *ayuntamiento* (town hall) has a lovely arched facade and faces across the square to **Iglesia de Nuestra Señora del Azogue**, a pretty village church which was first built in the 12th century. If you're staying the night, the **Posada Real La Cartería** (lacarteria. com) captures the essence of Puebla de Sanabria's medieval appeal with rooms and a restaurant.

06 TORO

With a name that couldn't be more Spanish and a picaresque history that overshadows its present, Toro is your archetypal Castilian town. It was here that Fernando and Isabel cemented their primacy in Christian Spain at the Battle of Toro in 1476. The town sits on a rise high above the north bank of Río Duero and has a charming historic centre with half-timbered houses and Romanesque churches. The high point, literally, is the 12th-century **Colegiata Santa María La Mayor**, which rises above the town and boasts the magnificent Romanesque-Gothic Pórtico de la Majestad.

◎ THE DRIVE

Return to the east–west N122 road that lies east of Toro and continue to Tordesillas (46km).

07 TORDESILLAS

Commanding a rise on the northern flank of Río Duero, this pretty little town has a historical significance that belies its size. Originally a Roman settlement, it later played a major role in world history when, in 1494, Isabel and Fernando sat down with Portugal here to hammer out a treaty determining who got what in Latin America. Portugal got Brazil and much of the rest went to Spain. Explaining it all is the excellent **Museo del Tratado del Tordesillas**. Not far away, the heart of town is formed by the delightful porticoed and cobbled **Plaza Mayor**, its mustard-yellow paintwork offset by dark-brown woodwork and black grilles.

◎ THE DRIVE

From Tordesillas, E80 sweeps northeast, skirts the southern fringe of Valladolid and then continues east as the N122, through the vineyards of the Ribera del Duero wine region all the way into Peñafiel (83km).

MANFRED GOTTSCHALK/GETTY IMAGES ©

Castillo de Peñafiel

08 PEÑAFIEL

Peñafiel is the gateway to the Ribera del Duero wine region and it's an appealing small town in its own right. **Plaza del Coso** is one of Spain's most picturesque plazas. This rectangular 15th-century 'square' is considered one of the most important forerunners to the plazas mayores across Spain. It's still used for bullfights on ceremonial occasions. But no matter where you are in Peñafiel, your eyes will be drawn to the **Castillo de Peñafiel**, one of Spain's longest and narrowest castles. Within the castle's crenulated walls is the state-of-the-art **Museo Provincial del Vino**, the local wine museum.

THE DRIVE
The N122 continues east of Peñafiel. At Aranda del Duero, turn north along the E5 and make for Lerma, an ideal place to stop for lunch. Sated, return to the E5 and take it all the way into Burgos (108km).

09 BURGOS

Dominated by its Unesco World Heritage–listed cathedral but with plenty more to turn the head, Burgos is one of Castilla y León's most captivating towns. The extraordinary Gothic **Catedral** (catedraldeburgos.es) is one of Spain's glittering jewels of religious architecture and looms large over the city and skyline. Inside is the last place of El Cid and there are numerous extravagant chapels, a gilded staircase and a splendid altar. Some of the best cathedral views are from up the hill at the lookout, just below the 9th-century Castillo de Burgos. Elsewhere in town, two monasteries – the **Cartuja de Miraflores**

(cartuja.org) and the **Monasterio de las Huelgas** (monasteriodelas huelgas.org) – are worth seeking out, while the city's eating scene is excellent.

THE DRIVE
Take the E5 south of Burgos but almost immediately after leaving the city's southern outskirts, take the N234 turnoff and follow the signs over gently undulating hills and through green valleys to the walled village of Covarrubias (42km from Burgos).

10 COVARRUBIAS

Inhabiting a broad valley in eastern Castilla y León and spread out along the shady banks of Río Arlanza with a gorgeous riverside aspect, Covarrubias is only a short step removed from the Middle Ages. Once you pass beneath the formidable stone archways that mark the village's entrances, Covarrubias takes visitors within its intimate embrace with tightly huddled and distinctive, arcaded half-timbered houses opening out onto cobblestone squares. Simply wandering around the village is the main pastime, and don't miss the charming riverside pathways or outdoor tables that spill out onto the squares. Otherwise, the main attraction is the **Colegiata de San Cosme y Damián**, which has the evocative atmosphere of a mini cathedral and Spain's oldest still-functioning church organ. Also note the gloriously ostentatious altar, fronted by several Roman stone tombs, plus that of Fernán González, the 10th-century founder of Castilla. Don't miss the graceful cloisters and the sacristy with its vibrant 15th-century paintings by Van Eyck and tryptic *Adoración de los Magos*.

THE DRIVE
The N234 winds southwest of Covarrubias through increasingly contoured country all the way to Soria (111km). En route there are signs to medieval churches and hermitages marking many minor roads leading off into the trees.

DETOUR
Santo Domingo de Silos
Start: 10 Covarrubias

Nestled in the rolling hills just off the Burgos–Soria (N234) road, this tranquil, pretty village is built around a monastery with an unusual claim to fame: monks from here made the British pop charts in the mid-1990s with recordings of Gregorian chants. Notable for its pleasingly unadorned Romanesque sanctuary dominated by a multidomed ceiling, the **church** is where you can hear the monks chant. The **monastery**, one of the most famous in central Spain, is known for its stunning **cloister** (abadiadesilos.es), a two-storey treasure chest of some of Spain's most imaginative Romanesque art. For sweeping views over the town, pass under the Arco de San Juan and climb the grassy hill to the south to the Ermita del Camino y Via Crucis.

11 SORIA

In the heart of the Castilian countryside, Soria is one of Spain's smaller provincial capitals. It's a great place to escape 'tourist Spain', with an appealing and compact old centre and a sprinkling of stunning monuments across the town and down by the Río Duero. The streets of the old town centre are pretty enough, but by the river is the **Monasterio de San Juan de Duero**, Soria's most striking sight, and it's a pretty 2.3km walk to the **Ermita de San Saturio** hillside chapel. The stroll is especially pretty in autumn.

31

Logroño has
some of the
best tapas bars
in Spain.

Roving La Rioja Wine Region

DURATION	DISTANCE	GREAT FOR
2–3 days	145km / 90 miles	Wine, history

BEST TIME TO GO	September and October when the grapes are being harvested.

Tapas, Logroño

La Rioja is home to the best wines in Spain and on this short-and-sweet road trip along unhurried back roads you'll enjoy gorgeous vine-striped countryside and asleep-at-noon villages of honey-coloured stone. But the overriding interest is reserved for food and drink: winery tours, cutting-edge museums and some of the best tapas in Spain make this drive an essential for any food-and-wine lover.

Link your trip

29 Northern Spain Pilgrimage

Follow the path of pilgrims on the road to Santiago de Compostela. You can join The Way in Logroño.

30 Historic Castilla y León

A quick skip south to Soria will let you do this captivating inland tour in reverse.

01 LOGROÑO

Small, low-key Logroño is the capital of La Rioja. The city doesn't receive all that many tourists and there aren't all that many things to see and do, but the historic centre makes for pleasant strolling and there is a monumentally good selection of *pintxo* (tapas) bars. In fact, Logroño is quickly gaining a culinary reputation to rival anywhere in Spain.

Rioja Trek (riojatrek.com), based 2.5km southeast of the city centre, offers a wide range of customisable winery tours (which can include visiting a traditional

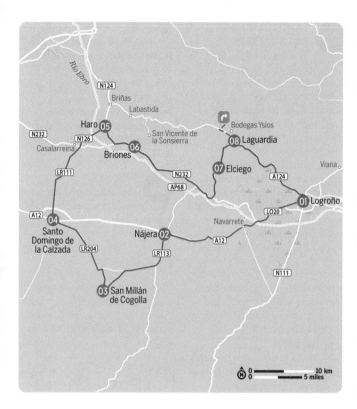

Tapas in Logroño

Make no mistake about it: Logroño is an eater's delight. There are several very good restaurants, and then there are the tapas (which here are often called by their Basque name, *pintxos*). Few cities have such a dense concentration of excellent tapas bars. Most of the action takes place on Calle Laurel and Calle San Juan. *Pintxos* cost around €2 to €4, and most of the bars are open from about 8pm to midnight, Tuesday to Sunday. Here are some of our favourites:

Bar Torrecilla The best pintxos in town? You be the judge. Go for the melt-in-your-mouth foie gras or the mini-burgers, or anything else that takes your fancy, at this modern bar on buzzing Calle Laurel.

Tastavin (www.facebook. com/tastavinbardepinchos) On *pintxo*-bar-lined San Juan, stylish Tastavin whips up some of the tastiest morsels in town, including smoked trout and lemon cream cornets, fried artichokes, tuna tataki and braised oxtail. The wines are outstanding.

Bar Soriano This venerable bar has been serving just one tapa, a mushroom stack topped with a prawn, since 1972.

---

vineyard and bodega and even doing some wine-making yourself), as well as wine tastings, tapas tours, hikes along some of La Rioja's fabulous mountain trails and activities for families with children.

THE DRIVE
It's only a short drive of 28km (25 minutes) from Logroño to Nájera, starting along the LO20, which transforms into the A12 motorway around the halfway point.

02 NÁJERA
The main attraction of this otherwise unexciting town, which lies on the Camino de Santiago, is the Gothic **Monasterio de Santa María la**

Real and, in particular, its fragile-looking, early-16th-century cloisters. The monastery was built in 1032, but was significantly rebuilt in the 15th century.

THE DRIVE
The dry landscapes around Nájera become greener and more rolling as you head southwest along the LR113 and LR205 for 18km (20 minutes) to San Millán de Cogolla. In the far distance rise the 2000m-plus mountains of the Sierra de la Demanda – snow-capped in winter.

03 SAN MILLÁN DE COGOLLA
The hamlet of San Millán de Cogolla is home to two remarkable monasteries, which between

them helped give birth to the Castilian (Spanish) language. On account of their linguistic heritage and artistic beauty, they have been recognised by Unesco as World Heritage sites.

The **Monasterio de Yuso** (monasteriodesanmillan.com/yuso) contains numerous treasures in its museum. You can only visit as part of a guided tour (in Spanish, with English and French information sheets available). Tours last 50 minutes and run every half-hour or so.

A short distance away is the **Monasterio de Suso** (monasteriodesanmillan.com/suso). It's believed that in the 13th century a monk named Gonzalo de Berceo wrote some of the first Castilian words here. Again, it can only be visited on a guided tour. Tickets include a short bus ride up to the monastery from the Monasterio de Yuso, whose reception area sells them; you can't arrive independently.

THE DRIVE
It's a 20km (20-minute) drive along the delightfully quiet LR206 and LR204 to Santo Domingo de la Calzada. The scenery is a mix of vast sunburnt fields, red-tinged soils, vineyards and patches of forest.

04 SANTO DOMINGO DE LA CALZADA
The small, walled old town of Santo Domingo is the kind of place where you can be certain that the baker knows all his customers by name and that everyone will turn up for María's christening. Santiago-bound pilgrims have long been a part of the fabric of this town, and that tradition continues to this day, with most visitors being foot-weary pilgrims. All this helps to make Santo Domingo one of the most enjoyable places in La Rioja. The biggest attraction in town, aside from the very worthwhile pursuit of just strolling the streets and lounging in the main old-town plaza, is a visit to the monumental **cathedral** (catedral santodomingo.com).

THE DRIVE
The LR111 (becoming the N126) goes in an almost ruler-straight line across fields of crops and under a big sky to the workaday town of Haro (20km, 20 minutes).

05 HARO
Despite its fame in the wine world, there's not much of a heady bouquet to Haro, La Rioja's premier wine-producing town. But it has a cheerful pace, and the compact old quarter, leading off Plaza de la Paz, has some intriguing alleyways with bars and wine shops aplenty.

There are plenty of wine bodegas in the vicinity of the town, some of which are open to visitors (but almost always with advance reservation). One of the more receptive to visitors is **Bodegas Muga** (bodegasmuga.com), which is just after the railway bridge on the way out of town to the north. It gives guided tours and tastings, in Spanish and English, daily except Sunday.

THE DRIVE
Briones is almost within walking distance of Haro. It's just 9km away (10 minutes) along the N124 and N232.

06 BRIONES
One man's dream has put the small, obscenely quaint village of Briones firmly on the Spanish wine and tourism map. The sunset-gold village crawls gently up a hillside and offers commanding views over the surrounding vine-carpeted plains. It's on these plains where you will find the fantastic wine museum **Vivanco** (Museo de la Cultura del Vino; vivancocultura devino.es). Over several floors you will learn all about the history and culture of wine and the various processes that go into its production. All of this is done through interesting displays brought to life with computer technology. The treasures on display include Picasso-designed wine jugs, Roman and Byzantine mosaics, and gold-draped, wine-inspired religious artefacts. Various guided tours take you behind the scenes of the winery and include tastings.

THE DRIVE
It's 23km (30 minutes) along the N232, LR211 and A3210 to Elciego. The scenery, which is made up of endless vineyards, will delight anyone who enjoys wide open spaces (and vine leaves). In the distance are strange, sheer-faced, table-topped mountains.

07 ELCIEGO

Rioja wine's most flamboyant flourish lurks in the village of Elciego (Eltziego in Basque) in the showstopping form of the **Hotel Marqués de Riscal** (hotel-marquesderiscal.com) – not unlike a rainbow-hued Guggenheim museum (not surprising, perhaps, as both buildings were designed by Canadian Frank Gehry). Casual visitors are not welcome at the hotel, but if you want to see it, you have three options. The easiest is to join one of the **Marqués de Riscal winery tours** (Vinos de los Herederos del Marqués de Riscal; marquesderiscal.com) – there's at least one English-language tour a day, but it's best to book in advance. You won't get inside the building, but you will get to see its exterior from some distance. A much closer look can be obtained by reserving a table at one of the two superb in-house restaurants: the Michelin-starred **Restaurante Marqués de Riscal** (restaurante marquesderiscal.com) or the **1860 Tradición** (hotel-marquesderiscal.com). For the most intimate look at the building, you'll need to reserve a hotel room for the night.

Photo Opportunity

Waving at the camera from in front of the Hotel Marqués de Riscal.

THE DRIVE

It's only 10 minutes (7km) along the A3210 from Elciego to wonderful Laguardia, which rises up off the otherwise flat, vine-striped countryside.

Hotel Marqués de Riscal, Elciego

08 LAGUARDIA

It's easy to spin back the wheels of time in the medieval fortress town of Laguardia, or the 'Guard of Navarra' as it was once appropriately known, sitting proudly on its rocky hilltop. As well as with memories of long-lost yesterdays, the town further entices visitors with its wine-producing present. **Bodegas Palacio** (bodegas palacio.com), just 800m south of Laguardia, arranges tours and tastings by appointment. Check the website for details of its wine courses (from €35 for one hour). On the southeast edge of town is the **Centro Temático del Vino Villa Lucía** (villa-lucia. com), a wine museum and shop selling high-quality wine from a variety of small, local producers. Museum visits are by guided tour only and finish with a 4D film and wine tasting.

⮎ DETOUR
Bodegas Ysios
Start: 10 Laguardia

Just a couple of kilometres north of Laguardia is **Bodegas Ysios** (bodegasysios.com), architecturally perhaps the most gobsmacking bodega in Spain. Designed by Santiago Calatrava as a 'temple dedicated to wine', it features a cedar exterior with an aluminium wave for a roof that matches the flow of the rocky mountains behind it – and looks best after dark when pools of light flow out of it. Tours provide an insight into wine production; book ahead.

MARISA ESTIVILL/SHUTTERSTOCK ©

Wine barrels, La Rioja

THE WEALTH OF THE GRAPE

La Rioja, and the surrounding areas of Navarra and the Basque province of Álava, comprise Spain's best-regarded wine-producing region. The principal grape of Rioja is the tempranillo. The first taste of a tempranillo is of leather and cherries, and the wine lingers on the tongue.

The Riojans have had a long love affair with wine. There's evidence that both the Phoenicians and the Celtiberians produced and drank wine here and the earliest written evidence of grape cultivation in La Rioja dates to 873 CE. Today, some 250 million litres of wine burst forth from the grapes of La Rioja annually. Almost all of this (around 85%) is red wine, though some quality whites and rosés are also produced. The Riojan love of wine is so great that in the town of Haro they even have a fiesta devoted to it. It culminates with a messy 'wine battle', in which thousands of litres of wine get chucked around, turning everyone's clothes red in the process. This takes place on 29 June.

How to find a good bottle? Spanish wine is subject to a complicated system of classification, similar to the ones used in France and Italy. La Rioja is the only wine region in Spain classed as *Denominación de Origen Calificada* (DOC), the highest grade and a guarantee that any wine labelled as such was produced according to strict regional standards. The best wines are often marked with the designations 'Crianza' (aged more than two years, with at least one year in an oak barrel), 'Reserva' (aged for at least three years, at least one of them in an oak barrel) or 'Gran Reserva' (aged for at least two years in an oak barrel and three years in the bottle).

PUYALROYO/SHUTTERSTOCK ©

Praia de Odeceixe (p259)

Portugal

Explore

Portugal

Portugal's mix of the medieval and maritime makes it a superb place for a road trip. A turbulent history of invasions by the Moors, Spanish and Napoleonic French has left its interior scattered with walled towns and formidable castles, while pounding Atlantic surf has sculpted a coastline of glorious coves and wide, sandy beaches.

There's terrific eating and drinking too, with several wine regions and restaurants cooking up succulent grilled pork and fresh locally caught fish.

Comparatively short distances are a further bonus, meaning you'll spend fewer hours behind the wheel and have more time to explore.

Lisbon

Lisbon, Portugal's capital and most populous city, is the country's principal gateway. Draped across steep hillsides on the banks of the Rio Tejo, the city is well worth a few days' exploration before you hit the road – northwards to Coimbra, Porto and the Doura Valley, and southwards to the Algarve and its tantalising beaches. You can take in the Castello de São Jorge and hilltop Alfama district, search out old-school bistros in Baixa, and see the night out in bohemian bars and riverside clubs.

To get to Lisbon, international flights serve the city's airport about 6km north of the centre. To leave, the A1 toll road heads north to Porto and the A2 leads south to Faro and the Algarve.

Porto

Most trips to northern Portugal pass through Porto, the country's second-largest city and a major transport hub. Flights arrive at its international airport while long-distance trains pull into Campanhã station, about 3km east of the city centre. By road, the A1 auto-estrada arrives from the south and the A4 runs in from the Spanish border. The Doura Valley is accessible via the scenic N108.

Porto is well set up for visitors with plenty of accommodation, sumptuous food and wine and a brilliant bar scene. Many big sights are huddled together in the Ribeira and Aliados districts, both of which can easily be covered on foot.

WHEN TO GO

Blooming wildflowers and mild sunny weather make spring a prime time for city visits and outdoor activities. Autumn is another top period, especially for wine lovers who can enjoy the fruits of the grape harvest. Summer brings sweltering temperatures and high season prices as holidaymakers flock to popular resorts and beaches in the sun-drenched Algarve.

Faro

Faro is the first port of call for many visitors to the Algarve. Travellers fly into the city's busy airport but few linger in town, preferring to head on to their booked resorts. But stay a day or two and you'll discover it has an attractive marina and picturesque *cidade velha* (old town). It's also well equipped with accommodation and has some great seafood restaurants and lively bars.

For onward travel, Lisbon is about 2½ hours away via the A2. For coastal drives, the N125 is the main go-to road.

Coimbra

The attractive medieval city of Coimbra makes a prime base for central Portugal. Home of the country's most prestigious university, its handsome hilltop centre cascades down a steep hillside to the banks of the Rio Mondego, hosting a lively bar and restaurant scene. To stay, there are some excellent guesthouses and a few traditional hotels.

The city, which kicks off our Highlands & History in the Central Interior drive, can be reached by train from Porto or Lisbon.

TRANSPORT

Portugal is well connected to North America and Europe by air. Most international flights arrive in Lisbon, though some also serve airports at Porto in the north and Faro in the Algarve. Alternatively, buses and trains run in from neighbouring Spain where you can connect with services to/from other European destinations.

 WHAT'S ON

Queima das Fitas

(May) Burning of the Ribbons marks the end of the academic year in Coimbra with concerts, parades and copious drinking.

Festa de Santo António

(June) The Festival of St Anthony is celebrated with feasting, merry-making and dancing in Lisbon's Alfama and Madragoa districts.

Festa de São Jão

(June) Elaborate processions, music and food take centre stage as Porto parties in the name of St John.

Resources

Portugal Tourism *(visit portugal.com)* Portugal's official tourist website with plenty of information and inspiration.

Solares de Portugal *(solares deportugal.pt)* Find your ideal holiday home on the listing site of the Turihab accommodation association.

Wines of Portugal (winesof portugal.info) For an overview of Portugal's wine scene with info on regions, grape varieties and wine routes.

 WHERE TO STAY

Accommodation is plentiful in Portugal, particularly in coastal resorts and the main towns and cities. Note, however, that some places on the coast and in rural areas close over winter, typically from March to April. As well as the usual array of hotels, guesthouses, campgrounds, private rooms and holiday rentals, Portugal has some excellent hostels, often housed in heritage buildings. Further up the budget scale, you can book rooms in rural cottages, farmhouses and manor houses through an association known as Turihab. And then there are the *pousadas*, top-end hotels housed in renovated castles, monasteries and palaces.

32

Douro Valley Vineyard Trails

DURATION	DISTANCE	GREAT FOR
5–7 days	381km / 237 miles	Wine, outdoors

BEST TIME TO GO	Spring for wildflowers, early autumn for the grape harvest.

Ponte de Dom Luís I, Porto

You're in for a treat. This Unesco World Heritage region is hands-down one of Portugal's most evocative landscapes, with mile after swoon-worthy mile of vineyards spooling along the contours of its namesake river and marching up terraced hillsides. Go for the food, the fabulous wines, the palatial *quintas* (estates), the medieval stone villages and the postcard views around almost every bend.

Link your trip

33 Alentejo & Algarve Beaches

Do one trip in reverse: about four hours south from Porto are great beaches and towns with Moorish heritage.

34 Highlands & History in the Central Interior

Dip south of Porto 120km to Coimbra for a foray into Portugal's history-crammed interior and inspiring Serra da Estrela mountains.

01 PORTO

Before kick-starting your road trip, devote a day or two to Porto, snuggled on the banks of the Río Douro, where life is played out in the mazy lanes of the medieval Ribeira district. From here, the double-decker bridge **Ponte de Dom Luís I**, built by an apprentice of Gustav Eiffel in 1877, takes the river in its stride. Cross it to reach Vila Nova de Gaia, where grand 17th-century port lodges march up the hillside. Many open their barrel-lined cellars for guided tours and tastings – usually of three different ports – that will soon help you tell your tawny

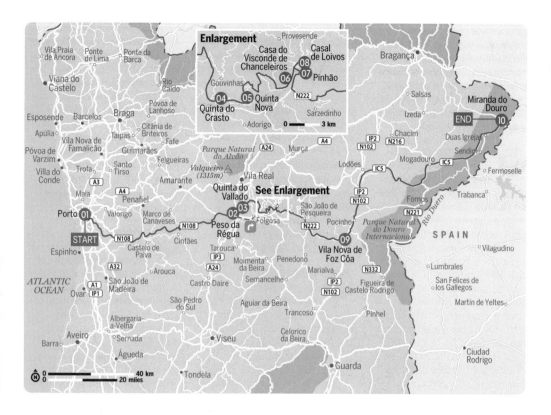

from your late-bottled vintage. Top billing goes to British-run **Taylor's** (taylor.pt) with their immense 100,000L barrel, **Graham's** (grahams-port.com) and **Calém** (calem.pt).

🚗 THE DRIVE

There are quicker ways of getting from A to B, but for immersion in Douro wine country, you can't beat the three-hour (137km) drive east on the N108. The serpentine road shadows the Río Douro, with views of vine-clad hillsides, little chapels and woodlands spilling down to the sparkling river.

02 PESO DA RÉGUA

Terraced hills scaled with vines like a dragon's backbone rise around riverside Peso da Régua. The sun-bleached town is the region's largest, abutting the Río Douro at the western end of the demarcated port-wine area. It grew into a major port-wine entrepôt in the 18th century. While not as charming as its setting, the town is worth visiting for its **Museu do Douro** (museudodouro.pt). Housed in a beautifully converted riverside warehouse, the museum whisks you through the entire wine spectrum, from impressionist landscapes to the remains of an old flat-bottomed port hauler. Down at the pier, you'll find frequent 50-minute boat trips to Pinhão, offered by **Tomaz do Douro** (tomazdodouro.pt), for instance.

🚗 THE DRIVE

Take the first exit onto the N2 at the roundabout at the end of Rua Dr Manuel de Arriaga, then the third exit at the next roundabout to join the N313. Turn right onto the N313-1 when you see the yellow sign to Quinta do Vallado. It's around a 5km drive.

🔸 DETOUR

DOC
Start: ② Peso da Régua

Architect Miguel Saraiva's ode to clean-lined, glass-walled minimalism, **DOC** (docrestaurante.pt) is headed up by Portuguese star chef Rui Paula. Its terrace peering out across the river is a stunning backdrop. Dishes give a pinch of imagination to seasonal, regional flavours, from fish *açordas* (stews) to game and wild mushrooms (plus good vegetarian options) – all of which are paired with carefully selected wines from the cellar. It's in Folgosa, midway between Peso da Régua and Pinhão, on the south side of the river. Take the N2 south of Peso da Régua, then hook onto the N222 heading east.

03 QUINTA DO VALLADO

Ah, what views! The vineyards spread picturesquely before you from **Quinta do Vallado** (quintadovallado.com), a glorious 70-hectare winery. It brings together five rooms in an old stone manor and eight swank rooms in an ultramodern slate building, decked out with chestnut and teak wood, each complete with a balcony. They all share a gorgeous pool. Guests get a free tour of the winery, with a tasting. Have a fine wine-paired meal and stay the night. The staff can also help arrange activities like cycling, hiking, fishing or canoeing.

THE DRIVE
From Quinta do Vallado, the N313-2, CM1258 and N322-2 take you on a 29km drive east through the curvaceous wine terraces of the Alto Douro, past immaculate rows of vines and chalk-white hamlets, with tantalising glimpses of the river below. After Gouvinhas, the wiggling road takes you south to Quinta do Crasto.

04 QUINTA DO CRASTO

Perched like an eyrie on a promontory above the Río Douro and a spectacular ripple of terraced vineyards, **Quinta do Crasto** (quintadocrasto.pt) quite literally takes your breath away. The winery is beautifully set amid the lyrical landscapes of the Alto Douro, a Unesco World

Heritage Site. Stop by for a tour and tasting or lunch. It produces some of the country's best drops – reds that are complex, spicy and smooth, with wild berry aromas, and whites that are fresh, with a mineral nose and tang of citrus and apples. Designed by Portuguese starchitect Eduardo Souto de Moura, the plunge pool here appears to nosedive directly into the valley below.

THE DRIVE
From Quinta do Crasto it's an easy 4km drive east along the mellow banks of the Río Douro to Quinta Nova via the N322-2 and CM1268.

05 QUINTA NOVA

Set on a ridge, surrounded by 120 hectares of ancient vineyards, overlooking the Douro river with mountains layered in the distance, **Quinta Nova** (quintanova.com) is simply stunning. Besides plush lodgings in a beautifully restored 19th-century manor, it offers romantic grounds, a pool gazing out across rolling vineyards, a restaurant, wine tours, tastings and some of the region's top walking trails – the longest of which is three hours.

THE DRIVE
It's a 10km drive east from Quinta Nova to Casa do Visconde de Chanceleiros on the CM1268, tracing the contours of the emerald-green vines unfurling around you.

06 CASA DO VISCONDE DE CHANCELEIROS

Fancy staying the night up in the hills of the sublime Alto Douro? **Casa do Visconde de Chanceleiros** (chanceleiros.com) is a gorgeous 250-year-old manor house, with spacious rooms

featuring classic decor and patios. The expansive views of the valley and lush terraced gardens steal the show, but so does the outdoor pool, tennis court, Jacuzzi, and sauna in a wine barrel. Delicious dinners (€38) are served on request.

THE DRIVE
A gentle 7.5km drive east along the M590, with spirit-lifting views across the terraced vineyards, the deep-green Douro and family-run *quintas*, brings you to Pinhão.

07 Pinhão

Encircled by terraced hillsides that yield some of the world's best port – and some damn good table wines too – little Pinhão sits on a particularly lovely bend of the Río Douro. Wineries and their competing signs dominate the scene and even the delightful train station has *azulejos* (hand-painted tiles) depicting the grape harvest. The town, though cute, holds little of interest, but makes a fine base for exploring the surrounding vineyards. From here, you can also cruise upriver into the heart of the Alto Douro aboard a traditional flat-bottomed port boat with **Douro-a-Vela** (douroavela.pt). Catch the boat from the Folgosa do Douro pier. Or enjoy sublime views over two rivers while wine tasting at **Quinta do Tedo** (quintadotedo.com).

THE DRIVE
Veer slightly west of Pinhão on the N323 and turn right onto the M585, following the sign for Casal de Loivos, 4.5km away. The country road weaving up through the vines, with the river below, later becomes the cobbled Rua da Calçada, passing *socalcos* (stone-walled terrace) vineyards.

Quinta do Tedo

08 CASAL DE LOIVOS

It's a tough call, but Casal de Loivos has hands-down one of the most staggeringly beautiful views in the region. From the *miradouro* (viewpoint), the uplifting vista reduces the Douro to postcard format, taking in the full sweep of its stone-walled terraced vineyards, stitched into the hillsides and fringing the sweeping contours of the valley, and the river scything through them. To maximise on these dreamy views, stay the night at **Casa de Casal de Loivros** (casadecasaldeloivos.com). The elegant house has been in this winemaking family for nearly 350 years. The halls are enlivened by museum-level displays of folkloric dresses, and the perch – high

Photo Opportunity

The staggering view of the Douro vineyards from Casal de Loivos' *miradouro* (lookout).

above the Alto Douro – is spectacular. Swim laps in the pool while peering down across the vines spreading in all directions.

THE DRIVE

Backtrack on the N323, then pick up the N222 south of the river for the 64km drive southeast to Vila Nova de Foz Côa. The winding road takes you through some picture-book scenery, with whitewashed hamlets and *quintas* punctuating vines, orchards and olive groves.

09 VILA NOVA DE FOZ CÔA

Welcome to the heart of the Douro's *terra quente* (hot land). This once-remote, whitewashed town has been on the map since the 1990s, when researchers, during a proposed project for a dam, stumbled across an astounding stash of Paleolithic art. Thousands of these mysterious rock engravings speckle the Río Côa valley. Come to see its world-famous gallery of rock art at the **Parque Arqueológico do Vale do Côa** (arte-coa.pt). The three sites open to the public include Canada do Inferno, with departures at around 9.30am from the park museum in Vila Nova de Foz Côa, which is the ideal place to understand just how close these

ZDENEK MATYAS PHOTOGRAPHY/SHUTTERSTOCK ©

Views from Casal de Loivos

aeons-old drawings came to
disappearing.

🚗 THE DRIVE
Wrap up your road trip by driving
120km northeast to Miranda do Douro
via the N102, IP2 and IC5. Closer to the
Spanish border you'll notice the shift
in scenery, with lushness giving way
to more arid, rugged terrain, speckled
with vineyards and olive groves.

10 MIRANDA DO DOURO

A fortified frontier town
hunkering down on
the precipice of the Río Douro
canyon, Miranda do Douro was
long a bulwark of Portugal's
'wild east'. While its crumbling
castle and handsomely severe
16th-century cathedral still lend
an air of medieval charm, modern-day Miranda now receives
weekend Spanish tourists, as
opposed to Castilian attacks. For
an insight on the region's border
culture, including ancient rites
such as the 'stick dancing' of
the *pauliteiros,* visit the **Museu
da Terra de Miranda**. If you'd
rather get a taste of the rugged
nature on Miranda's door-
step, **Europarques** (Crucero
Ambiental Arribes del Duero;
europarques.com) runs one- and
two-hour riverboat trips along a
dramatic gorge. Boats leave from
beside the dam on the Portuguese side. Stop by the **Parque
Natural do Douro Internacional Office** (natural.pt) for the
inside scoop on hiking among
the woods and towering granite
cliffs of the 832-sq-km park. It's
home to bird species including
black storks, Egyptian vultures,
peregrine falcons, golden eagles
and Bonelli's eagles.

KIYECHKA90/SHUTTERSTOCK ©

Portuguese wine tasting

WINES OF THE DOURO

The Douro has been world-famous for port wines for centuries, but
only recently has the region carved out a reputation for its equally outstanding table wines. The region's steep, terraced slopes, schist soils
(allowing good drainage), blisteringly hot summers and cold winters,
and old, established vines are a winning combination.

Dozens of grape varieties – nearly all of which are red and uniquely
Portuguese – are grown in the region, but the top five grapes are the
touriga nacional, tinta barroca, tinto cão, tinta roriz (tempranillo in
Spain) and touriga franca. Alone or as a blend, these grapes produce
well-structured, tannic and powerful wines, with finesse, length
and ripe-fruit flavours. The more expensive ones kept for ageing are
usually labelled 'Reserva' or 'Grande Reserva' and these are big, gutsy
wines – complex, oaky and full of jammy dark-fruit flavours.

White grapes account for a tiny proportion of wine production, but
they have also come on in leaps and bounds. Grapes such as malvasia,
viosinho, gouveio and rabigato produce pale whites that are crisp-
edged, minerally, fresh and fruity. Those kept for ageing are gold-hued
and more complex, with oaky, nutty flavours.

33

Alentejo & Algarve Beaches

DURATION	DISTANCE	GREAT FOR
4–6 days	360km / 224 miles	Food, outdoors, family travel

BEST TIME TO GO	Good all year, but crowded in July and August.

Odeceixe

Portugal's southern coasts offer a Mediterranean ideal, with fragrances of rosemary and pine drifting over some absolutely stunning beaches. Only this isn't the Mediterranean, it's the Atlantic, so add surfable waves, important maritime history and great wildlife-watching opportunities to the mix. This drive takes in some of the finest beaches in the region, and explores the intriguing towns, which conserve their tight-knit Moorish street plans.

Link your trip

28 Costa del Sol Beyond the Beaches

From Cacela Velha, head 350km east and southeast to Gibraltar, then journey east along Spain's southern coast.

32 Douro Valley Vineyard Trails

Combine this trip in reverse with a straight shot north from Vila Nova de Milfontes to Porto for wines and more.

01 VILA NOVA DE MILFONTES

One of the loveliest towns along this stretch of the coast, Vila Nova de Milfontes has an attractive, whitewashed centre, sparkling beaches nearby and a laid-back population who couldn't imagine living anywhere else. Milfontes remains much more low-key than most resort towns, except in August when it's packed to the hilt with surfers and sunseekers. It's located in the middle of the beautiful **Parque Natural do Sudoeste Alentejano e Costa Vicentina** and is still a port (Hannibal is said to

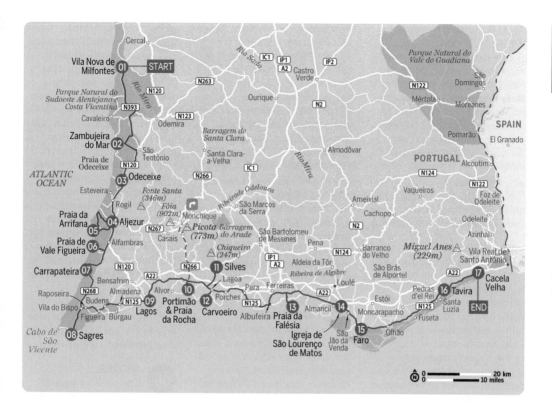

have sheltered here) alongside a lovely, sand-edged limb of estuary.

Milfonte's narrow lanes, tiny plazas and beach harbour offer varied eating and drinking options. The town beach is sheltered but can get busy; the best strand in the vicinity is fantastic **Praia do Malhão**, backed by rocky dunes and covered in fragrant scrub, around 7km to the north.

🚗 THE DRIVE

It's a 26km drive through protected parkland on the N393 south to Zambujeira do Mar.

02 ZAMBUJEIRA DO MAR

Enchantingly wild beaches backed by rugged cliffs form the setting of this sleepy seaside village. The main street terminates at the cliff and paths lead to the attractive sands below. Quieter than Vila Nova, Zambujeira attracts a backpacker, surfy crowd, though in August the town is a party place and hosts the massive music fest, **Festa do Sudoeste**. The high-season crowds obscure Zambujeira's out-of-season charms: fresh fish in family-run restaurants, blustering clifftop walks and a dramatic, empty coast.

🚗 THE DRIVE

Cutting back to the main road, you then head south on the N120. It's about 25km to Odeceixe through beautiful coastal woodland.

03 ODECEIXE

Located just as you cross into the Algarve from the Alentejo, Odeceixe is an endearing whitewashed village cascading down a hill below a picture-perfect windmill on the southern side of the Ribeira de Seixe valley. It's a sleepy town, except in summer, when it fills with people keen on its nearby beach. This tongue of sand is winningly set at a river-mouth and flanked by imposing schist cliffs (try saying that with a mouthful of porridge...). It's a particularly good option for families, as smaller children can paddle on the peaceful river side of the strand while older kids tackle the waves on the ocean side. The beach is 3.5km from Odeceixe itself, along a charming country road. At the beach, a small village has eating and surfing options. The **Rota Vicentina**, a long-distance walking path that leads right to the southwestern tip of Portugal, passes through Odeceixe, and there are great day walks in the vicinity.

THE DRIVE
It's an easy 15km down the N120 to Aljezur, through woodland and shrubland patched with heather and gorse.

04 ALJEZUR
The old part of Aljezur is an attractive village with a Moorish feel. A collection of cottages winds down the hill below a ruined 10th-century hilltop **castle**. Aljezur is close to some fantastic beaches, edged by black rocks that reach into the white-tipped, bracing sea – surfing hotspots. The handsomest beach in the Aljezur area, on the north side of the picturesque river mouth and backed by wild dunes, is **Praia da Amoreira**. It's 9km by road from Aljezur, signposted off the main road north of town.

THE DRIVE
A couple of kilometres south of Aljezur, the beaches of Monte Clérigo and Arrifana are signposted off to the right. At the top of the hill, head right (towards Monte Clérigo) for the full coastal panorama before winding your way south to Arrifana.

05 PRAIA DA ARRIFANA
Arrifana is a seductive fingernail-shaped cove embraced by cliffs. Just to add to the picturesqueness, it also sports an offshore pinnacle and a petite traditional fishing harbour. The beach is wildly popular with

surfers of all abilities and there are several surf schools in the area. The beach break is reliable, but there's also a right-hand reef break that can offer some of the Algarve's best surfing when there's a big swell. There's a small, very popular beachside restaurant, and clifftop eateries near the ruined fortress up above, which offers breathtaking vistas. Good diving is also possible here.

THE DRIVE
Praia de Vale Figueira is reached by a rough, partly paved road that runs some 5km from the main road at a point 10km south of Aljezur. Before reaching the turn-off, you must turn right off the N120 onto the N268.

06 PRAIA DE VALE FIGUEIRA
One of the remoter west-coast beaches, this is a long, wide and magnificent stretch of whitish sand with an ethereal beauty, backed by stratified cliffs hazy in the ocean spray. It's reached by a rough, semi-paved road and there are no facilities. The beach faces due west and has pretty reliable surf, especially when a southeaster is blowing. It's one of those lonely, romantic beaches that's great to stroll on even when the weather's nasty.

THE DRIVE
Head back to the main road (N268) and turn right onto it. It's about 10km from here to Carrapateira.

07 CARRAPATEIRA
Surf-central Carrapateira is a tranquil, pretty, spread-out village offering two fabulous beaches with spectacular settings and turquoise seas. **Bordeira** is a mammoth swath of sand merging into dunes 2km from the north side of town. **Amado**, with even better surf, is at the southern end. The circuit of both from Carrapateira (9km) is a visually stunning hike (or drive), with lookouts over the beaches and rocky coves and cliffs between them. In town, the **Museu do Mar e da Terra da Carrapateira** (cm-aljezur.pt) is an intriguing place to visit, with great views.

THE DRIVE
The N268 barrels on right down to Portugal's tip at Sagres (22km), via the regional centre of Vila do Bispo.

08 SAGRES
The small, elongated village of Sagres, with a rich nautical history, has an appealingly out-of-the-way feel. It sits on a remote peninsula amid picturesque seaside scenery with a sculpted coastline and stern **fortress** (monumentosdoalgarve.pt) leading to a stunning clifftop walk. It also appeals for its access to fine beaches and water-based activities; it's especially popular with a surfing crowd. Outside town, the striking

---

THE SAGRES FOOD SCENE

A closely packed string of surfer-oriented places on **Rua Comandante Matoso** in Sagres offer a bit of everything, whether it's a coffee or a caipirinha you're after. They are cafes by day, restaurants serving international favourites by night, whatever time hunger drags you away from the beach and lively bars. Further down the same street, near the port, is a cluster of more traditional Portuguese restaurants.

Path to Praia da Bordeira, Carrapateira

WHY I LOVE THIS TRIP

Andy Symington, writer

I can't think of a more impressive series of beaches than those of Portugal's south; they are simply magical. There's a wild and unspoiled romance to the seasprayed west-coast strands, while a succession of sun-baked golden sands in the south includes intriguing island beaches only reachable by boat. I love wandering the region's tight-knit old towns, trying to detect which lane that delicious aroma of grilling fish is coming from...

cliffs of **Cabo de São Vicente**, the southwesternmost point of Europe, make for an enchanting visit, especially at sunset. Make sure you pop into the small **museum** here, which has interesting background information on the Algarve's starring role in the Age of Discovery. From Sagres' harbour, worthwhile excursions head out to observe dolphins and seabirds. **Mar Ilimitado** (marilimitado.com) is a recommended operator.

THE DRIVE

Head back to Vila do Bispo and turn right onto the N125 that will take you to Lagos, a total drive of 34km. Promising beach detours include Zavial and Salema.

09 LAGOS

Touristy, likeable Lagos lies on a riverbank, with 16th-century walls enclosing the old town's pretty, cobbled streets and picturesque plazas. A huge range of restaurants and pumping nightlife add to the allure provided by fabulous beaches and numerous watery activities. Aside from the hedonism, there's plenty of history here: start by visiting the lovably higgledy-piggledy **Museu Municipal** (cm-lagos. com), which incorporates the fabulous baroque church **Igreja de Santo António**. Heading out on to the water is a must, perhaps cetacean-spotting with **Algarve Water World**

IVARS ANDRUPS/SHUTTERSTOCK ©

Igreja de Santo António, Lagos

(algarvewaterworld.com), paddling with **Kayak Adventures** (kayakadventureslagos.com) or learning to surf with **Lagos Surf Center** (lagossurfcenter.com). East of town stretch the golden sands of **Meia Praia**, backed by worthwhile beach restaurants.

🚗 **THE DRIVE**
Portimão is really just along the coast from Lagos, but it's a 24km detour inland via the N125 in a car.

10 PORTIMÃO & PRAIA DA ROCHA
The Algarve's second-largest town, Portimão's history dates back to the Phoenicians before it became the region's fishing and canning hub in the 19th century. Though that industry has since declined, it's still an intriguing port with plenty of maritime atmosphere. Learn all about the town's fishing heritage in the excellent **Museu de Portimão** (museudeportimao.pt), before strolling through the no-frills sardine restaurants of the fishers' quarter of Largo da Barca near the road bridge. At the southern end of Portimão stretches the impressive resort beach of Praia da Rocha, backed by numerous restaurants and nightlife options.

🚗 **THE DRIVE**
The N125 leads east to the junction with the N124-1 that takes you north to Silves. It's a drive of only 20km.

🔗 **DETOUR**
Monchique
Start: 10 Portimão

High above the coast, in cooler mountainous woodlands, the picturesque little town of Monchique makes a lovely detour, with some excellent options for day hikes, including climbing the Algarve's highest hills, Picota and Fóia, for super views over the coast.

Monchique and the surrounding area have some excellent eating choices and nearby **Caldas de Monchique** is a sweet little spa hamlet in a narrow wooded valley.

The N266 heads north from the N124 north of Portimão; it's a 27km drive from Lagos to Monchique, then another 30km on to Silves.

11 SILVES
Silves is one of the Algarve's prettiest towns and replete with history: it was an important trading city in Moorish times and preserves a tightly woven medieval centre. At the top of the town, its sizeable **castle** (cm-silves.pt) offers great views from the ramparts. Originally occupied in the Visigothic period, what you see today dates mostly from the Moorish era, though the castle was heavily restored in the 20th century. Below this, the atmospheric **cathedral** is the region's best-preserved Gothic church. The **Museu Municipal** (cm-silves.pt) gives good background on the city's history and is built around a fascinating Moorish-era well, complete with spiral staircase. The old-town streets are great for strolling.

Photo Opportunity

The rock formations at Praia da Marinha.

🚗 **THE DRIVE**
Cruise 14km straight down the N124-1 to the beach at Carvoeiro.

12 CARVOEIRO
Carvoeiro is a cluster of whitewashed buildings rising up from tawny, gold and green cliffs and backed by hills. This diminutive seaside resort is prettier and more laid-back than many of the bigger resorts. The town beach is pretty but small and crowded – there are lots of other excellent options in the area. The most picturesque of all, with stunning rock formations, is **Praia da Marinha**, 8km east of Carvoeiro. On foot, it's best reached by the **Percurso dos Sete Vales Suspensos** clifftop walk, beginning at Praia Vale Centianes, 2.3km east of town.

🚗 **THE DRIVE**
Head back to Lagoa to join the N125 eastwards. After 25km, turn right and head towards the coast, emerging atop the long beach. It's a 37km total drive.

13 PRAIA DA FALÉSIA
This long, straight strip of sand offers one of the region's most impressive first glimpses of coast as you arrive from above. It's backed by stunning cliffs in white and several shades of ochre, gouged by weather into intriguing shapes and topped by typical pines. The areas near the car parks get packed in summer (especially as high tides

cover much of the beach), but as the strip is over 3km long, it's easy enough to walk and find plenty of breathing room. It's a good beach for strolling, as the cliffscape constantly changes colours and shapes, and there's a surprising range of hardy seaside plants in the cracks and crevices.

THE DRIVE
Head back to the N125 and continue eastwards. Just after bypassing the town of Almancil, there's an exit to 'Almancil, São Lourenço, praias'. The church is signposted from here.

14 IGREJA DE SÃO LOURENÇO DE MATOS

It's worth stopping here to visit the marvellous interior of this small **church** (Church of St Lawrence of Rome; diocese-algarve.pt), built over a ruined chapel after local people, while digging a well, had implored the saint for help and then struck water. The resulting baroque masterpiece, built by fraternal master-team Antão and Manuel Borges, is wall-to-wall *azulejos* inside, with beautiful panels depicting the life of the Roman-era saint, and his death by roasting. In the 1755 earthquake, only five tiles fell from the roof.

THE DRIVE
Back on the N125, head south-eastwards and after 12km you're in Faro.

15 FARO

The capital of the Algarve has a distinctly Portuguese feel and plenty to see. Its evocative waterside old town is very scenic and has several

Mercado Municipal

Faro's impressive modern **market building** (mercado municipaldefaro.pt) is a great place to wander, people-watch, buy fresh produce, sit down on a terrace with a coffee, or lunch at one of the several worthwhile eateries.

interesting sights, including the excellent **Museu Municipal** (cm-faro.pt), set in a former convent. The area is centred around Faro's **cathedral**, built in the 13th century but heavily damaged in the 1755 earthquake. What you see now is a variety of Renaissance, Gothic and Baroque features. Climb the tower for lovely views across the walled town and estuary islands. Part of the **Parque Natural da Ria Formosa**, these islands can be explored on excellent boat trips run by **Formosamar** (facebook.com/formosamar). The cathedral has a small bone chapel, but much spookier is the one at the **Igreja de Nossa Senhora do Carmo** (diocese-algarve.pt), built from the mortal remains of over a thousand monks.

THE DRIVE
It's 35km east along the N125 to Tavira. Despite the road's proximity to the coast, you won't see much unless you turn off: Fuseta is a pleasant waterside village to investigate, with boat connections to island beaches.

16 TAVIRA

Set on either side of the meandering Rio Gilão, Tavira is a charming town. The ruins of a hilltop **castle**, now housing a pleasant little botanic garden; the **Renaissance Igreja da Misericórdia** (diocese-algarve.pt); and the **Núcleo Islâmico** (cm-tavira.pt) museum of Moorish history are among the attractions. It's ideal for wandering; the warren of cobblestone streets hides pretty, historic gardens and shady plazas. Tavira is the launching point for the stunning, unspoilt beaches of the **Ilha de Tavira**, a sandy island that's another part of the Parque Natural da Ria Formosa.

THE DRIVE
Cacela Velha is 14km east of Tavira: head along the N125 and you'll see it signposted. It's 1km south of the N125.

17 CACELA VELHA

Enchanting, small and cobbled, Cacela Velha is a huddle of whitewashed cottages edged with bright borders, and has a pocket-sized fort, orange and olive groves, and gardens blazing with colour. It sits above a gorgeous stretch of sea, with a characterful local bar, plus other restaurants, a church and heart-lifting views. From nearby **Fábrica**, you can get a boat across to the splendid Cacela Velha beach, which has a low-key LGBTIQ+ scene in summer.

Igreja de São Lourenço de Matos

34

Highlands & History in the Central Interior

DURATION	DISTANCE	GREAT FOR
5–7 days	770km / 480 miles	History, outdoors

BEST TIME TO GO	May to October for the best temperatures.

Casa dos Repuxos, Conímbriga

History is tangible at every turn in Portugal's interior and this route combines some of the nation's most evocative historic sights, from the venerable university library of Coimbra or Viseu's cathedral, to picture-perfect traditional villages like Piódão or Idanha-a-Velha. Sturdy fortress towns such as Almeida and Trancoso shore up the border with Spain, while the Serra da Estrela mountains offer superb vistas and glorious hiking opportunities.

Link your trip

30 Historic Castilla y León

Visit some of Spain's most appealing cities north and west of Madrid.

32 Douro Valley Vineyard Trails

Head to Porto, from where you can easily dip into the terraced vineyards and outstanding wineries of the Unesco World Heritage Douro.

01 COIMBRA

While Porto and Lisbon take the headlines, the university town of Coimbra, between the two, is one of Portugal's highlights. Its atmospheric historic centre cascades down a hillside above the Rio Mondego: a multicoloured assemblage of buildings covering a millennium of architectural endeavour.

The spiritual heart of the old town is the **Universidade de Coimbra** (uc.pt/turismo), whose stunning 16th- to 18th-century buildings surround the Patio des Escolas square. The **Biblioteca**

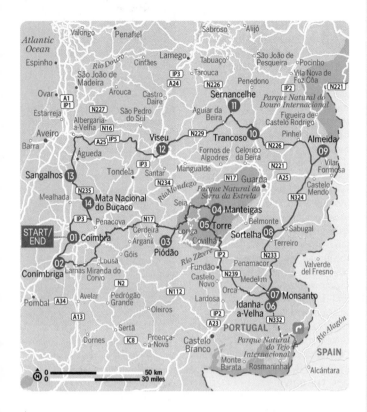

Coimbra Fado

If Lisbon represents the heart of Portuguese fado (traditional Portuguese melancholic song), Coimbra is its head. The 19th-century university was male-only, so the town's womenfolk were of great interest to the student body. Coimbra fado developed partly as a way of communicating with these heavily chaperoned females, usually in the form of serenades sung under the bedroom window. For this reason, fado is traditionally sung only by men, who must be students or ex-students.

The Coimbra style ranges from hauntingly beautiful serenades and lullabies to more boisterous students-out-on-the-piss type of songs. The singer is normally accompanied by a 12-string *guitarra* (Portuguese guitar) and perhaps a Spanish (classical) guitar too. Due to the clandestine nature of these bedroom-window concerts, audience appreciation is traditionally indicated by softly coughing rather than clapping.

There are several excellent venues in Coimbra to hear fado, including **À Capella** (acapella.com.pt).

Joanina library is the sumptuous highlight. Within a short stroll are two other Coimbra masterpieces: the **Sé Velha** (Old Cathedral) is one of Portugal's finest Romanesque buildings, while the altogether more modern **Museu Nacional de Machado de Castro** (museu machadocastro.pt) presents an excellent collection of art, as well as taking you down to the city's Roman origins.

🚗 THE DRIVE
It's a short drive southeast along the IC3/N1 some 16km to Condeixa-a-Nova, on whose outskirts sit the Roman ruins of Conímbriga.

02 CONÍMBRIGA
Hidden amid humble olive orchards in the rolling country southwest of Coimbra, Conímbriga boasts Portugal's most extensive and best-preserved **Roman ruins** (conimbriga.pt), and ranks with similarly lauded sites on the entire Iberian Peninsula.

To get your head around the history, begin at the small **museum** near the entrance. Displays present every aspect of Roman life from mosaics to medallions. Then, head out to the ruins themselves. A massive defensive wall running right through the site speaks of times of sudden crisis. In contrast, the extraordinary mosaics of the **Casa dos Repuxos** speak of times of peaceful domesticity.

🚗 THE DRIVE
It's two hours in the car to the next stop. The most interesting

route is to take the N342 east, turning north onto the N236, then taking the N17 and IC6 northeast. The last stretch on the N230 is a spectacular if occasionally nerve-racking drive, following valleys with breathtaking views, sheer drops and tight curves.

 03 PIÓDÃO

Remote Piódão offers a chance to see rural Portugal at its most pristine. This tiny traditional village clings to a terraced valley in a beautiful, surprisingly remote range of vertiginous ridges, deeply cut valleys, rushing rivers and virgin woodland called the Serra de Açor (Goshawk Mountains).

Until the 1970s you could only reach Piódão on horseback or by foot, and it still feels as though you've slipped into a time warp. The village is a serene, picturesque composition in schist and slate; note the many doorways with crosses over them, said to offer protection against curses and thunderstorms.

Houses descend in terraces to the square, where you'll find the fairy-tale parish church, the **Igreja Nossa Senhora Conceição**, and a low-key touristy scene selling local liqueurs and souvenirs.

THE DRIVE

It's only 66km to the next stop, but with the winding roads, spectacular scenery and intriguing villages en route, it may take you some time. Retrace your steps, then head northeast on the N338. The N231 takes you to Seia; from there the N339 then N232 is one of Portugal's great drives, through typical landscapes of the Serra da Estrela and down a vertiginous descent into Manteigas.

 04 MANTEIGAS

In the heart of the Serra da Estrela, Portugal's loftiest and most spectacular highland region, this is the most atmospheric of the mountain towns hereabouts. Cradled at the foot of the beautiful Vale do Zêzere, with high peaks and forest-draped slopes dominating the horizon in all directions, Manteigas enjoys a spectacular natural setting. There are lots of good marked walks in the surrounding area, so you may want to set aside a day to explore the mountain landscapes on foot. Walk through the glacial valley above town and you'll still encounter terraced meadows, stone shepherds' huts and tinkling goat-bells, while in Manteigas itself cobblestone streets and older homes still hold their own against the high-rise development that has taken root on the Serra da Estrela's fringes.

THE DRIVE

The drive from Manteigas to Torre (22km, around 35 minutes) is especially breathtaking, first following the N338 along the Vale do Zêzere. After turning right onto the N339 towards Torre, you pass through the Nave de Santo

TOP TIP:

Views to Stop For

At Penhas Douradas, at the top of the hill before the long descent into Manteigas, don't miss the stunning view from a stub of rock called **Fragão do Corvo**; just follow the signs.

Walks from Manteigas

The **Trilhos Verdes** (manteigas trilhosverdes.com) is an excellent network of marked trails in the Manteigas area. Each route is viewable online and has its own leaflet available at the park information office in town.

The relatively easy ramble (11km one way) through the magnificent, glacier-scoured **Vale do Zêzere**, one of the park's most beautiful and noteworthy natural features, is a highlight. It's quite exposed in summer.

António – a traditional high-country sheep-grazing meadow – before climbing through a surreal moonscape of crags and gorges. Visible near the turn-off for Torre is Cântaro Magro, a notable rock formation, rising 500m straight from the valley below.

 05 TORRE

In winter, Torre's road signs are so blasted by freezing winds that horizontal icicles barb their edges. Portugal's highest peak, at 1993m, Torre ('Tower') produces a winter freeze so reliable that it has a small ski resort with mainly beginners' slopes.

Outside the snow season (mid-December to mid-April), Portugal's pinnacle is rather depressing, though a park visitors centre with displays about the region's natural and cultural history is worthwhile.

Photo Opportunity

Piódão's tiny cluster of buildings and terraces.

Even if you give Torre itself a miss, it's worth the drive here to survey the astoundingly dramatic surroundings.

THE DRIVE

Retrace your steps from Torre and continue straight on along the N339 to eventually descend steeply into Covilhã. Take the IP2/A23 motorway south, then the N18 and N239 roughly eastwards, finally reaching the N332, which takes you the last stretch to Idanha-a-Velha. It's a drive of around 90km.

06 Idanha-a-Velha

Extraordinary Idanha-a-Velha is a very traditional small village with a huge history. Nestled in a remote valley of patchwork farms and olive orchards, it was founded as the Roman city of Igaeditânia (Egitania). Roman ramparts still define the town, though it reached its peak under Visigothic rule: they built a **cathedral** and made Idanha their regional capital. It's also believed that their legendary King Wamba was born here.

Moors were next on the scene, and the cathedral was turned into a mosque during their tenure. They, in turn, were driven out by the Knights Templar in the 12th century. It's believed that a 15th-century plague virtually wiped out the town's inhabitants. Today a small population of shepherds and farmers live amid the Roman, Visigothic and medieval ruins.

Wandering this picturesque village is an enchanting trip back in time.

THE DRIVE

Head north up the N332 again, then turn right at the N239. The turn-off to Monsanto is clearly marked. It's only a 15km drive. Passengers who want to stretch their legs could walk the pretty 7km trail from Idanha to Monsanto.

▶ DETOUR

Parque Natural do Tejo Internacional
Start: 6 Idanha-a-Velha

Still one of Portugal's wildest landscapes, this 230-sq-km park shadows the Rio Tejo (Tagus), the border between Portugal and Spain. It shelters some of the country's rarest bird species, including black storks, Bonelli's eagles, royal eagles, Egyptian vultures, black vultures and griffon vultures.

The best-marked hiking trail, the **Rota dos Abutres** (Route of the Vultures),

Idanha-a-Velha

TLF IMAGES/SHUTTERSTOCK ©

descends from Salvaterra do Extremo (34km southeast of Idanha-a-Velha) into the dramatic canyon of the Rio Erges. It's an 11km circuit that includes a vulture colony viewing point, and great views of a castle over in Spain.

07 MONSANTO

Like an island in the sky, the stunning village of Monsanto towers high above the surrounding plains. A stroll through its steeply cobbled streets, lined with stone houses that seem to merge with the boulder-strewn landscape, is reason enough to come. But to fully appreciate Monsanto's rugged isolation, climb the shepherds' paths above town to the abandoned and crumbling hilltop **castle**. This formidable stone fortress seems almost to have grown out of the boulder-littered hillside that supports it. It's a beautiful site, windswept and populated by lizards and wildflowers. Immense vistas include Spain to the east and the Barragem da Idanha dam to the southwest. Walkers will also appreciate the network of hiking trails threading through the vast cork-oak-dominated expanses below.

THE DRIVE

Sortelha is about 60km north of Monsanto across a variety of hilly landscapes. Head due north from Monsanto, eventually linking up with the N233. Turn off in the village of Terreiro, following the brown signs for Sortelha.

08 SORTELHA

Perched on a rocky promontory, Sortelha is the oldest of a string of fortresses guarding the frontier in this region. Its fortified 12th-century castle teeters on the brink of a steep cliff, while immense walls encircle a village of great charm. Laid out in Moorish times, it remains a winning combination of stout stone cottages, sloping cobblestone streets and diminutive orchards.

'New' Sortelha lines the Santo Amaro–Sabugal road. The medieval hilltop fortress is a short drive, or a 10-minute walk, up one of two lanes signposted 'castelo'.

The entrance to the fortified old village is a grand, stone Gothic gate. From here, a cobbled lane leads up to the heart of the village, with a *pelourinho* (pillory) in front of the remains of a small castle and the parish church. Higher still is the bell tower – climb it for a view of the entire village. For a more adventurous and scenic climb, tackle the ramparts around the village (beware precarious stairways and big steps).

THE DRIVE

Head east to Sabugal, then turn north, following the N324 north before joining the N340 for the final run northeast to Almeida. It's a drive of around 65km.

09 ALMEIDA

After Portugal regained independence from Spain in the 1640s, the country's border regions were on constant high alert. Almeida's vast, star-shaped fortress is the handsomest of the defensive structures built during this period.

The fortified old village is charming, with enough history and muscular grandeur to set the imagination humming.

Most visitors arrive at the fortress via the **Portas de São Francisco**, two long tunnel-gates separated by an enormous dry moat.

The long arcaded building just inside is the 18th-century **Quartel das Esquadras**, the former infantry barracks.

Not far away, the interesting **Museu Histórico Militar de Almeida** is built into the *casamatas* (casemates or bunkers), a labyrinth of 20 underground rooms used for storage, barracks and shelter for troops in times of siege. Piles of cannonballs fill a central courtyard of the museum, with British and Portuguese cannons strewn about nearby.

Make sure you also see the attractive **Picadero d'el Rey**, once the artillery headquarters, and what's left of the castle, blown to smithereens during a French siege in 1810.

THE DRIVE

Retrace your steps down the N340, then head northwest on the N324. At Pinhel, turn westwards onto the N221/N226, all the way to Trancoso, around 60km in total.

10 TRANCOSO

A warren of cobbled lanes squeezed within Dom Dinis' mighty 13th-century walls makes peaceful Trancoso a delightful retreat from the modern world. The walls run intact for over 1km around the medieval core, which is centred on the main square, Largo Padre Francisco Ferreira. The square, in turn, is anchored by an octagonal *pelourinho* dating from 1510. The Portas d'El Rei (King's Gate), surmounted by the ancient coat of arms, was always the principal entrance, whose guillotine-like door sealed out unwelcome visitors. On a hill in the northeast corner of town is the tranquil **castle**, with its crenellated towers and the distinctively slanted walls of the squat, Moorish **Torre de Menagem**, which you can climb for views.

🚗 THE DRIVE
Head 30km northwest along the N226 to reach the next stop, Sernancelhe.

11 SERNANCELHE
Located 30km northwest of Trancoso, Sernancelhe has a wonderfully preserved centre fashioned out of warm, beige-coloured stone. Sights include a 13th-century **church** that boasts Portugal's only free-standing Romanesque sculpture, an old Jewish quarter with crosses to mark the homes of the converted, and several grand 17th- and 18th-century town houses. The finest manor of all is the **Solar dos Carvalhos**, believed to be the birthplace of the famed 18th-century statesman and strong-armed reformer Marquês de Pombal. Just outside of town are hills that bloom with what are considered to be Portugal's best chestnuts.

🚗 THE DRIVE
The N229 leads you 55km southwest through increasingly fertile countryside to Viseu.

12 VISEU
One of central Portugal's most appealing cities, Viseu has a well-preserved historical centre that offers numerous enticements to pedestrians: cobbled streets, meandering alleys, leafy public gardens and a central square – **Praça da República**, aka the 'Rossio' – graced with bright flowers and fountains. Sweeping vistas over the surrounding plains unfold from the town's highest point, the square fronting the 13th-century granite **cathedral**, whose gloomy Renaissance facade conceals a splendid 16th-century interior, including an impressive Manueline ceiling.

🚗 THE DRIVE
It's a drive of 90km to the next stop. The quickest way is to take the A25 motorway west, turning south onto the IC2.

13 SANGALHOS
In the village of Sangalhos, in the Bairrada wine-producing region between Aveiro and Coimbra, the extraordinary **Aliança Underground Museum** (bacalhoa.pt) is part *adega* (winery), part repository of an eclectic, enormous and top-quality art and artefact collection. Under the winery, vast vaulted chambers hold sparkling wine, barrels of maturing *aguardente* (distilled spirits; firewater) and a series of galleries displaying a huge range of objects. The highlight is at the beginning: a superb collection of African sculpture, ancient ceramics and masks, but you'll also be impressed by the spectacular mineral and fossil collection and the beauty of some of the spaces. Other pieces include *azulejos,* a rather hideous collection of ceramic and faience animals, and an upstairs gallery devoted to India. The only complaint is that there's no information on individual pieces, and you don't have time to linger over a particular item. Phone ahead to book your visit, which can be conducted in English and includes a glass of sparkling wine.

🚗 THE DRIVE
It's an easy 20km drive down the N235 to the town of Luso and on up the hill to the Buçaco forest.

14 MATA NACIONAL DO BUÇACO
This famous, historic **national forest** (fmb.pt) is encircled by high stone walls that for centuries have reinforced a sense of mystery. The aromatic forest is criss-crossed with trails, dotted with crumbling chapels and graced with ponds, fountains and exotic trees. In the middle, like in a fairy tale, stands a royal palace. Now a luxury hotel, it was built in 1907 as a royal summer retreat on the site of a 17th-century Carmelite monastery. This wedding cake of a building is over-the-top in every way: outside, its conglomeration of turrets and spires is surrounded by rose gardens and swirling box hedges in geometric patterns; inside (nonguests are more or less prohibited entry) are neo-Manueline carvings, suits of armour on the grand staircases and *azulejos*.

Nearby, **Santa Cruz do Bussaco** (fmb.pt) is what remains of a convent where the Duke of Wellington–to-be rested after the Battle of Bussaco in 1810. The atmospheric interior has decaying religious paintings, an unusual passageway right around the chapel, some guns from the battle and the much-venerated image of *Nossa Senhora do Leite* (Our Lady of Milk), with ex-voto offerings.

Outside the forest walls lies the old-fashioned little spa town of **Luso**.

🚗 THE DRIVE
Heading back to Coimbra, ignore your GPS and make sure to take the lovely foresty N235, which later joins the IP3. It's a picturesque drive.

Santa Cruz do Bussaco

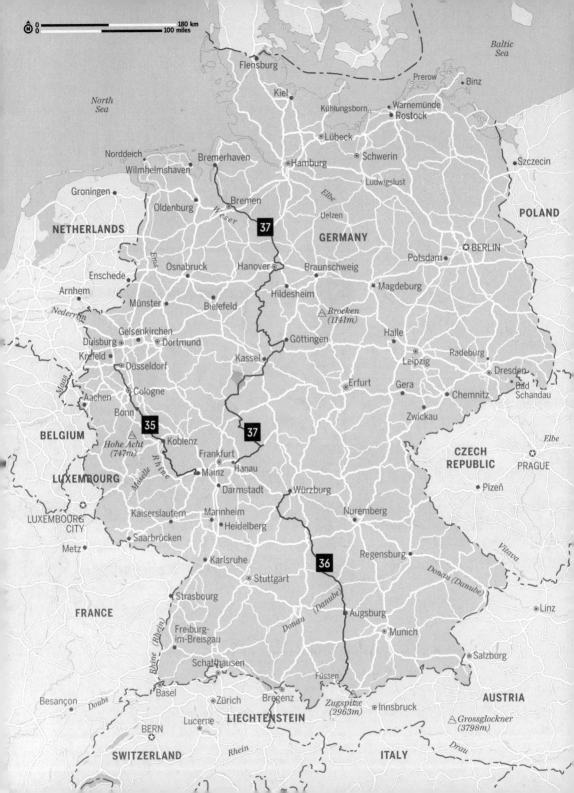

Tauberbischofsheim (p287)

Germany

Explore

Germany

Powerhouse cities, storybook villages, vine-stitched valleys and bucolic landscapes that beg you to leap out of the car and whoop for joy – road-tripping in Germany is a mesmerising kaleidoscope of dramatic landscapes and exciting experiences.

The trips in this chapter promise headline sights and romantic hideaways, steering you from Germany's confident, sophisticated cities to fabled Rhine vineyards and the medieval walled towns of Bavaria. So whether you want to cruise past castles, sip a glass or two of Riesling or climb into the foothills of the Alps, we have a trip for you.

Frankfurt

Glinting with glass and steel, Frankfurt am Main is one of Europe's principal financial centres, home to the European Central Bank. It's also a major transport hub. Its airport is one of Europe's busiest and you might well find yourself passing through even if Frankfurt isn't your final destination. However, take a day or two to explore the city and you'll discover it has an unexpectedly traditional side with half-timbered buildings, cosy taverns and beautiful parks. Art masterpieces adorn its Städel Museum and there are dizzying views to be enjoyed from the Kaiserdom cathedral.

To the east of the city, Hanau (starting point of the German Fairy Tale Road drive) is a mere 20km away. To the west, Mainz (on the Romantic Rhine tour) is about 44km away.

Munich

Germany's southern powerhouse, Munich is the capital and principal gateway to Bavaria, whose timeless towns can be explored on the Romantic Road drive. A hugely popular destination, the city is well set up for visitors with ample accommodation, museums showcasing everything from artistic masterpieces to technological innovations, cosmopolitan restaurants, bars for all tastes and a kicking nightlife scene. A few days will give you the chance to take in headline sights such as the Neues Rathaus, the city's impressive Gothic town hall, the palatial Residenzmuseum art museum and the Englischer Garten, Munich's vast central park.

Munich is served by a major international airport and trains from German cities and neighbouring countries. To connect with our Romantic Road tour,

WHEN TO GO

You can expect warm, sometimes hot, weather in summer, particularly in July and August when roads and resorts are busy, accommodation is in demand and the festival season is going strong. Come in spring or autumn and you'll find the weather ideal for road-tripping and outdoor pursuits. Winter heralds the ski season and plenty of cultural activity in the cities.

head to Augsburg, an hours' drive west on the A8 autobahn.

Hamburg

To explore northern Germany, Hamburg is the ideal base. The country's second-largest city and biggest port is a cosmopolitan place whose forward-looking vision is brilliantly encapsulated in the extraordinary Elbphilharmonie concert hall. There's plenty to see, from art treasures in the Hamburger Kunsthalle to seafood stalls in the epic Fischmarkt, and a bewildering selection of restaurants, bars and clubs for all tastes and pockets.

The city has its own airport, otherwise trains run in from across Germany. Bremen, the penultimate stop on our Fairy Tale Road trip, is an 80-minute drive southwest.

Berlin

Germany's capital is some way off the routes we cover in this chapter but it's well worth a de-

TRANSPORT

Most travellers arrive in Germany by air, or by rail and road from neighbouring countries. The country's main international airport is at Frankfurt but you can also fly direct to various other cities including Munich, Hamburg and Berlin. If you're travelling overland, trains and long-distance buses run to German cities from destinations across Europe.

tour. A few days will be enough to take in its major historic monuments and experience the indie spirit and anything-goes energy that permeates this once-divided Cold War city. To link with the German Fairy Tale Road tour, Berlin is a 3¼-hour drive along the A2 autobahn from Hanover.

WHERE TO STAY

Accommodation is plentiful in Germany, and while it's generally not necessary to reserve in advance, you'll need to book ahead for high season, major festivals and city trade fairs. The range of places runs the gamut: designer city hotels and indie hostels, traditional thatch-and-timber guesthouses and revamped castles. In rural areas, *Pensionen* (B&Bs) are prevalent and farm stays are popular, particularly with families looking to enjoy the countryside. Another rural favourite are inns known as *Gasthäuser* or *Gasthöfe*. Often set in lovely locations, these offer the chance to immerse yourself in local culture and sample authentic regional cuisine.

 WHAT'S ON

Karneval/Fasching

(February) Pre-Lent, carnival is celebrated with costumed street parties, parades and general revelry.

International Händel Festival

(May; haendel-festspiele.de) Opera and classical music fill the air during Göttingen's International Händel Festival.

Oktoberfest

(September; oktoberfest.de) Munich's legendary beer-swilling, stein-swinging fest rolls into town.

Christmas Markets

(December) *Glühwein* (mulled wine), gingerbread biscuits and shimmering decorations star in Germany's much-loved festive markets.

Resources

German National Tourist Office *(germany.travel)* Get the lowdown on every aspect of travel in Germany, with handy maps, tips and links to other useful sites.

Deutsche Welle *(dw.com)* The latest news in English from Germany's international broadcaster.

Deutschland Online *(deutschland.de)* Insightful features on culture, business and politics.

35

Rhine Valley Discovery

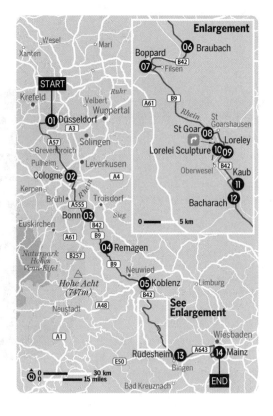

DURATION	DISTANCE	GREAT FOR
5–7 days	250km / 155 miles	History

BEST TIME TO GO	April to October offers the best weather, but July and August can be busy.

Boats gliding down the Rhine give passengers mesmerising views of the medieval villages, craggy hillsides and castle after castle floating past. But on this trip you'll get up close to its mightiest sights, hike through its high-perched vineyards, and discover hidden treasures and romantic hideaways you'd never see from the water. (Though you'll have plenty of opportunities en route to board a cruise, too.)

Link your trip

36 The Romantic Road

This ribbon of historical quaintness starts at Würzburg, two hours (153km) east from Mainz.

37 German Fairy Tale Quest

Get on the trail of the Brothers Grimm 65km east of Mainz in Hanau.

 DÜSSELDORF

01 Survey the mighty Rhine from Düsseldorf's **Medienhafen**. This old harbour area continues to attract red-hot restaurants, bars, hotels and clubs. Crumbling warehouses have transformed into high-tech office buildings, rubbing shoulders with bold new structures designed by celebrated international architects, including Frank Gehry.

Of course, no visit to Düsseldorf is complete without exploring its **Altstadt** (old town), which claims to be the 'longest bar in the world'.

PHOTOFIRES/SHUTTERSTOCK ©

BEST FOR OUTDOORS

Hike through the vines above Rüdesheim.

Cologne

THE DRIVE
It's a 43km drive south via the B1 and the A57 to Cologne. (Fear not: although this section travels through built-up areas and industrial estates, later stages become much more scenic.)

02 COLOGNE
A walking tour is the best way to appreciate this engaging city (Germany's fourth largest) on the Rhine. Must-sees include Cologne's world-famous **Dom** (Cologne Cathedral; koelner-dom.de), whose twin spires dominate the skyline, as well as superb museums such as the **Römisch-Germanisches Museum** (roemisch-german

isches-museum.de); sculptures and ruins displayed outside its entrance are the overture to its symphony of Roman artefacts found along the Rhine.

THE DRIVE
Drive south along the B51 on the Rhine's west bank before joining the A555 (30km all-up).

03 BONN
In a beautiful riverside setting, Ludwig van Beethoven's home town warrants a stop to visit the **Beethoven-Haus Bonn** (beethoven-haus-bonn.de), where the great composer was born in 1770. Other landmarks include the

soaring **Münster Basilica** (bonner-muenster.de), built on the graves of the two martyred Roman soldiers who later became the city's patron saints.

Bonn's old government quarter dates from its time as West Germany's 'temporary' capital, between 1949 and 1991 (when a reunited German government decided to move to Berlin). For a romp through recent German history from the end of WWII, pop by the **Haus der Geschichte** (hdg.de).

THE DRIVE
Take the B9 southeast for 24km. Once you leave the German state of North Rhine–Westphalia and

enter Rhineland–Palatinate, the road returns to the river's west bank; on your right you'll see the hilly wildlife park, Wildpark Rolandseck, as you approach Remagen.

04 REMAGEN

Remagen was founded by the Romans in 16 CE as Rigomagus, but the town would hardly figure in the history books were it not for one fateful day in early March 1945. As the Allies raced across France and Belgium to rid Germany of Nazism, the Wehrmacht tried frantically to stave off defeat by destroying all bridges across the Rhine. But the Brücke von Remagen (the steel rail bridge) lasted long enough for Allied troops to cross the river, contributing significantly to the collapse of Hitler's western front. One of the bridge's surviving basalt towers now houses the **Friedensmuseum** (bruecke-remagen.de), with a well-presented exhibit on Remagen's pivotal role in WWII.

THE DRIVE
Take the B9 southeast for 40km. The Rhine winds back and forth away from the road until you reach Koblenz. Stay on the B9 until you've crossed the Moselle to the town centre, or risk getting lost in a maze of concentric flyovers.

05 KOBLENZ

Koblenz sits at the confluence of the Rhine and Moselle Rivers – marked by the expansive **Deutsches Eck** ('German Corner'), adjoining flower-filled parks and promenades – and the convergence of three low mountain ranges (the Hunsrück, the Eifel and the Westerwald). Its roots go back to the Romans, who founded a

military stronghold (Confluentes) here because of the site's supreme strategic value.

On the Rhine's right bank, the 118m-high fortress **Festung Ehrenbreitstein** (tor-zum-welterbe.de) proved indestructible to all but Napoleonic troops, who levelled it in 1801. To prove a point, the Prussians rebuilt it as one of Europe's mightiest fortifications. It's accessible by car, on foot and by cable car.

Inside Koblenz' striking glass **Forum Confluentes**, the **Mittelrhein-Museum** (mittelrhein-museum.de) spans 2000 years of the region's history, including 19th-century landscape paintings of the Romantic Rhine by German and British artists.

THE DRIVE
Take the B49 to the Rhine's east bank and travel south on the B42; it's 13km to Braubach. At this point of the drive, you leave the cityscapes behind and enter an older world of cobblestones, half-timbered villages, densely forested hillsides and ancient vineyards.

06 BRAUBACH

Framed by forest, vineyards and rose gardens, the 1300-year-old town of Braubach centres on its small, half-timbered **Marktplatz**. High above are the dramatic towers, turrets and crenellations of the 700-year-old **Marksburg**

(marksburg.de), which is unique among the Rhine's fastnesses as it was never destroyed. The compulsory tour takes in the citadel, the Gothic hall and a grisly torture chamber.

THE DRIVE
Hug the Rhine's east bank for 11km as it curves around to the car-ferry dock at Filsen. It's a five-minute crossing to charming Boppard.

07 BOPPARD

Idyllically located on a horseshoe bend in the river, Boppard (pronounced 'bo-part') is one of the Romantic Rhine's prettiest towns, not least because its riverfront and historic centre are both on the same side of the railway tracks.

Boppard's riverfront promenade, the **Rheinallee**, has grassy areas for picnicking and a children's playground.

Many of the town's half-timbered buildings house cosy wine taverns, including its oldest, **Weinhaus Heilig Grab** (heiliggrab.de). In summer, sip local Rieslings under the chestnut trees, where live music plays on weekends.

Fantastic hiking trails fan out into the countryside, including the **Hunsrück Trails**, accessed by Germany's steepest scheduled railway route, the **Hunsrückbahn** (hunsrueckbahn.de). Around the **Vierseenblick**, a

---

CROSSING THE RHINE

No bridges span the Rhine between Koblenz and Mainz; the only way to cross the river along this stretch is by *Autofähre* (car ferry). The available crossings include **Bingen–Rüdesheim** (bingen-ruedesheimer.de), **Boppard–Filsen** (faehre-boppard.de), **Niederheimbach–Lorch** (mittelrhein-faehre.de), **Oberwesel–Kaub** (faehre-kaub.de) and **St Goar–St Goarshausen** (faehre-loreley.de).

WHY I LOVE THIS TRIP

Catherine Le Nevez, writer

The romance along this stretch of the Rhine is timeless. Poets and painters, including Lord Byron and William Turner, are among those who have been inspired by this castle-crowned, forest-and-vineyard-cloaked valley. A fabled stop on the original European Grand Tour, the riverscape here is now a designated Unesco World Heritage Site. It doesn't get more classic than that.

panoramic outlook reached by **Sesselbahn** (chairlift; sessel bahn-boppard.de) creates the illusion that you're looking at four separate lakes rather than a single river.

THE DRIVE
Take the B9 south for 14km, passing Burg Maus across the river near the village of Wellmich. Shortly afterwards, you'll spot Burg Rheinfels on the west bank above St Goar.

08 ST GOAR
Lording over the village of St Goar are the sprawling ruins of **Burg Rheinfels** (st-goar.de), once the Rhine's mightiest fortress. Built in 1245 by Count Dieter von Katzenelnbogen as a base for his toll-collecting operations, its size and labyrinthine layout are astonishing. Kids (and adults) will love exploring the subterranean tunnels and galleries (bring a torch). From St Goar's northern edge, follow the Schlossberg road to the castle.

THE DRIVE
Take the five-minute car ferry across to the little village of St Goarshausen. From St Goarshausen's Marktplatz, follow the L338 as it twists steeply uphill through thick forest for 1.2km and turn right onto the K89 for 2.5km to reach Loreley.

DETOUR
Oberwesel
Start: ⑧ St Goar

It's a quick 7.8km south from St Goar along the B9 to the village of Oberwesel.

Every April, Oberwesel crowns not a *Weinkönigin* (wine queen), as in most Rhine towns, but a *Weinhexe* (wine witch) – a good witch, of course – who is said to protect the vineyards. Photos of all the *Weinhexen*

crowned since 1946 are displayed in the cellar of Oberwesel's **Kulturhaus** (kulturhaus-oberwesel.de), along with 19th-century engravings of the Rhine and models of its riverboats.

Hidden sky-high up a vineyard-striped hillside, the flagstone terrace of **Günderode Haus** (guenderode filmhaus.de) is incredible for a glass of wine, beer or brandy, with sweeping views over the Rhine. The adjacent 200-year-old half-timbered house was used as a film set for *Heimat 3* (2004); it now hosts a cinema room and hosts live music and literary events, as well as wine tastings. From Oberwesel, take the K93 east for 600m, turn right (north) onto the K95; after 1km, the Loreley car park's on your right.

09 LORELEY
The most storied spot along the Romantic Rhine, Loreley is an enormous, almost vertical slab of slate; it owes its fame to a mythical maiden whose siren songs are said to have lured sailors to their death in the river's treacherous currents. Heinrich Heine told the tale in his 1824 poem 'Die Lorelei'.

On the edge of the plateau 4km southeast of the village of St Goarshausen, the visitor centre **Loreley Besucherzentrum** (loreley-besucherzentrum.de) covers the Loreley myth and local flora, fauna, shipping and winemaking traditions. A 300m gravel path leads to a **viewpoint** at the tip of the Loreley outcrop, 190m above the river.

THE DRIVE
Return to the B42 at the bottom of the hill; on your left, you'll see Burg Katz. Travel south for 2km to the car park by the breakwater for the next stop, the *Lorelei* sculpture.

Cat & Mouse

Two rival castles stand either side of the village of St Goarshausen. **Burg Peterseck** was built by the archbishop of Trier to counter the toll practices of the powerful Katzenelnbogen family. The latter responded by building a much bigger castle high on the other side of town, **Burg Neu-katzenelnbogen**, which was dubbed Burg Katz, meaning 'Cat Castle'. Highlighting the obvious imbalance of power between the Katzenelnbogens and the archbishop, Burg Peterseck was soon nicknamed Burg Maus ('Mouse Castle'). Both are closed to the public.

10 LORELEI SCULPTURE
At the tip of a narrow breakwater jutting into the Rhine, a bronze sculpture of Loreley's famous maiden perches atop a rocky platform. From the car park, you can walk the 600m out to the sculpture, from where there are fantastic views of both riverbanks. Be aware that the rough path is made from jagged slate (wear sturdy shoes!) and the gentler sandy lower path is often underwater.

THE DRIVE
Take the B42 south for 8km to the little village of Kaub; park next to the ferry dock.

11 KAUB
Kaub is the gateway to one of the river's iconic sights. As if out of a fairy tale, 1326-built, boat-shaped toll castle

Pfalzgrafenstein (burg-pfalz grafenstein.de), with distinctive white-painted walls, red trim and slate turrets, perches on a narrow island in the middle of the Rhine. A once-dangerous rapid here (since modified) forced boats to use the right-hand side of the river, where a chain forced ships to stop and pay a toll. The island makes a fabulously scenic picnic spot.

Alongside Kaub's car-ferry dock you can hop on a little **Fährboot** (faehre-kaub.de) passenger ferry (it only runs from this side of the river).

THE DRIVE
Take the car ferry across to the Rhine's west bank and head south on the B9 for 3km.

12 BACHARACH
Tiny Bacharach conceals its considerable charms behind a 14th-century wall. Enter

Photo Opportunity
Boat-shaped toll castle Pfalzgrafenstein on a Rhine island.

one of the thick arched gateways under the train tracks and you'll find yourself in a medieval old town filled with half-timbered mansions. It's possible to walk almost all the way around the centre on top of the walls. The lookout tower on the upper section of the wall provides some panoramic views.

Dating from 1421, **Zum Grünen Baum** (weingut-bastian-bacharach.de) serves some of Bacharach's best whites in rustic surrounds. Its nearby *vinothèque*, **Weingut Fritz Bastian**, by contrast, is state of the art.

Owner Friedrich Bastian is a renowned opera singer, so music (and culinary) events take place year-round, including on Bastian's private river-island with its own vineyard.

THE DRIVE
Head south on the B9, passing Burg Reichenstein then Burg Rheinstein on your right. Then, on your left, in the river itself, you'll pass the Mäuseturm, a fortified tower used as a signal station until 1974. Drive through Bingen to the car-ferry dock at its eastern edge, and cross the river to Rüdesheim.

13 RÜDESHEIM
Depending on how you look at it, Rüdesheim's town centre – and especially its most famous feature, the tunnel-like medieval alley **Drosselgasse** – is either a touristy nightmare or a lot of kitschy, colourful fun. There's

MARCOCIANNAREL/SHUTTERSTOCK ©

Pfalzgrafenstein, Kaub

also wonderful walking in the greater area, which is part of the Rheingau wine region, famed for its superior Rieslings.

For a stunning Rhine panorama, head up the wine-producing slopes west of Rüdesheim to the **Niederwald Monument**. Erected between 1877 and 1883, this bombastic monument celebrates the Prussian victory in the Franco-Prussian War and the creation of the German Reich, both in 1871. To save climbing 203 vertical metres, glide above the vineyards aboard the 1400m-long **Seilbahn cable car** (seilbahn-ruedesheim. de). A worthwhile network of hiking trails extends from the monument.

THE DRIVE
Head east on the B42 for 23km then turn south on the A643 to cross the bridge over the Rhine. It's then 13km southeast to the centre of Mainz.

14 MAINZ
The Rhine meets the Main at lively Mainz, which has a sizeable university, pretty pedestrian precincts and a *savoir vivre* dating from Napoleon's occupation (1797–1814). Strolling along the Rhine and sampling local wines in a half-timbered **Altstadt** tavern are as much a part of any Mainz visit as viewing the sights. Try the 1791 **Weinstube Hottum** for wines purely from the Rheingau and Rheinhessen regions, or vine-draped **Weingut Michel**, Mainz' only *Weingut* (winery) to exclusively serve its own wines.

Highlights you won't want to miss include the fabulous **Mainzer Dom** (mainzerdom.bistum mainz.de), the ethereal windows by Chagall in **St-Stephan-Kirche**

Köln-Düsseldorfer cruise boat

CRUISING THE RHINE

If you'd like to let someone else drive for a while and get a different perspective of the Rhine, it's easy to park up and hop on a cruise boat.

From around Easter to October (winter services are very limited), passenger ships run by **Köln-Düsseldorfer** (k-d.com) link Rhine villages on a set timetable. You can travel to the next village or all the way between Mainz and Koblenz.

Within the segment you've paid for (for example, Boppard–Rüdesheim), you can get on and off as often as you like, but make sure to ask for a free stopover ticket each time you disembark. Return tickets usually cost only slightly more than one way.

Children up to the age of four travel free, while those up to age 13 are charged a flat fee of €6 regardless of distance. To bring a bicycle, there's a supplement of €3.

A few smaller companies, including Bingen-Rüdesheimer (bingen-ruedesheimer.de), Loreley Linie (loreley-linie.com) and Rössler Linie (roesslerlinie.de), also send passenger boats up and down the river.

(st-stephan-mainz.bistummainz. de), and the first printed Bible in the **Gutenberg-Museum Mainz** (gutenberg-museum.de). This museum commemorates native son Johannes Gutenberg, who ushered in the information age here in the 15th century by perfecting movable type.

Also well worth a visit is the dungeon-like, brilliantly illuminated Roman archaeological site **Heiligtum der Isis und Mater Magna** (roemisches-mainz.de). The easy-to-miss entrance is on the Römer Passage mall's ground floor, just inside the western entrance.

Niederwald Monument, Rüdesheim

36

The Romantic Road

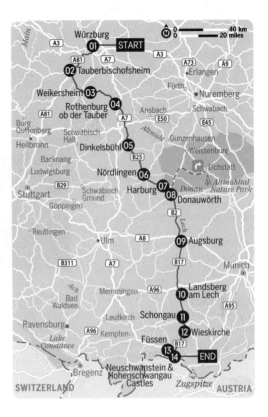

DURATION	DISTANCE	GREAT FOR
10 days	350km / 217 miles	Family travel, history

BEST TIME TO GO	January and February, when the route is blanketed in snow.

From the vineyards of Würzburg to the foot of the Alps, the Romantic Road (Romantische Strasse) is by far the most popular of Germany's touring routes. This well-trodden trail cuts through a cultural and historical cross-section of southern Germany, coming to a crescendo at the gates of King Ludwig II's crazy castles. The route links some of Germany's most picturesque towns, many appearing untouched since medieval times.

Link your trip

35 Rhine Valley Discovery

Würzburg is two hours (154km) from Mainz, at the end of this castle-lined riverside jaunt.

40 Grossglockner Road

It's a hop and a skip from Füssen to either end of this exhilarating journey through the Austrian Alps.

WÜRZBURG

01 This lively city in Bavaria's northeastern corner straddles the Main River and is renowned for its art, architecture and delicate wines. A large student population keeps things busy and hip nightlife pulsates through its cobbled streets.

Top billing here goes to the **Würzburg Residenz** (residenz-wuerzburg.de), a vast Unesco-listed palace built by 18th-century architect Balthasar Neumann as the home of the local prince-bishops. It's one of Germany's most important and beautiful baroque

BEST TWO DAYS

Find the most romantic towns of the Romantic Road between stops 4 and 6.

Würzburg Residenz

palaces. The wonderful zig-zagging Treppenhaus (Staircase) is capped by the world's largest fresco, a masterpiece by Giovanni Battista Tiepolo depicting allegories of the four then-known continents (Europe, Africa, America and Asia). The **Dom St Kilian** (dom-wuerzburg.de) is a highly unusual cathedral with a Romanesque core and baroque Schönbornkapelle, also by Neumann.

THE DRIVE
Take the B19 south to join the A3 motorway; follow this to meet the A81, which goes all the way to Tauberbischofsheim (37km).

02 TAUBERBISCHOFSHEIM
The main town in the pretty Tauber Valley, this small settlement has a picturesque marketplace dominated by a neo-Gothic town hall and lined with typical half-timbered houses. Follow the remains of medieval town walls to the Kurmainzisches Schloss, housing the **Tauberfränkisches Landschaftsmuseum** (tauberfraen kisches-landschaftsmuseum. de), where you can learn about Tauberbischofsheim's past.

THE DRIVE
The 33km dash to Weikersheim along the B290 and L2251 passes

through Lauda-Königshofen, a pretty stop in the Tauber Valley.

03 WEIKERSHEIM
Top billing in under-visited Weikersheim is **Schloss Weikersheim** (schloss-weikersheim.de), the Romantic Road's finest palace. Renaissance to the core, it's surrounded by beautiful formal gardens inspired by Versailles. Highlights include the enormous Knights Hall dating from around 1600 and over 40m long. The rich decor includes a huge painted ceiling, each panel depicting a hunting scene, and the amazingly

ornate fireplace. The unforgettable rococo mirror cabinet, with its gilt-and-red decor, is also part of the guided tour, after which you can wander the elegantly laid-out gardens.

THE DRIVE

The short 28km journey between Weikersheim and Rothenburg ob der Tauber follows minor country roads all the way. You could also detour via Creglingen, a minor stop on the Romantic Road.

04 ROTHENBURG OB DER TAUBER

A meticulously preserved historical town, touristy Rothenburg ob der Tauber is the Romantic Road's most popular stop. Once you're finished with the main sights, there are some less obvious attractions here.

You'll often see the **Plönlein** in brochures and tourist bumf, a gathering of forks in the cobbled road (Obere Schmiedgasse) occupied by possibly the quaintest, most crooked half-timbered house you'll ever see.

Hidden down an alley is the **Alt-Rothenburger Handwerkerhaus** (walburga-rothenburg. de), where numerous artisans – coopers, weavers, cobblers and

TOP TIP:

Guest Cards

Overnight anywhere in the Alps and your hotel should issue a free Gästekarte, which gives free bus travel plus many other discounts on admission and activities.

---

potters – have their workshops, and mostly have had for their house's 700-plus-years' existence. It's half museum, half active workplace; you can easily spend an hour or so watching the artisans at work.

THE DRIVE

The quickest way to Dinkelsbühl is the A7 motorway (50km). For a slower and longer experience, follow the official Romantic Road route (44km) along country roads via Schillingsfürst, another quaint halt.

05 DINKELSBÜHL

Immaculately preserved Dinkelsbühl is arguably the Romantic Road's most authentically medieval halt. Like Rothenburg, it is ringed by medieval walls, boasting 18 towers and four gates. The joy of Dinkelsbühl is aimless wandering through the crooked lanes, but for a history lowdown visit the **Haus der Geschichte** (hausdergeschichte-dinkelsbuehl. de), in the same building as the tourist office.

THE DRIVE

Just 32km separate Dinkelsbühl from Nördlingen along the B25, accompanied by the Wörnitz River for the first part of the journey. A few kilometres short of Nördlingen is Wallerstein, a small market town with the beautiful Church of St Alban, also a Romantic Road stop.

---

06 NÖRDLINGEN

Charmingly medieval, Nördlingen lies within the Ries Basin, a massive impact crater gouged out by a meteorite more than 15 million years ago. The crater – some 25km in diameter – is one of Earth's best preserved, and has been declared a special 'geopark'.

Nördlingen's 14th-century walls, all original, mimic the crater's rim and are almost perfectly circular: **Rieskrater Museum** (rieskratermuseum.de) tells the story. Next door is the **Stadtmuseum** (stadtmuseum-noerdlingen.de), giving an interesting rundown of Nördlingen's story so far.

On a completely different note, the **Bayerisches Eisenbahn museum** (bayerisches-eisenbahn museum.de) near the train station is a retirement home for locos that have puffed their last. The museum runs steam trains up to Dinkelsbühl, Feuchtwangen and Gunzenhausen several times a year; the website has details.

THE DRIVE

The 18km drive to Harburg is along the arrow-straight B25.

07 HARBURG

Looming over the Wörnitz River, the medieval covered parapets, towers, turrets, keep and red-tiled roofs of 12th-century **Schloss Harburg** (burg-harburg.de) are so perfectly

preserved they almost seem like a film set. Tours tell the Schloss' long tale and evoke the ghosts said to use the castle as a hang-out.

From the castle, the walk to Harburg's cute, half-timbered **Altstadt** takes 10 minutes, slightly more the other way (uphill). A fabulous village-and-castle panorama can be admired from the 1702 stone bridge spanning the Wörnitz.

THE DRIVE
From Harburg follow the B25 15km to Donauwörth.

08 DONAUWÖRTH
Sitting pretty at the confluence of the Danube and Wörnitz Rivers, the small town of Donauwörth had its heyday as a Free Imperial City in the 14th century. WWII destroyed 75% of the medieval old town but three gates and five town-wall towers still guard it today. The main street is Reichstrasse, which is where you'll discover the **Liebfraukirche**, a 15th-century Gothic church with original frescoes and a sloping floor that drops 120cm. Swabia's largest church bell (6550kg) swings in the belfry. The town's other major attraction is the **Käthe-Kruse-Puppenmuseum** (donauwoerth.de). In a former monastery, it's a nostalgia-inducing place of old dolls and dollhouses from world-renowned designer Käthe Kruse (1883–1968).

THE DRIVE
Augsburg is 47km away via the B2 and the A8 motorway. The scenic route via back roads east of the A8 passes close to the pretty town of Rain, another minor halt on the Romantic Road.

DETOUR
Eichstätt & Altmühltal Nature Park
Start: 8 Donauwörth

A short 55km off the Romantic Road from Donauwörth lies the town of Eichstätt, the main jumping-off point for the serenely picturesque 2900-sq-km Altmühltal Nature Park, which follows the wooded valley of the Altmühl River. Canoeing is a top activity here, as are cycling and camping. The park is an ideal break from the road and a relaxing place to spend a few days in unspoilt natural surroundings. Eichstätt itself has a wealth of architecture, including the richly adorned medieval **Dom** (eichstaetter-dom.de), with its museum; the baroque **Fürstbischöfliche Residenz**, where local prince-bishops once lived it up; and the **Willibaldsburg**, a 14th-century castle that houses a couple of museums.

Ballenhaus, Schongau

09 AUGSBURG

Augsburg is the Romantic Road's largest city and one of Germany's oldest, founded by the stepchildren of Roman emperor Augustus over 2000 years ago. This attractive city of spires and cobbles is an engaging stop, though far less quaint than others along the route.

Augsburg's top sight is the **Fuggerei** (fugger.de), Europe's oldest Catholic welfare settlement, founded by banker and merchant Jakob Fugger in 1521. Around 200 people inhabit the complex today; see how the residents of yesterday lived by visiting the **Fuggereimuseum**.

Two famous Germans have close associations with Augsburg. Protestant Reformation leader Martin Luther stayed here in 1518 – his story is told at **St Anna Kirche** (st-anna-augsburg.de). The birthplace of poet and playwright Bertolt Brecht is now a museum, the **Brechthaus** (brecht haus-augsburg.de;).

THE DRIVE

Drive 43km to Landsberg am Lech along the B17. The route mostly follows the valley of the Lech River. Look out for signs to the saucily named town of Kissing.

10 LANDSBERG AM LECH

A walled town on the Lech, lovely Landsberg has a less commercial ambience than others on the route. Just like the Wieskirche further south, the small baroque **Johanniskirche** was created by baroque architect Dominikus Zimmermann, who lived in Landsberg and served as its mayor. **Neues Stadtmuseum** (museum-landsberg.de) tells

Landsberg's Dark Literary Connections

Landsberg am Lech can claim to be the town where one of the German language's best-selling books was written. Was it by Goethe, Remarque, Brecht? No, unfortunately, it was by Adolf Hitler. It was during his 264 days of incarceration in a Landsberg jail, following the 1923 beer-hall putsch, that Hitler penned his hate-filled *Mein Kampf*, a book that sold an estimated seven million copies when published. The jail later held Nazi war criminals and is still in use.

Landsberg's tale from prehistory to the 20th century.

THE DRIVE

The 28km drive along the B17 to Schongau should take 30 minutes. En route you pass through Hohenfurch, a pretty little town regarded as the gateway to the Pfaffenwinkel, a foothill region of the Alps.

11 SCHONGAU

One of the lesser-visited stops on the Romantic Road, attractive Schongau is known for its largely intact medieval defences. The Gothic **Ballenhaus** served as the town hall until 1902 and has a distinctive stepped gable; it now houses a cafe. Other attractions include the **Church of Maria Himmelfahrt**, with a choir by Dominikus Zimmermann.

THE DRIVE

Take the B17 south until you reach Steingaden. From there country roads lead east and then south to Wies. This is where Bavaria starts to take on the look of the Alps, with flower-filled meadows in summer and views of the high peaks when the air is clear.

12 WIESKIRCHE

Located in the village of Wies, the **Wieskirche** (wieskirche.de) is one of Bavaria's best-known baroque churches and a Unesco-listed site, the monumental work of legendary artist-brothers, Dominikus and Johann Baptist Zimmermann. In 1730, a Steingaden farmer claimed he'd witnessed his Christ statue shedding tears. Pilgrims poured into the town in such numbers over the next decade that the local abbot commissioned a new church to house the weepy work. Inside the almost-circular structure, eight snow-white pillars are topped by gold capitals and swirling decorations. The unsupported dome must have seemed like God's work in the mid-17th century, its surface adorned with a pastel ceiling fresco celebrating Christ's resurrection.

THE DRIVE

Backtrack to Steingaden and rejoin the B17 to reach Füssen (32km). The entire journey is through the Alps' increasingly undulating foothills, with gorgeous views of the ever-nearing peaks along the way.

13 FÜSSEN

Nestled at the foot of the Alps, tourist-busy Füssen is all about the nearby castles

DPA PICTURE ALLIANCE ARCHIVE/ALAMY STOCK PHOTO ©

Museum der Bayerischen Könige

MUSEUM OF THE BAVARIAN KINGS

Palace-fatigued visitors to the Neuschwanstein and Hohenschwangau Castles often overlook the worthwhile **Museum der Bayerischen Könige** (hohenschwangau.de/museum-der-bayerischen-koenige), installed in a former lakeside hotel 400m from the castle ticket office (towards Alpsee Lake). The big-window views across the beautiful lake (a great picnic spot) to the Alps are almost as amazing as the Wittelsbach bling on show, including Ludwig II's famous blue-and-gold robe. The architecturally stunning museum is packed with historical background on Bavaria's first family and is well worth the extra legwork. A detailed audioguide is included in the ticket.

until you see signs for Hohenschwangau. Parking is at a premium in summer. However, as the castles are a mere 4km from Füssen's centre, it's probably not worth driving at all. RVO buses 78 and 73 (dbregiobus-bayern.de) run there from Füssen Bahnhof.

14 NEUSCHWANSTEIN & HOHENSCHWANGAU CASTLES

The undisputed highlights of any trip to Bavaria, these two castles make a fitting climax to the Romantic Road.

Schloss Neuschwanstein (neuschwanstein.de) was the model for Disney's *Sleeping Beauty* castle. King Ludwig II planned this fairy-tale pile himself, with the help of a stage designer rather than an architect. He envisioned it as a giant stage on which to recreate the world of Germanic mythology, inspired by the operatic works of his friend Richard Wagner.

It was at nearby **Schloss Hohenschwangau** (hohen schwangau.de) that King Ludwig II grew up and later enjoyed summers until his death in 1886. His father, Maximilian II, built this palace in a neo-Gothic style atop 12th-century ruins. Less showy than Neuschwanstein, it has a distinctly lived-in feel, where every piece of furniture is a used original. It was at Hohenschwangau where Ludwig first met Wagner.

The castles can only be visited on 35-minute guided tours. Buy timed tickets from the **Hohenschwangau Ticket Centre** at the foot of the castles. In summer, arrive as early as 8am to ensure you get in that day.

of Neuschwanstein and Hohenschwangau, but there are other reasons to linger. The town's **historical centre** is worth half a day's exploration and, from here, you can easily escape the crowds into a landscape of gentle **hiking**

trails and Alpine vistas. Or take an hour or two in Füssen's very own castle, the **Hohes Schloss**, today home to an art gallery.

🎱 THE DRIVE
To drive to King Ludwig II's castles, take the B17 across the river

Schloss Neuschwanstein

WHY I LOVE THIS TRIP

Marc Di Duca, writer

This 350km-long ribbon of historical quaintness is the Germany you came to see, but things can get crowded in the summer months, taking away a bit of the romance. Do the trip in winter when Bavaria's chocolate-box towns look even prettier under a layer of snow.

37

German Fairy Tale Quest

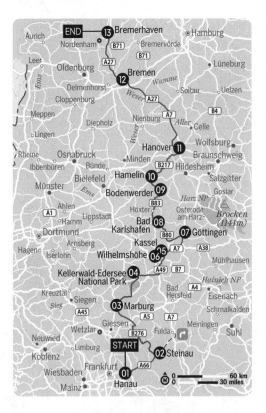

DURATION	DISTANCE	GREAT FOR
5 days	707km / 439 miles	Family travel

BEST TIME TO GO	May to September when the weather is best for outdoor sightseeing.

Tirelessly roaming the villages and towns of 19th-century Germany, the Brothers Grimm collected over 200 folk tales that had been passed down for countless generations. The stories they published often bear little resemblance to the sanitised versions spoon-fed to kids today; rather, they are morality tales with blood, gore, sex, the supernatural, magic and much more. See the locations of the stories and learn about the remarkable brothers on this trip, which includes a few non-Grimm fairy-tale sights as well.

Link your trip

35 Rhine Valley Discovery

Get your fill of castles and medieval villages: the end of the river trip is 65km west of Hanau.

36 The Romantic Road

Do one of the trips in reverse: the start of the quaint and historical Romantic Road is about an hour (110km) east of Hanau.

01 HANAU

A mere 20km east of Frankfurt on the Main River, Hanau is the birthplace of the Brothers Grimm (Jacob in 1785 and Wilhelm in 1786) and the perfect place to begin your trip. Strangely, their births are not overly commemorated here...

Located within Philippsruhe Palace, dating from the early 18th century, the **Historisches Museum Schloss Philippsruhe** (museen-hanau.de) has displays on town history, arts and crafts. The parks and gardens (free) are a beautiful stroll in snow or in summer.

BEST FOR FAMILIES

Grimmwelt, Kassel's attraction dedicated to all things Grimm.

Marburg

THE DRIVE
Hop on the A66 for a quick 50km run through the rolling hills to Steinau.

02 STEINAU
Steinau is situated on the historic trade road between Frankfurt and Leipzig. (The town's full name is 'Steinau an der Strasse', an important distinction when using your map app as there are several other Steinaus in Germany.)

The twin museums, **Brüder Grimm-Haus and Museum Steinau** (brueder-grimm-haus. de), inside the building where the Grimm family lived from 1791 to 1796, have exhibits on the brothers, their work and the history of Steinau.

THE DRIVE
Head west on the L3196 for 18km to the B276, where you'll turn north. Weave through the valleys for 64km to the junction with the L3166 and follow the Marburg signs along the L3127, L3089, L3048 and L3125. Picnic spots abound along the route.

03 MARBURG
Hilly, historic and delightful, university-town Marburg is 90km north of Frankfurt. It's a delight to wander the narrow lanes of the town's vibrant **Altstadt** (Old Town), sandwiched between a palace (above) and a spectacular Gothic church (below). On the south side of the focal Marktplatz is the historic **Rathaus**, dating to 1512. At the base of the Altstadt's Reitgasse is the neo-Gothic **Alte Universität** (1891), still a well-used and well-loved part of Philipps-Universität – the world's oldest Protestant university. Founded in 1527, it once counted the Brothers Grimm among its students.

Perched at the highest point in town, a steep walk up from St-Marien-Kirche or the Marktplatz, is massive **Landgrafenschloss** (uni-marburg.de/uni-museum), built between 1248 and 1300. It offers panoramic views of bucolic hills, jumbled Marburg rooftops and the **Schlosspark**.

DETOUR:

Fulda

START: ❷ **STEINAU**

Although it's not quite on the Fairy Tale Road, photogenic Fulda is well worth a side trip for those interested in sumptuous baroque architecture, historic churches and religious reliquaries. A Benedictine monastery was founded here in 744, and today Fulda has its own bishop.

Inside the baroque **Dom zu Fulda** (bistum-fulda.de), built from 1704 to 1712, you'll find gilded furnishings, plenty of putti (cherubs), dramatic statues (eg to the left of the altar) and the tomb of St Boniface, who died a martyr in 754.

Fulda's history started in the **Michaelskirche**, one of Germany's oldest churches. A still-standing reminder of the abbey that made this town, this remarkable structure was the monastic burial chapel. Beneath classic witch's-hat towers, a Carolingian rotunda and crypt recall Fulda's flourishing Middle Ages, when the abbey scriptorium churned out top-flight illuminated manuscripts.

Don't miss Fulda's spectacular **Stadtschloss**, built from 1706 to 1721 as the prince-abbots' residence. It now houses the city administration and function rooms. Visitors can enter the ornate **Historiche Räume** (Historic Rooms), including the grandiose banquet hall, and the octagonal **Schlossturm** for great views of the town and magnificent **Schlossgarten** (palace gardens), where locals play *pétanque* (boules) and sunbathe.

The palace's fairy-tale qualities capture the era's extravagance. Don't miss the amazing **Speigelkabinett** (Chamber of Mirrors) and grandiose **Fürstensaal**, a banquet hall decorated with reliefs of tipsy-looking wine queens. There are also pretty views from the **Green Room** over the gardens to the Orangerie.

Fulda is 40km northeast of Steinau on the A66.

THE DRIVE

Head north on the B3; after 18km turn north on the L3073. Continue north for 37km through Gemunden and Frankenau to Edertal, where you'll find the park. Note how the forest gets thicker and darker as you go.

04 KELLERWALD-EDERSEE NATIONAL PARK

This **national park** (nationalpark-kellerwald-edersee. de) encompasses one of the largest extant red-beech forests in Central Europe, the **Kellerwald**, and the **Edersee**, a serpentine artificial reservoir 55km northeast of Marburg and about the same distance southwest of Kassel. A decade ago this park, along with Hainich National Park in Thuringia and a cluster of other parks and reserves with large beech forests, became a Unesco World Cultural Heritage Site.

On a fairy-tale trip, it's fitting to wander into the deep woods, never forgetting that if your name is Grimm, nothing good is bound to happen. If you're lucky, you may see larger land animals like red deer; overhead, you might spot eagles and honey buzzards and, at night, various species of bat. (The brothers would surely approve.)

For information, head to the striking **visitors centre** (national parkzentrum-kellerwald.de) at the western end of the Edersee.

THE DRIVE

Drive east on the L3332, B485 and the B253 for 28km until you reach the A49 autobahn and zip along northeast until you reach Kassel.

05 KASSEL

Visitors to this culture-rich, sprawling hub on the Fulda River discover a pleasant, modern city.

Occupying a prime position atop the Weinberg bunker in the scenic **Weinbergpark** is the truly unmissable attraction on this trip, Kassel's **Grimmwelt** (grimmwelt. de). It could be described as an architect-designed walk-in sculpture housing the most significant collection of Brothers Grimm memorabilia on the planet. Visitors are guided around original exhibits, state-of-the-art installations and fun, hands-on activities, aided by entries from the Grimms' German dictionary: there was more to these brothers than just fairy tales, didn't you know?

Billed as 'a meditative space for funerary art', the **Museum für Sepulkralkultur** (Museum for Sepulchral Culture; sepulkral museum.de) aims to bury the taboo of discussing death.

THE DRIVE

The shortest leg of the trip takes you 6km west through Kassel's leafy suburbs. Take Wilhelmshöher Allee.

06 WILHELMSHÖHE

Wilhelmshöhe is the classy end of Kassel. You can spend a full day exploring the spectacular baroque parkland, **Bergpark Wilhelmshöhe**, which takes its name from **Schloss Wilhelmshöhe** (museum-kassel. de), the late-18th-century palace inside its expanse. Amble through the forest, enjoy a romantic picnic and explore the castles, fountains, grottoes, statues and water features; the **Herkules** statue and Löwenburg castle are also here.

The palace could star in any fairy tale. Home to Elector Wilhelm and later Kaiser Wilhelm II, the opulent complex today houses one of Germany's best collections of Flemish and Dutch baroque paintings in the **Gemäldegalerie** (painting gallery), featuring works by Rembrandt, Rubens,

Fairy Tale Road

The 600km **Märchenstrasse** (Fairy Tale Road; deutsche -maerchenstrasse.com) is one of Germany's most-popular tourist routes, with over 60 stops along the way. It's made up of cities, towns and hamlets in four states (Hesse, Lower Saxony, North Rhine-Westphalia and Bremen), which can often be reached via a choice of roads rather than one single route. The towns are associated in one way or another with the works of Wilhelm and Jacob Grimm. While most towns can be easily visited using public transport, a car lets you fully explore the route.

Jordaens, Lucas Cranach the Elder, Dürer and many others.

🚗 THE DRIVE

Retrace your 6km drive on Wilhelmshöher Allee back into Kassel and take the busy A7 up to Göttingen.

07 GÖTTINGEN

With over 30,000 students, this historic town nestled in a corner of Lower Saxony near the Hesse border offers a good taste of university-town life in Germany's north. Incredibly, since 1734, the **Georg-August Universität** has sent more than 40 Nobel Prize winners into the world. As well as all those award-winning doctors and scientists, it also produced the fairy-tale-writing Brothers Grimm (as German-language teachers).

Stroll around the pleasant **Markt** and nearby Barfüsser-

Herkules statue, Bergpark Wilhelmshöhe

strasse to admire the *Fachwerk* (half-timbered) houses. If you fancy, pop into a pub and make some new friends.

The city's symbol, the **Gänseliesel**, little goose girl, statue on the Marktplatz is hailed locally as the most kissed woman in the world – not a flattering moniker, you might think, but enough to make her iconic.

THE DRIVE
Take the L561 22km west to the B80, then head northwest for another 27km to Bad Karlshafen. Enjoy the curving panoramas as you follow the Weser River, which links several of the Fairy Tale Road towns and cities.

08 BAD KARLSHAFEN
Bad Karlshafen's orderly streets and whitewashed baroque buildings were built in the 18th century for local earl Karl by French Huguenot refugees. The town was planned with an impressive harbour and a canal connecting the Weser and the Rhine to attract trade, but the earl died before his designs were completed. The only reminder of his grand plans is the tiny **Hafenbecken** (harbour basin) populated by a gaggle of swans.

Take a stroll around the town centre, on the sinuous Weser's south bank, with the Hafenbecken and surrounding square, **Hafenplatz**, at its western end.

The interesting **Deutsches Huguenotten Museum** (huguenot-museum-germany.com) traces the history of the French Huguenot refugees in Germany.

THE DRIVE
Stay on the B83 for the 58km to Bodenwerder. You'll enjoy Weser vistas for much of the journey – which might lure you to stop for a picnic.

ROLF G WACKENBERG/SHUTTERSTOCK ©

Grimm Brothers statue, Hanau (p294)

GRIM(M) FAIRY TALES

In the early 19th century, the Grimm brothers travelled extensively through central Germany documenting folklore. Their collection of tales, *Kinder- und Hausmärchen*, was first published in 1812 and quickly gained international recognition. One thing you'll note about the 209 tales is that the original Grimm versions are much bloodier, more violent and earthier than today's ultra-sanitised, Disneyfied versions. It includes such fairy-tale staples as:

Hansel and Gretel
A mother tries to ditch her son and daughter, a witch tries to eat them and Gretel outsmarts her. Kids and father reunited and all are happy (the evil mother had died).

Cinderella
The story that gave stepsisters a bad name. Still, when the prince fits the shoe onto our heroine, all is good with the world, although in the Grimm version, the stepsisters are blinded by vengeful doves.

Rapunzel
An adopted girl with very long hair, a prince who goes blind and some evil older women are combined in this morality play that ends with love when the prince stumbles upon an outcast Rapunzel and his sight is restored. In the first edition of the Grimms' book, Rapunzel had children out of wedlock.

Although best known for their fairy tales, it should be noted that the Brothers Grimm were serious academics who also wrote *German Grammar* and *History of the German Language*, enduring works that populate reference shelves to this day.

WHY I LOVE THIS TRIP

Ryan Ver Berkmoes, writer

Did they give us nightmares or fantasies? Or both? Who can forget hearing the wild stories of the Brothers Grimm as a child? Evil stepmothers, dashing princes, fair maidens, clever animals, mean old wolves and more. With every passing year, these stories become more sanitised. But the real fairy tales are far more compelling, as you'll learn on this trip.

09 BODENWERDER

If Bodenwerder's most famous son were to have described his little hometown, he'd probably have painted it as a huge, thriving metropolis on the Weser. But then Baron Hieronymous von Münchhausen (1720–97) was one of history's most shameless liars (his whoppers were no mere fairy tales). He inspired the Terry Gilliam cult film, *The Adventures of Baron Munchausen* (1988).

Bodenwerder's principal attraction, the **Münchhausen Museum** (muenchhausenland.de), tackles the difficult task of conveying the chaos and fun associated with the 'liar baron' – a man who liked to regale dinner guests with his Crimean adventures, claiming he had, for example, tied his horse to a church steeple during a snow drift and ridden around a dining table without breaking one teacup. It holds paintings and displays of Münchhausen books in many languages.

THE DRIVE

The B83 again takes you north 23km to Hamelin, following the River Weser most of the way.

10 HAMELIN

According to the Brothers Grimm's *Pied Piper of Hamelin*, in the 13th century *Der Rattenfänger* (Pied Piper) was employed by Hamelin's townsfolk to lure its rodents into the river. When they refused to pay him, he picked up his flute and led their kids away. Today the rats rule once again – fluffy and cute stuffed rats, wooden rats and tiny brass rats adorning the sights around town.

Rodents aside, Hamelin (Hameln in German) is a pleasant town with half-timbered houses and opportunities for cycling along the Weser, on whose eastern bank lies Hamelin's circular **Altstadt**. The town's heart is its **Markt**.

Many of Hamelin's finest buildings were constructed in the Weser Renaissance style, which has strong Italian influences. Learn more at the town's **Museum Hamelin** (museumhameln.de).

THE DRIVE

Drive 47km northwest on the B217.

11 HANOVER

Known today for its huge trade shows, Hanover has an interesting past: from 1714, monarchs from the house of Hanover also ruled Great Britain and the British Empire for over a century.

Let your hair down at the spectacularly baroque **Herrenhäuser Gärten** (herrenhaeuser-gaerten.de), the grandiose Royal Gardens of Herrenhausen, which are considered one of the most important historic garden landscapes in Europe. Inspired by Versailles' gardens, they're a great place to slow down and smell the roses for a couple of hours, especially on a blue-sky day. With its fountains, neat flowerbeds, trimmed hedges and shaped lawns, the 300-year-old **Grosser Garten** (Great Garden) is the centrepiece of the experience.

THE DRIVE

Drive 47km northwest on the B217.

12 BREMEN

Bremen is well known for its fairy-tale character, a unique expressionist quarter and (it must be said, because Bremeners are avid football fans) one of Germany's most-exciting, if not overly successful, football teams.

With high, historic buildings rising up from this very compact square, Bremen's **Markt** is one of the most remarkable in northern Germany. The two towers of the 1200-year-old **Dom St Petri** (stpetridom.de) dominate the northeastern edge, beside the ornate and imposing **Rathaus**, which was erected in 1410. The Weser Renaissance balcony in the middle, crowned by three gables, was added between 1595 and 1618.

In front of the Rathaus is one of the hallmarks of Bremen, the city's 13m-high **Knight Roland statue** (1404). As elsewhere, Roland stands for a city's civic freedoms, especially the freedom to trade independently.

Photo Opportunity

Bremen's *Town Musicians of Bremen* sculpture.

On the western side of the Rathaus you'll find the city's unmissable and famous symbol of the Grimm fairy tale: the **Town Musicians of Bremen** (1951) by the sculptor Gerhard Marcks. The story tells of a donkey, a dog, a cat and a rooster who know their time is up with their cruel masters, and so set out for Bremen and the good life. On the way they encounter a forest cottage filled with robbers. They cleverly dispatch the crooks and, yes, live happily ever after. The statue depicts the dog, cat and rooster, one on top of the other, on the shoulders of the donkey. The donkey's nose and front legs are incredibly shiny, having been touched by many visitors for good luck.

THE DRIVE
A quick shot up the A27 autobahn for 65km will bring you to Bremerhaven and the North Sea.

13 BREMERHAVEN
Anyone who has had the fairy-tale dream of running away to sea will love Bremerhaven's waterfront – part trade machinery, part glistening glass buildings pointing to a more recent understanding of the harbour as a leisure spot.

Bremerhaven has long been a conduit that gathered the 'huddled masses' from the verdant but poor countryside and poured them into the world outside. Of the millions who landed in America, a large proportion sailed from here; an enticing exhibition at the **Deutsches Auswandererhaus** (German Emigration Centre; dah-bremerhaven.de), the city's prime attraction, allows you to share their history. The museum stands exactly in the spot where 7.2 million emigrants set sail between 1830 and 1974. Your visit begins at the wharf where passengers gathered before boarding a steamer. You then visit passenger cabins from different periods (note the improving comfort levels) before going through the immigration process at New York's Ellis Island.

ROSSHELEN/SHUTTERSTOCK ©

Town Musicians of Bremen statue

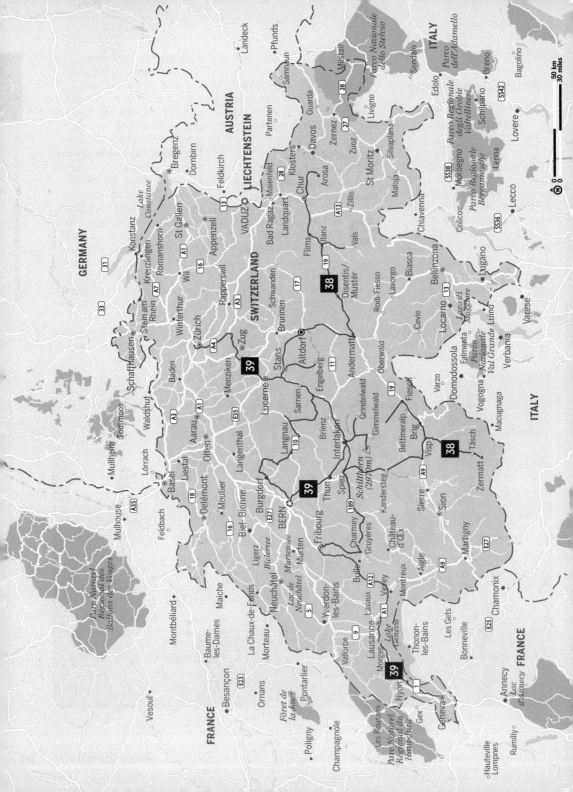

Engelberg (p308)

Switzerland

Explore

Switzerland

The epitome of heart-stopping Alpine beauty, Switzerland is made for slow travel. Its scenery is the stuff of travel legend, a dazzling mix of mighty snow-clad peaks, shimmering lakes and pristine pea-green valleys, while its dedication to efficiency makes getting around a breeze. And then there's the sport – year-round and pulse-quickening – and a choice of sophisticated, cultured cities.

Our road trips highlight the country's greatest hits and majestic heights, revealing legendary mountains, medieval towns, chocolate-box chalets and eye-catching contemporary architecture. Wherever you go in this spectacular country, you're never far from something extraordinary.

Geneva

Geneva, Switzerland's second-largest city, sits on the south-western tip of its namesake lake a few kilometres from the Swiss–French border. Slick and cosmopolitan, it's home to some 200 international organisations, including the World Trade Organization, the World Health Organization and the International Committee of the Red Cross, as well as a staggering number of hotels, boutiques, restaurants and chocolatiers.

Served by Switzerland's second-largest airport, the city is well connected for onward travel. The A1 skirts the northern shores of the lake as it leads to Lausanne, just under an hour away, and on to Fribourg, the second stop in our Geneva-to-

Zürich tour. But before riding out of town, take time for a stroll around the Vieille Ville (Old Town), where 18th-century philosopher Rousseau was born, and the buzzing, bar-heavy Quartier des Pâquis.

Zürich

If you're flying long-haul to Switzerland, you'll probably be headed to Zürich, the country's largest city. A wealthy financial centre, it enjoys an enviable lakeside location and a rich cultural life. It's got energy too and each summer the city thunders into life as thousands of revellers take to its streets for its celebrated street parade.

As a base, Zürich scores across the board: it has plenty of accommodation, interesting restaurants

WHEN TO GO

Switzerland's mountains are at their best – and busiest – during the ski season (between December and April) and in summer (July and August) when walkers and cyclists hit the high-altitude trails. Spring (April to June) can be idyllic with warm temperatures, blooming flowers and local produce, while September heralds the grape harvest, a good time for wine lovers.

and fashionable bars, as well as some fascinating places to explore. The Schweizerisches Landesmuseum (Swiss National Museum) is a great place to get a sense of the country, and the cobbled Altstadt (Old Town) and Niederdorf quarter both merit investigation. When it's time to move on, you can hire a car and join the Geneva to Zürich drive by heading southwest to Lucerne, just over 50km away.

Interlaken

Set between two lakes (Thun and Brienz) and surrounded by epic snowcapped peaks, Interlaken makes a superb base for both our Swiss trips. The town might be touristy but the surrounding Jungfrau region is home to some of the country's most famous mountains – including the Eiger, Mönch and Jungfrau – and the scenery is mind-blowing. Adrenalin seekers will also be in their element with any number of hair-raising outdoor pursuits to choose from.

TRANSPORT

Landlocked between France, Germany, Austria, Liechtenstein and Italy, Switzerland is easy to get to by land or air. Most international flights arrive in Zürich or Geneva, the country's two biggest airports, both of which offer the full gamut of services. Alternatively, you can drive in from neighbouring countries, or there are regular international trains to the main cities.

In town, there's a good range of accommodation and eating options, and car hire is available for onward travel. Bern is just under an hour away by train or via the A6 motorway.

WHAT'S ON

Lucerne Festival

(lucernefestival.ch) Classical music stars perform at Lucerne's world-class festival, split into spring, summer and autumn editions.

Swiss National Day

(1 August) Fireworks light up the country to celebrate Switzerland's birthday.

Zürich Street Parade

(mid-August; streetparade.com) Europe's largest street party rocks Zürich.

L'Escalade

Historical re-enactments, a running race, and mountains of chocolate feature during Geneva's popular event, held around 11 December.

Resources

My Switzerland *(myswit zerland.com)* Switzerland's official tourist website has everything from destination info to accommodation lists, railway timetables and thematic itineraries.

TCS *(tcs.ch)* Driving info in German, French and Italian, including real-time updates on the viability of the country's Alpine passes.

WHERE TO STAY

Switzerland boasts superlative accommodation. The main cities and popular resorts have a wide choice of hotels, B&Bs and hostels, as well as self-catering apartments, an increasingly popular choice. Note that many hotels in Zürich and Geneva are aimed at the business market so you can sometimes pick up great discounts for weekend stays. Out in the countryside, options include chocolate-box wooden chalets, family-friendly farm stays *(bauernhöfe)* and spartan Alpine huts *(hütten)*. Much frequented by hikers, these refuges are generally only open during the summer season (May or June to September).

38

The Swiss Alps

BEST FOR OUTDOORS

Whatever the season, the Alps offer activities galore.

DURATION	DISTANCE	GREAT FOR
7 days	537km / 333 miles	Family travel, outdoors

BEST TIME TO GO	Year-round, although certain mountain passes may be closed in winter.

Arosa

A natural barrier, the Alps are both a blessing and a burden when it comes to tripping around Switzerland. The soul-stirring views are stupendous, but you have to either get over or around the Alps, or go through them, to get to your next destination. Starting in Graubünden's Arosa and finishing in Valais' Zermatt, this trip visits five cantons via hairpin bends, valley highways, tunnels, passes and cable cars to bring you the best.

Link your trip

2 The Graceful Italian Lakes

A scenic two-hour drive (143km) across the Simplon Pass into Italy gets you to Stresa in the glorious Lake Maggiore region.

39 Geneva to Zürich

Arosa is a two-hour drive southeast (147km) on the A3 from Zürich, the end point of this bucolic ramble between Switzerland's biggest cities.

AROSA

01 Framed by the peaks of Weisshorn, Hörnli and moraine-streaked Schiesshorn, Arosa is a great Alpine all-rounder: perfect for downhill and cross-country skiing in winter, hiking and downhill biking in summer, and heaps of family activities year-round. Although only 30km southeast of Chur (Switzerland's oldest city), getting here involves 180-degree hairpin bends so challenging that Arosa cannot be reached by postal buses. Once here, you may want to revel in the beauty of the Mario Botta–designed **Tschuggen Bergoase Spa** (tschuggen.ch),

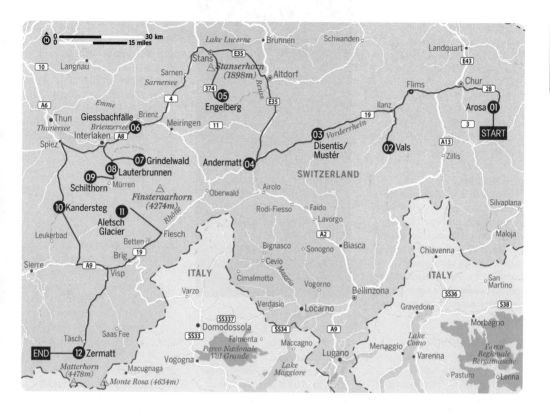

an architectural statement built at the foot of the mountains. The structure's recurring leaf-shaped motifs look particularly striking when illuminated at night.

🚗 THE DRIVE
The trip from Arosa to Vals is 79km and takes 1¾ hours. Head back towards Chur, then take Rte 19 to Ilanz for the delightful road that passes through Uors and St Martin before arriving at Vals (1252m). About 2km short of the village, you emerge into Alpine pastures, liberally scattered with chalets and shepherds' huts.

02 VALS
Shadowing the course of the babbling Glogn (Glenner) stream south, the luxuriantly green Valsertal (Vals Valley) is full of sleepy hamlets and thundering waterfalls. Vals stretches 2km along its glittering stream. The secret of this chocolate-box village and its soothing waters is out since Basel-born architect Peter Zumthor transformed **7132 Therme** (7132therme.com), formerly Therme Vals, into a temple of cutting-edge cool. Using 60,000 slabs of local quartzite, Zumthor created one of the country's most enchanting thermal spas. Aside from heated indoor and outdoor pools, this grey-stone labyrinth hides watery nooks and crannies, cleverly lit and full of cavernous atmosphere. Drift away in the bath-warm Feuerbad (42°C) and perfumed Blütenbad, sweat it out in the steam room, and cool down in the teeth-chattering Eisbad.

🚗 THE DRIVE
Return to Ilanz, then continue on Rte 19 to Disentis/Mustér (50km, 55 minutes).

03 DISENTIS/MUSTÉR
Disentis/Mustér's Benedictine monastery, **Kloster Disentis** (kloster-disentis.ch), rising like a vision above town, has a lavishly stuccoed baroque church attached. A monastery has stood here since the 8th century, but the present immense complex dates from the 18th century. Enter the **Klostermuseum**, crammed with

memorabilia, left of the church entrance. Head left upstairs to the **Marienkirche**, a chapel with Romanesque origins now filled with ex votos from people seeking (or giving thanks for) a miraculous intervention from the Virgin Mary. If you're peckish, a handy (and very good-value) on-site cafe-takeaway has soups, salads and specialities.

 THE DRIVE
Disentis is an exhilarating (40 minutes, 32km) drive along Rte 19 and the twisting Oberalp Pass (2044m), which connects Graubünden and Uri cantons. In winter, the pass is closed to cars, but a car train connects Sedrun on Rte 19 and Andermatt (three daily services in winter, two in spring). See matterhorngotthardbahn.ch for reservations.

04 ANDERMATT
Blessed with austere mountain appeal, Andermatt (Uri Canton) contrasts low-key village charm (despite a recent five-star development) with big wilderness. Once an important staging-post on the north–south St Gotthard route, it's now bypassed by the tunnel. It remains a major crossroads near four major passes (Susten, Oberalp, St Gotthard and Furka), making it a terrific base for **hiking** and **cycling**. The tourist office supplies free booklets.

One popular hike leads from the Oberalp Pass to sparkly **Lai da Tuma**, the source of the Rhine; the 11km round trip takes three to four hours, with 500m elevation gain. A walk around and along **Gotthardstrasse** reveals textbook dark-wood central-Swiss architecture, often weighed down with either geraniums or snow.

Zumdorf

If the grand scale of this trip seems overwhelming, the antidote surely lies in a quick detour to Switzerland's smallest village, Zumdorf: little more than a cluster of small buildings on the Furkastrasse with a population counted on one hand. Despite its diminutive size, it has **Restaurant Zum Dörfli** (zumdoerfli.ch), specialising in Swiss dishes (especially rösti) and venison (in season). You'll find it 6km southwest of Andermatt.

Skiers in the know flock to 2963m **Gemsstock** for the snow-sure winter slopes.

 THE DRIVE
Take Rte 2 to Göschenen, then get on the A2/E35 and follow the signs for Lucerne. The road skirts the bottom of Lake Uri for lovely water views. Continue to exit 33 (Stans-Süd), then follow Rte 374 to Engelberg (one hour, 77km in total).

05 ENGELBERG
Wonderful Engelberg (literally 'Angel Mountain') is divine, backed by the glacial bulk of **Mt Titlis** (titlis.ch), central Switzerland's tallest mountain, and frosted peaks, which feature in many a Bollywood production. After visiting the 12th-century Benedictine **Engelberg Monastery** (kloster-engelberg.ch), get closer to the heavens via the world's first revolving **cable car** (titlis.ch/en/tickets/cable-car-ride). It pirouettes over the dazzling **Titlis Glacier**, peaks rising

like huge spiky teeth ahead, before you step out onto Titlis station's **terrace** (3020m), with a panorama that stretches to Eiger, Mönch and Jungfrau in the Bernese Oberland. For even more thrilling views, take the adjacent **Cliff Walk** (titlis.ch/en/glacier/cliff-walk). Opened in 2012, this 100m-long, 1m-wide, cable-supported swinging walkway is Europe's highest suspension bridge.

There are some 360km of marked **hiking** trails in and around Engelberg. For gentle ambles and gorgeous scenery, head for **Brunni** across the valley. Its **cable car** (brunni.ch) goes up to Ristis at 1600m, where a chairlift takes you to the Swiss Alpine Club's refurbished **Brunni Hütte** (brunnihuette.ch). From here, you can choose to watch a magnificent sunset before spending the night.

 THE DRIVE
Retrace your route to the A2, heading west, before turning onto the A8 (direction Interlaken), and continuing alongside bright-blue Brienzersee to Giessbachfälle. The journey is one hour and 10 minutes, or 71km.

06 GIESSBACHFÄLLE
Illuminating the firs like a spotlight in the dark, the misty **Giessbachfälle** (Giessbach Falls) plummet 500m over 14 rocky ridges. Europe's oldest **funicular**, dating to 1879, creaks up from the boat station, but it's only a 15-minute walk up to the most striking section of the falls.

 THE DRIVE
Get back onto the A8 and follow it along the Brienzersee until exit 25 (Wilderswil/Grindelwald), then continue as the road winds its way through rural countryside up to Grindelwald (39km, 45 minutes).

Cliff Walk, Mt Titlis

07 GRINDELWALD

Grindelwald's sublime natural assets are film-set stuff – the chiselled features of Eiger's north face, the glinting tongues of Oberer and Unterer Glaciers and the crown-like peak of Wetterhorn. Skiers and hikers cottoned on to its charms in the late 19th century, making it one of Switzerland's oldest resorts. It has lost none of its appeal, with geranium-studded chalets and verdant pastures aplenty.

Turbulent waters carve a path through craggy **Gletscherschlucht** (Glacier Gorge; grindelwaldsports.ch), a 30-minute walk south of the centre. A footpath weaves through tunnels hacked into cliffs veined with pink and green marble. It's justifiably a popular spot for canyon and bungee-jumping expeditions.

Grindelwald is outstanding **hiking** territory, veined with trails that command arresting views to massive north faces, crevasse-filled glaciers and snow-capped peaks. Reach high-altitude walks by taking cable cars from the village.

THE DRIVE
Follow the signs to Lauterbrunnen, which is 20km (15 minutes) away by car.

08 LAUTERBRUNNEN

Laid-back Lauterbrunnen's wispy **Staubbachfall** (Staubbach Falls) inspired both Goethe and Byron to pen poems to their ethereal beauty. Today the postcard-perfect village, nestled in the valley of 72 waterfalls – including the **Trümmelbachfälle** (Trümmelbach Falls; truemmelbachfaelle.ch) – attracts a less highfalutin crowd. Hikes heading into the mountains from the waterfall-laced valley include a 2½-hour uphill trudge to car-free **Mürren** and a more gentle 1¾-hour walk to **Stechelberg**. In winter, glide past frozen waterfalls on a well-prepared 12km cross-country trail.

THE DRIVE
Head to Stechelberg (10 minutes, 6km), where you'll leave the car (paid parking available) and take the cable car to Schiltorn (adult/child return Sfr108/54).

09 SCHILTHORN

There's a tremendous 360-degree, 200-peak panorama from the 2970m Schilthorn, best appreciated from the **Skyline viewing platform** or the revolving restaurant **Piz Gloria** (schilthorn.ch). On a clear day, you can see from Titlis around to Mont Blanc, and across to the Black Forest in Germany.

Some visitors seem more preoccupied with practising their delivery of the line, 'The name's Bond, James Bond', because scenes from *On Her Majesty's Secret Service* were shot here in 1968–69. The **Bond World 007** interactive exhibition gives you the chance to pose for photos secret-agent style, and relive movie moments in a helicopter and bob sled.

AROUND GRINDELWALD: FIRST

From Grindelwald, a cable car zooms up to **First**, the trailhead for 100km of paths, half of which stay open in winter. You can trudge up to **Faulhorn** (2681m; 2½ hours), even in winter, via the cobalt **Bachalpsee** (Lake Bachalp). As you march along the ridge, the unfolding views of the Jungfrau massif are entrancing. Stop for lunch and 360-degree views at Faulhorn. You might like to continue to **Schynige Platte** (another three hours) and return by train.

Other great walks head to **Schwarzhorn** (three hours), **Grosse Scheidegg** (1½ hours), **Unterer Gletscher** (1½ hours) and **Grindelwald** itself (2½ hours).

First has 60km of well-groomed pistes, which are mostly wide, meandering red runs suited to intermediates. The south-facing slopes make for interesting skiing through meadows and forests. Freestylers should check out the kickers and rails at **Bärgelegg** or have a go on the superpipe at **Schreckfeld station**.

Faulhorn happens to be the starting point for Europe's longest **toboggan run**, accessible only on foot. Bring a sled to bump and glide 15km over icy pastures and through glittering woodlands all the way to Grindelwald via Bussalp. Nicknamed 'Big Pintenfritz', the track lasts around 1½ hours, depending on how fast you slide.

Year-round, you can get your pulse racing on the **First Flyer**, a staggeringly fast zip-line from First to Schreckfeld. The mountains are but a blur as, secure in your harness, you pick up speeds of around 84km/h.

The **First Cliff Walk** is a summit trail with a 40m-long suspension bridge, climbing stairs and an observation deck, with suitably impressive views of the local landscape and the jaw-dropping mountains.

THE DRIVE

After you descend to Stechelberg, head to Kandersteg via the road down to Interlaken. Get on the A8/Rte 11, then take exit 19 (direction Spiez/Kandersteg/Adelboden). The 60km trip takes one hour.

10 KANDERSTEG

Turn up in Kandersteg in anything but muddy boots and you'll attract a few odd looks. Hiking is the town's raison d'être, with 550km of surrounding trails. An amphitheatre of spiky peaks studded with glaciers and jewel-coloured lakes – such as **Blausee** (blausee.ch) and **Oeschinensee** (oeschinensee.ch) – creates a sublime natural backdrop to the rustic village of dark-timber chalets.

In winter there are more than 50km of cross-country **ski trails**,

including the iced-over Oeschinensee. The limited 15km of downhill skiing suits beginners while Kandersteg's frozen waterfalls attract ice climbers.

THE DRIVE

Take the BLS Lötschberg Tunnel, which connects with Goppenstein (in Valais) at regular intervals daily; it takes 15 minutes. From Goppenstein, head east from Rte 9. Once past Brig, the deep valley narrows and the landscape switches to rugged wilderness, with a string of bucolic villages of timber chalets and onion-domed churches (47km).

11 ALETSCH GLACIER

The Aletsch Glacier is a seemingly never-ending, 23km-long swirl of ice with deep crevasses that slices past thundering falls, jagged spires of rock, and pine forest. It stretches from

Valais Wine

The canton of Valais, which features so much of Switzerland's stunning Alpine scenery, is also the country's largest and best wine producer. Sampling it in situ at the end of a day's driving is a great idea.

Drenched in extra sunshine and light from above the southern Alps, much of the land north of the Rhône river in western Valais is planted with vines. Unique to the Valais are the *bisses* (narrow irrigation channels) that traverse the vineyards.

Dryish white Fendant, the perfect accompaniment to fondue and raclette, and best served crisp cold, is the region's best-known wine, accounting for two-thirds of Valais wine production. Dôle, made from Pinot noir and Gamay grapes, is the principal red blend and is full bodied, with a firm fruit flavour.

When ordering wine in a wine bar or restaurant, use the uniquely Swiss approach of *deci* (decilitre – ie a 10th of a litre) multiples.

SAHACHATZ/SHUTTERSTOCK ©

Piz Gloria, Schilthorn

Jungfrau in the Bernese Oberland to a plateau above the Rhône and is, justly so, a Unesco World Heritage Site.

Picture-postcard riverside **Fiesch** on the valley floor is the best place to access it. From the village, ride the **cable car** (eggishorn.ch) up to **Fiescheralp** and continue up to **Eggishorn** (2927m). Streaming down in a broad curve around the **Aletschhorn** (4195m), the glacier is just like a frozen six-lane superhighway. In the distance to the north rise the glistening summits of Jungfrau (4158m), Mönch (4107m), Eiger (3970m) and Finsteraarhorn (4274m). To the southwest of the cable-car exit, you can spy Mont Blanc and the Matterhorn.

THE DRIVE
It takes one hour (56km) to get to Täsch from Fiesch; first via Rte 19 to Visp and then the winding rural road to Täsch itself. Park the car here before boarding the train to car-free Zermatt.

12 ZERMATT
You can almost sense the anticipation on the train from Täsch. As you arrive in car-free Zermatt, the pop-up-book effect of the one-of-a-kind **Matterhorn** (4478m) works its magic. Like a shark's fin it rises above the town, with moods that swing from pretty and pink to dark and mysterious. Since the mid-19th century, Zermatt has starred among Switzerland's glitziest resorts. Today skiers cruise along well-kept pistes, spellbound by the scenery, while the style-conscious flash designer garb in the town's swish lounge bars.

Amble along the main-strip Bahnhofstrasse with its boutiques and stream of horse-drawn sleds or carriages and electric taxis,

Photo Opportunity
The incredible shark's fin jut of the Matterhorn.

then head towards the noisy Vispa river along Hinterdorfstrasse. This old-world street is crammed with archetypal Valaisian timber granaries propped up on stone discs and stilts to keep out pesky rats. Look for the fountain commemorating Ulrich Inderbinen (1900–2004), a Zermatt-born mountaineer who climbed the Matterhorn 370 times, the last time at age 90.

A walk in Zermatt's **Mountaineers' Cemetery**, in the garden of St Mauritius Church, is sobering. Numerous gravestones tell of untimely deaths on Monte Rosa, the Matterhorn and Breithorn. In July 2015 a **memorial** to 'the unknown climber' was unveiled to mark the 150th anniversary of the Matterhorn's first ascent.

The **Matterhorn Museum** (zermatt.ch/museum) provides a fascinating insight into Valaisian village life, the dawn of tourism in Zermatt and the lives the Matterhorn has claimed. Short films portray the first successful ascent of the Matterhorn on 14 July 1865, led by Edward Whymper, a feat marred by tragedy on the descent when four team members crashed to their deaths in a 1200m fall down the North Wall. The infamous rope that broke is on display.

THE HIGH LIFE

Charming as Zermatt is, heading out of town and up to the mountains is a rush like no other. Europe's highest cogwheel railway, the **Gornergratbahn** (gornergrat.ch), has climbed picture-postcard scenery to Gornergrat (3089m) – a 30-minute journey – since 1898. Sit on the right-hand side to gawp at the Matterhorn. Tickets allow you to get on and off en route; there are restaurants at **Riffelalp** (2211m) and **Riffelberg** (2582m). In summer an extra train runs once a week at sunrise and sunset – the most spectacular trips of all.

Views from Zermatt's cable cars are all remarkable, but the **Matterhorn Glacier Paradise** (matterhornparadise.ch) is the icing on the cake. Ride Europe's highest-altitude cable car to 3883m and marvel at 14 glaciers and 38 mountain peaks over 4000m from the Panoramic Platform (only open in good weather). Don't miss the **Glacier Palace**, an ice palace complete with glittering ice sculptures and an ice slide to swoosh down bum first. End with exhilarating snow tubing outside in the snowy surrounds.

WHY I LOVE THIS TRIP

Sally O'Brien, writer

Even though I now call Switzerland home, the Alpine scenery still has an otherworldly effect on me. The abundance of snow-capped peaks, mountains with fairy-tale names that 'pop up' at numerous vantage points, time-defying glaciers, gravity-defying railways. And then there's the moment you catch sight of the Matterhorn...

39

BEST FOR CULTURE

Zürich's mighty museums and relentless nightlife are intoxicating.

Geneva to Zürich

DURATION	DISTANCE	GREAT FOR
7 days	470km / 292 miles	Outdoors

BEST TIME TO GO	Late spring, summer and autumn when the light and weather are best.

Funiculaire de Fribourg (p316)

Rather than take a straight line from Geneva to Zürich, this trip gives you room to roam some of Switzerland's finest sights: small cities with charming Old Towns, heaven-sent lakes with dreamy views, winding roads through countryside bucolic and wild, an adventure capital with the perfect setting, a train ride to the top of Europe, and scenic ascents that will have you gasping – all book-ended by Switzerland's cultural capitals.

Link your trip

36 The Romantic Road

From Zürich, drive east via the A1 to Füssen in Germany, and do the gorgeous Romantic Road trip in reverse.

38 The Swiss Alps

It's a two-hour (147km) drive southeast from Zürich to Arosa, the starting point of the Swiss Alps whirl.

01 GENEVA

Cosmopolitan Geneva is a rare blend: a multicultural population chattering in every language under the sun, a distinctly French feel, one of the world's most expensive cities, a stronghold of the Protestant Reformation and a haven for dodgy bank accounts and humanitarian organisations.

With a whole day and night, schedule time for Geneva's magnificent **Old Town**. For waterside attractions, head for the emblematic **Jet d'Eau** and the egalitarian **Bains des Pâquis** (bains-des-paquis.ch).

Island Dining in Geneva

Genevan living is easy in summer: a constant crowd throngs the lakefront quays to hang out in pop-up terrace bars such as **La Terrasse** (laterrasse.ch), the fashionista spot by the water to see and be seen. Meander away from Quai du Mont-Blanc to uncover a beloved trio of summertime shacks on the water's edge.

The right-bank address is refreshingly casual: Rhône-side **Terrasse Le Paradis** (terrasse-paradis.ch) is the type of cafe that practically begs you to pull out a book and stay all day in deckchairs arranged down steps to the water, while sipping beakers of homemade *citronnade* (lemonade).

Le Bateau Lavoir (bateaulavoir. ch) is an eye-catching boat with rooftop terrace moored between the old market hall and Pont de la Coulouvrenière. Its cabin-size dining area cooks fondue and basic local dishes, the crowd is hip and there is a 360-degree lake view.

Then there's **La Barje** (labarje. ch), not a barge at all but a vintage caravan with tin roof and candy-striped facade, parked on the grassy banks of the Rhône near the Bâtiment des Forces Motrices. The beer and music are plentiful, outside concerts and art performances pull huge crowds, and proceeds go towards helping young people in difficulty.

Plenty of museums will tempt you: among the best are the **Musée d'Art Moderne et Contemporain** (mamco.ch), the **Musée International de la Croix-Rouge et du Croissant-Rouge** (International Red Cross & Red Crescent Museum; red crossmuseum.ch), and the lavish timepieces of **Patek Philippe Museum** (patekmuseum.com). For a behind-the-scenes glimpse of the UN, prebook a tour of the **Palais des Nations** (Palace of Nations; unog.ch).

THE DRIVE
Head west via the A1 until the A9 (follow signs to Vevey/Montreux). Take exit 11 and follow signs for Lutry. From Lutry, take Rte 9 (direction Vevey) until Cully, then head up Rte de la Corniche to Chexbres. Next follow Rte du Genevrex and get on the A9, followed by the A12 to Fribourg (143km total).

02 FRIBOURG
Nowhere is Switzerland's language divide felt more keenly than in Fribourg (Freiburg, or 'Free Town'), a medieval city where inhabitants on the west bank of the river Sarine speak French, and those on the east bank (of the Sanne) speak German. Sights that merit a look-see include the bohemian **Espace Jean Tinguely – Niki de Saint Phalle** (mahf.ch), the

FRIBOURG'S FUNICULAR

Nowhere else in Europe does a funicular lurch up the mountainside with the aid of sewage water (on certain days it smells as you'd expect). Constructed in 1899 and managed by the Cardinal Brewery until 1965 (when the municipality took over), the **Funiculaire de Fribourg** links the lower town with the upper. It runs every six minutes, and the ride in one of two counterbalancing water-powered carriages from the lower Pertuis station (121m; Place du Pertuis) to the upper station (618m; Rte des Alpes) takes two minutes.

evocative **Old Town** filled with Gothic facades, the **Musée d'Art et d'Histoire** (mahf.ch) and the outsize **Cathédrale de St Nicolas de Myre** (cathedrale-fribourg.ch) with its 74m-tall tower. Make time for a couple of the city's bohemian cafe-bars, such as **Le Port** (leport.ch) or **Café Culturel de l'Ancienne Gare** (cafeanciennegare.ch).

THE DRIVE
We've chosen a longish (103km, one hour and 50 minutes) scenic route along winding roads through lovely small towns and unspoiled countryside in Fribourg and Bern cantons. Head to the village of Charmey via Rte 189, then to Boltingen. Take Rte 11 to Speiz on Lake Thun, then follow Rte 8 to Interlaken.

03 INTERLAKEN
Interlaken once made the Victorians swoon with mountain vistas from the chandelier-lit confines of grand hotels; today it makes daredevils scream with adrenaline-loaded adventures. Straddling the glittering Lakes Thun and Brienz and dazzled by the pearly whites of Eiger, Mönch and Jungfrau, the scenery is mind-blowing. Check out views from **Harder Kulm** (jungfrau.ch/harderkulm), or try daredevil activities with **Outdoor**

Interlaken (outdoor-interlaken.ch) – organised in advance.

Leave the car in Interlaken after overnighting and head to the Top of Europe (Jungfraujoch) very early next morning.

THE DRIVE
From Interlaken it's a one-hour (54km) drive via Lake Thun's Seestrasse, past turreted Schloss Oberhoffen and art-nouveau-meets-neo-renaissance Schloss Hünegg. After Thun, you'll get to Bern quickly via the A6.

DETOUR
Jungfraujoch: The Top of Europe
Start: ③ Interlaken

Presided over by monolithic Eiger, Mönch and Jungfrau (Ogre, Monk and Virgin), the crown jewels of Bernese Oberland's Alpine scenery will make your heart skip a beat.

The 'big three' peaks have an enduring place in mountaineering legend, particularly the 3970m Eiger, whose fearsome north wall remained unconquered until 1938. Today it takes only 2½ hours from Interlaken Ost by train to Jungfraujoch (3454m), Europe's highest station.

From Kleine Scheidegg (the last stage of the journey), the train burrows through the Eiger before arriving at the **Sphinx meteorological station**. Opened in 1912, the tunnel took 3000 men 16 years to drill. Along the way, the Eigerwand and Eismeer stops have

panoramic windows offering glimpses across rivers of crevassed ice.

Good weather is essential for this journey; check beforehand on jungfrau.ch and always take warm clothing, sunglasses and sunscreen. Within the Sphinx weather station, there's a nice sculpture gallery, restaurants, indoor viewpoints and a souvenir shop. Outside there are views of the 23km-long Aletsch Glacier (p311). On cloudless days, the views stretch as far as the Black Forest in Germany.

When you tire (as if!) of the view, you can zip across the frozen plateau on a flying fox, dash downhill on a sled or snow disc, or enjoy a bit of tame skiing or boarding at the **Snow Fun Park**.

If you cross the glacier along the prepared path, in around an hour you'll reach the **Mönchsjochhütte** (moenchsjoch.ch) at 3650m, where hardcore rock climbers psych themselves up to tackle Eiger or Mönch.

04 BERN
Wandering through the picture-postcard **Old Town**, with its laid-back, riverside air, it's hard to believe that Bern (Berne in French) is the Swiss capital, but it is, and a Unesco World Heritage Site to boot. The flag-festooned, cobbled centre, rebuilt in grey-green sandstone after a devastating 1405 fire, is a delight, with 6km of covered arcades, cellar shops and bars, and fantastical folk figures frolicking on 16th-century fountains, such as the **Kindlifresserbrunnen**. Be sure to visit Bern's **Münster** (bernermuenster.ch), the famous **BärenPark** (Bear Park; tierpark-bern.ch), the architecturally daring **Zentrum Paul Klee** (zpk.org) and the well-endowed **Kunstmuseum** (Museum of Fine Arts; kunstmuseumbern.ch).

THE DRIVE

Leave via the A6 and take Krauchthalstrasse (35 minutes, about 24km) through verdant countryside to Burgdorf. From Burgdorf to Affoltern im Emmental, 6km to the east, is a scenic drive past old farmsteads bedecked with flower boxes, neat woodpiles and kitchen gardens. Rte 23 between Affoltern and Langnau im Emmental is 21km (25 minutes).

05 EMMENTAL REGION

After so much city time, the postcard-perfect landscapes of rural Switzerland beckon: time for the bucolic idyll of the Emmental region, where holey Emmental (Swiss cheese) is produced. To see the iconic cheese being made, head

Photo Opportunity

The verdant Emmental region exemplifies pastoral perfection.

to **Emmentaler Schaukäserei** (Emmental Open Cheese Dairy; emmentaler-schaukaeserei.ch) in Affoltern.

The region's gateway towns of **Burgdorf** and **Langnau im Emmental** preside over a mellow patchwork of quiet villages, grazing cows and fabulous farm chalets with vast barns and overhanging roofs, strung out along the Emme's banks. Burgdorf (literally 'castle village')

is split into an Upper and Lower Town. The natural highlight of the Oberstadt (Upper Town) is the 12th-century **Schloss** (castle), with its drawbridge, thick stone walls and trio of museums.

THE DRIVE

From Langnau im Emmental, take Rte 10 for 30 minutes (23km), crossing from Bern Canton to Lucerne Canton, to reach Schüpfheim, the heart of the Entlebuch biosphere.

06 UNESCO BIOSPHERE ENTLEBUCH

The 39,000-plus-sq-km **Entlebuch area** (biosphaere.ch), a mixed mountain-and-highland ecosystem, was declared a Unesco Biosphere Reserve in 2001. Far from being a lonely wilderness

MARKUS THOENEN/SHUTTERSTOCK ©

Emmental region

outpost, the reserve is home to some 17,000 people keen to preserve their traditional dairy-farming lifestyle. The landscape of karst formations, sprawling moors (some 25% of the area), Alpine pastures and mountain streams, which rise from 600m to some 2350m above sea level, makes for stirring scenery. The park office is in Schüpfheim.

THE DRIVE
Driving through Entlebuch from Schüpfheim, take the Pano-ramastrasse (which deserves to be more famous) to the town of Giswil (Obwalden Canton; 50 minutes, 37km). Next, follow the signs to Lucerne (Luzern in German) along the A8 (30 minutes, 30km).

07 LUCERNE
Recipe for a gorgeous Swiss city: take a cobalt lake ringed by mountains of myth (Pilatus, Rigi), add a well-preserved medieval **Old Town**, then sprinkle with covered bridges **Kapellbrücke** and **Spreuerbrücke**, sunny plazas, candy-coloured houses and waterfront promenades. Legend has it that an angel with a light showed the first settlers where to build a chapel in Lucerne, and today it still has amazing grace.

One minute it's nostalgic, with its emotive **lion monument**; the next it's highbrow, with concerts at acoustic marvel **Kultur und Kongresszentrum** (KKL; kkl-luzern.ch) and the peerless

Picasso collection of **Sammlung Rosengart** (rosengart. ch). Crowd-pleasers such as **Verkehrshaus** (Swiss Museum of Transport; verkehrshaus.ch) and the surrounding natural wonders never fail to impress, while balmy summers and golden autumns ensure this 'city of lights' shines constantly.

THE DRIVE
A fast 15-minute, 15km journey along the A2 will get you from Lucerne to Stans' Stansstader-strasse 19, for the journey up to Stanserhorn.

08 STANSERHORN
Looming above the lake, 1898m **Stanserhorn** (stanserhorn.ch) boasts 360-degree vistas of Lake Lucerne, Mt Titlis, Mt Pilatus and the Bernese Oberland, among others. Getting to the summit is half the fun. The journey starts with a ride on a vintage 19th-century funicular from Stans to Kälti. From here, the nearly transparent **CabriO**, launched in 2012 as the world's first cable car with an open upper deck, takes you the rest of the way, offering amazing on-the-go views.

On sunny days or when many travellers are expected, book an online 'boarding pass' to confirm your time of departure and subsequent return.

At the summit there's the star-shaped **Rondorama**, the region's only revolving restaurant,

which rotates 360 degrees every 43 minutes. Kids love the nearby **marmot park**, where the critters can be observed in a near-natural habitat.

THE DRIVE
Retrace your route along the A2 and head toward Lucerne before changing to the A4 and following the signs to Zürich (50 minutes, 65km).

09 ZÜRICH
Culturally vibrant, efficiently run and set at the meeting of river and lake, Zürich is constantly recognised as one of the world's most liveable cities. It's a savvy, hard-working financial centre, yet Switzerland's largest and wealthiest metropolis has an artsy, postindustrial edge. Much of the Old Town, with its winding lanes and quaint squares, is lovingly intact. Must-see sights include the glorious **Fraumünster** (fraumuenster. ch), with its Marc Chagall stained-glass windows, the **Grossmünster** (grossmuenster. ch) with its salt-and-pepper-shaker steeples, and the excellent **Kunsthaus** (kunsthaus.ch), which holds an impressive permanent art collection. For contemporary cool, walk around Züri-West.

In summer, the fun revolves around lake and river pools like **Seebad Utoquai** (bad-utoquai.ch), **Frauenbad** and **Männerbad**.

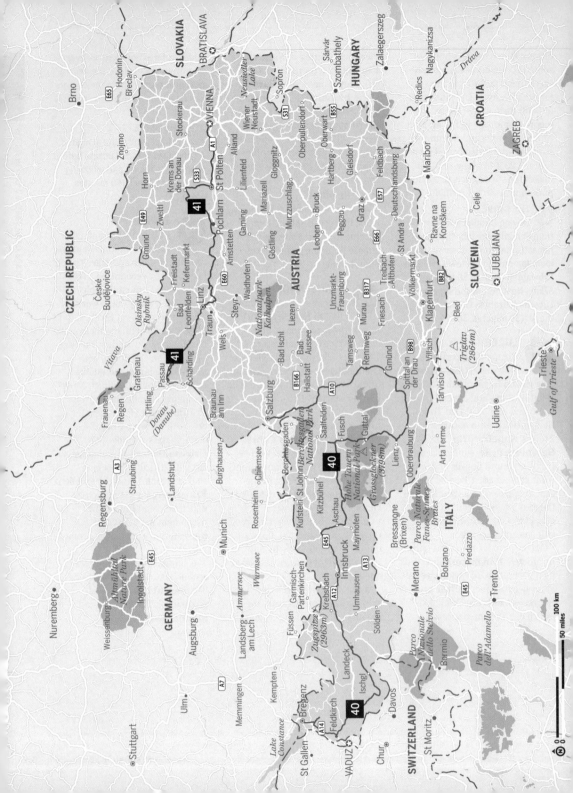

Gerlos Alpine Road (p328)

Austria

40 Grossglockner Road

Gasp at breathtaking Alpine scenery as you traverse three of Austria's most spectacular mountain passes. **p324**

41 Along the Danube

Follow the Danube River as it flows through forests and vineyards from neighbouring Germany to Vienna. **p330**

Explore

Austria

Austria is a road-tripper's dream destination. Not only do its spellbinding landscapes and story-book architecture create spectacular backdrops, but opportunities abound to get out and experience them for yourself. On our trips you can scale soaring peaks and ski powdery heights, raft white-water rapids and career down toboggan runs. When you're maxed out on thrills and spills, Austria's cultural highlights include medieval castles, monumental palaces, art-filled museums and magnificent churches. And then, for dessert, you can dig into cake in grand cafes and down monk-made beer in historic monasteries.

Vienna

A few days in Vienna will start your Austrian trip off in high style. The country's cultured capital makes an immediate impression with its imperial architecture and bombastic baroque displays, verdant parks and showcase squares. You can tour the Hofburg royal palace and take in artistic masterpieces at the Belvedere before adjourning for a slice of Sachertorte (chocolate cake) at one of the city's many coffeehouses.

Vienna, which is served by Austria's main international airport, is in the east of the country. When the time comes to hit the road, the A1 autobahn strikes west, shadowing the Along the Danube trip as it traverses the country to Linz, about two hours' drive away. Salzburg is a further 130km along the same road.

Salzburg

Straddling the fast-flowing Salzach River, the musical city of Salzburg has impeccable cultural credentials – Mozart lived here 250 years ago and it was in and around the city that *The Sound of Music* was filmed. Music lovers still flock to the city, especially in July for the celebrated Salzburg Festival. Classical music apart, the city is a handsome sight, guarded by a 900-year-old clifftop fortress, the Festung Hohensalzburg, and backed by brooding snow-capped mountains. As a visitor, you'll spend much of your time in the Altstadt (Old Town) exploring its museums, palaces and medieval squares.

WHEN TO GO

Austria's mountains are a year-round playground: the ski season runs from around mid-December to March while midsummer is best for high-altitude hiking and road-tripping. Summer, Austria's main holiday period, means long, hot days, festival fun and high-season prices. Spring and autumn are less crowded, and with mild, often dry weather these are good months for sightseeing and out-door pursuits.

The city, starting point for our epic Grossglockner Road trip, makes a great base for western Austria. It has a full range of accommodation and is well connected: European flights arrive at the city airport, and there are regular trains to/from Linz and Vienna.

Innsbruck

With the jagged spires of the Nordkette mountain range soaring into the air, Innsbruck is a sight to behold. Tyrol's capital makes a wonderful base for Austria's western Alps and the Grossglockner Road trip with a full range of accommodation, international restaurants and popular pavement cafes. In town, you can explore the late-medieval Altstadt before heading to the hills via a space-age funicular and series of cable cars. Up in the heights, you can pit yourself against the pistes, skiing and tobogganing in winter, and hiking and mountain biking in summer.

TRANSPORT

Landlocked Austria is well connected to the rest of the world. International flights serve Vienna and several regional capitals while trains and buses run in from destinations across Europe. By car, major highways enter from neighbouring countries, including Germany and Italy. It's also possible to enter Austria by riverboat from Hungary, Slovakia and Germany.

Innsbruck is on the east–west A12 motorway and the A13, which runs in from Italy. There are also European flights to its small airport and trains from neighbouring countries and Austrian cities.

 WHAT'S ON

Donauinselfest

(June; donauinselfest.at) Three days of rock, pop, hardcore, folk and country music on Vienna's river island.

Salzburger Festspiele

(July and August; salzburger festspiele.at) World-class opera, classical music and drama take Salzburg by storm.

Bregenzer Festspiele

(August; bregenzerfestspiele.com) Bregenz stages lakeside opera and classical music.

Christkindlmärkte

(December) Christmas markets bring festive sparkle, mulled wine and good cheer to Vienna and the rest of Austria.

Resources

Austria Info (austria.info) Austria's official multilingual tourist site is packed with useful, up-to-date information.

ÖAMTC (oeamtc.at/laender info/austria) Helpful info about driving in Austria and links to other useful sites.

Wien Info (wien.info) Vienna's official tourist website is comprehensive, easy to navigate and practical.

WHERE TO STAY

Whether you're after an urban design hotel or a traditional Tyrolean chalet, you'll find accommodation to suit your style. Austria's cities are well supplied with hotels, hostels, B&Bs and rental apartments, while countryside options include farm stays, chalets, mountain huts and camping grounds. Many places take sustainability seriously, including organic farms, which provide great family-friendly accommodation, often in bucolic rural settings. Up in the mountains, *Almhütten* (Alpine huts) are popular with hikers, providing spartan digs during the summer season (roughly May to September). Booking ahead is always recommended and imperative in high summer and the ski season.

40

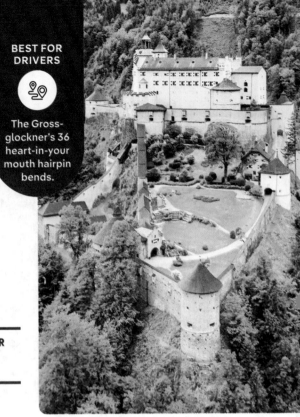

BEST FOR DRIVERS

The Gross-glockner's 36 heart-in-your mouth hairpin bends.

Gross-glockner Road

DURATION	DISTANCE	GREAT FOR
5-7 days	711km / 442 miles	Outdoors

BEST TIME TO GO	The peak time to tackle this trip is mid-summer.

Burg Hohenwerfen

Fair warning: if you're a faint-hearted driver (or passenger), this probably isn't the trip for you. But if you're up for a serious adventure, this Austrian classic provides an opportunity to experience epic scenery, invigorating alpine sports, and dizzying mountain passes with so many switchbacks they're used by high-performance car manufacturers and championship race drivers as test tracks.

Link your trip

36 The Romantic Road

Strike north after Innsbruck to find a ribbon of historical quaintness running through Bavaria's western reaches.

39 Geneva to Zürich

Mountains, pastures, lakes and small-town charm, book-ended by Switzerland's biggest cities.

01 SALZBURG

Salzburg's trophy sights huddle in the pedestrianised, Unesco World Heritage–listed **Altstadt**. The tangled lanes are made for a seren-dipitous wander, leading to hidden courtyards and medieval squares framed by burgher houses and baroque fountains. You'll also see plenty of icons from the evergreen musical *The Sound of Music*.

Beyond city strolling, there are plenty of oppor-tunities to get active, from swimming at **Freibad Leopoldskron**, Salzburg's biggest lido, with diving boards, water slides and volleyball, to hiking up

Salzburg's rival mountains, the 540m **Mönchsberg** and 640m **Kapuzinerberg**. Both mountains are thickly wooded and criss-crossed by walking trails, with photogenic views of the Altstadt's right bank and left bank respectively.

 THE DRIVE
It's 47km south from Salzburg on the B159 to Werfen, mostly along the Salzach River. After passing through a wide valley, you'll enter a tight, steep gorge; follow it until Werfen.

02 WERFEN
More than 1000m above Werfen in the Tennengebirge mountains is **Eisriesenwelt** (eisriesenwelt.

at). Billed as the world's largest accessible ice caves, this glittering ice spectacle spans 30,000 sq metres and 42km of narrow passages burrowing deep into the heart of the mountains. A highlight is the cavernous **Eispalast** (ice palace), where the frost crystals twinkle when a magnesium flare is held up to them. Wrap up warmly for subzero temperatures. Photography is not permitted inside the caves.

On a wooded clifftop beneath the majestic peaks of the Tennengebirge is the formidable fortress **Burg Hohenwerfen** (salzburg-burgen.at), dating from 1077. Time your visit to be there for the 3.15pm falconry show.

 THE DRIVE
Take the A10 south to the Millstätter See (which you can visit on a trip through the Carinthian Lakes) and turn west onto the B100/E66 through the Drau Valley to Lienz (166km in total).

03 LIENZ
Ringed by Dolomite peaks blushing reddish-pink at sunset, Lienz straddles the Isel and Drau Rivers, and lies just 40km north of Italy. An ancient **Roman settlement**, today it's a famed ski town (for its Zettersfeld and Hochstein peaks, and especially its 100km of cross-country trails), but it has an energetic vibe year-round.

If you want to get up into the mountains, **Bergstatt** has guides who can lead you on half-day, full-day and multiday rock climbing, via ferrata or summit trips.

THE DRIVE
Take the B107 north, passing picturesque villages including Winklern – 17km from Lienz, with a wonderful alpine hotel – and Heiligenblut – look for the needle-thin spire of its pilgrimage church – to the Grossglockner High Alpine Road toll gates (43km in total).

04 GROSSGLOCKNER HIGH ALPINE ROAD
A stupendous feat of 1930s engineering, the 48km **Grossglockner Road** (gross glockner.at) swings giddily around 36 switchbacks, passing jewel-coloured lakes, forested slopes and above-the-clouds glaciers as it traverses the heart of the Hohe Tauern National Park, peaking at the bell-shaped **Grossglockner** (3798m), Austria's highest mountain.

En route, flag-dotted **Kaiser-Franz-Josefs-Höhe** (2369m) has memorable views of Grossglockner and the rapidly retreating **Pasterze Glacier** (best appreciated on the short and easy Gamsgrubenweg and Gletscherweg trails). Allow time to see the glacier-themed exhibition at the visitor centre and the crystalline Wilhelm-Swarovski observatory.

Get your camera handy for **Fuscher Törl** (2428m), with super views on both sides of the ridge, and **Fuscher Lacke** (2262m), a gemstone of a lake nearby. A small exhibition documents the construction of the road.

A 2km side road corkscrews up to **Edelweiss Spitze** (2571m), the road's highest viewpoint. Climb the tower for staggering 360-degree views of more than 30 peaks topping 3000m.

Between toll gates, all attractions are free. Check the forecast before you hit the road, as the drive is not much fun in heavy

TOP TIP:
Alpine Road Tolls

Be aware that this trip's three top-draw drives – Grossglockner High Alpine Road, Gerlos Alpine Road and Silvretta High Alpine Road – incur hefty tolls. There's also a smaller toll on the detour to the Stubaital. Toll booths accept cash and credit cards.

Photo Opportunity
Europe's highest waterfalls, the three-tiered Krimmler Wasserfälle.

fog, snow or a storm. It's often bumper-to-bumper by noon, especially in July and August; beat the crowds by setting out early.

THE DRIVE
Descend the Grossglockner on the B107 to Bruck then take the B311 northeast to Zell am See.

05 ZELL AM SEE
Resort town Zell am See's brightly painted chalets line the shore of the deep-blue **Zeller See**, framed by the Hohe Tauern's snowcapped peaks.

Mountain breezes create ideal conditions for windsurfing on the lake; **Windsurfcenter Zell Am See** (supcenter-zellamsee. at) rents equipment and runs courses.

THE DRIVE
From the lake, it's 54km to the Krimmler Wasserfälle. Head west on the B168 and B165 to Krimml; when you arrive in town the waterfalls come into view.

06 KRIMMLER WASSERFÄLLE
Europe's highest falls, at 380m, are the thunderous, three-tier **Krimmler Wasserfälle** (wasserfaelle-krimml.at). The **Wasserfallweg** (Waterfall Trail), which starts at the ticket office and weaves uphill through mixed forest, has up-close viewpoints. It's 4km one way (about a 2½-hour round-trip walk).

Krimmler Wasserfälle

THE DRIVE
From the falls, it's 7.7km (and eight hairpin bends) to the Gerlos Alpine Road toll gates.

07 GERLOS ALPINE ROAD
Open year-round, the **Gerlos Alpine Road** (gerlosstrasse.at) winds 12km through high moor and spruce forest, reaching an elevation of 1630m. The lookout above the turquoise Stausee (reservoir) is a great picnic stop, with a tremendous vista of the Alps.

Take the 4.8km-long **Jodel Wanderweg** (Yodel Hiking Trail; jodelweg.at) in Königsleiten. You can go it alone and practise your high notes at eight stops with giant cowbells, alpine horns and listen-repeat audio clippings. Alternatively, join a free guided sing 'n' stroll hike with trail founder Christian Eder. The three-hour downhill ambles begin at 10.30am every Wednesday from late June to mid-September at the Dorfbahn cable-car station; call the tourist office by 5pm the previous day to reserve a spot.

THE DRIVE
Continue west on the B165, passing the reservoir Durlassboden, before descending to Zell am Ziller along six hairpin bends (63km in total).

08 ZELL AM ZILLER
At the foot of knife-edge Reichenspitze (3303m), Zell am Ziller is a former gold-mining centre and popular ski base.

Year-round, you can take a wild toboggan ride on the 1.45km-long **Arena Coaster** (zillertalarena.com), which incorporates both a 360-degree loop and a 540-degree loop. It's accessible by cable car, or a steep 1.5km walk.

Aktivzentrum Zillertal (aktiv zentrum-zillertal.at) offers summertime paragliding, white-water rafting on the Ziller, via ferrata climbing, canyoning and – one for the kids – llama trekking.

THE DRIVE
Zell am Ziller sits 60km from Innsbruck. Take the B169 north, then the A12 west to the city.

09 INNSBRUCK
Hit Innsbruck's cultural attractions, such as the **Volkskunst Museum**, then head up to its ski jump, the **Bergisel** (bergisel.info), for a spectacular city and mountain panorama. Rising above Innsbruck like a celestial staircase, the glass-and-steel structure was designed by the unconventional Iraqi architect Zaha Hadid.

Hadid also designed the space-age funicular **Nordketten-bahnen** (nordkette.com), which whizzes from the Congress Centre to the slopes every 15 minutes. Walking trails head off in all directions from Hungerburg and Seegrube.

THE DRIVE
Leave Innsbruck on the west-bound A12 and veer southwest on the B188, passing a string of ski towns, to the Silvretta High Alpine Road toll gates (118km all up).

10 SILVRETTA HIGH ALPINE ROAD
Silhouetted by the glaciated Silvretta range and crowned by the 3312m arrow of Piz Buin, the Montafon Valley remains one of the most serene and unspoilt in the Austrian Alps.

The 23km-long **Silvretta High Alpine Road** (silvretta-bieler hoehe.at) twists and turns beneath peaks rising to well over 2500m before climbing over the 2036m Bielerhöhe Pass via 34 knuckle-whiteningly tight switchbacks. At the top of the pass, the **Silvretta Stausee** (2030m), a startlingly aquamarine reservoir, mirrors the surrounding peaks on bright mornings.

 DETOUR:

Stubaital

START: 9 INNSBRUCK

Slip out of sandals and into skis at year-round skiing magnet, **Stubai Glacier** (stubaier-gletscher.com). A one-day summer ski pass (adult/child €42.50/21.30) covers 26 lifts accessing 62km of slopes. Ski shops are plentiful; ski or snowboard and boot rental costs around €30/15 per adult/child. Summer skiing is between 2900m and 3300m and is dependent on weather conditions.

Lower down in the Stubai Valley, the **Wildewasserweg** waterfall trail wends for 9.2km (one way) to **Sulzenau Glacier**. En route, it passes the spectacular Grawa falls; there's a cafe with a panoramic viewing deck at its base.

The Stubai Glacier is just 38km south of Innsbruck. Take the A13 south to the toll gates (per car including passengers €3); keep right to take the B183 southwest along the valley.

THE DRIVE

It's 100km to Rappenlochschlucht. Continue on the B188 and join the A14 at aromatic Bludenz (home to the Milka chocolate factory; there's an outlet shop but, alas, no tours). Continue northwest to Dornbirn, from where Rappenlochschlucht is 4km southeast on Gütlestrasse.

11 **RAPPENLOCHSCHLUCHT**

The Rappenlochschlucht (Rappenloch Gorge; rap penlochschlucht.at) was gouged out by the thundering Dornbirner Ache. From the car park, there's a 375m trail to the **Staufensee**, a turquoise lake ringed by forest.

At the bottom of the Rappenlochschlucht, a 19th-century cotton mill is the unlikely home of the world's largest collection of Rolls-Royces at the **Rolls-Royce Museum** (rolls-royce-museum.at).

THE DRIVE

Return to Dornbirn and head north on the B190 for 16km to Bregenz.

12 **BREGENZ**

Bregenz sits on the shores of **Lake Constance** (in German, Bodensee), Europe's third-largest lake. The views here are extraordinary: before you the mirror-like lake; behind you, the

1064m-high Pfänder mountain; to the right, Germany, to the left, Switzerland.

A **cable car** (pfaenderbahn.at) glides up the Pfänder. At the top, a 30-minute circular trail brings you close to deer, wild boar, ibex and whistling marmots at the year-round **Alpine Game Park Pfänder**.

Some 5km south of central Bregenz, where the Rhine flows into Lake Constance, is the nature reserve **Rheindelta** (rheindelta. org). Easily explored on foot or by bike, the reserve attracts more than 300 bird species, including rare black-tailed godwits.

SAIKO3P/SHUTTERSTOCK ©

Bergisel, Innsbruck

41

Along the Danube

DURATION	DISTANCE	GREAT FOR
2–4 days	320km / 198 miles	Wine, history

BEST TIME TO GO	Aim for summer; many places close between November and March.

Stift Engelszell, Engelhartszell an der Donau

Immortalised in the stirring 'Blue Danube' waltz by Johann Strauss II, this magnificent river ripples with the reflections of dense green forests, hilltop castles and ribbons of vineyards, particularly on its prettiest stretch, the Wachau, between Melk and Krems an der Donau. Along the river's course are plenty of surprises too, including the cutting-edge city of Linz, and two superb monasteries producing, respectively, sublime beer and wine.

Link your trip

36 The Romantic Road

Head west, skirting Munich, to this ribbon of historical quaintness running through Bavaria's western reaches.

40 Grossglockner Road

A hop and a skip south and you can twist and turn along three of Austria's most spectacular mountain passes.

01 PASSAU

Just inside the German border, Passau's pastel-shaded Altstadt sits atop a narrow peninsula jutting into the confluence of three rivers: the Danube, the Inn and the Ilz. Christianity generated prestige as Passau evolved into the largest bishopric in the Holy Roman Empire, as testified by the mighty cathedral, **Dom St Stephan**.

Stroll the old town, which remains much as it was when the powerful prince-bishops built its tight lanes, tunnels and archways with an Italianate flourish.

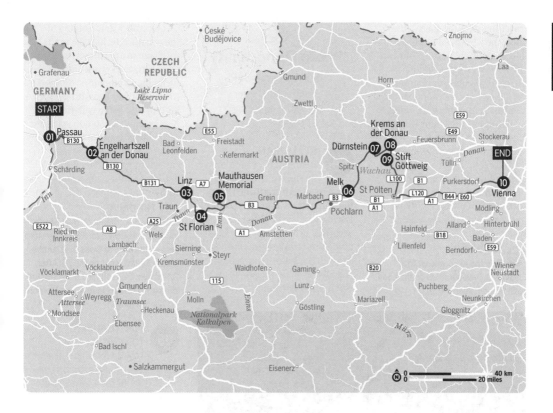

THE DRIVE
Cross the Inn River where it joins the Danube and head east on ST2125 which, 3.3km later, becomes the B130 on entering Austria, and follows the Danube's southern bank. On your right, you'll pass Burg Krempelstein, built on the site of a Roman watch house. It's 26km all up to Engelhartszell an der Donau.

02 ENGELHARTSZELL AN DER DONAU
The little riverside village of Engelhartszell an der Donau is home to one of only eight licensed Trappist breweries outside Belgium, and the only one in Austria. At the 1293-founded abbey **Stift Engelszell** (stift-engelszell.at),

you can purchase monk-made brews (dark Gregorius, amber Benno and blond Nivard); the

---

🚢 Danube Cruises

Floating past vine-covered banks crowned by castles gives you a different perspective of the river. From Passau and Linz, **Wurm & Noé** (donauschiffahrt. eu) operates cruises between Regensburg in Germany and Vienna from March to early November. Ticket prices vary according to how many stops you stay on board.

---

shop also sells liqueurs and cheeses produced here. Adjoining the shop is the abbey's gorgeous rococo church, completed in 1764.

THE DRIVE
Take the B130; at Aschach an der Donau, cross the river on the B131, and continue east to Ottensheim to join the B127 to Linz (52km in total).

03 LINZ
The Austrian saying *In Linz beginnt's* (It begins in Linz) sums up this technology trailblazer. Its leading-edge **Ars Electronica Center** (ars. electronica.art) has labs for interacting with robots, animating digital objects, converting your name to DNA and (virtually)

travelling to outer space. After dark, the LED glass skin kaleidoscopically changes colour. Directly across the Danube is Linz' world-class contemporary-art gallery, the glass-and-steel **Lentos** (lentos.at), with works by Warhol, Schiele and Klimt, among others.

But it's not all new in Austria's third-largest city: the **Mariendom** (dioezese-linz.at) is a neo-Gothic giant of a cathedral with a riot of pinnacles, flying buttresses and filigree-tracery windows.

THE DRIVE
Take the A1 southeast to Ebelsberg, then continue on the L564 to St Florian (21km all up).

Photo Opportunity

The kaleidoscopic ARS Electronica Center after dark.

04 ST FLORIAN
Rising like a vision above St Florian is its magnificent abbey, **Augustiner Chorherrenstift** (stift-st-florian.at). Dating to at least 819, it has been occupied by the Canons Regular, living under Augustinian rule, since 1071. Today its imposing yellow-and-white facade is overwhelmingly baroque.

Compulsory guided tours of the abbey's interior take in the resplendent apartments adorned with rich stuccowork and frescoes, including 16 emperors' rooms (once occupied by visiting popes and royalty) and a galleried library housing 150,000 volumes.

The **Stiftsbasilika** is an exuberant affair with an altar carved from 700 tonnes of pink Salzburg marble, and a gold 18th-century organ.

THE DRIVE
Head northeast on the L566 to join the B1. Follow it for 7.5km then turn east on the B123 to cross the Danube, before turning west on the B3. After 2.4km take the L1411 for 2.5 signposted kilometres to the Mauthausen Memorial (22km in total).

05 MAUTHAUSEN MEMORIAL
Nowadays Mauthausen is a peaceful small town on the north bank of the Danube, but in WWII the Nazis turned the quarrying centre into the **KZ Mauthausen** concentration camp. Prisoners were forced into slave labour in the granite quarry and many died on the so-called *Todesstiege* (stairway of death) leading from the quarry to the camp. Some 100,000 prisoners perished or were executed in the camp between 1938 and 1945. The complex is now a **memorial** (mauthausen-memorial.org); English-language audioguides relate its sobering history. It's not recommended for under 14s.

THE DRIVE
Travelling east for 76km brings you to Melk. Along the river at Grein, look out for the dramatic castle Greinburg rising to your left.

A G BAXTER/SHUTTERSTOCK ©

Ars Electronica Center (p331), Linz

MELK

06 Historically, Melk was of great importance to the Romans, and later to the Babenbergs, who built a castle here. In 1089 the Babenberg margrave Leopold II donated the castle to Benedictine monks, who converted it into the fortified **Stift Melk** (stiftmelk.at). Fire destroyed the original edifice; today its monastery church dominates the complex with its twin spires and high octagonal dome. The baroque-gone-barmy interior has regiments of cherubs, gilt twirls and polished faux marble. The theatrical high-altar scene depicts St Peter and St Paul (the church's two patron saints).

THE DRIVE

The Wachau is the loveliest valley along the mighty river's length: both banks here are dotted with ruined castles and terraced with vineyards. From Melk, follow the river northeast along the northern bank for 28km, passing medieval villages Spitz, Wösendorf in der Wachau and Weissenkirchen, to reach Dürnstein.

DÜRNSTEIN

07 Picturesque Dürnstein is best known for the **Kuenringerburg** – the now-ruined castle above the town where Richard the Lionheart (Richard I of England) was imprisoned from 1192 to 1193, before being moved to Burg Trifels in Germany.

Of the 16th-century buildings lining Dürnstein's hilly, cobbled streets, the **Chorherrenstift**

(stiftduernstein.at) is the most impressive. It's all that remains of the former Augustinian monastery originally founded in 1410, and received its baroque facelift in the 18th century.

THE DRIVE

Head east along the river on the B3 for 7.5km to reach Krems an der Donau.

KREMS AN DER DONAU

08 Against a backdrop of terraced vineyards, Krems has an attractive cobbled centre and gallery-dotted **Kunstmeile** (Art Mile; kunstmeile-krems.at). Its flagship is **Landesgalerie NÖ** (landesgalerie-noe.at), a futuristic structure from 2019 containing ever-changing exhibitions of edgy modern art and contemporary installations.

THE DRIVE

Leave Krems an der Donau on the B37 and cross the southbound L100. Stift Göttweig is well signposted (9km altogether from Krems).

STIFT GÖTTWEIG

09 Surrounded by grape-laden vines, Unesco World Heritage Site–listed **Stift Göttweig** (Göttweig Abbey; stiftgoettweig.at) was founded in 1083, but the abbey you see today is mostly baroque. Highlights include the Imperial Staircase, with a heavenly ceiling fresco painted by Paul Troger in 1739, and the over-the-top baroque interior of the Stiftskirche (which has a Kremser Schmidt work in the crypt). Best of all is the

opportunity to sip wine made here by the monks – including an exquisite Messwein rosé – on the panoramic garden terrace above the valley (you can also buy it at the abbey's shop).

THE DRIVE

From Stift Göttweig, it's 79km to Vienna. The most scenic route, through farmland and forest, is south on the L100 to St Pölten, then east on the L120 to join the eastbound B44 at Ebersberg. Continue through the Wienerwald (Vienna Woods) to the Austrian capital.

VIENNA

10 Renowned for its imperial palaces, baroque interiors, opera houses and magnificent squares, Vienna is also one of Europe's most dynamic urban spaces.

A wonderfully atmospheric (if touristy) way to experience the city is clip-clopping aboard a **Fiaker**, a traditional-style open carriage drawn by a pair of horses. Drivers point out places of interest en route. Lines of horses, carriages and bowler-hatted drivers can be found at Stephansplatz, Albertinaplatz and Heldenplatz at the Hofburg.

You can also survey the city from Vienna's 65m-high, 1897-built Ferris wheel, the **Riesenrad**. It's located at the **Prater** (wiener-prater.at), a sprawling park encompassing meadows, woodlands, and an amusement park, the Würstelprater, between the Danube and Danube Canal.

Arriving

Europe is one of the world's major destinations, served by flights from across the globe. Its busiest airports include London Heathrow, Paris Charles de Gaulle and Madrid Barajas (pictured), all of which offer modern services and excellent transport links for onward travel. Once in Europe, a comprehensive network of rail, road and ferry links connect countries, making getting around pretty straightforward.

Car Rental at Airports

Car rental is available at all of Europe's main airports. Agencies are often situated in arrivals halls or dedicated rental centres. Once you've got to your vehicle, which could involve a bus transfer to a distant car park, check it thoroughly and mark any bumps or scratches.

Prebooking is advisable. You'll get a better rate and have a wider choice of vehicle. Make sure to specify if you want an automatic car, as most

European cars are manuals (stick shifts).

As a rule, it's not worth hiring a car for time you'll be spending in big cities. In fact, a car can often be more hassle than it's worth in city centres – you'll have to deal with stressful traffic, access restrictions, one-way systems and extortionate parking. Better to wait and hire as you head out of town.

Airport pick-ups usually cost more than from city-centre locations.

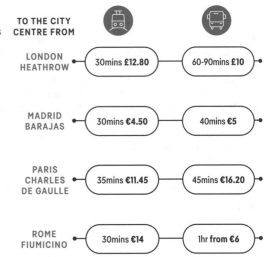

TO THE CITY CENTRE FROM	🚊	🚌
LONDON HEATHROW	30mins £12.80	60-90mins £10
MADRID BARAJAS	30mins €4.50	40mins €5
PARIS CHARLES DE GAULLE	35mins €11.45	45mins €16.20
ROME FIUMICINO	30mins €14	1hr from €6

VISA-FREE STAYS

EU nationals can travel freely within the Schengen zone; travellers from the UK, Canada, New Zealand, the US and Australia can stay for up to 90 days without a visa.

SCHENGEN AREA

Britain is not part of the Schengen area. Visas are not generally required for stays of up to six months – for detailed information, check gov.uk/browse/visas-immigration.

ETIAS

The European Travel Information & Authorisation System is due to start from 2024. Non-EU travellers from visa-exempt countries travelling to a Schengen member state will have to register online and pay a €7 fee.

WI-FI

Free wi-fi is generally available at airports, train stations (sometimes on trains, too), hotels, hostels, B&Bs and cafes. Signal quality varies and can be poor in more remote areas and in old, thick-walled buildings.

Getting Around

FILLING UP

Filling up at a petrol station is pretty straightforward. At some stations an attendant will fill up for you – just ask for the amount you want (€50, say) or for a full tank, and specify petrol or diesel. At self-service stations you either fill up first and pay a cashier, or pay first (at a machine if the station's unattended) and fill up at your selected pump. Most stations accept cards but some smaller places might insist on cash.

DRIVING INFO

Drive on the right in continental Europe; on the left in Britain and Ireland.

50

Speed limits: 50km/h in urban areas; 80–110km/h on secondary roads; 110–130km/h on motorways.

.05

Blood alcohol limit is 0.05% (0.08% in England and Wales).

Road Tolls

Many European motorways (*autoroutes, autostrade, autobahns* etc) are toll roads. Prices and payment systems vary from country to country: in some you pay at toll booths; in others you have to prepay. For a comprehensive overview, see tolls.eu.

City Driving Zones

Driving regulations are common in European cities. These include low emission zones, in which older

vehicles are banned or charged for entering, and limited traffic zones in which unauthorised traffic is prohibited. Access is often monitored by security cameras.

Parking

Parking can be a headache. Car parks fill quickly and on-street parking usually requires payment, either at a meter (with coins or cards) or through an app. Always check for coloured lines on the road and local signs.

Driving Styles

Driving styles vary across Europe and you might find attitudes to speeding, overtaking and using the horn are not what you're used to. Drivers can be aggressive and in some countries you'll almost certainly encounter lane hopping, late breaking and high-speed tailgating.

TRAVEL COSTS

Car rental
€30–150 per day

Petrol
€1.56–1.87 per/litre

EV charging
€0.20–0.95 per kWh

Train ticket
Paris–Milan
€54–149

Accommodation

REGULATION FOR RENTALS

The so-called 'airbnbisation' of many European cities has become a hot political issue in recent years. The exponential growth of short-term rentals – which now account for almost a third of the EU's supply of tourist accommodation – has been accused of driving locals out of city centres and pushing rental prices up, particularly in heavily visited cities. To address this, civic, national and European authorities are currently looking at ways to regulate the sector and introduce legislation. To make your own small contribution, consider diversifying the types of accommodation you stay in on your trip.

HOW MUCH FOR A NIGHT IN A...

parador
€75–300

farm stay
€40–100

mountain hut
free–€30

Country Inns

For a taste of genuine hospitality, consider staying in a country inn. Ranging from historic British and Irish pubs to timber-clad German *Gasthäuser,* these provide simple accommodation, often in lovely rural locations, and the chance to spend long evenings getting to grips with the local food and drink.

Agriturismi

Farm stays, known as *agriturismi* in Italy, are popular across Europe. Comfort levels, facilities and prices vary but the best offer top-notch accommodation as well as the chance to sample authentic local cuisine. They are perfect for families, for relaxing, and for trying activities such as foraging, olive harvesting and cookery classes.

Mountain Huts

Hikers are well catered to in Europe with a network of mountain refuges and huts, most open only in the summer. In the remote wilds of Scotland, northern England and Wales, you can overnight in spartan shelters known as bothies. These barebone cabins are generally free to use so long as you respect the 'bothy code' (mountainbothies.org. uk/bothies/bothy-code).

Eco Hotels

Bio- or *Öko-* ('eco') hotels are widespread in Austria. Many are located in picturesque rural settings and offer wellness facilities such as saunas and steam baths, as well as skiing and other outdoor activities. Generally speaking, you'll need your own wheels to get to them.

UNIQUE OPTIONS

To sleep like royalty in Spain, check out the country's *paradores*. These state-run hotels are often housed in former castles, convents or palaces, and while they're generally top end, they often cost less than you might imagine, especially if you book online and far in advance. Portuguese *pousadas* are similar, offering memorable stays in historic surroundings.

Cars

HOW MUCH TO HIRE...

a mid-size car

€30–110
per day

an EV

€50–160
per day

a campervan

€60–175
per day

Car Rental

Car-hire agencies are widespread and you'll find the big international firms at airports and major train stations, as well as city locations. Smaller local outfits often offer cheaper rates, but it pays to check user reviews for reports of past experiences with them.

You'll generally have the option of returning your car to a different location, but you will be charged extra for this.

To rent, you'll need a credit card, valid driver's licence (with IDP if necessary) and passport. You'll also need to be over 25. Some places

do hire to 21- to 25-year-olds, but supplements will apply.

Rates typically include mandatory third-party liability insurance and sometimes also a basic collision damage waiver (CDW).

Electric Vehicles

Electric vehicles (EVs) currently constitute around 15–20% of Europe's rental fleet.

As a rule, EVs are best suited to shorter day trips rather than long-distance touring. Mid-size cars have a range of about 200km, but you probably won't get that when driving at higher speeds.

To fully charge a car generally takes three to four hours on a slow charger (11–22kWh) or about 45 minutes on a fast charger (110kWh). Vehicles often come with maps showing charger locations; otherwise you'll find chargers at petrol stations, supermarkets and public car parks. Accommodation providers may also have them. Always check with your rental agency how to use chargers as you might have to download an app and set up an account.

OTHER GEAR

Hire cars generally come with the equipment you're legally obliged to carry, such as warning triangles, reflective vests and first-aid kits. Snow chains and/or all-weather tyres are obligatory in some areas in winter, so check whether these are included. Child seats, sat navs and other accessories are charged as extras.

Health & Safe Travel

Health Care

Health care is readily accessible throughout Britain and Europe. EU and Brit nationals are entitled to reduced-cost, sometimes free, medical care with a valid EHIC (or GHIC) card; non-EU citizens should take out medical insurance. Pharmacists can advise on medical matters and sell medications for minor illnesses.

Weather

Recent years have seen an increase in severe weather events. Summer 2022 was Europe's hottest ever and many countries suffered heatwaves,

droughts and raging wildfires. Storms and torrential rain have also caused problems, leading to fatal landslides and devastating floods in 2022 and spring 2023. If you're caught in a fire or flood, follow evacuation orders immediately.

Theft

Europe is generally safe but petty theft can be a nuisance, particularly in tourist hot spots and major transport hubs. Always lock your car and never leave anything visible, especially when parking overnight. In case of theft, report the incident to the police within 24 hours and ask for a statement.

Security

The Russian invasion of Ukraine in February 2022 has raised concerns about the safety of travelling in Europe. The nine countries covered in this book are all considered safe, but for the latest advice check your national government travel advisory site.

INSURANCE

It's foolhardy to travel without insurance to cover theft, loss and medical problems. There are a wide variety of policies, so check the small print. Some policies specifically exclude 'dangerous activities', which can include scuba diving, motorcycling, winter sports, adventure sports or even hiking. Check that the policy covers ambulances or an emergency flight home, and that it provides adequate liability coverage for where you will be driving.

IN CASE OF EMERGENCY

The number 112 can be dialled free for emergencies in all EU states.

CAR BREAKDOWN

In the event of a breakdown, call your car-hire company. Roadside assistance might be included in your rental contact or it might be available as a paid extra – check before you go.

National motoring organisations, and in France, the ASFA motorway company, also provide 24-hour roadside assistance, though there will generally be a fee to pay.

Responsible Travel

Climate Change

It's impossible to ignore the impact we have when travelling, and the importance of making changes where we can. Lonely Planet urges all travellers to engage with their travel carbon footprint. There are many carbon calculators online that allow travellers to estimate the carbon emissions generated by their journey; try resurgence.org/resources/carbon-calculator.html. Many airlines and booking sites offer travellers the option of offsetting the impact of greenhouse gas emissions by contributing to climate-friendly initiatives around the world. We continue to offset the carbon footprint of all Lonely Planet staff travel, while recognising this is a mitigation more than a solution.

Biohotels
biohotels.info
Lists sustainable accommodation in Germany, Austria and Italy.

Slow Food
slowfood.com
Grassroots organisation promoting local food cultures.

Blue Flag
blueflag.global
Ecolabel for beaches meeting environmental standards.

EAT LOCAL & SEASONAL

Seasonal, zero-kilometre produce is the bedrock of Europe's national and regional cuisines. To sample the best for yourself, pick up picnic provisions at farmers markets and dine in local family-run restaurants.

CHOOSE TO REFILL

You don't need to splash out on bottled water. Tap water is generally safe to drink and many European cities have free drinking fountains where you can fill up your reusable water bottle.

VISIT OFF-PEAK

Overtourism is increasingly an issue in heavyweight destinations such as Venice and Barcelona. Visit at quieter off-peak times, and you'll avoid the worst of the crowds and pay less for your accommodation.

Nuts & Bolts

Time Zone
Britain, Ireland, Portugal GMT/UTC; mainland Europe UTC plus one hour

Population
198 million (Western Europe)

Emergency number
112

CURRENCIES:
BRITISH POUND (£), EURO (€), SWISS FRANC (CHF)

Digital Payments

Contactless digital payment is widespread in Europe but some smaller shops, restaurants, museums and tourist sites may insist on cash payment. ATMs are available in towns and cities; less so in rural areas. Major credit cards are widely accepted.

Tipping

In restaurants, a service charge is often added to your bill, meaning tipping is not strictly necessary. However, diners often still leave a small tip, usually around 5% to 10%. If service isn't included, 10% to 15% is fine. As a rule, it's best to tip in cash.

ELECTRICITY

Europe generally runs on 220V, 50Hz AC, but there are exceptions. The UK runs on 230/240V AC, and some old buildings in Italy and Spain have 125V (or even 110V in Spain). The continent is moving towards a 230V standard. If your home country has a vastly different voltage, you will need a transformer for delicate and important appliances.

The UK and Ireland use three-pin square plugs. Most of Europe uses the 'europlug' with two round pins. Italy and Switzerland use a third round pin in a way that the two-pin plug usually – but not always – fits. Buy an adapter before leaving home; those on sale in Europe generally go the other way, but ones for visitors to Europe are also available – airports are always a good place to buy them.

VAT

A VAT sales tax – about 21% and included in the sales price – is levied on many goods and services sold in the EU. Non-EU travellers leaving the EU can claim a tax refund provided they've spent more than a set amount in shops offering duty- or tax-free shopping.

Weights & Measures

Europe uses the metric system so fuel and drinks are priced by the litre and distances are given in kilometres. Britain, exceptionally, uses miles on its road signs and pint glasses to serve its beer.

Drinking & Smoking

The legal drinking age in most European countries is 18. Smoking bans are widespread, typically prohibiting smoking on public transport and in restaurants, bars, shops, and enclosed public spaces.

Toilets

You'll find toilets at train stations, museums, tourist sites, shopping centres and motorway service stations. Some are free; others charge a fee, typically €1 to €1.50.

HOW MUCH FOR...

an espresso
€1–4

0.5L beer
€1.30–8

a midrange meal
€20–35

Index

Road Trips 000
Map Pages 000, 000

Road Trips 000
Map Pages 000, 000

Road Trips 000
Map Pages 000, 000

Road Trips 000
Map Pages 000, 000

THE WRITERS

This is the 3rd edition of Lonely Planet's *Best Road Trips Europe* guidebook, updated with new material by Duncan Garwood. Writers on previous editions whose work also appears in this book are included below.

Duncan Garwood

Based near Rome, Duncan is a travel writer and guidebook author specialising in Italy and the Mediterranean. Over the past two decades he has clocked up hundreds of thousands of kilometres driving through his adopted homeland and exploring its far-flung reaches. He has worked on a host of Lonely Planet guidebooks and contributed Italy chapters to books on epic drives and world food. He has also written about Italy for newspapers, websites and magazines. *@DuncanGarwood*

Contributing writers

Isabel Albiston, Oliver Berry, Stuart Butler, Jean-Bernard Carillet, Fionn Davenport, Marc Di Duca, Belinda Dixon, Peter Dragicevich, Anthony Ham, Paula Hardy, Catherine Le Nevez, John Noble, Sally O'Brien, Josephine Quintero, Kevin Raub, Daniel Robinson, Brendan Sainsbury, Regis St Louis, Andy Symington, Ryan Ver Berkmoes, Kerry Walker, Nicola Williams, Neil Wilson

SEND US YOUR FEEDBACK

We love to hear from travellers – your comments keep us on our toes and help make our books better. Our well-travelled team reads every word on what you loved or loathed about this book. Although we cannot reply individually to your submissions, we always guarantee that your feedback goes straight to the appropriate writers in time for the next edition. Each person who sends us information is thanked in the next edition.

Visit **lonelyplanet.com/contact** to submit your updates and suggestions or to ask for help. Our award-winning website also features inspirational travel stories and news.

Note: We may edit, reproduce and incorporate your comments in Lonely Planet products such as guidebooks, websites and digital products, so let us know if you are happy to have your name acknowledged. For a copy of our privacy policy visit **lonelyplanet.com/legal**.

BEHIND THE SCENES

This book was produced by the following:

Commissioning Editor Darren O'Connell

Production Editor Saralinda Turner

Book Designer Virginia Moreno

Cartographer Chris Lee-Ack

Assisting Editors Janet Austin, Melanie Dankel, Gabrielle Innes, Graham O'Neill, Maja Vatric

Cover Image Researcher Norma Brewer

Product Development Amy Lynch, Marc Backwell, Katerina Pavkova, Fergal Condon, Ania Bartoszek

Thanks to Ronan Abayawickrema, Karen Henderson

ACKNOWLEDGMENTS

Cover photograph Amalfi Coast, Italy; IgorZh/Shutterstock ©